REFLECTIVE HISTORY SERIES

Barbara Finkelstein and William J. Reese, Series Editors

Schooled to Work:
Vocationalism and the American Curriculum,
1876–1946
HERBERT M. KLIEBARD

Moral Education in America:
Schools and the Shaping of Character
from Colonial Times to the Present
B. EDWARD MCCLELLAN

The Failed Promise of the
American High School, 1890–1995
DAVID L. ANGUS & JEFFREY E. MIREL

SCHOOLED TO WORK

Vocationalism and the American Curriculum, 1876–1946

Herbert M. Kliebard

TEACHERS COLLEGE PRESS

Teachers College, Columbia University
New York and London

Published by Teachers College Press, 1234 Amsterdam Avenue, New York, NY 10027

COVER ILLUSTRATION. Forging class, Mt. Berry, Georgia. *Courtesy Library of Congress.*

Library of Congress Cataloging-in-Publication Data
  Kliebard, Herbert M.
    School to Work: Vocationalism and the American Curriculum, 1876–1946 /
  Herbert M. Kliebard.
      p.   cm.   — (Reflective history series)
    Includes bibliographical references (p.) and index.
    ISBN 0-8077-3867-0 (cloth : alk. paper)
    ISBN 0-8077-3866-2 (pbk : alk. paper)
      1. Education—United States—Curricula—History. 2. Vocational education—
  United States—Curricula—History. 3. Interdisciplinary approach in education—
  United States—History. I. Title. II. Series.
  LB1570 .K587 1999
  370.11'3'0973—dc21   99-21307

ISBN 0-8077-3866-2 (paper)
ISBN 0-8077-3867-0 (cloth)

Printed on acid-free paper

Manufactured in the United States of America

06 05 04 03 02 01 00 99   8 7 6 5 4 3 2 1

To my parents, Yetta and Morris Kliebard,

May their memory be a blessing

CONTENTS

FOREWORD

"Man the Reformer" was the title of the address that Ralph Waldo Emerson presented to the Mechanics' Apprentices' Library Association in Boston on January 25, 1841. As one of the leading lights of Transcendentalism, Emerson offered his listeners an intellectual feast, choice words to savor as he appraised the reform movements that then seemed to define the age. Every institution, from schools to churches, was being held up to new moral standards. Every familiar idea faced greater scrutiny. Abolitionists taught citizens that the sugar in their tea came from Cuban plantations where slaves gave their lives and precious freedom to help satisfy the consumer's sweet tooth. Even the division of labor—so celebrated by Adam Smith and political economists—had an ambiguous influence upon the lives of free laborers, a point surely not lost upon the apprentices in the audience. It led to untold advances in productivity as well as a gnawing sense of discomfort, or what radical theorists would later call alienation.

The difficulties of slaves and free workers alike, Emerson remarked, were obvious, leading many people to proclaim that "manual labor" should be the foundation in the education of "every young man." Indeed, direct contact with "the soil and nature, and abstaining from whatever is dishonest and unclean," inspired many utopian experiments of the early nineteenth century, from Brook Farm to the Shakers, the latter now only remembered for their fine chairs and craftsmanship, not their wholesale indictment of the larger society. As Emerson explained, the relationship of the individual to work was a troubling, difficult one, though he affirmed that "labor is God's education; that he only is a sincere learner, he only can become a master, who learns the secrets of labor, and who by real cunning extorts from nature its scepter."

Not every poet, novelist, and publicist in the nineteenth century spoke in such mystical ways. But anxieties about the changing nature of work and personal identity, about the widening gap between intellectual and manual labor, and about the connection between learning and earning a living proved enduring. Work itself was puzzling. Was it a curse from God after the Fall? Simply a regrettable reality? Or the path to worldly or spiritual redemption? In a democratic age, many citizens understandably feared that the division of labor meant separating those who worked with their heads from those who labored with their hands and did the drudge work of society. Machines had destroyed many traditional crafts, along with apprenticeships, fueling further debate about the nature and meaning of work and the purposes of schools as the century wore on. Little wonder, then, that many manual training schools promised to train the head, heart, and hand, a noble ideal in a world of mechanized parts, smooth-running machines, and alienated labor.

In a sweeping reinterpretation of the rise of vocational education and ultimate triumph of "vocationalism," Herbert M. Kliebard explains how Americans came to grips with social change as they increasingly turned to public schools for answers to the vexing problems of an urban, industrial society. Oriented around academic subjects, from the elementary grades through the high schools, public schools had always taught the values of punctuality, hard work, application, and the familiar virtues of Poor Richard. But they never promised to prepare people for work alone; indeed, most educators assumed that the common schools taught moral character, trained the mind through the teaching of basic subjects, and offered civic instruction appropriate to a republic. A child typically attended school only for a few years, and one learned to work primarily by working. All that was about to change as manual training courses entered some urban schools in the late nineteenth century, and as society's expectations about education expanded. Manual training gave way to a full-fledged movement for vocational education, which provided the basis for an all-embracing vocationalization—the idea that every school subject had to justify itself by its occupational utility. Public understanding of the purposes of mass education would never be the same.

The leading historian of curriculum of his generation, Kliebard deftly uses history to help us understand a host of enduring problems first raised in the nineteenth century, when markets and industry redefined the economic basis to American society. Issues that perplexed Emerson's generation—about the nature of work, education, and democracy—live with us still, despite the historical distance we have traveled. Kliebard offers us much needed perspective as citizens debate anew the meaning of public education and the transition from "school to work." Without question, he laments the continual erosion of respect in this century for academic, humanistic education and the undemocratic consequences that often resulted. Yet his is not a nostalgic longing for an irretrievable, imperfect past but an attempt to paint in bright as well as dark hues the many individuals and groups that competed in the making of the twentieth-century curriculum. He reconstructs how the champions of manual training and vocational education envisioned school and society at the turn of the century. Most importantly, he shows how school innovations often served important symbolic functions, fulfilling psychic needs during times of severe social change.

Many citizens in this century expected schools to preserve revered values such as the "work ethic" while simultaneously preparing youth for the modern workplace. It mattered not that factory labor, efficiency experts, and industrial managers had effectively destroyed everything that work and the work ethic once represented. Home economics and shop class, in the end, may not have reached the ends desired. That is almost beside the point. What mattered was that many citizens applauded the reality that educators seemed to be doing something tangible and constructive.

Readers of this volume will meet an array of fascinating reformers, members of voluntary groups, and also those who dissented from vocationalization, such as W. E. B. Du Bois, Ella Flagg Young, William Bagley, and especially John Dewey. Dewey's nuanced critique both of the traditional academic curriculum and of the vocationally minded reformers of the first half of the twentieth century forms an important part of the analysis. *Schooled to Work*, however, deals not only with famous intellectuals but also with the nitty-gritty politics of curricular reform. Chapters co-authored with Carol Judy Kean examine reform movements and strategies in Milwaukee, an important industrial city at the turn of the century. Other chapters explore the politics of vocational education and vocationalization in different regions of the country, developments on the state and national level, and the professional activities of an emerging vocational education establishment.

According to Kliebard, the purposes and popular understanding of the meaning of public schools underwent a major transformation between the decades following the Civil War and 1946. During these years, despite a series of often devastating economic depressions, America became the world's leading industrial power. Simultaneously, a variety of reformers taught Americans to think about their schools in new ways that made the links between education and jobs explicit. Lost was a world that believed that academic, humanistic learning was an inherent democratic right. To understand what took its place and why is the focus of this imaginative interpretation of a fundamental aspect of our educational past. This book is the starting point for anyone curious about the perennial questions surrounding the nature of work and education in American culture.

William J. Reese
Madison, Wisconsin

✦✦✦ PREFACE ✦✦✦

Recent Gallup polls have indicated that when Americans are asked to state the purpose of public schooling, they overwhelmingly respond with answers like "to get better jobs," "to make more money," and "to achieve financial success." When asked specifically how they would rate the importance of the goal of becoming economically self-sufficient, a full 78 percent of Americans answered "very important," and another 18 percent "quite important." These polls also report that when respondents are asked to approve or disapprove of such other educational purposes as citizenship and promoting cultural unity, they also respond favorably.[1] That Americans expect a great deal of their schools should come as no surprise, but it is dramatically evident that when they are confronted with the question of what education is for, they spontaneously frame their response in terms of jobs, and when that goal is mentioned directly, a mere 4 percent of Americans (including those who respond "don't know") attach no particular importance to economic reward as the purpose of schooling. Whatever else public schooling may mean to Americans, it is above all a training ground for the workplace. That conviction is also reflected in a series of urgent political pronouncements over the past several years which overwhelmingly stress the importance of education in the economic sphere.

The effects on the education of young people have been devastating. Recently, a professor of communications at the University of Michigan reported that surveys of his students (mostly juniors and seniors) over the past ten years revealed that only 7 percent could identify the state's two senators, only about a third knew the name of the U.S. secretary of state, and fewer than half knew when World War Two began and ended. This, sadly, is old news. What is remarkable and revealing in this case is the reason these "bright, inquisitive" college students in a highly selective university offered for their lack of elemental knowledge: "They said they wouldn't need the information in their future jobs."[2] Jobs are everything. Being educated, or at least well-informed, is simply beside the point.

Other reasons have been adduced for the failure to educate. Critics like E. D. Hirsch, for example, blame John Dewey and a succession of other educational reformers, as well as schools of education for allegedly adopting their ideas.[3] These criticisms miss the mark. As most teachers can testify, they do

xiii

teach the kind of knowledge and information that reflect Hirsch's sense of what cultural literacy entails. The question is not why American schools do not teach these things; it is why students reject that knowledge. I hope that this book provides the basis of a more plausible explanation for the failure.

This book is an attempt to trace the evolution of job training as an educational ideal. It begins with the drive to install manual training in American schools, proceeds next to vocational education, and then to *vocationalization*, which includes vocational education but incorporates the idea that the curriculum as a whole, not just a part of it, exists for the purpose of getting and holding a job. These three stages overlap. Manual training, for example, was principally seen as a moral corrective and a pedagogical reform, but training for the workplace was never absent as the drive to install manual training into the curriculum proceeded. Vocational education was, first and foremost, skill training for the workplace, but it also included the promise of preserving treasured values related to the work ethic and to improving school practice generally. At the same time that vocational education was occupying an increasingly important role in the American curriculum, vocationalism was establishing itself as the central purpose of American schooling. The greatly expanded role of vocational education in the curriculum is itself a highly significant development in American education; the idea that the curriculum as a whole ought to be directed toward vocational purposes is an even more far-reaching phenomenon.

Chapters 1 and 2, which review national trends and issues relating to manual training and vocational education up to around 1912, are followed by two chapters that deal specifically with the way in which manual training and then vocational education were implemented in the Milwaukee, Wisconsin public schools during the same period. Chapters 3 and 4 examine in a kind of case study the political and practical obstacles that the installation of manual training and then vocational education entailed as well as the processes by which those obstacles were overcome in one large industrial city. In these chapters, I relied very extensively on comparable chapters from the Ph.D. dissertation of one of my former graduate students, Carol Judy Kean,[4] and she is therefore listed as the coauthor of those two chapters. Her research was extremely useful in developing certain themes in the book, and chapters 1 and 2 also reflect her work. I am very grateful to her for the graciousness she showed in allowing me to make such liberal use of her dissertation.

The other debts I owe in connection with the writing of this book are far reaching, and I can never fully acknowledge them, but I shall try to mention at least the most conspicuous, beginning with the dedication. The reflections on the nature of work that prompted this book began, I suspect, with my parents' experience with it. My father earned his living as a sewing machine operator in the sweatshops of New York City, and in hard times, my mother did as well when her health permitted. My childhood recollections of the Great Depression center mainly on my father's inability to find work and the despair this created in the family. On occasion, when he found piece-work, he would come home almost too exhausted to talk. To be honest, then, my antipathy to what Frederick Winslow Taylor called the "piece-rate system" and to efforts generally to squeeze the last ounce of productivity from the worker has its roots in my own life history. It is in this regard that I hope I can be excused for reflecting a touch of skepticism about the so-called dignity of work. Undoubtedly, satisfaction may be derived from the work of the hands, but I sometimes think that the conviction that all work has dignity regardless of the circumstances has served to inhibit attempts to improve conditions in the workplace and to stave off efforts somehow to humanize it. When all work, even under the most degrading conditions, is declared to be ennobling, the need to reform the workplace somehow seems much less urgent.

My debt to my wife, Bernice, is so great that I can never truly acknowledge it fully, and my children, Diane and Ken, have always been a continuing source of inspiration and delight to me, as now my grandchildren are.

I would also like to acknowledge the teachers in vocational schools and in schools everywhere whose dedication and competence often under extremely adverse circumstances are greatly underappreciated. My first full-time teaching job was in 1952 at the Bronx Vocational High School in the South Bronx, and my two years of teaching there was an experience I shall always remember and even treasure despite my all too obvious limitations in overcoming the obstacles I faced. My subsequent six years of teaching in a suburban junior-senior high school served only to heighten the contrast in my mind between the two kinds of education America's schools provide. If bifurcation as it relates to the split between vocational and general education becomes an ugly word in this book, that also may stem from my own experience with it. The opportunity gap tied to social class as well as race and gender is an all too obvious fact of American life, but it seems to me now that our system of education needlessly exaggerates it, and that became a familiar refrain in this book.

From the time I became an assistant professor at the University of Wisconsin, Madison, in 1963 to the present, I have considered myself incredibly lucky to find work that is exactly suited to my temperament and in a setting that is on one hand humane and, on the other, one that encourages exacting rigor from its students and faculty. In time, my work became almost indistinguishable from play. In that sense, I suppose that I found a measure of dignity in my own work after all, but labor that is not only drudgery but unrewarding and even demeaning remains for me an ever-present concern.

I owe a particular debt of gratitude to my close colleague and a coeditor of the series in which this book appears, Bill Reese, who provided me with great advice as to sources and directions. I am also happy once again to acknowledge the sound advice and encouragement provided by my former major professor, Arno A. Bellack. He undertook to review drafts of chapters and provided me with the benefit of his keen insight and criticism. Donna Schleicher cheerfully offered to check the manuscript for errors, and I am once again very grateful to her for her invaluable assistance and the moral support she provided. Members of the support staff in my departments such as Darcy Holmes, Mary Jo Gessler, and Gail Geib helped in numerous other ways. In the research for this book, I was assisted by able and resourceful graduate assistants, whose aid over the long period of gestation proved instrumental in its completion. They include Clif Tanabe, Carole Trone, Eric Houck, and Amy Shuffleton. Ms. Shuffleton was tremendously helpful in the preparation of the reference section. I should also like to thank Barry Franklin, Daniel Pekarsky, and Francis Schrag for reading drafts of some chapters and providing me with the benefit of their suggestions.

In the course of conducting the research for this book, I discovered a number of excellent sources that dealt with issues closely related to my main subject of vocationalism. To cite one example, in chapter 7, which deals with vocationalism during the period of the Great Depression and the New Deal, I found the interactions between various government agencies and educational policy-makers to be so fascinating that I had to resist being lured into matters unrelated to vocationalism per se. Fortunately, fine general treatments of the depression period in relation to education and youth are available. The older and widely cited doctoral dissertations by George P. Rawick (1957) and Harry Zeitlin (1958) hold up very well, and I also found the more recent Ph.D. dissertation by Andre R. O'Coin (1988), which is expressly related to vocational education in the depression era, to be extremely comprehensive and well researched. In fact, I wrote to O'Coin to congratulate him on a fine piece of work only to discover that he died tragically only a few years after being awarded the Ph.D. I have tried to acknowledge his contributions to this work as well as those of other excellent scholars whose research and findings I drew upon, but the conventions of footnoting do not really do justice to the debt involved. Excellent published sources on the period of the Great Depression include David Tyack, Robert Lowe, and Elizabeth Hansot's *Public Schools in Hard Times: The Great Depression and Recent Years* (1984) and Richard A. Reiman's *The New Deal and American Youth: Ideas and Ideas in a Depression Decade* (1992). I recommend these works to readers whose interest on the subject extends beyond the impact of the depression on American vocational education in particular. Throughout this book, the reader will find references to other fine works on vocational education and related topics, such as Harvey

A. Kantor's *Learning to Labor: School, Work, and Vocational Reform in Califor-nia, 1880–1930* (1988), John L. Rury's *Education and Women's Work: Female Schooling and the Division of Labor in Urban America, 1870–1930* (1991), and most conspicuously, the wonderful collection of essays edited by Harvey A. Kantor and David B. Tyack, *Work, Youth, and Schooling: Historical Perspectives on Vocationalism in American Education* (1982), all of which I found to be immensely stimulating. I also recommend Berenice Fisher's *Industrial Educa-tion: American Ideals and Institutions* (1967) and Arthur G. Wirth's *Education in the Technological Society: The Vocational-Liberal Studies Controversy in the Early Twentieth Century* (1972), which cover some of the same ground in a perceptive and provocative way.

Herbert M. Kliebard
Madison, Wisconsin

SCHOOLED TO WORK

Vocationalism and the American Curriculum, 1876–1946

 1

"YOUNG VULCANS, BARE-ARMED, LEATHER-APRONED . . . HONEST SWEAT"

Manual Training and the American Work Ethic, 1876–1905

*I firmly believe that in most of our schools there is too much same-
ness and monotony; too much intellectual weariness and subsequent torpor. Hence, if we abridge somewhat the hours given to
books, and introduce exercises of a widely different character, the
result is a positive intellectual gain. There is plenty of time if you
will but use it aright. Throw in the fire those modern instruments of
mental torture, the spelling and defining books. Banish English
grammar, and confine to reasonable limits geography and word-
analysis. Take mathematics, literature, science, and art in just proportion, and you will have time enough for drawing and the study
of tools and mechanical methods.*

*Manual exercises, which are at the same time intellectual exer-
cises, are highly attractive to healthy boys. Go, for instance, into
our forging-shop, where metals are wrought through the agency of
heat. A score of young Vulcans, bare-armed, leather-aproned with
many a drop of an honest sweat stand up to their anvils with an
unconscious earnestness which shows how much they enjoy their
work. What are they doing? They are using brains and hands.*

Calvin M. Woodward, 1885[1]

With the bloody fighting of the Civil War behind them, Americans were
facing another kind of upheaval. The Industrial Revolution was not
only transforming the workplace; its effects were serving to remake social

1

institutions and to recast social relations. In the process, the day-to-day lives of Americans—even their images of themselves—were profoundly altered. Changes in their world were now becoming visible everywhere. Railroads were bringing heretofore secluded parts of the country close to urban centers and delivering the products of the new industrialized society to Americans everywhere. With the rapid expansion of railroads and ease of travel came a renewed awareness that America was changing. Everything was becoming bigger, faster, and more impersonal. First the telegraph and then the telephone were used to coordinate business transactions in America's growing industrial economy. After the introduction of the rotary press in 1875, newspaper prices dropped sharply, bringing mass circulation.[2] Magazines like *Ladies Home Journal* were developing a huge readership, and advertising was creating new markets. After a century as a political reality, a new American national identity was being forged.

Americans were also becoming more prosperous. The standard of living was rising steadily, and manufactured products were becoming more widely available. As food prices began to fall, workers were better able to afford manufactured goods, such as ready-made clothing. But there were also psychic tensions and uncertainties. A depression struck in 1873 and continued until 1878. This was followed by an economic boom in the 1880s, although in 1883 more than twenty banks failed and many railroads declared bankruptcy. A major depression struck again in 1893 and persisted until 1897; once more there were wage cuts and layoffs. Workers were increasingly being faced with the threat of unemployment, and the growth of cities brought a squalor and degradation of life that was profoundly troublesome. That a major transformation had been wrought was becoming obvious, not simply in terms of manufacture but in the lives of most Americans. For many, this meant prosperity previously undreamed of; yet even as the standard of living was rising, a gnawing anxiety began to take hold.

As mass markets were being created by new means of transportation and technological changes in communication, entrepreneurs were devising new techniques of production requiring a change not simply in how work went forward in manufacturing plants but ultimately in the way in which the nature of work was conceived and understood. Much of this changed conception of work was related to the fact that rapid industrial and economic growth increasingly depended on specialization and division of labor. Since a particular conception of the dignity of work lay at the core of morality in Protestant America, this changing conception of work brought with it a confusion about a value structure that had been forged in the world of preindustrial capitalism. "The work ethic" as it evolved in an earlier era, says Daniel Rodgers, "belonged to a setting of artisans' shops, farms, and countinghouses."[3] It was not driven by Bessemer converters, continuous assembly lines, or the stopwatches of efficiency engineers. The new industrialism carried with it not just a transformation in America's economic arrangements and in its social institutions; it precipitated a moral crisis.

The process of manufacturing became increasingly divorced from design and management. Management as well as labor was becoming specialized, creating sharp divisions within the corporate structure and establishing new patterns of corporate governance. At the same time, new ways of controlling the production process were creating different expectations as to what kind of work was to be valued. Skilled labor was not as highly prized as it had been, and as a result, new relationships developed between labor and management. In 1885, for example, when managers and unionized workers at the McCormick plant were at odds, management installed new molding machines and dismissed the entire workforce, hiring unskilled workers in their place.[4] Not only was skilled labor itself being devalued in the new industrial economy; a new antagonism, a new anonymity, and a growing alienation were replacing the earlier relationships between managers and workers and even between worker and worker.

These changes in the workplace carried with them implications for a new conception of the nature of work itself. The natural rhythms of work in a dawn to dusk preindustrial society gave way to the regimen of the clock. What was at times a kind of easy fellowship in the workplace was abandoned in favor of the discipline of exacting work rules. Propelled by wage incentives, the pace of work was no longer controlled by vagaries of human energy and proclivities but by rigorous production standards and the exactitude of the stopwatch. A new economic order, most visible in large-scale plants in northern cities, was demanding profound changes in the relationship between workers and workers, between workers and management, between workers and the workplace, and between workers and work.

THE EMERGENCE OF A NATIONAL
MANUAL TRAINING MOVEMENT

Manual training as a national reform movement in schools began to take shape as a response, albeit an ambiguous one, to radical transformation of working relationships and the nature of work itself. According to some accounts, the movement had its formal inception at the Philadelphia Centennial Exposition of 1876, although philanthropic and social welfare traditions of manual training reach back into the antebellum period.[5] At the 1876 exposition, John D. Runkle, a mathematics professor and president of the Massachusetts Institute of Technology, first examined the pedagogical innovations on display at the Russian tool exhibit. Runkle later described his experience almost as a kind of divine revelation:

> At Philadelphia, in 1876, almost the first thing I saw was a small case containing three series of models—one of chipping and filing, one of forging, and one of machine-tool work. I saw at once that they were not parts of machines, but simply graded models for teaching the manipulations in those arts. In an instant, the problem I had been seeking to solve was clear to my mind; a plain distinction between a mechanic art and its application in some special trade became apparent.[6]

What came to be called the "Russian system" was an outgrowth of social and political conditions in the latter part of nineteenth-century Russia. With industry having become established in the eighteenth century after the reign of Peter the Great, Russia faced a growing need for trained workers, but lacking the Western European tradition of well-organized guilds, systematic trade training was not widely available. After the emancipation of the serfs in 1861, large factories began competing with artisan industry, and systematic instruction in the use of tools became a high priority. The development of such instruction was relatively unimpeded because those guilds that did exist were not powerful enough to mount effective opposition.[7]

The Russian system of graded exercises in the use of tools was developed by Victor Della Vos at the Imperial Technical School in Moscow beginning around 1868. His central idea was that through systematic instruction, the skills of a trade would be taught independently of the actual creation of the product. His new system not only took less time than apprenticeships but was designed to convey the necessary skills to many students at once. Upon viewing Della Vos's graded exercises at the Philadelphia exposition, Runkle realized that this separation of the learning of work skills from the tangible process of production represented a viable school-based alternative to the apprenticeship system. As an apprentice, one learned the required skills by actually participating in the work required to do the job under the tutelage of a master of that trade. Under Della Vos's system, the student *prepared* for work by learning discrete skills through carefully designed lessons.

Runkle's first impulse was to use the "Russian Tool System" as a way of improving the training of future engineers, and in that regard, he organized a group of instruction shops as a secondary school which was adjacent to and essentially a preparatory school for the Massachusetts Institute of Technology. Within a year after seeing Della Vos's system at the Philadelphia Exposition, he opened his School of Mechanic Arts, a secondary school whose motto was "Arts, not trades; instruction, not construction," thereby announcing that the purpose of the school was educative, not for producing goods. Emphasis was placed on introducing students to the properties of certain materials such as wood, clay, and iron, and toward providing instruction in such basic shop activities as chipping, filing, and forging. A regular academic curriculum existed alongside these forms of instruction.[8]

Runkle's enthusiasm for the principles on which his School of Mechanic Arts was based, however, soon led him to become an ardent advocate for their introduction into public schools. In 1877, only a year after the Philadelphia Exposition, Runkle arranged for an exhibit of the Russian system of tool instruction at the Louisville, Kentucky, meeting of the National Education Association. In his home state, he urged the Massachusetts Board of Education to incorporate manual training into the curriculum of public high schools, arguing that the conventional curriculum was successful neither in promoting high culture nor in preparing the new generation for the world of industry. By contrast, his new manual arts curriculum would both instill the traditional respect for manual labor and prepare graduating students to make their way successfully in the new industrial world. Runkle evidently saw the new manual training as a bridge between the older values associated with the honest toil that had been the hallmark of the independent artisan so revered earlier in the nineteenth century and the mechanized forces being unleashed by the new and restructured industrial society.

In this sense, the emerging manual training movement embraced two almost contradictory justifications. At the same time that manual training seemed to preserve the values associated with the Protestant work ethic that had their origins in a preindustrial society, it promised to address the needs of the new industrialism. In fact, however, that work ethic was in many ways at odds with the new industrial order. Under the older system, "In a world remote from the time clock and the efficiency expert," Rodgers says, "the work ethic was not a certain rate of busyness but a way of thinking."[9] Work not only had dignity; it was a moral imperative. Whatever its merits as a way of teaching work skills, the new manual training seemed to tap a nostalgia for those older values giving a measure of comfort to Americans disconcerted by the rapid rise of the factories and the consequent decline of the artisan system. In his report to the Board of Education of the State of Massachusetts for 1876–77, for example, Runkle was careful to introduce his proposal by urging that schools find "the means to elevate and dignify the labor of our country," even suggesting that schools as then constituted "through habit" often teach children to "despise" labor.[10] If work was being debased under the regime of the new factory system, it could at least be esteemed and perhaps even ennobled in the schools.

At the same time, manual training in schools appeared to be an eminently appropriate response to a changing economic system where apprenticeship no longer seemed to fit. Although Runkle was usually careful to emphasize the educational and moral benefits rather than the practical value of manual training, even he could not resist justifying it in terms of occupational preparation as well. "When the student has become familiar with the use of tools in the few fundamental arts" he argued, "then he will apply his knowledge in production ... [and thereby] furnish an opportunity for the application in manufacture."[11] In this way, a kind of rarified and purified form of labor could be introduced into the schools, labor that was morally uplifting and at the same time a preparation for work in the real world. The school was, in effect, being proposed as a mediating institution between an intimate and familiar world marked by traditional values and the increasingly impersonal and remote world of modern industry. As a vehicle for resurrecting and preserving nineteenth-century ideals and as a way of coming to terms with the new industrial society, manual training had a powerful appeal.

CALVIN WOODWARD JOINS THE CAMPAIGN FOR MANUAL TRAINING

Almost as soon as Runkle had undertaken a national leadership role in the manual training movement, he was joined in his campaign by a powerful ally, Calvin M. Woodward, a professor at the O'Fallon Polytechnic Institute at Washington University in St. Louis. Woodward had earlier experimented with his own system of graded shop exercises in an effort to overcome what he regarded as a dismal lack of practical knowledge about tools among his own students. Although, like Runkle, Woodward at first regarded Della Vos's innovations as aiding specifically in the training of engineers, he too began to envision a more far-reaching overhaul of American education. In effect, the campaign for manual training became a kind of morality play in which the mythic American hero was portrayed as a vigorous, "bare-armed" worker (see Figure 1). As the drama unfolded, that representation of the ideal American, a modernized version of the antebellum noble artisan, was to do battle with bookish, ink-stained rivals for most of the twentieth century. The plot of the drama pitted Woodward's "young Vulcans," the muscular "mechanics, engineers, and manufacturers" in spirited conflict with their traditional enemies, "the clerks, book-keepers, salesmen, poor lawyers, murderous doctors, whining preachers, penny-a-liners, or hardened 'school-keepers'."[12] The theater in which this play was enacted was the American public school.

By 1878, only two years after the Philadelphia Exhibition, Woodward was able to present a full-fledged pedagogical rationale for manual training. In a paper read before the St. Louis Social Science Association, he declared at the outset that "the object of education has been the same in all ages; the development of those powers and faculties which combine to form the ideal man of the age," but he was also careful to quote Carlyle to the effect that, "Man is a tool-using animal,"[13] thus establishing the centrality of tools to the development of those powers. A master publicist, Woodward was also able to evoke the convictions that lie at the core of American life and the fear that those

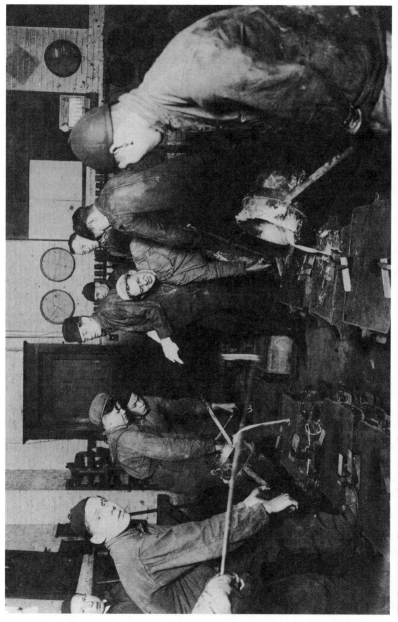

FIGURE 1. Forging class, Seattle, Washington. Calvin M. Woodward's image of his students as "young Vulcans" symbolically contrasted manual training with what he regarded as the effete and bookish education of his time. *Courtesy Seattle Public Schools.*

central values are in danger of becoming eroded—"the ambitious young wife who cannot endure cooking. . . . the man who turns up his nose at the rough palm of the joiner or the soiled fingers and greasy apron of the machinist."[14] These attitudes, he feared, might even be reinforced by the kind of education that exists. The remedy, of course, was manual training, but there were obstacles to its incorporation into the American curriculum. "Although indenture and regular apprenticeship have passed away forever," there was "the tyranny of Trade Unions [that] is felt in every trade," unions who "for the purpose of increasing the value of their own labor and skill . . . , combine to keep others out of their shops."[15] In this regard, Woodward was careful to dissociate such training from trade training, objecting, for example, to "special education . . . that begins too early and limited to the absolute needs of the trade."[16] For Woodward, the answer lay in instruction in tool use in the public schools in the absence of actual construction of products. Referring to Della Vos's system, he declared that "to Russia belongs the honor of having solved the problem of tool instruction."[17] At the same time that valuable skills were being learned, the value of honest labor would be esteemed and education enlivened.

Although at first Woodward emphasized manual training as a way of introducing his own students to the "alphabet of tools,"[18] like Runkle, he soon began to see this curriculum as embodying a broader pedagogical vision. Throughout the 1880s, Woodward continued to promote manual training, not simply as an improvement in the preparation of engineers or industry managers, but as a new form of secondary education, one in which shop work would become as commonplace in the curriculum as the traditional academic subjects. Rather than finding its place on the periphery of the curriculum, manual training would occupy center stage. That emphasis was manifest in the curriculum of Woodward's Manual Training School of Washington University in St. Louis when it began operation in 1880. The three-year program of studies centered on joinery, foundry work, and machinery, combining this shop work with pure and applied mathematics, science, penmanship, and drawing. As his enthusiasm for manual training grew, his arguments began to reflect a threefold emphasis: manual training as moral regeneration, as pedagogical reform, and as preparation for the workplace in the new industrial society.

It is partly through Woodward's evolving and occasionally contradictory ideas as to the role manual training would play in the schools that the ambiguous and sometimes puzzling nature of the movement can be traced. Although Woodward wanted to use manual training exercises as a form of skill training by introducing his students first to wood and then to "brass, iron, and steel turning, fitting and finishing," he was reluctant to define this work as preparation for a trade.[19] His enthusiasm for learning skills involved in manual labor notwithstanding, Woodward was conscious that European-style trade training, where future workers and future professionals, academics, and business leaders were housed in different institutions, had antidemocratic overtones. He argued that the European arrangement might be suited to the European social system where the lives of workingmen were predestined to "run smoothly in grooves cut for them before they were born." In American society, as he saw it, "every boy is a natural candidate for the office of president, and no one shall dare to place any bounds to his aspirations and social possibilities." European-style training, except for its use in charitable and reformatory schools, had no place in America, "at least for the present." These qualifications aside, Woodward continued to stress the nation's need for technically trained workers. "General culture," he declared, was often a euphemism for learning "a little of everything and nothing deep," although he found some benefit in offering general training to insure "a wholesome intellectual culture."[20]

As his campaign gathered momentum, Woodward began to direct his message more specifically to an audience of professional educators. Through a series of addresses delivered to conventions of the National Education Association (NEA) in the latter part of the nineteenth century, Woodward found a national platform for publicizing the reforms he had introduced in St. Louis. The NEA was at the time the nation's most important forum for debating educational policy and a place where local school people could become acquainted with what was going on in leading urban centers such as Boston and Chicago. In that setting, Woodward softened his message. Instead of pitting manual training against education for general culture, he promoted manual training as part of general education. He once characterized traditional education as a two-legged stool, needing the leg of manual training to make it stable.[21] Manual training was not a rival to traditional education; it completed it.

In one form or another, the message that Woodward was delivering was being heard in large cities. In 1884, the Commercial Club of Chicago founded the Chicago Manual Training School. In that same year, Baltimore established the first manual training school to be publicly supported. In 1885, the city of Philadelphia opened the second public manual training high school. Toledo followed suit that same year, as did St. Paul in 1888.[22] Manual training was also being incorporated into public school programs of study. Moreover, as Woodward liked to point out, elements of manual training had been introduced in schools even when manual training courses *per se* were not offered. As evidence of manual training's success, he argued that "whenever manual training [had] been judiciously tried," the result was an extension in the period of schooling. Pointing to his own school as an example, he claimed that experience in manual training had resulted in "a stronger taste for study and a greater zeal for higher education." In his Manual Training High School, for example, 87 of the 239 graduates had embarked on careers in teaching, law, medicine (dentistry and surgery), architecture, and engineering, all requiring higher education. At Washington University, about half of the freshman and sophomore classes in the previous year, 1888, were graduates of his school.[23] In its early incarnations, manual training clearly was being advertised not as an alternative to academic and professional education, but as complementary to it and a way of enhancing it.

In this form, manual training's growing popularity in schools was greeted by nearly universal acceptance among professional educators. Only in the case of someone like William Torrey Harris, the superintendent of schools in St. Louis, who was rapidly developing a reputation as a hidebound conservative in educational matters, would one hear reservations expressed. If the career of manual training can be traced through its expression in the determined advocacy of Runkle and Woodward, then the opposition—the expression of a rival educational ideal—can be illustrated in Harris's opposition to it. Actually, Harris was not so much an outright opponent of manual training as he was skeptical of what he regarded as the grandiose claims made in its behalf. His objections were expressed at the NEA convention in 1889 (shortly before he was to assume the post of U.S. Commissioner of Education), when he reported as chair of the Committee on Pedagogics. According to Harris, manual training had emerged as a central concern of the committee because of the "strong claims set up for it by its advocates," because it "serves to unite the critics of the educational system already existing" including "its uncompromising enemies," and because of the claim that manual training "is educational in the same sense as the branches of science and literature." For Harris, the last argument in particular raised serious questions about the course of study in American schools, and, therefore, the committee sought to untangle the educational claims that proponents had been making in behalf of manual training. The committee also sought to determine the economic value of manual training because, as they saw it, "the popularity of the movement has its foundations in the conviction that if the schools teach manual training, all pupils will be fitted for useful industries before the age of leaving school for business."[24] Harris's Committee of Pedagogics, in other words, had undertaken the formidable task of assessing the range of pedagogical and economic claims being put forward by leaders of the burgeoning movement.

Harris was not antagonistic to the idea that manual training in some form could become a reasonable alternative to apprenticeship, but he did not see it as establishing itself as integral to the curriculum in public schools. If introduced at all, it should appear rather late and only after suitable attention had been given to intellectual culture. The committee recommended, therefore, that the introduction of manual training be postponed until the pupil had reached the age of twelve. This would insure proper attention to "the intellectual branches of school-work, namely, in reading, writing, arithmetic, geography, grammar, and history." Harris went on to suggest that postponing manual training until the fifteenth year was even more desirable because the student's increased maturity would enhance the effectiveness of the instruction, but he seemed most concerned that manual training would somehow detract from the intellectual and spiritual functions of schooling.

Harris liked to view the school as providing a special environment free of vicissitudes that characterize the world outside of school. He acknowledged that "the great majority of children are destined to earn their living by manual labor," but to him this did not mean that the school should devote itself to prepare its students for this work. In fact, because many children face "a life of drudgery" in their adult lives, childhood should all the more be "devoted to spiritual growth, to training the intellect and will, and to building the basis for a larger humanity." With some prescience, he called into question the idea that it was the school's responsibility to "forecast the horoscope of the child," which in his view could result in putting limitations on the child's intellectual and spiritual development. The effect on the child would be to "make sure of his inability to ascend above manual toil,"[25] thus raising the possibility that such training could eventuate in a self-fulfilling prophecy.

In terms of economic considerations, Harris's report also questioned the growing conviction that preparation for a future job should be exalted above other factors, contending instead that it was "but a small part of the total functions of anyone's life." "What does one need," Harris asked, "besides his trade?," arguing that good citizenship was a more noble ideal for schools to pursue. The first prerequisite of citizenship was literacy. He defined literacy, however, not simply in terms of reading and writing but in terms of the "knowledge and thoughts that make up the conventional view of the world— such ideas and opinions as one learns in studying geography and history, and especially literature."[26] To Harris, education was a process of opening up what he liked to call the "windows of the soul" (mathematics, geography, grammar, history, and literature) to intellectual culture in the interest of creating an enlightened citizenry. Manual training, with its emphasis on the work of the hands, seemed to be only peripherally related to that task.

In his NEA address that same year, "The Intellectual Value of Tool Work," Harris expressed a willingness to concede a "permanently valid place for the manual training school side by side with apprentice schools for youths who are old enough to enter a trade," but, he continued to insist, "Cultivate the humanities first, and afterwards the industrial faculties."[27] Reiterating his persistent theme of the "windows of the soul," he compared the value of those studies represented in the traditional school curriculum with the value of tool work and found the latter definitely wanting. Manual training simply would not open up any new window. While he was willing to make some room for manual training, it could come only after the job of intellectual training was accomplished. Increasingly, however, Harris's was becoming very much a lonely voice.

Woodward was almost alone in confronting Harris directly at the NEA meeting,[28] but he subsequently undertook a vigorous rebuttal of the main contentions of the Committee on Pedagogics. As he saw it, the report, having been "published five or six times, and no doubt . . . widely read,"[29] could not go uncontested. Woodward appeared most concerned with the position taken by the committee that manual training was "devoted to the business of educating the youth in the essential of his trade or occupation." In defining manual education in that way, Woodward argued, the committee was simply constructing a "straw-man for the exquisite pleasure of seeing it topple under their vigorous blows."[30] Woodward wanted manual training seen in the same way as the standard elements of the curriculum and not as an ornamental appendage. "No trade," he declared, "is included in our tool-work just as no occupation is included in science and mathematics."[31] On the other hand, he was appalled that Harris's committee found it necessary to recommend that no instruction in manual training be begun before the age of twelve. "*No manual training school that I know of,*" he said, "*admits pupils till they are thirteen or fourteen years old*" (original emphasis).[32] While not exactly denying the value of manual training for job purposes, Woodward was eager to convey the impression that such economic advantages were incidental to manual training's benefits in terms of intellectual development. Harris, on the other hand, took those economic benefits to be the underlying basis of manual training. The ambiguity as to whether manual training should be interpreted primarily as a pedagogical reform or as a necessary avenue to learning job skills for the new industrial age was never resolved. In a sense, this dual justification may have actually added to its appeal. Supporters tended to see in the reform what they wanted to see.

By 1893, the national movement in behalf of manual training was in full swing, and Woodward, in an assessment of its new stature, was able to marshal a full array of supporters and their endorsements. Although he acknowledged that one source of its growth was the tradition of the trade school, the second, "from which manual training has gained its chief vigor, has been the conviction, now very widespread, that at school more than books should be studied." In Woodward's words, its rise to new prominence was nothing less than "the natural product of our advancing civilization."[33] With uncommon skill, Woodward, over time, was able to present manual training not as narrow trade training, appealing as that was in certain quarters, but as an overall reform that would address the very real shortcomings of traditional education. The pedagogical argument was a powerful one when it came to winning over professional educators and school managers to the cause, but it was not the appeal that was most attractive to industrialists or, for that matter, the general public.

MANUAL TRAINING FOR AFRICAN AMERICANS
AND AMERICAN INDIANS

From its earliest manifestations but persisting throughout its history, manual training was seen as especially beneficial for those segments of American society that were believed to require remedial treatment for one reason or another. Even before the Civil War, manual training was widely prescribed for delinquent children in northeastern cities, and it was the education of choice for children with physical disabilities. The poor as a class were also among the earliest target groups for the supporters of manual training since their impoverished condition was in part deemed to be a function of defective values. Increasingly, manual training was also believed to have curative powers for immigrants as well as for various ethnic and racial minorities. As Joseph Lee, the respected Boston philanthropist, once put it, "It is interesting to see how invariably the men who take up the whole subject for a given class of people,—whether they be the blind, the deaf-mutes, deformed children, or youthful criminals; or whether they are the boys of a particular parish or club; or whether they are a whole race like the negroes or the jews,—are at the present time including industrial training among the things which they find themselves called upon to provide."[34]

By the time Lee expressed his views in 1902, manual training was already being widely promoted as a source of moral and social enrichment, especially with respect to the virtues associated with the work ethic, and those views already had an established tradition in the arena of African American education. In fact, black industrial education was already in place by the eighteenth century.[35] By 1830, it had been embraced by black intellectuals such as Samuel Cornish as well as by Northern white philanthropists who were pressing to create manual arts colleges for African Americans. These early efforts, however, met with little success. As James Anderson summed up the ill-fated antebellum drive for black industrial schools in the Northeast, "A manual labor college or trade school . . . would not so much solve labor-market problems as make them apparent."[36] Racism in the job market made the idea of skilled black workers as an integral part of the job force only a remote possibility.

The drive for manual training for blacks, however, was rekindled after the Civil War. During Reconstruction, the effort to provide manual training for African Americans was being seen by white reformers in particular not so much as an avenue for teaching valuable job skills but as a socializing instrument through which the newly freed slaves would acquire the virtues of industry and hard work. The founding of Hampton Normal and Agricultural Institute in 1868 is one indication of the success of that drive. Hampton Institute was the brainchild of Samuel Chapman Armstrong, who was born in Hawaii of missionary parents and had served as a commander of black troops during the Civil War. Armstrong's position as editor of the journal *Southern Work- man* put him in a position to disseminate to the white power structure his ideas on the role of African Americans in the South. At times, his message took on the form of a stern warning. Referring to the ex-slave, he once said that "In his mental, moral, and material destitution, he has as much power as any- body to make the next President, or to decide on questions of tariff, currency, or war," implying of course that, even in their degraded condition, they could acquire and exercise great political power. The problem lay essentially in the ex-slave's defects of character. "His low ideas of life and duty, his weak con- science, his want of energy and thrift, his indolent, sensuous tropical blood," he said, "are, rather than mere ignorance, the important and unfortunate facts about him."[37] Drawing on his experience in the Hawaiian Islands, Armstrong saw both Polynesians and African Americans as lacking important character traits. "The negro and the Polynesian," he said, "have many striking similar- ities. Of both it is true that not mere ignorance, but deficiency of character is the chief difficulty, and that to build up character is the true objective point in education." The answer he believed lay in overcoming their natural ten- dency toward idleness. "In the weak tropical races," he reported, "idleness, like ignorance, breeds vice."[38] Fortunately, as Armstrong saw it, these defects of character could be corrected through the sort of manual training that Hamp- ton would provide. Accordingly, the Hampton Institute was not founded pri- marily to train black workers for skilled jobs; it was designed as an institution for teaching appropriate attitudes toward work and thereby correcting the moral failings of an American underclass.

After a time, Hampton's program of industrial education was extended to American Indians, although that decision was quite controversial. Students in the school were wary of the move, and Armstrong himself worried as to whether the Indians were quite civilized enough to accept the school's instruc- tion.[39] According to Armstrong, however, American Indians were in need of moral training quite as much as African Americans:

> Indians are easily taught, for their minds are quick; their bodies are a greater care than their brains; but morals are the chief concerns of their teachers. Hence their education should be first for the heart, then for the health, and last for the mind, reversing the custom of placing mind before physique and character. This is the Hampton idea of their education.[40]

Toward this end, Indian boys were taught farming and such trades as black- smithing, shoemaking, and harness repair. One problem, according to Arm- strong, was that "they soon tire, for their muscles are not trained to steady day's work." He was able to report, however, that after two years' training,

Indian boys could accomplish a full ten hours of labor. Girls were taught to mend and make clothing, washing, ironing, and cooking. Armstrong reported that Indian girls were particular in washing dishes and setting tables but rather slow about it.[41]

In 1892, a report on the progress of the Hampton Institute indicated that the student population now included a total of "633 colored students," of whom 430 were boys and 233 girls, but in addition there were 128 Indian pupils, of which 91 were boys and 37 girls. Like the African American students, American Indian boys were given instruction "in the use of carpenter's, wheelwright's, and blacksmith's tools in order that they may be able to repair everything that their knowledge of civilized life will make essential on their return home."[42] The boys also had access to a paint shop, a tin shop, a knitting room, and a printing office. The industrial education of Indian girls was described as "chiefly educational rather than remunerative," but in practice it seemed to concentrate on maintenance and decorating:

> Each Indian girl does her own sewing, washing, and mending, scrubs and sweeps her own room and takes care of all her personal belongings. The care of the halls and corridors is allotted among the girls and the spacious assembly hall and chapel of Winona, tastefully decorated with hanging baskets of vines and ferns in the windows and wreathed with green garlands at Christmas, is kept neat and orderly by their willing hands.[43]

For both African Americans and American Indians, much emphasis was also placed on the virtues of working the land, although alleged differences in their natural tendencies were sometimes taken into account. "The Negro's social instinct," it was noted, "draws him to manufacturing centres, where a trade will bring him ample support, and he is prone to regard agriculture as a reversion to former conditions of poverty and depressing labor among ignorant and degraded of his own people, while the Indian both by nature and tradition is averse to tilling the soil and he quickly feels the strain of long continued, arduous labor in this as in other occupations."[44] Whatever their differences, however, it was believed that the deficiencies in both groups could be corrected through their experiences at Hampton, and in this regard, working with the soil and the raising of farm animals were thought to be especially effective.

The so-called Hampton model was widely emulated in the South in the sense that industrial training schools for newly freed slaves as well as for the American Indian population sprung up in many states, but the term "Hampton model" can be misleading. At least some of these institutions, while emphasizing industrial education generally, tended to give that kind of education a distinctively different slant from that of Hampton's. Tuskegee Institute, probably the most renowned of these institutions, is a case in point.

Because its founder and guiding spirit, Booker T. Washington, was a graduate of Hampton, it is easy to assume that both institutions were ideologically
of one piece. Washington, however, succeeded in putting his own stamp on
Tuskegee. For one thing, the faculty at Tuskegee was African American, and
in its time, this represented a significant departure from the white missionary tradition in black education that Armstrong represented. Washington
drew his faculty not only from Hampton but, in the case of academic teachers, from Fisk University as well as from the pool of black graduates of northern universities.

Of considerable importance as well is that the balance in terms of pedagogical emphasis tilted more toward skill training in the interest of creating
an independent class of black artisans than toward moral redemption. The
association of manual training with the Protestant work ethic inevitably came
through in Washington's public statements, but the main impetus at Tuskegee
was industrial education's economic rather than moral benefits. Although
Washington was capable of saying that "all forms of labor are honorable, and
all forms of idleness disgraceful," a moral pronouncement, he was more concerned that blacks, who had once been skilled and proficient workers, had
begun to lose those skills and, as a result, were not realizing their economic
potential. In the twenty years after emancipation, he said, "Many were trained
in Latin, but few as engineers and blacksmiths," and he often laced his
speeches with anecdotes designed to illustrate how economically worthless a
literary education was for African Americans. While always careful not "to
apologize for the curse of slavery," he liked to emphasize by way of contrast
that, under slavery, blacks were responsible for doing the work that needed
to be done:

> In most cases if a Southern white man wanted a house built he consulted a
> Negro mechanic about the plan and about the actual building of the struc-
> ture. If he wanted a suit of clothes made he went to a Negro tailor, and for
> shoes he went to a shoemaker of the same race. In a certain way every slave
> plantation in the South was an industrial school.[45]

Although such ability to get things done was not monetarily rewarded under
the system of slavery, Washington contended that, once free, blacks could use
their skills to achieve a measure of economic independence. His image of the
blacks under slavery—competent, resourceful, energetic—was the virtual
antithesis of the image that Armstrong presented of the ex-slave as shiftless,
indolent, and lethargic.

At his 1895 speech at Fisk University, Washington elaborated on this
theme and tried to dispel the notion that industrial education was somehow
opposed to a literary education. He was quick to add, however, that "it requires

as quick a mind to build a Corliss engine as it does to write a Greek grammar." As was usually the case, he emphasized the economic rather than the moral advantages of an industrial education. "Ninety per cent. of any race on the globe earns its living in the common occupations of life," he said, "and the Negro can be no exception to this rule."[46] For the most part, Washington was careful not to disparage academic and professional education, but he believed that the key to the blacks' economic emancipation lay in industrial education. "The Negro has the right to study law," he said in what is perhaps his best book, "but success will come to the race sooner if it produces intelligent, thrifty farmers, mechanics, and housekeepers to support the lawyers."[47]

Over the course of his life, Washington was always respectful of "General Armstrong" as he called him, and undoubtedly he shared something of Armstrong's moral fervor, but his primary concern was not in using manual training to mitigate the African American's alleged aversion for work. Washington saw in industrial education the opportunity to help blacks become economic assets to the new South and, not incidentally, to achieve economic independence for themselves. "Almost the whole problem for the Negro in the South," he declared in his autobiography, "rests itself on the question as to whether he makes himself such an indispensable service to his neighbor, to the community, that no one can fill his place better in the body politic."[48] It should not be surprising that Washington relegated the alleged redemptive powers of manual training to secondary importance at Tuskegee. Ministering to innate moral failings and defects of character is most appealing when the objects of those ministrations are groups other than one's own.[49] Washington, unlike Armstrong, was dealing with his own people.

Although much has been made of the contrast in the messages of the two great black leaders of the time, Washington and W. E. B. Du Bois, Du Bois had considerable sympathy for Washington's effort to create an education for African Americans that would insure their economic independence, providing, of course, that the education of their "souls" was not neglected. Much of his well-known criticism of Washington, especially as expressed in *Souls of Black Folk,* was directed at Washington's apparent neglect of the education of the group Du Bois liked to call the "talented tenth," the future leaders of his people, but he was also skeptical about some of the claims being made in behalf of industrial education.[50] When Du Bois was invited to address Hampton students in 1906, he confronted this issue directly. Summing up what he regarded as the philosophy of industrial education for the millions of black people, he said that its underlying message was, "Take the eyes of these millions off the stars and fasten them in the soil; and if their young men will dream dreams, let them be dreams of corn bread and molasses."[51] So long as industrial education becomes the sum total of the education they receive, he believed, they would never achieve the measure of equality that was their right. Anticipating that industrial education would not simply take the form of a skill-training adjunct to the academic curriculum, Du Bois feared that other educational ideals could become obliterated. He sharply opposed, therefore, "A distinct philosophy of education which makes the earning of a living the center and norm of human training and which moreover dogmatically asserts that the subject matter and methods of work particular to technical schools are the best for all education—that outside them there is properly no higher training."[52] For a great many Americans—not only African Americans—this is just what education became.

The problem as Du Bois saw it was not simply that a technical education was beginning to overshadow all other educational ideals; it was also that the kind of technical education that African Americans were receiving at institutions like Hampton and Tuskegee did not in fact provide the job skills that modern industry required. Du Bois's coauthored study, *The Negro American Artisan*, seemed to accept Washington's assessment of the role of the black artisan under slavery. "So far as the South was concerned," Du Bois declared, "the Negro slave had been for years the actual artisan,"[53] and he even went on to say that blacks continued to function in that role for a while after emancipation. Certain factors in the contemporary situation, however, made a restoration of that once vital role unlikely. One factor, for example, was the competition from white artisans which, while present to some extent in the antebellum period, had become sharply intensified after the Civil War. Secondly, he believed that African Americans' drive for political power, ironically, had had a deleterious effect on their effort to achieve economic independence. Perhaps most important, however, was that the new industrial system no longer depended on the expert skills that the independent artisan possessed. In other words, industrial education was teaching skills that were not nearly as remunerative as they once had been. As Du Bois put it, "*Negro youth are being taught the technique of a rapidly disappearing age of hand work*" (original emphasis).[54] More than others in his time, black and white, Du Bois was aware that manual training's actual economic value would be minimal in the twentieth century. Industrialization had simply made hand work obsolete in many cases (see Figure 2). As he summed up his case, "The industrial school is facing an age of machinery. The teaching of mere hand work, save in limited amounts for educative purposes, is not training for modern industry."[55]

In support of this position, Du Bois amassed an array of statistical data on black employment at skilled trades as well as a wide range of anecdotal evidence he had collected through surveys of black artisans. When African American artisans were asked how they received their training, 41 percent cited apprenticeship, 37 percent "picked up" their trade, and only 21 percent attended trade school.[56] Du Bois observed in that regard that some of the most successful artisans were those in the first two categories. He also concluded

FIGURE 2. Basket weaving at Tuskegee Institute, Tuskegee, Alabama, 1902. W. E. B. Du Bois believed that the hand crafts being taught in black industrial schools had little economic value. Photograph by Frances Benjamin Johnson. *Courtesy Library of Congress.*

that somewhere between "half and two-thirds of the Negroes trained in industrial schools do not follow their trades,"[57] indicating a limited economic return on their investment in industrial education. In the end, Du Bois perceived a disparity between the moral and pedagogical benefits being claimed for manual training and its purported economic rewards. If industrial education was to have economic value, Du Bois believed, it would have to be overhauled in keeping with the new realities of the workplace. The key to the problem, however, was not so much the school training needed to get a job but the discrimination directed toward African Americans in the workplace. Labor historian Walter Licht, for example, has pointed out that, in the late nineteenth and early twentieth century, black children "attended and remained in school in disproportionately large numbers." Moreover, it was not simply young blacks who were not represented in the workplace, as Du Bois had indicated; Philadelphia's blacks, young and old, were systematically denied employment because of color until around World War Two.[58]

In the context of the debate over black education, a significant contradiction seemed to be emerging between the principal assumptions upon which manual training rested. Some moral and pedagogical benefits could conceivably accrue from an emphasis on the kind of hand labor so revered in antebellum America, but its economic rewards would then be meager. Economic benefits could possibly be achieved by attuning industrial education to the demands of modern industry, but that would merely reproduce the drudgery of the new factory system in schools and diminish its value in the moral and pedagogical sphere. In any case, such job training would certainly not address the discrimination that blacks were experiencing in the workplace.

That fact notwithstanding, the drive to provide industrial education for African Americans continued unabated. The unresolved tension between the moral message as reflected in Armstrong's position and Washington's economic message was real enough, but politically, there was no reason the two messages could not be delivered in tandem. Like Runkle and Woodward, Armstrong and Washington were capable of crafting their messages to their audiences, and Washington in particular was a master of ambiguity. Although his sympathies lay chiefly with economic benefits, he was aware that the success of institutions such as Tuskegee depended on northern philanthropists and on the good will of the white power structure in the South. Manual training as a remedy for various defects of character not only had a long history but a wide appeal to those groups. If anything, the economic and moral messages, although incompatible in one sense, complemented each other in terms of their public appeal. Just as the national leaders in the manual training movement like Woodward and Washington could shift from one message to another or simply present both at the same time, so could their audiences accept either one or both, depending on their ill-defined and sometimes even contradictory hopes and anxieties. While Americans were concerned with an erosion of the traditional work ethic in the wake of industrialization, they were also made anxious by the way new industries and the transformation in the nature of work would affect their earning power and that of their children. Both justifications were to endure well into the twentieth century and were to affect the course that the American curriculum actually took.

Although the tension between manual training's alleged redemptive powers and its promise of economic returns was especially conspicuous in the arena of African American education, it was present as well wherever manual training was discussed. Whether at the national level or in the specific context of the education of minorities both in the North and the South, that tension was never fully resolved. In particular instances, the balance would shift first one way then the other, depending on who was articulating the position or particular circumstances. In general, Washington's position to the contrary, the moral justification tended to prevail when particular, presumably benighted, target groups such as African Americans and American Indians were involved, and increasingly, when manual training was prescribed for the general population, economic and pedagogical rationales assumed greater prominence.

MANUAL TRAINING AS A SUCCESSFUL INNOVATION

The success of a curricular innovation such as manual training is obviously difficult to measure. By the standard of whether manual training schools were established in large numbers along the lines of Woodward's, its achievement was limited but not inconsequential. In 1894, there were fifteen manual training high schools with a combined enrollment of 3,362 students. By 1913, there were already fifty-one such schools, enrolling 50,975 students, approximately three-quarters of whom were boys.[59] In addition, although there were relatively few public manual training high schools, 13,000 students were enrolled in independent schools by 1897.[60] Even the introduction of specific courses of study within the curriculum of regular public high schools does not fully account for its impact. As Woodward liked to point out, much of the idea of manual training had been introduced without it being specifically labeled as such.

A little known concomitant to the expansion of manual training in elementary and secondary schools was its effect on the curriculum of normal schools. Although normal schools are commonly regarded as narrow teacher training institutions, in fact, as Christine A. Ogren has shown, for most of their existence, they exercised an intellectually stimulating and educationally liberating function particularly for women of modest means. Beginning around 1910, however, she argues, "state normal schools began to move away from fostering intellectualism in female students." Although manual training and domestic science courses were quite common in black normal schools as early as the 1880s, they did not become firmly established in the curriculum of white normal schools until the second decade of the twentieth century. In the Geneseo, New York, normal school, for example, an industrial arts department was initiated in 1914, followed by a department of domestic science in 1917. Even in black normal schools, despite the influence of the Tuskegee tradition in the South, liberal arts subjects predominated until around 1910. These new subjects not only competed with the liberal arts for resources; they also contributed to gender segregation. "Students in different courses had fewer academic classes in common," Ogren reports, "which contributed to a decline in the extent to which the schools' academic climate fostered intellectualism in women students."[61] As commonly justified, manual training was not supposed to compete with liberal education, but in some cases, it obviously did.

The diverse set of justifications for manual training put forward by leaders of the movement, such as Woodward, may have led to some inconsistencies and was sometimes subject to direct criticism. One commentator, for example, observed that among the supporters of manual training, "there seemed no body of pedagogical principles that was common to all or even a majority."[62] Manual training was, in other words, an educational innovation that could take on different forms and could be rationalized in a variety of ways, both in terms of the virtues that were attributed to it and the ways in which it was actually being put into practice. Rather than weakening its force, however, such ambiguity probably contributed in the end to manual training's widespread acceptance. With enthusiastic support emanating from within the professional education community and with the general public, the main question, it seemed, was not whether manual training ought to be implemented in schools but which justification would prevail and, therefore, what direction it would take.

One direction it took was as a kind of concomitant to the arts and crafts movement. Beginning in the 1860s, the English socialist William Morris began to stress the joys of handicrafts, contrasting the beauty of the creations of hand labor with the ugliness of mechanized manufacture. After meeting Morris in 1892, Elbert Hubbard took up the cause in the United States and aggressively publicized the virtues of wood, metal, and leather handicrafts through his wide-ranging publications and his Roycroft Shops. Aesthetically, the arts and crafts movement had a significant impact on American design. Its influence, for example, was prominent on the work of Gustav Stickley, who helped create and popularize the first American style of furniture by emphasizing simple motifs, rugged good looks, the natural beauty of the wood grain, and quality in construction. In addition, the great American architect Frank Lloyd Wright incorporated much of the arts and crafts aesthetic not only in the design of his buildings but in their furnishings. As a practical response to industrialization, however, the impact of the movement was limited.

Some lasting effect of the new interest in handicrafts, however, was felt in schools through the incorporation of industrial arts courses into the curriculum. As it evolved, industrial arts had little to do with industry and much to do with art. As one of its leaders, Frederick G. Bonser proclaimed its creed: "Primary emphasis will not be placed upon the production of industrial commodities, but rather upon intelligence and cultivated taste in their choice and use."[63] As envisioned by Bonser, then, industrial arts would accomplish many of the pedagogical purposes associated with manual training. In teaching the craft of book making, for example, no effort would be made to prepare children to become bookbinders. "The purpose," he said, "is rather to develop insight into an industry whereby the race has put itself on record for untold generations."[64] In this regard, Bonser was not only reflecting some of the early ambitions for manual training but giving them something of a Deweyan twist. Industrial arts did become a fixture in American schools, but contrary to the hopes and expectations of manual training's proponents, it found its place only on the periphery of the curriculum.

At best, the drive in behalf of manual training achieved mixed results in terms of implementation in schools, but its ultimate success reached beyond enrollments and the efficacy of its programs. For many educational leaders and members of the general public alike, manual training represented a symbolic but nevertheless compelling way of addressing the disturbing changes that had occurred in American life, offering a measure of reassurance as to what the future held in a time of great uncertainty. Under the pressure of industrialization, the once-proud independent artisan was being transformed into an interchangeable part. Whatever that transformation meant in terms of the debasement of labor, the myth of the dignity of work needed to be preserved. Manual training's claim to having the power to reinvigorate the ennobling power of work and to correct moral defects was a dubious argument at best, and even its alleged value as preparation for the workplace was at least debatable; but in acknowledging and honoring the role of manual labor, manual training's symbolic message struck a responsive chord in many Americans. The contradictions and exaggerated claims of the manual training movement notwithstanding, it was comforting for Americans to believe that the problems associated with the transformation of the workplace could be addressed in schools. Somehow the new, puzzling, impersonal world that the Industrial Revolution had wrought seemed less threatening.

Not the least of the concerns that disturbed the tranquility of Americans on Main Street was the extent to which African Americans and American

Indians as well as other outsider groups, such as immigrants and the poor, could be redeemed from moral squalor. Here again, manual training was being proposed as a remedy. Whether manual training actually delivered on these promises almost did not matter. What mattered most was whether the values that Americans had traditionally treasured were being represented and affirmed in the public discourse about the curriculum. Instrumental effects aside, certain status interests were being validated.

The strength of manual training as an educational reform resided largely in the fact that it looked backward and forward at the same time—backward to the era of the independent artisan and to the dignity of the work associated with preindustrial America, and forward to the society that was being wrought by the new industrialism. At one and the same time, manual training combined the symbolic reassurance that traditional values were not being displaced with the utilitarian prospect that it could somehow equip America's youth with the skills that a new industrial society demanded. For the time being, this left the matter of the movement's eventual direction somewhat uncertain. While these two rationales could easily coexist in the public discourse, however, the actual programs of study required a central focus, as the different emphases of Hampton and Tuskegee illustrated.

The moral and pedagogical arguments persisted and continued to lend force to the movement, but as the new century began, manual training, including its symbolic associations with the work ethic, was perceptively mutating into vocational education, the training required in the new workplace. The distinction between manual training and vocational education, however, can be overdrawn. In 1893, for example, Woodward himself explicitly claimed that manual training would meet the needs of the job market. "By multiplying manual-training schools," he said, "we solve the training of all the mechanics our country needs."[65] Manual training can be distinguished from vocational education not in terms of absolute lines of demarcation but in terms of the balance that each reflected. In that regard, Licht observes,

> Advocates of practical study... drew a sharp distinction between manual training and trade training, generally favoring the former as part of a general education—the hand and the mind had to be exercised simultaneously—and opposing the latter as too narrow and potentially at odds with the goals of the common school system. The lines drawn, however, were often hazy.

The resolution of this ambivalence, he concludes, "guaranteed that matters would be resolved in a hybrid way."[66] Manual training as a curricular reform achieved first respectability, then prominence, and finally acceptance in the councils of educational leaders and with the public generally because it was associated with moral redemption and pedagogical renewal, but the economic message was never absent. Vocational education projected a distinctly more explicit commitment to economic benefits both to the individual and to the nation, but it also promised to shore up traditional virtues associated with the Protestant work ethic as well as to remake the school curriculum in line with the needs and interests of the growing school population.

In the end, however, it was the economic message that attracted the crucial support of a coalition of politically powerful interest groups. The consensus that these interest groups reached and their successful efforts to initiate programs of study and to enlist local, state, and federal support for them served to determine manual training's main direction. Within a short time after manual training was so favorably received in educational circles, the balance both in terms of the national debate and in the way industrial education was being implemented began to shift from its value as a moral corrective and a pedagogical reform to practical job skills. In the minds of many, this was precisely what the new industrial society required. In the course of propelling manual training in the direction of the economic imperative, those interest groups helped transform the fundamental purposes of American schooling.

 2

FITTING YOUTH "FOR THEIR LIFE-WORK"

From Manual Training to Vocational Training, 1895–1912

> *In the first burst of their enthusiasm over the new-found man-*
> *ual-training idea it was claimed that boys who had taken the man-*
> *ual-training work in elementary school and high school would*
> *receive a basic training in industrial education which would enable*
> *them to adapt themselves to the varied demands of different pro-*
> *ductive callings. The failure of manual training to realize these*
> *claims has been the thing which has brought most discredit upon*
> *the movement and most opposition to its further development.*
>
> *...Manual training has not met and cannot meet the need of*
> *industrial education. Those who take the work do not enter produc-*
> *tive employment, and if they did expect to, manual training is not*
> *the sort of education which they need to fit them for their life-work.*
>
> *Charles A. Prosser, 1912*[1]

The widespread public acceptance of manual training was one indication that a spirit of reform was in the air. It was a reform, it seemed, that all but the most hidebound of traditionalists could support. On the one hand, it addressed the growing feeling that education needed to become attuned to the new industrial society, and on the other, it posed no serious threat to the established order in education. It represented an adjustment, not a revolution. The niceties of the argument that manual training was merely "completing" a liberal education rather than supplanting it, however, tended to become lost in the enthusiasm generated by the idea that the curriculum could be reorganized so as to bring direct economic rewards. Perhaps the most enduring effect of the drive to install manual training in American schools was that it opened a breach in the academic fortress through which the assembled armies of vocational education could charge.

A new economic imperative had emerged in the wake of the Industrial Revolution. A steady supply of workers was now needed; with apprenticeship declining and few other sources of trade training available, the answer seemed to lie in a more drastic reordering of the school curriculum than manual training entailed. In the end, it was not so much manual training with its visionary but sometimes convoluted and contradictory promises that Americans turned to but to straightforward vocational education. At the same time, then, that manual training was achieving some success both in terms of national visibility and implementation in schools, dedicated proponents of vocational education like Charles Prosser were challenging its efficacy in meeting the requirements of the new industrial age. Manual training just did not provide the job training that the new industrial order required.

In varying degrees and in different ways, three national organizations spearheaded the drive to put vocational education in the forefront of the school curriculum: the National Association of Manufacturers (NAM), the American Federation of Labor (AFL), and the National Society for the Promotion of Industrial Education (NSPIE). Over time, and along with other interest groups, they formed a powerful coalition that eventuated in a major reordering of the school curriculum. Although each of these interest groups was motivated by different ideals, their interests seemed to coalesce in a vision of education that was tied to its direct economic advantages.

Probably the most salient economic motive was the desire of the leaders of American business and industry to make the United States preeminent in the international marketplace. Of particular concern was the excellence of Germany's manufactured goods, an advantage manufacturers attributed to the German system of vocational education. What America needed in their view was a plentiful reservoir of skilled labor similar to what presumably existed in Germany. Labor's interest, however, lay in advancing personal prosperity and the quality of life for workers. To the struggles for a minimum wage, limitation of working hours, safe working conditions, workmen's compensation, and the abolition of child labor there was added a growing conviction on the part of labor leaders that public education could under the right circumstances be used as a lever for personal advancement. Working people generally began to look to the schools to provide an education that would alleviate their economic anxieties and prepare their children to function successfully in the new industrial regime. Finally, a growing professional cadre in education, as represented principally by NSPIE, saw in the prospect of an expanded vocational education the chance to make the curriculum function much more directly and more visibly in the lives of Americans. Not incidentally, the professional status of educators would be greatly enhanced in the process.

Education would become not merely a way to master a restricted range of academic subjects and thereby in some vague way promote intellectual development; at one and the same time, public education would become an indispensable instrument for addressing matters vital to the national interest and
to individual success. Although their interests did not coincide, these groups
eventually joined in a coalition that made direct trade training a means to
realize their aspirations.

THE NATIONAL ASSOCIATION OF MANUFACTURERS
MOUNTS ITS CAMPAIGN

The National Association of Manufacturers (NAM) was the first to enter the
fray. Founded two years after the panic of 1893, NAM found itself facing the
most serious depression in American history. With this third depression in
three decades, some prominent Americans were beginning to express doubts
as to whether an unregulated economy would survive into the twentieth century. As NAM's membership sought to extricate themselves from their economic difficulties, the problem of overproduction emerged as a leading concern. Speakers at NAM conventions in its first few years pointed out that the
rapid expansion of railroads in the 1870s and 1880s had stimulated an over-
expansion of industry. As an antidote, NAM's leaders sought not only to
expand domestic markets but also to achieve a much stronger foothold in foreign markets, particularly in Latin America.

One obstacle in competing for those foreign markets as well as increasing domestic ones was the perceived shortage of skilled labor. The inadequacy
of the apprenticeship system for training workers for an expanding industrial
economy was evident, but the nature of the training that should replace it
was unclear. In some industries, a technologically advanced division of labor
had obviated the need for craft labor, and many workers were simply picking
up the skills they needed on the job. Industries such as machine tools had
become so specialized that it became difficult for an apprentice to learn the
trade in anything like a systematic way.

New approaches to dealing with the problem gradually emerged. Beginning around the 1870s, large firms systematically shifted their apprentices
from one specialization to another so that they could be introduced to the
variety of skills needed on the job. In many cases, they also required a form
of company-sponsored vocational education to supplement on-the-job training. Certain firms, such as General Electric and Allis-Chalmers, even established their own schools as part of what was being increasingly called the "new
apprenticeship" system. General Electric also pioneered the use of what they
called an "apprentice supervisor" who was principally concerned with the

training of apprentices; as the practice was adopted by other plants, they also assumed responsibility for teaching apprentices in schools created for this purpose.[2] Clearly, manufacturers were beginning to rely more and more on organized vocational training either to supplement or to replace the declining system of apprenticeship. NAM leaders looked longingly to the technical education that was available in Germany and in England, and they began to formulate an educational policy that would put them in a competitive position vis-à-vis those leading industrial countries. The German system came in for particular admiration, and in 1898, following England's example, NAM began to send representatives to observe German schools. In his 1898 annual report, NAM's president, Theodore C. Search, concluded his comments on the subject by declaring, "There is hardly any work we can do or any expenditures we can make that will yield so large a return to our industries as would come from the establishment of educational institutions which would give us skilled hands and trained minds for the conduct of our industries and our commerce."[3]

Admiration for the German system of education, however, was not universal. Labor organizations, educators, and social welfare workers among others were continually raising questions about the class bias embedded in European education. Other concerns were who would administer a separate vocational system and who would finance such a system. Nevertheless, as early as 1900, NAM leaders were ready to embark on a concerted campaign to institute a full-scale system of industrial training in American schools. In the initial stages of that campaign, they faced scattered opposition from organized labor. Labor was particularly concerned with the extent to which the new vocational education would be controlled by the manufacturers and used to create an oversupply of workers. The growing union movement was seeking to gain some measure of control over working conditions and at the same time was interested in reducing the supply of cheap labor. Runkle and Woodward's vigorous campaign for manual training notwithstanding, neither manufacturers nor trade unions were particularly interested in manual training as a way of invigorating the traditional American curriculum.

Conflict between labor and management was particularly bitter in this period, partly because unions were experiencing tremendous growth. In 1897, union membership was only 447,000; by 1904, it reached 2,072,700. Fearing the unions' growing power, NAM under the leadership of its president, David Parry, sought to forestall the AFL's attempts to get an anti-injunction bill passed and to include an eight-hour-day provision in government contracts. Identifying strikes with open rebellion, Parry described union members as "men of muscle, rather than of intelligence, and commanded by leaders who are at heart disciples of revolution."[4] Union limitations on the number of apprentices, according to Parry, had forced employers to find new ways of training workers "in the hope of obtaining that supply of new blood for their workshop, which is essential to the prevention of dry rot."[5] In the context of this concern for a fresh supply of skilled labor, combined with a conviction that unions were artificially restricting access to training, NAM formed its Committee on Industrial Education.

At NAM's 1895 convention, the Committee on Industrial Education singled out the public schools for particular criticism. Alluding to the fact that 80 percent of students in public schools dropped out before high school, the committee framed its argument in terms of concern for the poor who, with apprenticeships now in very short supply, simply had no place to go. "The outrageous antagonism of organized labor to the apprenticeship system," the report stated, "is itself a crime against the youth of the whole nation." The answer was a system of technical and trade schools along the German model. The report went so far as to say that the establishment and maintenance of such a system of trade schools in order to impart "the practical and technical knowledge of a trade is the most important issue before the American people today."[6]

Throughout the first decade of the twentieth century, NAM sought to refine and extend its policy of instituting a system of trade schools. Widespread general criticism of the public schools was one thing, but actually implementing particular changes was quite another. The United States, after all, had been in the forefront in creating a system of common schooling. Looking to Europe for leadership in terms of educational policy, with its strong class divisions and emphasis on state supremacy, would undoubtedly be viewed with suspicion. Moreover, even if some forms of trade training could be introduced into public schools, it was not clear what particular kinds of trades could be successfully taught. Most pressing was the issue of who would finance what promised to be a very expensive reform. That such a major undertaking could not succeed without major federal support was becoming clear in NAM councils, but here again such federal intervention in educational affairs ran contrary to longstanding American traditions of local control and financing of education. Although the drive for manual training had opened the way for some kind of restructuring of the curriculum in American schools, its inherent ambiguities left the direction of changes open. The stands that the NAM adopted on those issues helped shape the form that these new programs of study took.

In ensuing years, NAM's Committee on Industrial Education continued to report regularly to the membership. In large part, their reports concentrated on reviewing the successes that various independent, industry sponsored, and philanthropically supported trade schools had achieved. The 1906 report, for example, described the programs of the New York Trade School, which already had 900 pupils, and the founding of a Trade School for White Boys in Gadsden, Alabama, where the boys "become skilled sufficiently to produce articles of value." The achievements of the trade school branch of Winona Technical Institute in Indianapolis, Indiana, were complimented, as were the recently established Milwaukee Trade School and trade schools in Palo Alto, California; Buffalo, New York; Columbus, Georgia; and Cincinnati and Cleveland, Ohio.[7] In the course of praising Milwaukee's new trade school, the report cited a letter by F. W. Sivyer indicating NAM's position on vocational education was instrumental in making the case for the new trade school, quoting him that "we thought it to be a very good argument for our school," and concluding that the school was "a decided success." Sivyer's letter went on to reflect pride that the teachers in the school were "practical men," thus alluding indirectly to the often expressed view that school people generally were too academically oriented to be entrusted with trade training. A fundamental difference in orientation and outlook between school personnel and teachers of practical skills was something that Woodward and other supporters of manual training sought to minimize but would, as vocational education policy developed, become an important point of contention. It was one of the factors contributing eventually to a decided bifurcation between academic and vocational education. Clearly elated by Sivyer's account, the committee predicted "a glorious future" for the school. Members were so stirred by the report that they moved to send copies to every school board in cities of 30,000 inhabitants or over.[8]

At the 1907 NAM meeting, the standing Committee on Industrial Education continued its practice of reporting on the successes of new trade schools in various parts of the country. This time, Philadelphia was singled out for being the first city to incorporate its trade school into the public school system. Wisconsin was also commended for being the first state to pass a statute explicitly providing for trade schools. Anthony Ittner, chair of the Committee on Industrial Education, returned to the issue of union restrictions on trade training, once again strongly condemning the practice and declaring that "every young man living in that portion of the earth's surface covered by the protecting folds of 'Old Glory' [should] have the widest and fullest opportunity to learn the trade of his choice" and that the "right to learn a trade should be as free as air and sunlight."[9] The 1907 meeting also addressed the appropriate age for training, an issue William Torrey Harris had raised a few years earlier. The period between the ages of fourteen and sixteen was selected because "this would provide for that brief period in their lives when their characters are being formed, for the years which are so often spent in idleness and evil associations, when so many form bad habits which not seldom remain with them through life."[10] Apparently, NAM leaders were mindful of the longstanding connection between manual labor and character building.

In the early years of their campaign for vocational education, the NAM focused on the creation of independent trade schools, but by 1911, association leaders recognized that, if their hopes for vocational education were to be realized, they would need to shift their emphasis to the public schools. Creating independent trade schools was simply too costly and cumbersome. By NAM standards, however, the public schools themselves were clearly inadequate to the task they had in mind. "Efficiency," they declared, "is the best test of education, and by this test American common school education doesn't educate."[11] Reflecting the continuing suspicion of professional educators, H. E. Miles from Racine, Wisconsin, added his voice to the mounting criticism of the public schools, particularly emphasizing the unrealistic aspirations of professional educators. A realistic appraisal of the state of schooling, he argued, would find that schools are based on "theories and not upon realities, upon dreams of things as they might be, not upon the actualities of things as they are." Miles pointed out that only one-half of the children in school completed the sixth grade, one in three completed the grammar school course, and one in thirty finished high school, but the public schools were providing virtually nothing suitable for this group.[12] A familiar criticism was being heard. The public school curriculum with its traditional emphasis on academic subjects was meeting the needs of only a small minority of youth.

At NAM's 1912 annual meeting, Miles, reporting once again for the Committee on Industrial Education, divided youth into three distinct classes: the "abstract-minded and imaginative children," the "concrete or hand-minded children," and "the great intermediate class," thus anticipating the threefold division of the secondary school curriculum in the years to come. Miles argued that the "hand-minded," constituting according to his estimate "one-half the youth of the land," were most sorely neglected by the existing system of schools. For these youth, the system "has been horribly unmindful, uninformed and inconsiderate," and consequently, many of them leave school at an early age.[13] One solution, however, was at hand. Continuation schools on the German model should be provided for both boys and girls between the ages of fourteen and sixteen. At a minimum, five hours of instruction per week should be provided, and employers would pay the continuation student's wages during instruction. The curriculum would focus on a specific industry. Courses such as mechanical drawing, shop math, pattern making, molding, machine shop, and carpentry would be taught in connection with the actual construction of products. For girls, courses would be provided in such areas as dressmaking, millinery, and domestic science. Instruction in citizenship would be included "to make an industrial worker who is a good citizen, wise to his rights and obligations."[14]

It was imperative, of course, that instructors and supervisors be drawn from the ranks of "practical men" not just in continuation schools but for vocational education generally. Professional educators were just too closely tied to impractical academic ideals to be entrusted with instituting an effective vocational alternative. In this regard, Wisconsin's dual system of administrating vocational and academic education was singled out for special commendation. Wisconsin had established a State Board of Industrial Education in 1911, with the nine members divided equally among representatives of employers, employees, and educators. Local city boards were similarly structured. This arrangement insured that "the work shall be particularly practical."[15]

The 1912 report also mentioned the virtues of "pre-vocational" programs and manual training in elementary schools. In addition, what were then called "intermediate high schools" along the lines of those in Los Angeles were cited with approval. In those schools, academic, commercial, and industrial curricular options were provided, the latter two serving to "round out and fit for their occupations the children who can stay in school until they are sixteen years of age."[16] Finally, the 1912 Committee on Industrial Education report recommended that the proposed new system of industrial education be supported by vocational guidance centers since, according to their estimate, 85 percent of children who enter the workforce at age fourteen find themselves in "blind alley" occupations.[17] At the time, vocational guidance was a small and relatively insignificant movement, but by the 1920s, it had become an important concomitant in the drive to vocationalize the American curriculum (see Chapter 6).

Making policy recommendations on the floor of NAM conventions was one thing, but actually bringing about radical changes in American schools was quite another. Cost continued to be a critical issue, and in this regard a concerted political campaign needed to be mounted. Early in their campaign to transform American education, NAM leaders already realized that major federal aid for vocational education would be necessary to support their programs. As precedents, they cited federal legislation in behalf of agriculture, such as the Morrill Act of 1862 and the Hatch Act of 1887. With bills such as those already part of legislative history, NAM leaders believed they could lobby successfully for federal resources to be made available for industry in the form of industrial education. In 1907, for example, they threw their support behind the Davis Bill, which included provisions for agricultural education and home economics as well as for industrial education. The solution, it appeared, lay in allying themselves with other interest groups. If, with their help, political opposition to federal financing of industrial education could be overcome, the success of their efforts would be assured.

THE DOUGLAS COMMISSION HELPS SPUR A NATIONAL MOVEMENT

One of the signal events in the drive to institute a national system of industrial education was the 1906 report issued by the Commission on Industrial and Technical Education, generally known as the Douglas Commission. A year earlier, the Massachusetts Senate and House of Representatives had passed a bill authorizing Governor William L. Douglas to appoint a commission to "investigate the needs for education in the different grades of skill and responsibility in the various industries of the Commonwealth."[18] The Commonwealth of Massachusetts, in other words, was to take the lead in linking its school system to the needs of industry. Composed of nine prominent citizens of Massachusetts, including one representative of the public schools, the commission proceeded expeditiously to hold twenty public hearings throughout the state. Written largely by Susan M. Kingsbury (described in the report as "a trained student of sociological problems"), the report reflected a genuine concern for the well-being of the working poor. Over the course of its investigation, the commission came to provide strong support for the contention that schools were out of tune with the times. As the report saw it, the public school system was simply inadequate in terms of "modern industrial and social conditions," clinging instead to an outmoded humanistic tradition. The remedy was to move in the direction of industrial trade training.

The Douglas Commission noted, however, that labor unions had evidenced suspicion and hostility to creating trade schools at public expense. "The opposition to such schools," they reported, "is based on the fear that they would furnish workmen in numbers sufficiently large to affect the labor market, and bring about a lowering of wages."[19] They also felt that, in the event of strikes, these schools would become "scab factories." In contrast to trade schools, technical schools were apparently well received by labor. Technical schools were defined as "schools which would offer to men already engaged in industries the opportunity to broaden their knowledge of the principles of the trade."[20] Technical schools, in other words, did not offer quite the same threat that trade schools did since they were designed to augment the capacities of the existing workforce rather than expanding it.

That distinction, however, tended to get lost under the weight of evidence reported by the commission that existing schools failed to address the needs of most students. The report focused particularly on adolescents between fourteen and sixteen, seeing that group as representing "the most important question which faces the educational world today." Since the compulsory school age at that time was fourteen, Kingsbury found that 25,000 children in Massachusetts were either working or "idle." This situation was exacerbated by the fact that few apprenticeships were available. Five-sixths of those children had not graduated from grammar schools, one-half of them had not gone beyond the seventh grade, and one-quarter had less than six years of schooling. Many of these students were at work, largely in "dead-end" jobs which had no possibilities for advancement.[21] When Kingsbury examined the reasons given for their dropping out of school, she found that the common belief that parents put children to work was "not tenable, except for the foreign element." Quite the contrary. The findings indicated that it was the children themselves who made the decision to leave. "It is the dissatisfaction of the child which takes him from school," she found, "and ignorance on the part of the parent which permits him to enter the mill." The state's largest textile mill employers reported that they did not need to, or even want to, employ children in their industry. In the end, the commission found that the responsibility for this deplorable state of affairs rested squarely on the schools. Kingsbury consulted thirty-five to forty school superintendents, and all except three felt the blame was in "the system, which fails to offer a child of fourteen continued schooling of a practical character." The 25,000 students who were apparently cast adrift by the public schools became a way of symbolizing the failure of the schools of the day.[22]

Girls fared no better than boys, according to the report. The teaching of sewing came in for particular criticism. Grammar schools, for example, moved "too rapidly to . . . complex problems," whereas they would be advised to "confine their work to instilling the simple principles of sewing, cutting and construction of articles, with the right use of the proper tools, including the machine as well as the needle." The teaching of housekeeping and cooking to girls was more favorably treated by the commission, although they believed that instruction in these subjects did not begin early enough. The report also declared that evidence from the work of philanthropic organizations, such as the Boston Women's Educational and Industrial Union, in such trades as sales, wire frame making, and hat making "has shown that definite training for an industry which requires skill makes the girl more responsible, more reliable and more womanly."[23] All in all, the report advocated training in particular vocational skills as educationally desirable for girls as well as boys.

With the appearance of the Douglas Commission report, the main terms of the industrial education debate began to shift somewhat from its alleged value to the national economy to the beneficial effects that would accrue to American education generally and to a distressed segment of the youth population in particular. The argument that manual training would somehow "complete" a liberal education, however, was losing its force. Instead, the general idea that the older education was simply not working began to take hold. Traditional education did not need to be supplemented; it needed to be replaced, at least for large numbers of America's schoolchildren.

ORGANIZED LABOR STRUGGLES TO ENUNCIATE A POLICY

Although the National Association of Manufacturers was moving aggressively in the area of industrial education and its cause was being advanced by state agencies, the AFL found it difficult to formulate a comprehensive position. Union growth and successes in certain areas had aroused a concerted opposition on the part of business, making the formulation of educational policy seem less than important. The strike by the Amalgamated Association of Iron and Steel Workers against three subsidiaries of United States Steel in 1901, for example, resulted in a severe setback for unions. When the United Mine Workers struck anthracite mines in Pennsylvania in 1902, major violence erupted, and miners' strikes in Colorado in 1903 and 1904 eventuated in the dispatch of federal troops. Manufacturers, often with the aid of local officials, were developing effective anti-union measures such as lockouts, black lists, and the use of citizens' alliances to thwart union interests. Union leadership seemed preoccupied with this growing animosity and with the success that some corporations, such as U.S. Steel, had achieved in resisting union demands. Although unions had made some early attempts to develop their own forms of industrial education as a response to new technologies, these attempts were not greeted with great enthusiasm by the membership. After the Linotype was introduced in 1890, for example, the New York local of the International Typographers Union recommended that typographer's unions use their own machines to teach the new skill, but the plan fizzled.[24]

By the time NAM launched its campaign in behalf of industrial education, the older more radical unions such as the National Labor Union and the Knights of Labor had been succeeded by the American Federation of Labor. Beginning in 1881 as the Federation of Organized Trades and Labor Unions, it was reorganized in 1886, with Samuel Gompers, a former cigar maker, becoming its first president after winning the battle for control of the organization over socialist rivals. Under his leadership, the AFL focussed much more directly on material benefits, such as higher wages and an eight-hour day, than with class issues and revolutionary ideals.

By the 1890s, labor suffered some disastrous setbacks, most notably the Homestead strike of 1892, a series of unfavorable court rulings, and the severe depression of 1893. These events prompted the AFL to undertake concerted political action, but it was still slow to develop a fully articulated position with regard to education generally and to industrial education in particular. Some labor stands emerged here and there. At least initially, organized labor simply contradicted longstanding NAM complaints that it was artificially restricting the labor supply. "The limitation of apprentices," said one article in the *American Federationist* in 1900, "which has caused so many to shed crocodile tears . . . is absolutely false and groundless." That persistent charge, the article went on, is intended to force "men to walk the street in idleness while their places are filled with cheap child labor."[25]

The AFL was relatively silent on industrial education until 1907, when Gompers joined the newly formed National Society for the Promotion of

Industrial Education (NSPIE). It was in that year that Charles R. Richards, NSPIE's secretary, addressed the AFL's annual convention. Almost immediately thereafter, the delegates passed a resolution alluding to the "misapprehension [that] exists in many quarters" as to organized labor's position on industrial education and formally endorsing "any society or association having as its object the raising of the standard of industrial education and the teaching of the higher techniques of our various industries."[26] A year later, Gompers appointed a committee to look into the issue, and in 1909, the AFL special committee on industrial education cautiously endorsed vocational training: "Organized labor favors the plan of industrial training that will give our boys and girls such a training as will help them to advance after they are in industry." The preliminary report went on to give particular attention to the appropriate age at which vocational education should take place, taking the position that "if such industrial education took children between the ages of fourteen and sixteen when they are of little value in a business way, at a time when the education they received is of advantage so far as it goes, but hardly fits them for actual working places, that it would serve to give them proper training to prepare and enter some branch of actual vocational work."[27] Evidently, labor was still extremely wary of the possibility that large-scale vocational training in schools would have the effect of flooding the labor market with cheap labor. Restricting as much as possible the age at which such training would take place would serve to mitigate that problem.

Reporting to the membership at the 1909 convention, Gompers took particular pains to warn of the dangers of industrial education remaining in "the power of private interests where there is sure to be the danger of exploitation for private profit and wilful rapacity." Vocational education under public control was a far better alternative although, even there, there were dangers. One of the principal dangers was the possibility that vocational education would dominate the curriculum for large numbers of students. Gompers was careful, for example, to declare himself "emphatically against the elimination from our public schools system of any line of learning now taught," and he endorsed industrial education only as "supplementary" to the existing program of studies. What he was seeking, he said, was an educational system which would "make better workers of our future citizens, better citizens of our future workers."[28] Clearly, organized labor harbored a strong suspicion that industrial education would simply be substituted for general education, thus depriving one segment of the population of the kind of education best suited to active and effective citizenship; but given the momentum that industrial education had generated, labor could hardly be counted in the opposition. Their best option was to join in the movement in order to gain some control over it. As one delegate at the 1912 convention put it, "We cannot stop the trend in the

direction of this kind of education in the schools; but we can, if we co-oper-
ate with the educators, have it come out our way."[29]

As part of its campaign against child labor, the AFL supported compulsory attendance in school. Recognizing, however, that compulsory education
would be effective only up to a point, they also endorsed continuation schools
somewhat along the lines that NAM had recommended. In 1911, a year
before its endorsement by NAM, the AFL recommended three types of continuation education: one during the day for young children, one in the evening
for adult workers, and trade training for youth between fourteen and sixteen.[30]
Four years later, they proposed compulsory continuation school for all youth
fourteen to eighteen for a minimum of five hours per week. As NAM had proposed in 1912, the salaries of these youth would be paid by employers during
their instruction.[31]

At the 1912 AFL meeting, the Committee on Industrial Education was
ready to present a preliminary report. Strong opposition was voiced to any
vocational content in the curriculum before the age of fourteen, although
manual training was deemed acceptable. Manual training and particularly
manual training high schools as well as commercial high schools were regarded
as directed toward general education and, therefore, not much of a threat. The
committee was also suspicious of the growing trend toward prevocational education. Like most NAM leaders, the report also strongly endorsed that vocational courses be taught by teachers with practical trade experience, even
going so far as to say that "We insist that such courses be given by men
tutors."[32] Although the interests of manufacturers and organized labor on the
issue of industrial education clearly diverged in certain major respects, some
basis for a compromise was beginning to appear.

Between 1907 and 1912, the outlines of a labor position on industrial
education took shape. First, vocational training needed to be wrested from
private control where such training could easily become a training ground for
"scabs." The only realistic alternative was the public schools. Secondly, once
industrial education was installed in public schools, its governing bodies
needed to have labor representation on at least an equal basis with representatives of manufacturing. (This became a key provision in the crafting of the
Smith-Hughes Act.) Finally, whatever the form of governance, vocational
training should not be regarded as providing full competence in any trade.
While it should be directed toward the development of job skills, it should
be supplementary to the general curriculum, and not regarded as making for
fully qualified workers. In this way, vocational trainees would not be in direct
competition with experienced workers for jobs. Labor also endorsed a somewhat higher age for vocational training to begin than was usually being proposed (around fourteen) in order to insure that curricular differentiation
should not begin too early.

By January 1913, Gompers was ready to join in the consensus that was building on industrial education. Alluding to the widely reported statistics regarding the high rate of dropping out of school and to a system of schooling that establishes "mental 'straight jackets,'" he reiterated the now familiar argument that schools were failing "to connect with life, practical affairs and needs." But Gompers once again stopped short of endorsing vocational education as an alternative to general education. "Organized labor," he said, "would not detract from or abolish cultural instruction for we can not make education complete by leaving out that which gives breadth, vision and understanding." The answer lay not in creating two distinct forms of education but in seeking some form of integration. "To combine the intellectual and the practical," he concluded, "must be the next advance of the public school." As a practical matter, however, he strongly endorsed the Page Bill then pending before Congress, which supported industrial education and home economics as well as instruction in agriculture and agricultural extension. "The American Federation of Labor," Gompers reported to the membership, "has already devoted much time to securing its adoption."[33] The main configuration of a powerful coalition in behalf of federal funding for industrial education was now in place.

THE NATIONAL SOCIETY FOR THE PROMOTION OF INDUSTRIAL EDUCATION BUILDS A COALITION

Since 1895, the National Association of Manufacturers had been arguing that a system of vocational education would help to expand domestic markets and improve America's position in world markets, but the report of the Douglas Commission drew national attention to another important ingredient in the debate over vocational education—a faltering system of schooling. By 1906, many educators were already in agreement with Kingsbury's contention that the educational system was failing a large proportion of its children. Faced with continuing criticisms, educators could ill afford to maintain the status quo.

On June 6, 1906, very soon after the Douglas Commission reported its findings, the Engineers Club in New York City became the setting for the formation of a national society that was to play a critical role in moving industrial education from the arena of policy-making and reports to its implementation into the curriculum of public schools. On that day, James P. Heany, Director of Art and Manual Training in New York City, and Charles R. Richards, then a professor of manual training at Teachers College, Columbia University, and soon to be president of Cooper Union, convened a group of sixteen men for the purpose of making the dream of a national system of industrial education a reality. From the beginning, it was clear to them that, to succeed, the new organization would have to bridge the lines of narrow interest and forge a broad spectrum of support. A committee was quickly formed, and at its first organizational meeting at Cooper Union in early 1907, about 250 representatives of labor, manufacturing, and the professions were in attendance. The diversity within the group was testimony to the broad appeal that industrial education was enjoying, but it also posed an enormous task for the organizers. Somehow the wide range of interests that was represented had to be reconciled and an effective political coalition established.[34]

At that 1907 meeting, admiration for the German system of industrial education was once again expressed. The vice president of the National City Bank, for example, was confident that with a system of industrial education in place, America's competitive position with Germany would be enhanced. One sign of the success of that meeting was the appearance of Jane Addams, director of Hull House and national leader in the social settlement movement, but the position she actually took in the cause of industrial education was a considerable departure from the usual arguments. Addams believed that industrial education should be directed to the well-being of the worker. "Let America, by all means, keep the lead in the application of science to industry," she said, "but let us also enter a new field, to see what may be accomplished for industry by cultivating the workman himself, so that his mind, his power of variation, his art instinct, his intelligent skill, may ultimately be reflected in the industrial product." Addams, like others before her, praised the German system and urged governmental support for industrial education. In her view, however, what America needed to emulate was not industrial efficiency but the German system of old age pensions, unemployment relief, and Germany's acceptance of "human welfare [as] a legitimate object for governmental action."[35] Evidently, what Addams admired in the German system was quite different from what NAM had long envied. Her position, however, was clearly outside the mainstream of the movement for industrial education.

At NSPIE's second organizational meeting in 1907, Nicholas Murray Butler, long a central figure in education policy-making and the president of Columbia University, was invited to chair the conference. Butler assured the membership that NSPIE had "taken hold of one of the most important and far-reaching of our social and industrial problems," but this meant that the differences in the interests represented needed to be reconciled. While he was fundamentally in sympathy with the desire of manufacturers to become more competitive with Germany, he also assured the representatives of labor that they, too, stand to gain from the expansion of industrial education. "If we can make labor worth more," he said, "labor is perfectly sure to get more." Butler was also conscious of the uneasiness that many professional educators were experiencing over the possibility of a fundamental shift in the school's center of gravity. In this regard, he appeared sympathetic to Harris's position that the primary purpose of American education was citizenship, not trade training. He warned against the introduction of industrial education at too early an age, but at the same time held that such early education needed to lay "a sound foundation for the special trade and industrial education which is to follow."[36] By addressing some of the most commonly expressed objections, Butler was giving voice to the increasingly widespread opinion that a broad range of interest groups all had something to gain from a system of industrial education.

Reporting at the same 1907 meeting was the Sub-Committee on Industrial Education for Women. The report alluded to what would become a source of some uncertainty and indecision within the industrial education movement. On the one hand, it was clear that women were entering the industrial workforce in great numbers, and this implied trade training for women as well as men. (The census for 1900 indicated that more than 23,000,000 women in the United States were over the age of sixteen. Of these, about 5,000,000 were employed outside the home.) On the other hand, the feeling persisted that job training for women was inconsistent with women's traditional role, and this implied teaching domestic skills rather than industrial education. As the report put it, "While there is the generally accepted opinion that all women must be trained for the home, we are confronted with almost insurmountable difficulties as to how this shall be accomplished, since we find the number of women who are obliged to earn their living constantly increasing." The report tried to make the case that industrial education could actually "make for better women and better homes" and was careful to add that the pleas for industrial education for women was not really "an attempt to break down the theory that women's place was in the home."[37] In general the motives behind providing home economics and forms of vocational education for women varied and were quite complex and often contradictory. As historian Geraldine Joncich Clifford characterized the problem,

> Vocational courses for girls represented an accommodation by schoolmen to a variety of realities: the continued commitment to women's prime (that is domestic) vocation; the desire to "do something" for the girls while the boys went off to their "real" vocational courses; the practical scheduling problems of balancing vocational boys' offering and girls' offerings so as to preserve the basic coeducational mix in the rest of the curriculum; the hope of prolonging school attendance by adding nonacademic subjects; and the goal of Americanizing the daughters of immigrants.[38]

Over time, new values associated with industrial productivity tended to come into conflict with traditional norms and values in the vocational education of women, and they tended to be resolved largely in terms of the latter.

If indeed the new education was to be a direct and specific preparation for one's future social and economic role, there were already some indications that predicting a woman's future role was not as easy as some educational reformers supposed. The program of studies that balanced the new industrial training for boys but sent a symbolic signal that women's role would remain relatively unchanged was home economics. Since the early nineteenth century, after all, women's groups had urged the introduction of courses that would prepare girls for their domestic duties. For the most part, however, a common curriculum for males and females prevailed in nineteenth-century schooling. Now, not just a course or two, but an entire program of studies was being promoted in order to preserve and enhance household skills. In time, the injection of home economics into the American curriculum early in the twentieth century became what historian John Rury has called "probably the most important feature of the new high school curriculum developed for women."[39]

At NSPIE's next meeting, in 1908, a report grandly announced that the society would bring together industrialists, manufacturers, schoolmasters and "the great American public itself" in the interest of promoting industrial education.[40] To be successful, the new movement had to reconcile the diverse positions of interested parties but enlist the support of the general population. To this end, NSPIE committed itself to keeping the public informed as to developments in both Europe and the United States and would seek not only to reconcile diverse interests but to establish and support polices that promised concrete change. While some success had been achieved using private funding, such a fundamental alteration in the purpose of American schooling required generous governmental support, and this implied broad public acceptance.

The most startling development at NSPIE's 1908 meeting occurred in the course of the opening address by Charles W. Eliot, who a year later was to conclude his distinguished forty-year reign as president of Harvard University. Now a senior statesman in the educational policy arena, Eliot had in 1892 chaired the widely discussed Committee of Ten, and he had long championed the case for an academic education for all, regardless of their future social or vocational roles. The centerpiece of the Committee of Ten report,[41] for example, presented four model programs of study for American high schools, none of which included any manual training or vocational education. In his 1908 NSPIE address, Eliot referred to the peril which confronted the nation as a result of the high rate of dropouts, something that the Douglas Commission report had emphasized in his home state of Massachusetts only two years before. To remedy this situation, he proposed not only a radical solution but one that was antithetical to his longstanding position. Eliot suggested nothing less that a dual system of education that would include trade schools on one side and regular public schools on the other. Going even further, he then raised the question, "But how shall the decision be made that certain children will go into industrial schools, others into ordinary high schools, and others again into mechanics arts high schools?" His response was, "The teachers of the elementary schools ought to sort the pupils and sort them by their evident and probable destinies."[42] Eliot's dramatic proposal signaled major success for the vocational education movement. His complete reversal of position was all the more astonishing since only three years earlier he had published an impassioned plea against "prognostication" as a basis for determining curricular paths.[43]

Apparently anticipating that his new position might strike some members of his audience as antidemocratic, Eliot went on to argue that,

> If democracy means to try to make all children equal or all men equal, it means to fight nature, and in that fight democracy is sure to be defeated. There is no such thing among men as equality of nature, of capacity for training, or of intellectual power. . . . We must get rid of the notion that some of us were brought up on, that a Yankee can turn his hand to anything. He cannot in this modern world; he positively cannot. . . .[44]

Even for Eliot, long a champion of humanist causes and normally sensitive to making invidious distinctions among human beings, the new industrial regime required a fundamental alteration not only in the education of children, but also in our very image of ourselves as Americans and in the way democracy itself was conceived.

Between 1907 and 1910, NSPIE undertook to survey influential leaders and to circulate their responses in a series of bulletins. Bringing NAM and organized labor into the fold presented an especially formidable task. Labor, of course, had long been suspicious that industrial education would be used to create an oversupply of workers and thereby bring down wages. Union leaders were calling for a strong voice for labor in setting public policy in this regard, but NAM was at this time extremely hostile to organized labor and reluctant to make concessions. When, for example, in 1909, word reached NAM's Committee on Industrial Education that NSPIE was seeking involvement by unions in their campaign, their response was impassioned: "to invite labor leaders affiliated with the American Federation of Labor to become members of the Society would be tantamount to inviting the devil and all his imps to participate in a movement for the promotion of the Christian Religion as taught by the lowly Nazarene while on earth!"[45] Nevertheless, to build an effective coalition, NSPIE leaders realized that participation by organized labor was critical. NSPIE was determined to achieve it, and the publication of their bulletins served to reconcile some of the differences between business and labor leaders.

At a minimum, both groups agreed that industrial education should be supported at public expense, although the question of dual control remained a contentious issue. Moreover, whatever the ambiguity of the term "industrial education," both groups came to interpret it as learning the skills of a trade. In the end, the criticism of dissenters like Jane Addams and John Dewey had little effect. For the vast majority of Americans, industrial education as the development of what Addams and Dewey called "industrial intelligence" meant little.

Other organized interest groups followed the lead of the NSPIE mainstream. In vocational training under public auspices, they had found something of a middle ground; a consensus began to build, with professional educators now joining in the campaign. As early as 1907, the National Education Association called for the establishment of trade schools at public expense "whenever conditions justify their establishment."[46] In the same year, the AFL adopted a resolution endorsing any policy or association which had as its goal "raising the standard of industrial education and the teaching of the higher techniques of our various industries."[47] With such influential support coming from virtually all sides, the time seemed propitious for a concerted effort to achieve long sought federal support for vocational education.

SCIENTIFIC MANAGEMENT APPLIED TO SCHOOLS

At the same time that the political battle was being waged for installing vocational programs in the public schools, the conceptual apparatus for understanding the nature and purposes of schooling was being quietly overhauled. The impetus for that change came partly from the world of manufacture. Changes in the manufacturing process began to exercise influence beyond factories and even beyond the efforts to maintain and support trade training in public schools. As vocational education was replacing manual training in the minds of school reformers as well as in the schools themselves, efforts to control the manufacturing process, particularly the system of production that came to be known as scientific management, were now influencing the fundamental assumptions and criteria of excellence that vocationalism as an emerging educational ideal required. Incorporating efficient practices simply in the day-to-day operations of the school had relatively few serious implications for the way schools were perceived, but efficiency, defined in terms of what was actually appropriate or inappropriate to study, transformed the way Americans thought about the purposes of schooling.

The key to that transformation was the adoption of the principle that education, more than anything, was a form of preparation. Just as the modern factory required exacting blueprints for the products to be produced and predetermined production goals in order to be truly efficient, so now did the schools require exacting determination of the outcomes to be achieved in relation to the raw material. Although education in some vague sense had always been considered a way of somehow getting ready for what lay ahead, under the growing influence of vocationalism precise predictions as to one's future social role and to the demands that that role entailed became the principal basis on which a curriculum was to be built. If vocational education were to succeed, what one studied had to be tied expressly to the predicted activities that one would one day be called upon to perform. Given that imperative, manufacturing processes and industrial management were beginning to supply the metaphors critically needed to transform the way the curriculum was conceived and understood.

Although the transformation of the process of manufacture proceeded slowly at first, the dramatic rise in the sheer size of manufacturing establishments after 1880 accelerated the process of change, bringing with it a change in the style of management whose effects reached far beyond the manufacturing process itself. The growth in the sheer size of factories was indeed dramatic. As Daniel Nelson has illustrated this point, in 1870 the McCormick factory in Chicago was reputed to be the largest factory in the United States, but there were at that time only 400–500 workers employed there; by 1900, 1,063 factories employed more than 500 workers. This phenomenal growth in the size of factories brought with it new modes of production and employee relations. For most of the nineteenth century, the control of manufacture was in the hands of skilled workers, often with a foreman as supervisor in charge. Owners of small workshops were often so concerned with the financing of their businesses that they gave little attention to the actual operation of the plant. Trained managers whose job it was to deal with personnel were largely a phenomenon of the period after 1880.[48]

As manufacturing establishments grew in terms of size, scientific management began to challenge the old order of foreman-controlled production. That shift was stimulated by a change in the professional status of engineers, who were beginning to assume managerial as well as technical functions in modern industry. "Rather than restricting their attention to technical matters," argues David Noble, "they consciously undertook to structure the labor force and foster the social habits demanded by corporate capitalism."[49] This new breed of engineer-managers was not so much interested in the mundane overseeing of work on the job as they were in applying a *system* of improving production. The "premium plan," introduced in the 1880s by Frederick A. Halsey, for example, was one of several schemes that sought to restructure the traditional salary system by offering workers additional wages in return for higher productivity. Throughout the late-nineteenth century and extending into the twentieth, engineers were increasingly critical of the inefficiency of older approaches to manufacture and proclaimed the new doctrine of the elimination of waste.[50]

Easily the most prominent of the new class of professional engineer-managers emerging in the 1880s was Frederick Winslow Taylor, the "father of scientific management." Two years after his graduation from the Stevens Institute of Technology in 1883, Taylor delivered his first paper before the American Society of Mechanical Engineers, introducing his own version of what later came to be known as piecework, the "piece-rate system."[51] Like Halsey, Taylor sought to address in a systematic way the issue of productivity through the introduction of a monetary reward system, but Taylor also brought a large measure of moral rectitude to his plan. The problem as he saw it was "soldiering" (avoiding work),[52] and the answer lay simply in *requiring* an honest day's work. "If a man won't do what is right," he once said, "*make* him."[53] Taylor was convinced that the key to making workers do what they are told was economic incentive. Under Taylor's system of scientific management, foremen would be replaced by efficiency experts, an exacting standardization of work, and the stopwatch as a mechanism of control. Workers would then be expected to submit to the strict regulation that Taylor imposed in return for higher wages. Efficiency was Taylor's watchword, but economic incentive was the key to the success of his system.

Around the turn of the century, Taylor was joined in his efforts to transform production techniques by Frank B. Gilbreth, whose bricklaying experiments led Taylor to abandon more or less his incentive wage plans and concentrate instead on time-motion studies. Gilbreth had chosen bricklaying as the trade he would investigate because, as he saw it, the techniques of bricklaying were essentially the same as they were thousands of years ago, and learning the art of bricklaying was imbedded in a grossly inefficient system of apprenticeship. The question that he sought to answer was whether both the work itself and the process of learning that ancient and skilled trade could now be controlled by such modern production criteria as efficiency and standardization. For Gilbreth, the enterprise also entailed a strong moral dimension. "The work of a bricklayer," he said, "is generally indicative of his personal character. If he is dishonest he will do dishonest work and cover it up before the flaw is seen."[54]

The fruits of Gilbreth's studies of the art of bricklaying took the form of a long series of exacting rules for management to follow in obtaining the maximum output from the workers. Gilbreth recommended, for example, that what he called an "athletic contest" be used in which two gangs of workers are pitted against one another and a score kept. Higher wages would be awarded in instances of extraordinary productivity. In what he called the "Gilbreth Packet System," he promulgated a series of efficiency measures for piling bricks upon packets. He prescribed, for example, that "The packets shall be made of two pieces laid lengthwise, and so spaced that the outside edges of the packet are spaced exactly the length of the average brick to be carried. The space between the two pieces shall be wide enough to permit room for the men's fingers to clear without jamming."[55] Gilbreth also divided the art of bricklaying into twelve standard processes, each minutely described. Apprentices could then be taught to perform each of these tasks without wasted motion. "Tapping brick down to grade with the trowel," Gilbreth proclaimed, "should not be necessary if the mortar is of the right consistency, the brick is wet enough and the joints of the right size; but if tapping is necessary, tap the brick one hard tap instead of several light taps."[56] To Taylor, such exacting control over the operations to be performed was a model of how all work could be organized.

By the time Taylor published *The Principles of Scientific Management* in 1911, he was already an American cultural hero. His *Shop Management*, published by the American Society of Mechanical Engineers in 1903, had been widely admired, and he was in demand as a consultant to a wide range of corporations. Labor remained suspicious, however. His methods led all the foremen at the Simonds Rolling Machine Company to resign, but Taylor instituted a system of supervisors, including a "speed boss," an "inspector," and a "disciplinarian" to replace them.[57] Ideas such as these brought him to the forefront of his profession. In 1906, Taylor was elected president of the American Society of Mechanical Engineers.

Although his major emphasis lay in the kind of efficiency that would be created through his time and motion studies, Taylor continued to stress moral issues. "Soldiering" in the workplace was not only inefficient but morally repugnant, and that an inferior worker should receive the same wages as a "first class man" wounded his ethical sensibilities. Taylor argued, for example, that any pity for the inferior worker by the "philanthropically inclined [was] entirely misplaced" since inferior workers could easily find other jobs. Their pity, he contended, should be reserved for the "first-class men" who were deprived of earning wages commensurate with their productivity. He also believed that scientific management, once introduced, would usher in a new era of harmony between labor and management. The only instance in which a strike might be unavoidable would be if union members "were so stubborn that they would be unwilling to try any other system, even though it assured them larger wages than their own."[58] In general, Taylor argued, "scientific management . . . has for its very foundation the firm conviction that the true interests of [employees and employers] are one and the same." Under his system, the interests of the worker and of management, Taylor asserted, "become identical"[59]

Given the growing concern about labor unrest at this time, Taylor's message of common interest between management and workers may have carried more appeal to his audience of corporate executives, factory managers, and the public generally than the exacting precision with which he approached the process of manufacture. Taylor's expressions of concern for labor's well-being, however, are open to question. In 1906, for example, he proposed to an official of the American Locomotive Company that he set a up a non-union foundry which, using Taylor's methods, would be in a position to underbid the union foundry and then lay off the union workers. Nor was Taylor's claim that scientific management would produce labor peace borne out in practice. In the same year that *Scientific Management* was published, molders at the Watertown Arsenal struck in protest against the introduction of Taylor's techniques, an action that prompted a House of Representatives committee to investigate the problem. The testimony of the workers seemed to focus less on technical changes than on the use of the stopwatch and the bonus system.[60]

Efficiency, however, remained Taylor's touchstone, and in *The Principles of Scientific Management*, he included high praise for Gilbreth's analysis of bricklaying. By detailed standardization of each step of the bricklaying process, Taylor claimed, Gilbreth had succeeded in transforming a trade "continuously practised since before the Christian era" into a scientifically controlled operation. Using scientific management techniques, the number of motions entailed in the work of bricklayers was reduced from eighteen to five, thus dispensing with useless motions that had been around for centuries. According to Taylor, Gilbreth revolutionized the training of bricklayers by teaching, for example, that a completed motion with the right hand should be followed with a motion with the left hand, thus speeding the operation and increasing productivity.[61] By extending the application of scientific management to all work, Taylor argued, similar beneficial results would be achieved.

Taylor's system was equally applicable to unskilled work. His famous illustration of how he dramatically increased the productivity of a "pig handler" at the Bethlehem steel plant is a case in point. The man he called Schmidt (actually Henry Noll) was "of the mentally sluggish type . . . , so stupid that he was unfitted to do most kinds of laboring work."[62] Nevertheless, according to his highly questionable account,[63] Taylor was able to increase his pig-handling productivity (moving heavy slabs of pig iron from one place to another) from 13 tons to 45 tons a day by raising his salary a mere 55 cents. By increasing Schmidt's salary from $1.15 to $1.70 a day, Taylor was now free to instruct him in the most efficient way to do his job. In doing so, he reinforced the belief that even in the most menial of labor there was a "best way" that could be conveyed through a combination of monetary inducement and training in the right methods. Workers still needed to be trained in how to work according to scientific principles. In an odd way, faith in scientific management was serving to blur the distinction between skilled and unskilled work. The complex art of bricklaying was purportedly reduced to a series of simple tasks, while the mundane labor of lifting and carrying slabs of pig iron was elevated to a job requiring scientific analysis and instruction in its fine points. Thus, whatever had been the effects of industrialization in terms of de-skilling the workplace, an education of sorts was required in order to achieve maximum efficiency.

In terms of actually improving the efficiency of the workplace, Taylor's system had less impact than is commonly believed. In a detailed review of the impact of Taylorism on the management of manufacturing plants, Daniel Nelson examined twenty-nine plants that had introduced scientific management between 1901 and 1917. He concluded that although its introduction had resulted in some changes, rarely if ever did it entail a complete reorganization along the lines that Taylor recommended. Typically, the Taylorizing of a manufacturing plant involved a modification in the physical organization, something of a change in the way the foremen functioned, but only a modest alteration in the way the workers actually performed. Nelson concludes that "to describe scientific management in these plants as a 'partial solution to the labor problem' or a radical revision of the worker's role . . . is both inappropriate and misleading."[64]

The changes that scientific management actually wrought in the workplace, particularly in relation to Taylor's grandiose claims, were apparently quite modest, but there is no question that efficiency generally became a staple of reform by the second decade of the twentieth century. Although organized labor remained deeply suspicious of scientific management, efficiency was undertaken as a popular cause by leading middle-class reformers. Prominent progressives such as Louis Brandeis, Herbert Croly, and Walter Lippmann embraced many of the efficiency principles.[65] Taylor's overall influence was so great that historian Peter Drucker maintains it is Taylor, and not Marx, who should stand alongside Darwin and Freud as the principal shapers of modern sensibility,[66] and Christopher Lasch saw Taylor's ideas as constituting "a new interpretation of the American dream."[67] Taylor's work, in fact, exerted a strong international influence, exciting the admiration of such diverse historical figures as V. I. Lenin, Benito Mussolini, and Antonio Gramsci. If Taylor did not succeed entirely in bending the operation of the modern factory to his exacting strictures, he did succeed magnificently in infusing efficiency into the consciousness of millions, making his methods virtually synonymous not only with scientific precision but with competence and efficacy. As historian Sean Wilentz sums up Taylor's impact, "What began as a blueprint for rearranging authority in the workplace turned into a design for modern living itself."[68]

It should not be surprising, then, that the application of Taylor's efficiency principles extended far beyond the management of factories to a variety of different spheres including, very prominently, the construction of curricula. In some cases, the relationship between the techniques that Taylor advanced and their counterparts in curriculum-making was almost surely indirect. In *Scientific Management*, for example, Taylor introduced a principle that was to become a standard feature of curriculum-making in the twentieth century. "There is no question," he said, "that the average individual accomplishes the most when he either gives himself, or some one else assigns him, a definite task, namely a given amount of work which he must do within a given amount of time."[69] The idea that a curriculum should consist of a series of highly specific goals to be achieved by explicitly specified practices within standardized time periods was to become common wisdom wherever curricular planning was undertaken, but this is probably attributable to the hyper-rationality that both Taylorism and scientific curriculum-making embodied rather than to a conscious application of Taylor's principles to curricular design.

In other cases, however, the link between scientific management and a new way of seeing the processes of schooling was direct and conspicuous. One of the most widely admired and frequently cited works in the early part of the twentieth century, for example, was Leonard Ayres's *Laggards in Our Schools*.[70] With support from the Russell Sage Foundation, Ayres undertook an extensive review of the problem of what was then called "retardation" and "elimination"—the failure of "laggards" to make normal progress in school (repeating grades) and what is now called dropping out. Published in 1909, Ayres's study reflected the same concern raised only three years before in the Douglas Commission report as to the schools' failure to address the needs of an important segment of its population; but while the Douglas Commission incorporated a tone of concern for the well-being of the 25,000 adolescents in Massachusetts for whom schooling apparently had so little relevance that they dropped out, Ayres was now examining that problem and the related issue of "retardation" from the new perspective of efficiency. He found, for example, that in the cities he sampled, "one-sixth of all the children are repeating and we are spending about $27,000,000 in this wasteful process of repetition in our cities alone." The causes of such waste were manifold. Health problems, adenoids in particular, were implicated. (A widespread belief at the time was that adenoids obstructed the flow of blood to the brain, thus impairing mental efficiency.) The performance of "different races" was also a factor, with Germans having the best records, followed by Americans, Russians, English, Irish, and Italians.[71] To reduce waste, Ayres appealed to the standards then presumably employed in industry:

> In this country there are perhaps 8,000,000 people engaged in the manufacturing industries. The teachers and pupils in our schools number about 19,000,000. Yet when we turn from the field of applied mechanics to that of educational administration the transition as regards standards and measures of comparison is too often from science, knowledge, and precision to conjecture, opinion, and chance.[72]

Schools, Ayers insisted, needed to adopt the scientific methods then employed in industry in order to reduce the inefficiency that "retardation" and "elimination" represented.

In that regard, Ayres constructed his Index of Efficiency, by which school systems could measure their rates of productivity as a prelude to curricular and structural change. Initially, a determination was made as to the number of children who enter each school year in relation to how many remained until the final year of elementary school. "Such a factor," Ayres explained, "would show the relation of the finished product to the raw material." The number of beginning students indicates "the number of children who under conditions of maximum theoretical efficiency should be in each grade." The size of the actual school system would then be compared to its theoretical size. After actual size was compared with actual product, the Index of Efficiency would be arrived at, and this would "give us a means of rating different school systems on the basis of efficiency."[73] Of thirty-one cities subjected to his Index of Efficiency, Ayres found that Medford and Waltham, Massachusetts, ranked at the top, while two "colored" schools in Wilmington, Delaware, and Memphis, Tennessee, ranked at the bottom. For many years after its publication in 1909, Ayres's work was widely cited as a pioneer work and a model of scientific thinking applied to education.

A SCIENTIFICALLY MANAGED CURRICULUM

A further indication of a direct influence of scientific management on schooling was the publication in 1912 of an article by John Franklin Bobbitt entitled, significantly, "The Elimination of Waste in Education." Although the appearance of a book here and an article there can hardly be construed as establishing a major trend, the ideas and principles that both Ayres and Bobbitt reflected in their work were not only exquisitely representative of their time but became common wisdom in planning a curriculum for decades thereafter. Moreover, Bobbitt's emergence as one of the preeminent leaders in the field of curriculum studies shortly after the article was published is further indication of the appeal and popularity of those ideas. In his 1912 article, Bobbitt took as his case in point the school system in Gary, Indiana, which under the leadership of its superintendent, Willard Wirt, was already achieving some renown.[74] Although the city had been "practically created by the United States Steel Corporation," its schools faced hard times financially according to Bobbitt because this new city had no "school plant" already functioning. To conserve resources, therefore, supreme efficiency became the order of the day.

According to Bobbitt, Wirt, whom he consistently refers to as an "educational engineer," was able to "create a thoroughly modern school plant" and "then to operate it according to recently developed principles of scientific management."[75] Bobbitt then proceeded to describe how Taylor's principles had been carried over to the operation of the Gary schools. At first the application of the principles was quite literal. "The first principle of scientific management," Bobbitt declared, "is to use all the plant all the available time." In that regard, Bobbitt pointed out that in a typical school, while classrooms were being used, other spaces in the school building such as the assembly room, the playground, and the science room were lying idle. Wirt (the "educational engineer") devised a plan, widely known as the platoon system, whereby children would be systematically shifted to the various spaces so that maximum utilization of the school plant would be achieved. Even with these farsighted measures in place, however, the school plant lay useless for much of the time. "The six-hour day is not enough," Bobbitt insisted; to eliminate this waste, "the plant might well be operated continuously from eight o'clock in the morning until six o'clock in the evening." Similarly, the school week needed to be reconsidered in the light of efficiency principles. "That an expensive plant should lie idle during all of Saturday and Sunday while 'street and alley time' is undoing the good work of the schools," Bobbitt observed, "is a further thorn in the flesh of the clear-sighted educational engineer. . . . Scientific management demands that the school buildings be in use on Saturdays and Sundays." In that regard, Bobbitt also introduced the possibility of an all-year school since closing the school for two months during the summer results in "a loss of some 16 percent, no small item in the calculations of the efficiency engineer."[76] At this point, Bobbitt was simply treating the school building like the physical space in a modern factory and prescribing its use in the interest of maximum efficiency.

When Bobbitt turned to what he claimed was the fourth principle of scientific management, however, the implications of applying Taylorism to schools became much more portentous:

> Work up the raw material into that finished product for which it is best adapted. Applied to education this means: Educate the individual according to his capabilities. This requires that the materials of the curriculum be sufficiently various to meet the needs of every class of individuals in the community; and that the course of training and study be sufficiently flexible that the individual can be given just the things he needs.[77]

Proposing to "meet the needs" of school children or advocating flexibility in the curriculum seems hardly noteworthy, but in practice this meant making important curricular decisions based on questionable assumptions as to what those needs were and exaggerating the curricular differentiation that was required in order to meet them. For an individual, for example, with a "motor type of mind," Bobbitt suggested that there may come a time when manual activities should not only be emphasized but when general studies would be omitted entirely. Since "the boys require masculine leadership in many of their activities, and the girls feminine leadership," some gender segregation also seemed desirable.[78] Bobbitt's article, published only a year after Taylor's *Scientific Management* appeared, reflected precisely the new thinking about the curriculum. The idea that school buildings should be run with maximum efficiency was merely a transference of the principles of scientific management to the running of the school "plant," and this carried with it manifold implications; but the idea that the curriculum should be governed by efficiency principles implied something much more far-reaching. Teaching subjects to children and youth who would not have occasion to make use of them in their adult lives was now regarded as a monumental waste.

At least as significant as Bobbitt's specific recommendations for creating a scientifically controlled curriculum was his introduction of a potent new vocabulary into curricular discourse, and this metaphorical language came to control what was deemed to be right and proper in curricular design. Derived directly from the manufacturing process, that language also served to define the overarching purposes of schooling. Proceeding from the root metaphor of the school as a factory and the curriculum as a production process, school children became "raw material" and the teacher the overseer of the production process, making sure that the products were constructed according to the specifications laid down and with a minimum of waste. School administrators, of course, were the "educational engineers" who not only designed the systems but were responsible for assessing the quality of the raw material and determining the best use to which it should be put. They and their staff of specialists also drew up the educational blueprints and exacting design specifications that predetermined the nature and quantity of the output. The success of the enterprise would be ascertained by the extent to which higher productivity could be achieved and whether the finished product met the specifications that had been expressly set forth.

In the context of Taylorism, these criteria made perfect sense. Over the next few years, in the course of rising to the forefront of the burgeoning field of curriculum studies, Bobbitt elaborated on those ideas. In *The Curriculum*,[79] the first book written on the curriculum, and the even more popular *How to Make a Curriculum*, he brought these ideas to an ever wider audience of teachers and administrators. In that latter work, for example, Bobbitt set forth a principle that became central to the process of schooling in the twentieth century: "Education is primarily for adult life, not for child life. Its fundamental responsibility is to prepare for the fifty years of adulthood, not for the twenty years of childhood and youth."[80] The child was, in other words, not so much a child as an adult in the making. The curriculum, in turn, became the mechanism by which the crude raw material of childhood was transformed into a fully-functioning adult. By 1912, vocational education was now not merely well established as an alternative to general education; its precepts were beginning to control the curriculum as a whole.

Bobbitt was not alone in promoting this new form of thinking about the curriculum. He was simply a leading representative of a new conception of curriculum-making, and therefore, someone who could articulate its underlying assumptions with clarity and force. Bobbitt along with Leonard Ayres, W. W. Charters, David Snedden, and a host of other so-called scientifically oriented curriculum-makers were now in the forefront of curriculum thinking. The principles that had their inception in sustaining a supremely efficient factory not only became the basis on which schools were to be managed but the foundation of how the curriculum was to be conceived and its purposes defined. To be sure, the new factory system demanded a steady supply of workers, which presumably vocational training would produce. At the same time that public schools were undertaking to fill that need, the new factory system was also providing the metaphors that a burgeoning school system would embrace. Vocational education as a prominent addendum to the standard curriculum represented a significant shift of emphasis in American schools; conceiving of schools *as* factories amounted to a pedagogical revolution.

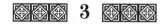 3

"A COLOSSAL ADVANTAGE"

Manual Training in Milwaukee, 1883–1906

Herbert M. Kliebard and Carol Judy Kean

> *At this time when every city of any importance in the country is expending money unsparingly in revising its course of study so as to include manual training in some form or other as complete as possible, Milwaukee ought, at least, not condemn, or go on record as opposed to this "new education" which has won its way to the front and has become in the words of Prof. James in the Atlantic Magazine "A Colossal Advantage" to the youth of the land in the schools which are preparing our future citizens for practical life.*
>
> *Milwaukee School Director, Frank Ellis, 1898[1]*

As the drama of industrial education was being enacted on the national stage, dozens of school districts were launching their own productions. To a very considerable extent, these local performances echoed the themes and points of contention that were being heard at the annual conventions of the NEA and enunciated by widely recognized actors on the national scene. At the same time, however, relatively obscure education professionals as well as local citizens' groups brought their own interpretations and inflections to the dramas being played out in their communities. The contentions of national leaders, such as Woodward, that manual training was an ideal vehicle for "completing" a liberal education, for example, carried a certain amount of weight, especially among education professionals, but local conditions frequently gave the many battles over manual training a special coloration. Not the least of these factors was that manual training was getting such a favorable reception at the national level that school districts could ill afford to be left behind. School administrators, to be sure, were reflecting their own instincts and ideologies as they considered the merits of manual training, but they were also eager to portray their schools as supremely up-to-date. In a sense, their reputations as school leaders were at stake. Along with the familiar justifications for manual training that were being proclaimed on every side, a powerful civic pride and a professional imperative were also operating. No city and no school administrator could afford to be seen as failing to keep up with the rapid changes that the Industrial Revolution had produced. The new breed of professional school leaders, like Milwaukee school director Frank Ellis, could not simply stand pat when other cities were already bestowing on their youth the "colossal advantage" that manual training now represented.

School officials, however, also had to deal with the day-to-day realities of implementing an idea that, while appealing in many respects, entailed considerable cost. Manual training, school leaders were discovering, required uncommon tools, equipment, and space, and then as now, the prospect of meeting the cost of school programs had considerable saliency whenever reforms were proposed. While national leaders could aim their message at the well-known benefits that manual training presumably provided, local leaders had to balance those alleged advantages against the reality of having to pay the bill. This required patience and compromise. The doubts of sometimes penurious citizens had to be overcome. A student constituency had to be identified. Competent teachers had to be hired. Special facilities and equipment had to be bought and paid for, and those costs had to be justified in terms of benefits to real students in real classrooms. Perhaps more than anything, influential interest groups had to coalesce around the reform and even, in some cases, take the initiative.

Beyond the matter of justifying costs and marshaling political support, local school officials had to face the formidable task of actually developing the programs of study that manual training entailed. The vague generalities that often accompanied the call for manual training had to be translated into the quotidian realities of teaching and learning. In certain significant respects, manual training represented a departure from the way schooling was normally conducted and required a new way of thinking about schooling. Fixed desks in orderly rows and oral recitation of lessons had to give way to bustling activity along with the noise entailed in such activity. These difficulties notwithstanding, school officials had to take into account Milwaukee's growth into a major industrial center and what that implied in terms of school practice.

MILWAUKEE'S INDUSTRIAL GROWTH

Despite some vagaries in the national economy, Milwaukee, like other American cities, was enjoying a boom in the late-nineteenth century. Manufacturing expanded substantially in the 1870s and 1880s as entrepreneurs looked for investments in industry. Real estate agencies were besieged with requests for manufacturing sites. Having heard that Milwaukee was a good place to obtain work, skilled mechanics from all parts of the country migrated to the city in large numbers. The *Evening Wisconsin* reported that the city's manufacturing interests were "expanding like a greenbay tree, and the amount of population which [was] pouring into the South Side, where most of the manufactories [were] being established [was] a marvel to the oldest citizens."[2] Between 1890 and 1910, manufacturing overtook trade and commerce as the driving force of Milwaukee's economy, the annual value of manufactured products increasing more than tenfold. Between 1899 and 1909 alone, the gross value of manufactured products grew by 88 percent, a gain almost equal to the increase in the preceding sixty years.

By 1892, manufacturing in Milwaukee had grown to such an extent that the Chamber of Commerce became convinced that the city's future depended upon further industrial expansion—that the time was past when purely commercial pursuits would support the population. The need to expand industry, however, created new anxieties, and the depression of 1893 lent credence to the fear that prosperity would not last. Five of the city's banks were forced to close and, although no failures occurred among the manufacturing plants, work was suspended for a time and wages reduced. Manufacturing gradually recovered; by 1897, employment was again high and some factories were working at full capacity. Foreign orders for heavy machinery swelled industrial profits in 1898. By 1899, these plants were being taxed beyond their capacity, and between 1904 and 1909 alone, profits increased 51 percent. In 1880, there were 13,782 industrial workers; by 1899, this number had grown to 45,297, and in 1909, the number of workers engaged in industry stood at 68,933. The consolidation of industrial management, already evident in the 1860s, continued and accelerated. Between 1870 and 1880, the number of firms in Milwaukee increased only 2 percent while the number of employed workers rose 147 percent. Between 1899 and 1909, the number of the city's different establishments increased by 24 percent while there was slightly less than a 50 percent increase in the number of persons engaged in factory work.[3]

The rapidly expanding industries had their foundations in the raw materials supplied by the farms and forests of Wisconsin and its neighboring states. This was especially true of the five predominant Milwaukee industries of this period: flour milling, meat packing, tanning, brewing, and the manufacture of iron and steel. Flour production in Milwaukee increased steadily from 1870 to 1892. Milwaukee still ranked as the third city in the nation in the value of flour manufactured in 1909, but the city's output was only 70 percent of what it had been in 1882, and it continued to decline thereafter. The brewing industry increased its output during this period from 142,000 barrels in

1871 to an astounding 3,700,000 in 1910. Five meat packing companies in the city continued to do business on a large enough scale throughout the period to maintain this industry's status among the top five. Tanning enterprises increased their production 400 percent, giving Milwaukee the distinction of being the world's largest producer of plain tanned leather in 1890.[4]

Milwaukee's geographical position, as well as the natural resources and production needs of regions to the north and west, supported the city's early development of its iron and steel industry. The two rolling mills and six blast furnaces of the Milwaukee Iron Company or Bay View Works were producing 45,000 tons of railroad iron in the early 1870s and employed more than a thousand workers. The Bay View Works was reorganized due to financial difficulties in 1878, becoming the property of the North Chicago Rolling Mill Company, which also leased the Minerva Furnace, Milwaukee's other major smelting plant. By 1885, the Bay View Plant was employing fifteen hundred men earning from $2.50 to $5.00 per day.

The increasing demand for the products of foundries and machine shops was an indicator of the rapid industrial development of the city. In 1900, foundries and machine shops led Milwaukee enterprises in value of goods produced. Local manufacturers, as well as those in many other cities of the Midwest, required millstones, engines, pumps, and machines. Milwaukee's most outstanding supplier of these products was the Reliance Iron Works. Founded in 1847, this millstone factory was taken over by Edward P. Allis in 1860. Between that date and his death in 1889, Allis transformed a business amounting to $31,000 annually into a large-scale enterprise reporting an annual production averaging more than $3 million per year. By the turn of the century, Milwaukee foundries were seeking a national and in some cases an international market as the companies' organization followed the prevalent trends toward financial and managerial consolidation. A reorganization in 1890 converted Edward P. Allis & Company into the Edward P. Allis Company, and in 1901, it was one of four enterprises that merged to form the Allis-Chalmers Company. With the completion of this consolidation, Allis-Chalmers's annual business exceeded $10 million, it employed five thousand workers in five plants, and it had branch offices in ten American cities as well as four outside the United States.

SUPERINTENDENT ANDERSON OPENS
THE MILWAUKEE CAMPAIGN

Terms such as "industrial arts," "industrial education," and "manual training" could be found in prior reports to the Milwaukee school board, but it was Superintendent William E. Anderson who in 1883 first attempted systematically to present the case for and against introducing "mechanical industries" in Milwaukee's common schools and to outline a plan as to how the Board of School Directors should proceed in this area. His report reviewed the most prevalent arguments being espoused by nationally prominent educational figures at the time. It is clear that what national leaders of the movement had to say was penetrating the educational policies and school practices of major cities throughout the United States. As Anderson put it in his first annual report to the school board in 1883, "Industrial training is just now attracting considerable attention from educators."[5] Educators, it is true, were supporting manual training with great enthusiasm on educational grounds, but the message being received in local school districts had much more to do with economic prosperity than with notions of "completing" an education through manual training.

Boys, according to Anderson, were being "educated away" from the mechanical arts, and the lucrative places in America's workshops were being filled by foreign workmen. National prosperity rested upon the development of manufacturing resources and a significant increase in the numbers and skill of the population engaged in manufacturing. As Anderson saw it, the national welfare depended upon the adaptation of the common schools to the purposes of industry. The public schools must, therefore, develop a new content and new teaching methods, without of course neglecting reading, writing, arithmetic, and other essential areas of the curriculum. There were also echoes of Woodward's image of the masculine ideal of the Young Vulcan in Anderson's report. The new industrial age demanded a larger, more "liberal," more "natural," and more "practical" preparation for life than was being provided in the bookish, "narrow ruts of present school work." The schooling that the new technological society required was as much physical and manual as it was intellectual and contemplative. The "true" common education, Anderson argued, must include both mental and manual training. In addition, the new trade schools and technical schools would open up an entirely new field of opportunity for the country's youth. These special schools and departments would furnish that "preparation for usefulness" and that positive disposition toward art and trade that would "elevate" the working classes and close the social gap between artisans and the other classes.[6]

Apparently, the charge that the standard curriculum was weaning youth away from the ideal of the noble artisan resonated in Milwaukee as well as in the national arena. Superintendent Anderson, however, took issue with the notion that the "oft-remarked repugnance of the youth of both sexes to work with their hands" could be charged directly to their schooling: "That [Milwaukee's schools] do not teach manual industries, I admit. That they inculcate habits which tend to indolence in after life, I positively deny."[7]

The ambiguity as to how manual training was to be justified, so evident at the national level, was also initially reflected in Milwaukee. Despite his references to the needs of industry, Anderson also seemed to accept the notion that manual training was not really a preparation for entering the workforce. He even rejected the argument that direct trade training should or could be assumed by the public schools. In his view, only a limited number of specific trades could be handled in the school setting, and these would be so costly to provide that the general efficiency of the school might be hindered, thus depriving the children of their opportunity to receive a good general education. Furthermore, he believed, the ultimate result of such specialized training would be to overcrowd a few trades with too many workers—a result which would expose the city's artisans to excessive labor competition, lower wages, and force them to find new occupations. Those branches of knowledge which were applicable to all industries and occupations were the ones that should be incorporated into the curriculum. Studies such as drawing, bookkeeping, the elements of physical and natural science, clay molding, geometrical constructions from cardboard, and mensuration had a direct bearing upon a multitude of occupations and, at the same time, could be said to constitute a very effective means of general training. Adding these studies to the elementary school curriculum, Anderson realized, would not "appease" the public demand for a new industrial education for youth ages six through fourteen years of age. What such an education should entail was still a mystery to him. He recommended, therefore, that "in the present unripe stage of opinion and experience, a society of inquiry, composed of ladies and gentlemen interested in this most important subject form as soon as possible."[8]

Anderson felt on surer ground when he turned his attention to the high school. Here, he asserted that the whole result of high school training was preparation for those professions whose basis was a "literary culture." Reflecting what was becoming a persistent theme in the drive for vocational education, Anderson argued that boys who were to become lawyers, doctors, theologians, or journalists received ample preparation for these vocations, but "those who would be bridge builders, draughtsmen, mechanical or civil engineers, or merchants find that the whole bent of the instruction is to them a 'disqualifying culture.'"[9] He concluded his report by stating that the analysis he had presented warranted an attempt to introduce a course of instruction in the high school which would include the necessary training for trades, shop work, or higher technical training.[10]

Following the recommendation of the superintendent, the Milwaukee Board of School Directors appointed a committee to examine industrial training and recommend the next steps to be taken in developing a program in the area. The school board's committee held two public meetings during the 1883–84 school year at which industrial education was discussed at length by interested educators and laypersons. The committee also studied the manual training system already in operation in cities such as St. Louis, Chicago,

Toledo, Worcester, and Boston and concluded that wherever manual training programs appeared to be successful, they had been developed for and implemented with classes of pupils who had, for the most part, completed their elementary or common school education. The committee took a cautious stand. "At present, the only change in the direction of industrial education, which seems practicable," concluded the special committee, "is in some rearrangement of the instruction in the grammar grades and high school."[11]

During the early 1880s, the uncertainty as to what manual training actually entailed plagued Milwaukee's school administrators as well as many others across the nation. By 1885, Anderson was ready to present his definition to the Board of School Directors: "[It] is best explained as being such a modification of both elementary and secondary instruction as will the better adapt the same to the purposes of general education, and at the same time afford a preparation which will be found of direct value and assistance in industrial life."[12] When faced with the alternatives of manual training as "completing" the standard curriculum or manual training as preparation for modern industry, Anderson, like nationally prominent educators and members of the public, simply accepted both. Manual training in his mind would require the elimination of a mass of superfluous detail that had crept into the basic curriculum under a mistaken notion of thoroughness. It would mean the adoption of practical and comprehensive methods of teaching all subjects—a system of training in which natural phenomena, objects, and materials would be systematically studied and the mind "exercised and invigorated" by actual experience, experiment, and observation. The elementary course of instruction would deal with natural objects and their special properties, including plants and animals, common minerals, vegetables useful as foods and as fabrics, rudiments of natural history, physics, chemistry, geometry (as used in the study of art forms), drawing, the making of simple apparatus to conduct simple experiments in physics, and mechanics. Few if any changes in buildings would be required in the district schools to put this system of instruction into operation, and the expense incurred would be minimal. At the high school level, industrial training would include systematic instruction in five areas: (1) mathematics; (2) applied mathematics and drawing; (3) science, including physics, mechanics, and chemistry; (4) language, including English and German, with options of Latin or French for pupils intending to go to polytechnic schools or the university; (5) regular work in wood and iron, the application of drawing to modeling, the use of typical tools, and the principles of machinery.[13]

At Anderson's urging, the Milwaukee Board of School Directors requested a sum of $5,000 from the Common Council during the 1885–86 school year for the purpose of "engrafting manual training upon the public schools." Interestingly, the request was denied at first because the school board did not present a specific plan for systematically introducing manual training elements into the curriculum, but the board continued to petition the Common Council for money to initiate an experiment in manual training until 1891. In that year, the Board of School Directors allocated some of its extra funds to implement a program of manual training in the public schools.

From the early 1870s on, when a number of Milwaukee's citizens began to complain that the schools provided no adequate preparation for their children to become artisans and tradesmen, the city's school managers had been grappling with the problem of bringing the schools into a closer relationship to the workplace. Everywhere, it seemed, school systems were introducing manual training programs into their curricula and claiming successful results. Although the exact nature of this reform often called industrial education rather than manual training remained elusive to Milwaukee's school leaders, they did not doubt that they too must initiate curriculum change along these lines. While the school managers debated and studied these issues among themselves, a citizens' group working outside the schools took the initiative and organized what was to become Milwaukee's first formal step in the direction of the "new" education.

COOKING IN MILWAUKEE'S PUBLIC SCHOOL CURRICULUM

The first breakthrough in the effort to introduce manual training into Milwaukee's curriculum occurred in the context of the education of girls, and it seemed prompted by the fear that traditional homemaking skills were declining in the new industrial society. As is often the case, the immediate impetus for that reform came from outside the professional education establishment. Worried that many girls were being allowed to grow up without the knowledge of the "housewifely arts" upon which the welfare and the comfort of the home depended, the Milwaukee Public School Cooking Association, a group of public-spirited women, was organized by Fannie J. Crosby. With dedication and skill, the association lobbied to convince public school officials that schools should teach the art of cooking, "which influences so largely through wholesome or unwholesome food, the health and welfare of the home."[14] In the fall of 1887, the Cooking Association petitioned the school board, requesting the use of rooms in the Seventh District school building for the purpose of giving free instruction in cooking and domestic economy. The board granted this request on November 1, and on March 6, 1888, the Milwaukee Public School Cooking Association made its first formal report on the progress of their instruction to the school directors.[15] The association had fifty applicants for its Seventh District Cooking School but was unable due to restricted time and space to accept more than twenty-four. These twenty-four applicants were divided into two classes of twelve each, and the first class met on November 12, 1887. Thereafter, one class met in the morning, the other in the afternoon each week.

According to the vice-president of the Cooking Association, the interest and average attendance of the pupils showed a steady improvement over time. A strict record was kept of attendance, behavior, and the number of dishes prepared in class and at home by the pupils. During the period covered by the vice-president's initial report, the pupils stated that they had reproduced 1,306 dishes, making an average of fifty-four dishes prepared at home by each pupil. A curriculum was emerging. Cooking instruction was directed toward the "perfect and most economical preparation" of simple dishes, the building of fires in stoves and ranges, the cleaning and care of cooking utensils, the selection and comparative values of food, simple tests for spoilage, the "practical teaching of the chemistry of cooking," neatness, and method of work. All instruction was designed to make pupils familiar with the ways in which to prepare wholesome, appetizing, and economical dishes, useful in giving variety to food, reducing waste, and thereby reducing the cost of living.

Members of the Cooking Association believed that students across the nation needed to learn the duty of economy in food selection and preparation if the health of America's rapidly increasing population was to be secured. In its view, the Europeans were far ahead of the United States, and the Cooking Association sought to prepare the pupils who enrolled in its cooking classes to deal intelligently with this matter in their homes and in their lives. Local response was enthusiastic. Classes of pupils who had obtained parental written permission to devote one afternoon each week to attend cooking classes had already formed in the First and Third Districts even though there were, as yet, no facilities. The association appealed to the school board, explaining that it had available five days in the week which could be used for cooking classes formed in the various school districts and conducted at the Seventh District School. No cost would be incurred by the city or the pupils. The women in the association wanted to extend the benefits of the new program throughout the public schools, but the present lack of space prevented them from so doing. Written testimonials as to the value of cooking school instruction had been received from many parents, and the public interest appeared strong. It was now up to the school board to determine whether this work would be continued.

In September, school director August Stirn, a strong proponent of manual training, presented a resolution in favor of continuing the cooking school program under certain conditions. Pupils would be allowed to attend cooking lessons only when excused by the superintendent, and they would be expected to "fully meet the requirements of the course of instruction" and "maintain their standing in the regular grade work of the school." Principals were required to report any pupils who proved "delinquent in their studies" during the period of attendance of cooking lessons. Neither the school board nor the pupils were to incur any costs as a result of cooking instruction. The resolution specified that cooking instruction would take place at the Second District School. No explanation was given for this change, but the Second District was slightly more centrally located than was the Seventh during this period and would, therefore, be a more suitable location for the Milwaukee Public School Cooking Association to establish its classes. In any event, the association was grateful to have the use of the two rooms for its cooking classes and began immediately to equip them "with great care following plans obtained from Boston."[16]

In accordance with the September 4 resolution of the school board, the building principals were asked to name students in the upper grades who might, in their opinion, be able to leave school for one-half day during the week "without detriment to their general standing and scholarship." In response to this request, 150 pupils were identified. The pupils were organized into ten classes, and each class was assigned a half day of cooking instruction to take place in the Second District School.[17] At the March 5, 1888, meeting of the Board of School Directors, Commissioner Desmond presented a resolution proposing that a committee of five and the president of the school board be appointed to examine the work being done in the cooking classes to determine whether the teaching of cooking in the public schools should be placed under the direct control of the board and whether the board should extend any financial assistance to the cooking school (for two years having been supported by private citizens). The Special Committee accomplished its work quickly and at the following meeting presented its report with accompanying exhibits. The committee concluded that the cooking school did not interfere at all with the academic program of the girls who participated in it, and that the instruction they received was valuable and desirable. On the basis of a financial report submitted by the Public School Cooking Association, the committee believed that the cooking school could be publicly supported at "very slight expense" and that, in assuming charge of the cooking school, the school board would "not be dealing with an experiment, or with an impracticable and visionary scheme of manual training." The committee then recommended that a sum not exceeding $1,300 be appropriated for the purpose of teaching the science of cooking and domestic economy.

Three exhibits were attached to the report. In the first, Superintendent Anderson described the basis on which the Cooking Association built its program. The culinary arts were taught in a "scientific" manner. Practical lessons in the preparation of common foods were given, and the rationale for the cooking processes was explained as the pupils proceeded with their work.

Whenever general principles of science were obvious, these were fully discussed. "In reasoning from cause to effect, in training to careful observation and the drawing of correct inferences upon observation, and even in the cultivation of the moral habits of neatness, diligence and order, the Cooking School is as efficient and available a means as is supplied in any department, grade, or feature of the elementary schools." Superintendent Anderson acknowledged that he might appear to be placing a high value upon an industry traditionally viewed as the "peculiar sphere of menials or of the less intelligent class," but he asserted that his estimate was in harmony with the change taking place in the prevailing views of a true standard of value in educational means and processes, or as he put it, "the respectability of all departments of human industry, especially where such industry rises to the dignity of art and is susceptible of being improved or perfected upon the application of the principles of science."[18] Anderson had no doubt that, tested by the standards of culture and utility, cooking instruction was valuable and should be retained.

Exhibit B, submitted by the Managers of the Public School Cooking Association, was a proposition stating that, if the school board was not yet willing to incorporate cooking into the regular curriculum of the schools, the association would continue to supervise the school, provide a thoroughly competent teacher, and use its own equipment, provided the expenses were met by the board. Included was an itemized accounting of the cost of the cooking school and a projected list of expenses for the coming year.[19]

Exhibit C contained excerpts from letters of the parents of girls who were attending the school, responding to a request for their opinions of the value of instruction. The report noted that thirty-six of the letters were "highly commendatory," while three were skeptical to disapproving. The majority of the letters included statements such as the following: "The [cooking] school imparts much useful information"; "the school promotes neatness and order in the kitchen"; "what I like most is the order and accuracy taught; very practicable and satisfactory"; "an essential branch for the public school"; "a good and lasting foundation has been so well laid that with practice at home, she will not only make herself useful, but will be able to direct the culinary department of a household whenever the opportunity may occur"; "as patrons and tax payers, we would like to see the work continued as part of the regular public school education"; "it seems to entirely eliminate from the child's mind the idea that the work is drudgery."[20] On the whole, parents whose daughters were participating in the cooking schools obviously believed that the training was helpful and appropriate. With an eager constituency in place, reservations with regard to the cooking school began to recede.

At first, care was taken not to let cooking school attendance interfere with academic studies. The superintendent and the principals who selected those students who could participate in the cooking classes supported this form

of manual training for girls so long as their academic studies did not suffer from
the half-day's weekly absence required by their attendance at the cooking
school. The principals helped to ensure this by selecting the more "able"
prospective students; to attend the cooking school was a privilege and something to be earned. At the end of this school year, both the president of the
school board and the superintendent were so pleased that they recommended
establishing at least two additional cooking schools on the east and south sides
of the city.[21]

When the school board decided to incorporate the cooking school program into the regular curriculum of the Milwaukee public schools, it appointed
Emeline Torrey as director of the department of training in cooking and
domestic science.[22] Torrey reported monthly to the board, citing such statistics as the numbers of pupils who were enrolled from each district, the number of absent and tardy students by district and the number of home dishes
prepared. Later, as more cooking school centers were added to the school system, the reports were condensed to include only total enrollment and average weekly attendance for each of the centers. These statistics were reported
to the school board at its monthly meeting by the superintendent.

Within two years of its existence, the cooking school had instructed
some 550 pupils. The curriculum of the school now consisted of twenty specific lessons, all combining practical demonstrations with such "scientific
instruction" as was needed to explain the reasons for a particular procedure.
The first exercises dealt with the most efficient and economical use of heat,
fuel, and fire. These lessons were followed by the general classification of the
elements of food and demonstrations on the effects of steam and boiling water,
illustrating the correct preparation of plain vegetables, rice, and starchy and
glutinous foods. The art of cooking a variety of meats followed next, and connected to this study was a series of lessons on using leftovers. Broiling, stews,
batters, and bread making were explained. Three lessons were devoted to the
cooking of poultry and fish. Some attention was given to cooking for invalids
and, if time permitted, to storing food and adapting food preparation to occupation and climate. Throughout the course of instruction, the care of kitchen
apparatus, the proper ways to serve food, and ways to economize were stressed.
"Scientific information" was not the only value of cooking school instruction,
although it was considered of prime importance. Some proponents of the
cooking school pointed to attitudes and behaviors as an important outcome
of the instruction. "Strange as it may appear to some," it was reported, "cooking is reducible to principles; and the business of the kitchen, though scouted
as a menial art, is based upon a knowledge of the elements of physics and
chemistry and the exercises of industrial virtues of no mean order, such as
patience, cleanliness, system and dexterity."[23] Moral virtues such as patience,
cleanliness, industry, and discipline had long been pointed out by school man-

agers as some of the positive results of public school training. The appeal to
"science" as a justification for including (or excluding) a particular subject in
the curriculum was a relatively new phenomenon, but its appearance in the
rhetoric of Milwaukee's school managers is not surprising. A widespread perception had emerged across the nation that America was entering the "scientific age." The new program in cooking, in this way, served not only to preserve traditional roles and values—a kind of female version of the noble
artisan—but it incorporated the idea that a scientifically based cooking program would bring with it such benefits as proper nutrition and hygiene.

Even so, the introduction of cooking was not without its detractors. During the school years 1890–91 and 1891–92, proposals were presented to abolish the cooking schools. The chief objection was that public funds were being
used to support special instruction for a small number of pupils. Some objected
to the "ornamental" part of the instruction such as cakes, fancy soups, hors
d'oeuvres, sweetmeats, and "luxuries." Others had the idea that the school's
purpose was to turn out chefs and were critical because it was not doing so.
Various committees of the school board held open meetings to hear arguments
for retaining and for abolishing the cooking school. Having heard both the
pros and the cons, the school board judged the cooking school not only worth
continuing but expanding. An evening cooking school was organized in
November 1891 in the Second District. A second school was opened in the
Fifth District on the South Side in February 1892.

Milwaukee's public cooking schools operated throughout the 1890s without much change or controversy. In 1902, a third cooking school was established on the East Side, thereby providing one school for each side of the city.
The curriculum did not vary during this period, and enrollments remained relatively stable. Periodic investigations of the cooking schools were made by
the various committees of the school board, the Board of Cooking School
Inspectors, and such nonschool organizations as the Woman's School Alliance
(a group of middle-class, reform-minded women who organized themselves in
the spring of 1891 for the purpose of promoting the best interests of children
in the Milwaukee public schools). In June 1897, the school board's Committee on Manual Training reported that the Woman's School Alliance had visited 111 mothers (also many fathers) and without exception the cooking
schools were greatly praised. The girls not only assisted their mothers in cooking but often could instruct them in how to get the best results. The good
moral influence of the cooking school curriculum was cited as important by
many mothers. As a result of this report, the committee not only approved
the continuation of the schools, but recommended that they be expanded as
soon as possible. The program continued to operate without any basic changes
until 1900, when the suggestion to extend the duration of the course from
twenty to forty weeks came to the school board from several different sources.

This request was initially denied because the board's Committee on Course of Instruction was uncertain as to what to do with the boys while the girls were in the cooking schools; the cooking school program by this time was highly organized and operating efficiently, but a program of manual training for boys was yet to be initiated. The concern given voice most prominently by the Douglas Commission as to the general appropriateness of the standard curriculum, particularly in the upper grades and the high school, was being expressed in Milwaukee as well. Pupils were starting to stay in school longer, and new groups of students—poor, working-class, and immigrant children— were entering the schools in greater numbers.

The manner in which cooking schools were introduced in Milwaukee may be indicative of a general pattern of curricular change. In certain notable cases at least, when reluctance to implement a proposed reform exists, outside groups undertake to initiate the change and actually develop the curriculum. Once the curriculum is in place, and the public reaction is favorable, then school leaders feel emboldened or obliged or even compelled to incorporate that change in the public schools. The success of the cooking schools served to convince Milwaukee's citizens that schools had the responsibility to provide more than an academic education. With popular reaction to cooking schools so strongly favorable, even the introduction of manual training, despite its costs, became much more politically palatable.

MANUAL TRAINING INTRODUCED INTO MILWAUKEE'S PUBLIC SCHOOLS

Throughout the 1880s, resolutions to introduce manual training into the high schools of Milwaukee were often made, but no definite action was taken until the 1890–91 school year. In that year, Milwaukee's school board formed a special committee to investigate the subject of manual training. After the committee contacted other cities which were experimenting with manual training programs, they recommended that a beginning in manual training be made as soon as practicable. The committee reported that many cities had "proved" manual training to be conducive to "good order and discipline," encouraged a "taste for manual labor at an early age," and retained the children from "one to three years longer in the schools." In line with the pronouncements of major leaders of the manual training movement at the national level, the committee took the stand that schools were not for the purpose of trade training. "The schools," the committee stated, "are not established for the purpose of teaching scholars how to make a living but to teach them how to live; they are not to teach trades, but to enhance a desire for education." If a teacher could succeed in winning a pupil's interest through manual training, then "even the dullest pupil" would become a "bright scholar."[24] The committee recommended an appropriation to "fit up a school or schools," as inexpensively as possible, in order to initiate manual training. This recommendation was referred to the Committee on Finance, which suggested that a sum of $1,500 should be appropriated to establish and operate a manual training department on an experimental basis for one year. The Board of School Directors voted 22 to 4 in favor of this resolution.

In time, the Committee on Art and Industrial Education recommended that the manual training room be established in the high school, and the High School Committee assumed the responsibility for hiring a manual training teacher and purchasing the necessary apparatus to equip the room.[25] Herbert M. Woodward was appointed as director of manual training in August 1891, and the manual training school opened its doors to thirty-eight pupils in September. The manual training department was located on the attic floor of the north wing of the high school building. The room was large enough to accommodate all the equipment but was difficult to get to and poorly lit. The department was equipped initially with twelve double carpenter's benches, allowing room for twenty-four boys to work at once, twenty-four sets of beach tools (tools, without sharp edges, used in ordinary joinery and which could be used by different pupils at different times), thirty sets of edge tools (for the individual use of thirty pupils), one set of occasional tools (for use of all in the shop at any one time), a band saw with 36-inch wheels, a grindstone, four 12-inch turning lathes, a 7-horsepower gas engine to furnish power, a 350-gallon tank to furnish a water supply for the engine and wash sink, and a sink large enough to accommodate twenty-four boys washing up at one time. The introduction of such equipment was a significant departure from what was taken to be a normal classroom and represented a considerable investment in the interest of sustaining the manual training program.

With the equipment in place, plans for a curriculum quickly followed. The first half of the year was devoted to learning and practice of all the elementary details of practical carpentry and joinery. The second semester was given over to wood turning. These activities were consistent with other beginning manual training programs being conducted at the high school level in various school districts across the nation. Simple exercises with the various turner's tools were mastered first, followed by the creation of practical and ornamental pieces. The goal was to develop the students' skill in the handling of tools along with a practical knowledge of materials and construction rather than the production of marketable items. Twenty-three pupils were in the first division, working in the shop from 9:30 A.M. until 10:55 A.M.; fifteen were in the second, working from 11:00 A.M. to 12:30 P.M. For some reason, Woodward believed that twenty-three was a good number and pointed out in his first report that there was room for eight more in the second division and a third division could be started during the afternoon session. Attendance figures were reported monthly to the school board beginning with thirty-eight in September but falling steadily until it reached twenty-nine in January.

Even with the steady decline in attendance, the school board apparently judged the manual training experiment a success, there being no discussion about discontinuing the program. Manual training would be offered as a high school course with the hope that Milwaukee could eventually establish a Mechanic Arts School modeled after the ones in St. Louis and Boston. In addition, the board quickly resolved the problem of under-enrollment in the manual training course by authorizing Superintendent Anderson to admit seventh- and eighth-grade pupils of the First District School, two to three times a week, into Woodward's classes.[26] Although at the national level elaborate rationales were often constructed as to the appropriate age to begin a given program of manual training, this issue was resolved in Milwaukee largely in terms of simple cost effectiveness.

Almost as soon as manual training was introduced into the high school curriculum, individuals and groups outside of the public schools began to press for expansion of the program. The major impetus in this case came from an interest group representing business. Milwaukee's Builders' and Traders' Exchange, composed of the city's leaders in these enterprises, adopted a resolution in April 1893, recommending "any movement tending to bring about the establishment of . . . manual training schools." They argued that this was "a matter of great importance to the entire community" because "owing to the lack of opportunity many bright boys are prevented from becoming mechanics in the trade of their choice, if at all,"[27] suggesting, perhaps, that craft unions were restricting access to the trades and thereby inhibiting Milwaukee's industrial growth. The city's manufacturing concerns were expanding, which brought a large influx of people seeking work and needing housing. The construction industry was booming, and skilled workers were needed to keep pace with these demands. Copies of the resolution were sent to the Regents of the State Board of Normal Schools and to Milwaukee Public School Superintendent Peckham as well as to the school board. In May of the same year, the Ninth Ward School Director requested access to rooms in the Ninth District school building be made available to those who wanted to teach "industrial and technical training" to interested adults. This was the beginning of a series of such requests over the next few years from individuals who were willing to volunteer their time to teach facets of manual training (sewing, carpentry, electrical work, needlework) to students below the high school age and to adults. In most instances, these requests were granted if the individuals were willing to provide all needed materials and to pay maintenance costs while using the rooms.

Once again, the impetus to a major curricular innovation was provided by nonschool agencies initiating programs at minimal cost. By 1900, thirteen individual and uncoordinated "industrial training rooms" were scattered throughout the Milwaukee public school system.[28] In the school year 1894–95, four years after manual training was introduced into the high school on the East Side, and the first year in which five manual training students graduated from the three-year course, the Milwaukee Board of School Directors created a standing Committee on Manual Training. The committee was to exercise general supervision over the department, to appoint (subject to character requirement and confirmation by the school board) all manual training instructors, and to recommend such changes which seemed desirable and practicable. All matters pertaining to manual training were to be referred to this committee before being acted upon by the entire school board.[29]

In October of the same school year, 1894–95, Professor H. H. Belfield and Colonel Augustus Jacobson, of the Chicago Manual Training School, visited Milwaukee at the request of the Milwaukee Manual Training Association and delivered several evening lectures in the auditorium of the East Side High School on the scope and value of manual training.[30] As a result of attending these "very entertaining and instructive lectures," James M. Pereles, an attorney and president of the school board, recommended in his presidential address that the work of the drawing department should more directly complement the work in manual training than it had heretofore, and further, that the study of drawing should be included in the high school normal, scientific, and English courses. At this time, the high schools offered four four-year courses (Ancient Classical, Modern Classical, English, and German Normal) and four three-year courses (English Normal, General Science, Business, and Manual Training).

Almost from the beginning, the introduction of manual training programs had the effect of differentiating the curriculum along the lines of probable destination. The four-year courses were directed to youth believed to be college bound, while the three-year courses were more likely to be taken by pupils who would presumably enter the job market directly from the high school. As part of the pervasive concern about cost-effectiveness, Pereles also suggested that introducing manual training in some of the upper grades would, in his opinion, increase the percentage of attendance in the schools. The dual problems of slow progress through the grades and dropping out of school early were becoming of increasing concern to Milwaukee's educators. These arguments for manual training and, more specifically, industrial education would appear more and more in the next two decades in the larger urban areas. Again the demand was to make the curriculum relevant to a rapidly increasing and diverse population, and this was interpreted as attuning the curriculum to one's eventual social and occupational role.

The desirability of providing manual training for the boys in the sixth, seventh, and eighth grades was raised periodically for the next few years, but no steps were taken to incorporate it into the curriculum of these grades. Instead, the school board, through its Manual Training Committee, directed its energies toward upgrading and expanding the high school program. In 1896, the Common Council agreed to appropriate funds to construct an addition to the East Side High School so that the manual training department could be moved out of its cramped quarters in the attic where it had been housed since 1891. Milwaukee's third high school, West Side High, opened its doors in the 1896–97 school year. The Manual Training Committee was kept busy the entire year purchasing machinery and awarding contracts to equip the new West Side Manual Training School and to re-equip and enlarge the original East Side school. Once this work was completed, the committee began to work on plans for a third manual training department in the proposed new South Side High School building. President of the school board A. J. Lindemann, a Milwaukee industrialist, commented in his annual address that the organization of these manual training schools at the high school level would constitute the second major step toward having manual training throughout the entire school system. It had been practiced in the kindergartens for many years and was now firmly established in the high schools. The next "improvement," as he saw it, was to introduce manual training into the primary and district schools. Lindemann suggested that the next school board send its Manual Training Committee to the Manual Training School, established by Senator J. H. Stout, at Menomonie, to learn how manual training could be successfully introduced into the entire school program and pursued in the ordinary classroom without disrupting other work.[31]

Superintendent Peckham resigned as superintendent of the Milwaukee Public Schools in 1896 and was succeeded by Henry O. R. Siefert, who had served since 1889 as assistant superintendent. During the first six months of Siefert's tenure in office, the manual training program began to assume greater prominence. First, the Committee on the Course of Study and Text Books revised the courses for the high schools, changing the arrangement so as to divide the scholastic year into two semesters. This was the first time that the Manual Training Course was published in the school board's official records.[32] The course took three years to complete and was organized as shown in Figure 3. The completion of these three-year courses did not mean that a student earned a high school diploma. Diplomas were granted only to those pupils who finished a four-year course of instruction. The subjects included in this course appear to have been fairly rigorous in the areas of English and mathematics and probably provided good academic training, but the absence of foreign language studies and the fact that only one science was required posed obstacles to any student who might seek admission to the University

First Year

    Semester I   Algebra, American Classics, Joinery, Mechanical Drawing
    Semester II   Algebra, Grammar, Turning, Mechanical Drawing

Second Year

    Semester I   Geometry, Rhetoric and Composition, Forging, Mechanical
                     Drawing
    Semester II   Geometry, Rhetoric and Composition, Moulding, Mechanical
                     Drawing and Pattern Making

Third Year

    Semester I   Trigonometry, Physics, Machine Shop, Mechanical Drawing
    Semester II   Advanced Algebra, Physics, Machine Shop, Mechanical
                     Drawing

FIGURE 3. Three-year manual training course. *Source:* Board of School Directors of the City of Milwaukee, *Proceedings* (1897–98): 45.

of Wisconsin. Evidently, this course was designed more with the idea of keeping young boys in the high school longer than preparing them for post-secondary education.

Second, the Committee on Manual Training reported that the Wisconsin state legislature had increased the state aid for the maintenance of the School for the Deaf with the specific intent of incorporating manual training into the curriculum of that school. By now the legislature, too, had apparently become convinced that manual training was a beneficial aspect of the curriculum, at least for some segments of the student population. The Board of School Directors undertook, therefore, to begin to fulfill the promises made to the state legislature by finding a manual training instructor for the School for the Deaf, by making the necessary building alterations to accommodate a manual training room, and by purchasing the necessary equipment and materials for carrying on the study in the school.

Third, Superintendent Siefert suggested that the school board seek an opinion from the city attorney as to the legality of establishing and maintaining manual training in the present form, as well as whether it was lawful to continue to teach typing and bookkeeping in the high schools and cooking in the common schools. His specific question was: "Does the charter permit the maintenance of special courses, such as the manual training course or the business course, or such special studies as cooking?" Siefert did not question the value or utility of any of these subjects, but he believed that if they were to be taught in the high schools, they should be a part of the regular course and every pupil should be obliged to take them.[33] The expense of equipping and maintaining manual training establishments in each of the three high schools was greater than Siefert believed could be justified, and because only a limited number of pupils would profit from them, he feared they might also be illegal. The school board referred Siefert's request to the Committee on Manual Training, and two months later, the committee sent it on to the city attorney. At the December meeting of the board, the committee presented the opinion of the city attorney as to the legality of manual training and cooking in the pubic school curriculum. The city attorney pointed out that section 496B of chapter 354 of the Laws of 1897 expressly authorized any Wisconsin high school to establish and maintain a department of manual training. Beyond the legalities of the issue, he added his own endorsement:

> I can see no reason why the cooking school should not be maintained if the Board so determines . . . cooking is something that every one is interested in; and it is not for the purpose of educating trained cooks that these lessons are given, but for the purpose of giving a wider knowledge of the proper method and treatment of culinary subjects and for the benefit of the health of the whole people. . . . I can see no reason why cooking, which every one is interested in, should not be taught as well as Greek, Latin, music or drawing, in which the people at large are by no means so directly interested.[34]

Having been assured that what the school board was doing was legal, some of its more zealous members renewed their efforts to carry manual training into the lower grades.

The Milwaukee Board of School Directors' most ardent advocate of manual training was probably School Director Frederick W. Sivyer, a prominent Milwaukee industrialist who served on the school board from 1894 to 1899. Sivyer had consistently urged the board to create a standing Committee on Manual Training. This accomplished, he soon began to agitate for expanding manual training into the upper elementary grades. As chair of the Manual Training Committee, he made inquiries into and solicited descriptions of elementary manual training programs operating across the country. In April 1898, Sivyer presented a resolution to the board requesting that the Committee on Manual Training report to the school board on the advisability of introducing manual training in the fourth, fifth, and sixth grades by the regular class teachers for one hour per week. The boys would be instructed in sloyd (a Swedish system of woodworking emphasizing carving) and the girls in sewing. The committee would also estimate the cost of such instruction, based on the number of pupils enrolled presently in those grades. Sivyer included with this resolution a statement from the nineteenth Annual Report of the Board of Education of the City of Minneapolis and a letter from Ida H.

Clark of Denver describing the elementary manual training work being car-ried out in these cities.[35]

Milwaukee's movement in behalf of manual training, however, began to run into financial problems. The City of Milwaukee and its public schools had to cut services and retrench in the wake of the depression of 1893. Between 1895 and 1898, the Board of School Directors abolished the entire reserve corps of teachers, dispensed with the services of a primary supervisor, three special calisthenics instructors, and the directors of music and drawing, cut the salaries of the German teachers, and abolished the evening schools alto-gether. In 1898, the Common Council refused to appropriate the amount of funds requested by the school board, and its Committee on Finance searched for additional areas where costs could be reduced without affecting the effi-ciency of instruction. When the committee discovered that there were only 147 pupils taking manual training instruction and that the annual cost for this one study was more than $30 per capita as compared to $15 per capita for all studies put together in the grammar grades, the Finance Committee recom-mended that all pupils taking the manual training course should be concen-trated in the new high school building located on the South Side. The com-mittee reasoned that the children of the large working-class population living in that area would be the most likely to take advantage of this study.[36] The idea that manual training was appropriate particularly for working-class chil-dren, although not often expressed, was probably widely shared by advocates of manual training in Milwaukee. (The popular notion that manual training was a subject worthy of every young boy's study was more often expressed.) The Finance Committee further argued that the South Side manual training facilities were the best of the three locations and that it would present no real hardship for West and East Side pupils to attend the South Side school. The Board of School Directors adopted the resolution to consolidate the manual training schools at the beginning of the next school year.

Almost immediately, fifty-one members of the Milwaukee Manual Train-ing Association signed a statement objecting "in the extreme" to the deci-sion to "abandon" manual training in the East and West Side high schools. They argued that the proposed consolidation would deal "a blow to this fea-ture of schoolwork from which it will take many years to recover, and which may even prove fatal." The association petitioned the school board to rescind its resolution and, if necessary, employ student assistants to help reduce the cost of maintaining the manual training departments in the high schools. The Woman's School Alliance added its protest the following month, also calling for the school board to rescind its resolution. Sivyer, in his resigna-tion submitted in May 1899, added his voice to those who wished the board to reconsider its decision. In July, the Joint Committee on Finance and Man-ual Training discovered that the cost of consolidation might actually exceed the cost of continuing the three manual training schools separately, and they recommended that the board rescind its resolution.[37] Whatever may have been the initial reservations as to cost, they were resolved once the coalition of interest groups made their presence felt.

Although the public schools were in a period of fiscal retrenchment, pressures to introduce a systematic approach to manual training in the grades continued to mount. These pressures came both from inside the public school system and from agencies outside the schools. Internally, the most active proponents were some of the school directors themselves. At the opening of the school year in September 1898, the school board adopted a resolution requesting the school principals to discuss and report their conclusions on two questions: "Is it desirable to introduce sloyd work for boys and sewing for girls as a part of the regular school work?" and "if so, in what grades and to what extent?"[38] In order to assist them in their deliberations, Superintendent Siefert developed a circular of inquiry and sent it to more than one hundred school superintendents in cities of 20,000 or more inhabitants. The superintendents were asked to respond to a series of twenty-six questions on the subject of manual training and its implementation. Siefert received responses from at least forty-seven cities in the country who offered manual training, and these data were turned over to the principals for study in their monthly meetings. In February, Siefert appointed a committee of five principals—two in favor of manual training, two opposed, and one undecided—to formulate resolutions and to report the consensus of the principals at the March meeting. The committee produced four different reports, one signed by two members, and three other reports each signed by one member. Not having any majority opinion to act upon, Siefert decided to take a voice vote at the March principals' meeting on the question, "Is it desirable to introduce sloyd work for boys and sewing for girls as a part of the regular school work?" The results were aye's 17, no's 30. Fiscal conservatism had temporarily won the day.

School Director Frank Ellis was not content to let the matter rest. Even though the wording of the initial resolution had left the principals the option of rejecting manual training in the grades (although the intent of the resolution may have been to discourage that choice), that response was clearly unsatisfactory to Director Ellis. There was always the danger in his view of Milwaukee's somehow falling behind the programs of the "new education" that other cities were providing and thereby losing the "colossal advantage" that manual training provided.[39] Accordingly, Director Ellis requested that Superintendent Siefert and First Assistant Superintendent Arthur Burch report their views on this subject within sixty days, at the same time furnishing estimates as to the per capita cost of introducing and maintaining sewing, cooking, woodworking, and the like in each grade of the Milwaukee public schools. Two months later the superintendents submitted their report to the Board of

School Directors. The report reviewed the work being carried out in other cities—the grades in which manual training was included in the curriculum, the subjects which comprised manual training, the costs—and pointed out that a Wisconsin statewide committee charged with investigating this subject and preparing a feasible plan for the introduction of this branch into the grammar grades had been appointed recently. This was, Siefert believed, a step in the right direction, and if the school board wished to investigate this matter further, then it should appoint a committee consisting of the president of the board, one director, the superintendent, the assistant superintendent, and two principals to visit some city where manual training was well established. (Cleveland was suggested.) The school board referred this report to its Committee on Finance and Manual Training.[40]

While the problem of introducing manual training into the grades was being studied and debated, the Committee on the Course of Study was busy revising the high school manual training course based upon recommendations from the principals of the East and West Side schools. The most important recommendation was to extend the studies of the manual training course to four years. As a three-year course, no pupil could receive a diploma under the rules of the school board, and no pupil could be admitted to the University of Wisconsin upon completion of the program. Cutting off a group of students from entrance to college proved troublesome. Adding a fourth year to the course would alleviate that problem. The committee, therefore, revised the course and submitted it to the Department of Engineering at the University of Wisconsin for approval before it presented the reorganized course to the board. German was now required where no foreign language had heretofore been included in the manual training course. Zoology, chemistry, and botany were added where, in the first course designed by the committee, only physics had been required. Three years of some form of English were now required, and two semesters of history were included as an option. Studies in mathematics, mechanical drawing, and the trades remained the same although their sequences were slightly altered. A student could now pursue further training at the university level without having to make up subject deficiencies. Under the new plan, electing to take the manual training course no longer hindered a pupil from pursuing further formal education after high school. In addition, in the school year 1899–1900, the Committee on the Course of Instruction revised the high school business course and extended it from three to four years in length. Soon after, the University of Wisconsin developed a department of commercial and business training, and the high school business course was repositioned to prepare students to enter the university in this area, too, if they desired to do so.[41]

The Milwaukee Manual Training Association became the most active interest group pushing the implementation of a K–12 system of manual training into the Milwaukee public schools. The association was organized in the last week of November 1886 with the object of seeing that steps be taken at once to provide industrial and manual training in the city.[42] In a sense, it was a local forerunner to the National Society for the Promotion of Industrial Education, and its advocacy in behalf of industrial training was no less ardent. The Manual Training Association included prominent merchants, businessmen, industrialists, brewers, educators, social workers—all civic-minded men and women who viewed manual training as embodying new, progressive educational principles. Until the mid-1890s, the association contented itself with informing its members on aspects of manual training and the various programs being developed in cities across the nation. By 1899, however, the Milwaukee Manual Training Association was ready to take concerted action. In May of that year, the association announced that it had prepared pamphlets on manual training, its nature, purpose, and relation to other branches of study, and its results in other cities, together with a suitable plan for its introduction in the grades of the Milwaukee public schools. These pamphlets were distributed with permission of the school board to every school official, principal, and teacher in the public school system. The announcement was only the first of a veritable barrage of recommendations to the Board of School Directors from the association.[43]

At the June school board meeting, the Joint Committee on Finance and Manual Training presented a memorandum from the Milwaukee Manual Training Association which detailed twenty separate suggestions on how to introduce manual training into the grades, what should be the content at various grade levels, how the teachers should be trained, what costs would be incurred, and the like. In August, the president of the association, A. J. Lindemann (who served on the Board of School Directors from 1894 to 1899 and was president of the board in 1896–97), wrote to praise the school board for its action of June 6, 1899, in favor of the gradual introduction of a "thorough system of correlative manual training into all the grades of the graded schools."[44] He went on to suggest that the board immediately make arrangements for a series of lectures with demonstrations and practical exercises in manual training to be given to all first-grade teachers in the first semester of the school year. These teachers would then be prepared to introduce the methods of manual training in their classrooms at the beginning of the second semester (February 1900).[45] School principals should also attend these training sessions so that they would be competent to supervise the program when it was implemented. During the second semester, the process would be repeated with the second-grade teachers, who would then begin manual training in their classrooms the first semester of 1900–01. At the same time, the manual training instructor would supervise the manual training exercises being conducted by the first-grade teachers. With this teacher training procedure in place, Lindemann predicted that a coherent and continual system of manual training could be operating in all the grades within four years. Conscious of the persistent concern for costs, Lindemann was careful to point out that the association's conception of an appropriate system of manual training did not require elaborate or expensive shops and equipment, nor a corps of special teachers. It did require a number of lines of work that could be taught by the regular class teachers using inexpensive materials, "in intimate correlation and coordination with the studies of the general curriculum, work that will enliven, make more interesting, and be in every way auxiliary to, the regular studies."[46]

As their promotional efforts continued, the Milwaukee Manual Training Association's campaign to establish a K–12 manual training curriculum in the city's public schools began to carry a note of urgency. They offered to "furnish data and all requisite information in their possession, and if desirable assist in securing the services of a pedagogue who is an expert and authority on this special work, for the purpose of training your teachers, and introducing the system."[47] The school board's Committee on Manual Training had no sooner reported favorably on Lindemann's memorandum to the board (and recommended that the Finance Committee find the funds to carry out the association's suggestions) when the committee received a further proposal from the Milwaukee Manual Training Association, presenting in a general way some of the manual features the association considered necessary but with no attempt to demonstrate in any detail their correlation with the rest of the curriculum. It proposed that physical culture exercises, modeling, nature and experimental science work, object lessons, drawing, and music should extend through the entire course and should be given to boys and girls alike. At about the fourth grade, some gender differentiation should begin with part of the manual work, the boys taking modified sloyd work while the girls took sewing in a more definite and systematic manner than had been given in kindergarten and the first three grades. The regular classroom teachers would conduct these exercises at least two hours per week in the fourth, fifth, and sixth grades. In the seventh and eighth grades, special teachers would be required because the boys would take woodworking using more sophisticated tools and the girls would take cooking. Having noted these general features, the association presented to the school board a tentative series of exercises for a K–8 course in sewing and promised that they would shortly produce similar curricula in cooking, tool work, drawing, and modeling.[48]

The November 1899 memorandum from the Milwaukee Manual Training Association not only was quite specific in detailing a curriculum, but its authors, Robert C. Spencer (of the Spencerian penmanship fame) and Albert K. Stebbins also took care to state some familiar pedagogical principles which led them to espouse manual training as a necessary component of the public school curriculum. "The child's experience," they argued, "should form the basis for a large part of the language and number work, and for other branches of study. . . . The closer we can bring the work of the school in touch with human interests and activities, and especially in contact with the home, the better for the child, the home, and society." Through manual training, the child's interest would be awakened and held, and children would learn to produce something useful. This knowledge would, in turn, aid them in developing "self-respect and a sense of power and efficiency." Spencer and Stebbins held that, especially in the lower grades, "arithmetic, language, geography, science and history must be founded upon sense experiences and motor activities."[49]

In February 1900, the Milwaukee Manual Training Association fulfilled its promise and presented outlines of elementary school curriculum content in drawing, modeling in clay and sand, wood carving, and cooking to the Board of School Directors.[50] All of these communications from the association were referred to the Manual Training Committee and, quite often, to the Finance Committee. These committees in turn recommended that as soon as the funds were available, the school board should introduce manual training into the grades, following the suggestions of the Milwaukee Manual Training Association. The Committee on Course of Instruction, however, was still reluctant to launch into manual training on a grand scale. On April 10, 1900, it reported that, "nothing is to be gained by a radical departure in this direction." The committee explained that "most enthusiastic exponents of manual training are not agreed as to methods and plans, and no two cities of the country . . . are pursuing parallel lines in furthering this branch of education." Until a consensus on the nature and purposes of manual training was achieved and financial restrictions on the operations of the schools were removed, the committee cautioned that the board should proceed slowly and carefully.[51] In the meantime, several significant changes took place in the manual training programs already provided.

The Committee on Course of Instruction twice revised the manual training course; first in September 1901, and again in December 1902. The course as finally approved by the Board of School Directors, in 1903, was as shown in Figure 4. Grammar was now a required subject in the first year because "pupils graduating from the manual training course and entering the state university are required to have a better knowledge of English than has sometimes been the case."[52] Two years of German were included as an option because this was an admissions requirement of the engineering course at the University of Wisconsin. English history and American history were now required, where heretofore students elected either history or German. The mathematics and science requirements remained unchanged. In order to graduate from the manual training program and be eligible for university admission, a student would need to take three years of mathematics, three years of English, two years of

First Year

    Semester I   Algebra, American Classics, Joinery, Freehand Drawing, Physical Geography, optional

    Semester II   Algebra, Grammar, Turning, Mechanical Drawing, Physiology, optional

Second Year

    Semester I   Geometry, Rhetoric and Composition, Mechanical Drawing, Pattern Making, German, optional

    Semester II   Geometry, Rhetoric and Composition, Cabinet Making, Mechanical Drawing, German, optional

Third Year

    Semester I   English, History, Physics, Mechanical Drawing, Forging, German, optional

    Semester II   American History, Physics, Mechanical Drawing, Forging and Moulding, German, optional

Fourth Year

    Semester I   Advanced Algebra, Zoology or Chemistry, English Literature, Machine Shop Work

    Semester II   Trigonometry, Botany or Chemistry, American Literature, Machine Shop Work

FIGURE 4. Four-year manual training course. *Source:* Board of School Directors of the City of Milwaukee, *Proceedings* (1902–03): 214.

German, one year of history, two years of science, probably one semester each of physical geography and physiology, three years of drawing (two and one-half of mechanical; one-half of freehand), and four years of various trade studies. If a student did not plan to go to college, the only significant difference in the course of study might be that he or she would not elect German.

    The second change that was made in manual training offerings was that cooking school classes, after several years of lobbying, were extended from twenty weeks to forty weeks. In addition, a new cooking school was established in the Seventh District school building on the East Side, following the same general plan and equipment of the West and South Side cooking schools. In the same resolution that initiated this new cooking school, the Manual Training Committee suggested that the cooking school attendance requirements be revised in order to ensure that "the greatest benefit may result from attendance at the cooking schools."[53]

The third change occurred when the State of Wisconsin passed legislation which encouraged the introduction of manual training into both elementary and secondary schools. In addition, Wisconsin normal schools began to develop and implement programs to qualify teachers for these programs.[54]

Finally, until this time, the principals of a number of schools, with permission of the school board, had organized classes in sewing for girls and in various forms of manual work for boys during one period each week (usually Friday afternoons), provided there was no expense to school system. In April 1903, a principal requested that the Manual Training Committee pay for such materials as were needed to carry out these activities. The committee brought the matter before the entire school board because it involved a departure from the manual training work sanctioned by the board. The board unanimously agreed to grant authority to the Committee on Manual Training, subject to the limitation of the funds provided for manual training purposes, to furnish upon request the needed materials to carry on the work in sewing and elementary manual training. With this decision, the Board of School Directors took its first tentative step toward paying the cost of manual training.[55]

In September 1903, the Committee on Manual Training presented three resolutions to the Board of School Directors which, when acted upon, launched manual training in grades one through six, thereby effecting a K–12 system of manual training in the Milwaukee public schools. The first resolution created the position of supervisor of elementary manual training at an annual salary of $1,200. The second proposed that the Finance Committee set aside $3,800 in the next apportionment of funds for equipment and materials required for manual training work in the first six grades. The third resolution requested that the Committee on Course of Instruction and Text Books modify the curriculum in order to permit the teaching of manual training in the first six grades for a period of one hour per week, the instruction to be given by the regular class teachers in their classrooms. These resolutions were referred respectively to the Committees on Rules, Finance, and Course of Instruction. While these committees were deliberating, the school directors authorized the superintendent to arrange for the introduction of elementary manual training in the schools where the principal and teachers were willing and ready to undertake the task.

On January 5, 1904, the Board of School Directors resolved that, beginning with the new semester on February 1, manual training instruction was to be made a standard part of the curriculum in all the grades. The work in kindergarten, in the seventh and eighth grades, and in the high schools was to be continued as it was; in grades one through six, it would be implemented according to a detailed plan formulated by Superintendent Siefert, which not only specified the nature of the work to be done and the materials required but also the actual outcomes of the instruction (see Figures 5 and 6). The time

FIRST, SECOND, AND THIRD GRADES

Time—One hour per week in periods of one-half hour each

Nature of work	*Materials*	*Models made in class*
Raffia-work	raffia, needles	Mats, hats, bags, baskets, needle cases, belts, napkin rings
Paper folding	common paper	envelopes, color charts, etc.
Weaving	wool, cotton	mats, rugs, simple holders, cushion covers
Clay modeling	clay	model dishes, animals, forms used in arithmetic, oblong, square, etc.

FOURTH GRADE

Time—One hour per week in one-hour periods

Nature of work	*Materials*	*Models made in class*
Raffia	raffia	simple baskets, school bags for books, market and waste baskets
Weaving	splints, wool yarns	baskets, small rugs on looms, table mats
Sewing	cotton cloth gingham	dusters, laundry bags, sewing on buttons

FIFTH AND SIXTH GRADES

Time—One hour per week in one-hour periods

Nature of work	*Materials*	*Models made in class*
Sewing	cotton, gingham lawn, flannel, needles, thread	aprons for cooking, sewing on buttons and making button holes, darning and patching, making shirtwaists and dress skirts, cutting patterns
Designing and making one basket of raffia		

Work for Boys

Mechanical drawing, a basis for the wood work. All models made from working drawings and then cut or whittled out in wood.

Time—One hour per week at the same time the girls sew.

Models made of pine, walnut, maple, poplar, or woods easily and cheaply purchased in Milwaukee.

Models made—penholders, checker boards, paper knives, calendars, picture frames, book racks, etc.

Equipment:	One set of scissors for each building
	One set of knives for each building
	One set of try squares for each building

FIGURE 5. Manual training course for grades one through six. *Source:* Board of School Directors of the City of Milwaukee, *Proceedings* (1903–04): 272–74.

FIGURE 6. Apron making in Vocational School, Green Bay, Wisconsin, 1919. Apron making became an official part of Milwaukee's manual training curriculum in 1904. *Courtesy State Historical Society of Wisconsin.*

set aside for manual training instruction in the first through sixth grades was to be scheduled by the principals of the schools in order to best meet each school's particular needs. At a special meeting called one week later (January 12, 1904), the school board agreed to allocate $2,500 from the manual training fund for the purchase of supplies and equipment to implement the grade work in manual training and, upon the recommendation of Superintendent Siefert, confirmed the appointment of Ida Hood Clark as Supervisor of Elementary Manual Training. Clark assumed her post on January 15, 1904, and quickly began to purchase and distribute supplies, plan the manual training program for each building, give demonstration lessons, and conduct teachers' meetings on the subject.[56]

One additional significant change took place in Milwaukee's manual training program in the spring of 1905. Periodic recommendations were made to the school board to eliminate selective admissions in the cooking and shop centers and open up these advantages to all the children in the seventh and eighth grades. In the academic year 1904–05, at the prodding of the new superintendent, Carroll G. Pearse, the Committee on Manual Training allocated funds to establish seven centers for instruction in cooking and the same number for instruction in woodwork. These centers were located around the city, with a cooking center and a woodworking shop paired at each location. This was done so that boys and girls of the same class could go to the same location for their manual training activities. This new arrangement provided adequate facilities to allow all of the boys and girls of the seventh and eighth grades to participate in cooking and woodworking classes. Thereafter, these studies became a required part of the curriculum.

THE MILWAUKEE EXPERIENCE WITH MANUAL TRAINING

After fourteen years of study, debate, and cautious piecemeal implementation, the public schools of Milwaukee could now boast a K–12 manual training curriculum. The ambiguity as to what manual training really was had not been resolved, but practically speaking, there was no compelling reason to do so. Placating powerful interest groups, justifying costs, and the development of concrete programs of study took precedence over the articulation of elaborate rationales.

Absolutely critical to the success of the implementation efforts was the mobilization of citizens' groups. Since the early 1870s, working-class parents had periodically raised questions as to whether schools were adequately preparing their children to become artisans or mechanics, and middle-class reformers questioned whether the curriculum was interesting or relevant to their children's needs and aspirations. In the Milwaukee setting, these aspirations needed to be translated into politically potent demands. As was the case nationally, citizen groups and industrial leaders were in the forefront of this effort. Once the Cooking Association was established and Milwaukee's merchants and manufacturers organized themselves into the Milwaukee Manual Training Association, they were in a position to exert considerable influence on the city's school managers. Their efforts paralleled on the municipal level the work of the American Association of Home Economics, the National Association of Manufacturers, and the National Association for the Promotion of Industrial Education in enlisting federal support for their programs. While the school board considered and debated what should be done for pupils ages six through fourteen, these interest groups not only began to exercise political pressure but actually to develop programs in these areas. In response to these compelling new demands, Milwaukee's school officials found it necessary to accelerate their efforts to implement a reform that was already capturing the imagination of nationally prominent educational leaders and was being implemented in cities of comparable size and demographics.

Political considerations aside, two urgent practical problems required resolution before implementing a comprehensive program of manual training in Milwaukee's schools. First, there was the mundane but pressing issue of cost. Although questions as to the cost of implementing manual training were occasionally heard at the national level, financing manual training seemed to have a special urgency in Milwaukee. Educational innovations of the scope of manual training brought with them considerable new expenditures, and Milwaukee's public schools did not have much money to spare. Equipment had to be purchased, and teachers and supervisors had to be paid. Space was a particularly formidable obstacle. With pupils entering the schools in ever increasing numbers and staying for longer periods of time, the city was experiencing difficulty in providing an adequate number of school buildings and classrooms. Temporary school housing was more the rule than the exception. Fiscal conservatism more than ideological or educational objections made the school board proceed cautiously in undertaking such a major curricular revision.

Even as the last component of the manual training system in Milwaukee, the required cooking and shop courses at the seventh and eighth grades level, was being put into place, strong complaints were voiced as to whether the public was getting results commensurate with the money being put into manual training. Charges were made that the high school course led nowhere—that it provided neither good preparation for the university nor adequate training for skilled occupations. The high school program, the elementary course in manual work, and the cooking and shop centers for the seventh and eighth grades were "all running at their own sweet wills, with no direction other than that being given by the Committee on Manual Training, and with no power delegated to anyone . . . to control or unify them."[57] Whatever the merits of these accusations, however, the momentum was on the side of innovation.

The second practical problem that needed to be overcome was the actual creation of a curriculum for manual training. Making grand pronouncements about the abstract benefits of manual training was one thing; it was quite another to translate these alleged benefits into an intelligible and workable program of studies. For this task, pedagogical expertise had to be solicited and concrete steps undertaken so as not to undermine existing programs. Kindergarten programs were quickly installed, but planning coherent and potentially effective programs for the elementary grades (first through eighth) presented considerable difficulty. At the high school level, the need for industrial training in the interest of easing the transition to the workplace seemed more plainly evident, but even there, adjustments were needed. Omitting German from the new manual training program, for example, meant that its graduates would not be eligible for admission to the University of Wisconsin's Engineering School. That concern led initially to the inclusion of a foreign language requirement in manual training programs at the secondary school level, and for the time being, that adjustment forestalled a sharp division between academic and manual training programs at least in terms of eligibility for college.

In the end, the practical problems were resolved. The combination of initiatives taken by local citizens' groups and business interests and the pressure simply to be seen as a progressive and enlightened city proved too strong to be denied. With cities all over the country reporting on their successes in implementing manual training, Milwaukee's civic pride was at stake. By 1905, no school manager in Milwaukee could afford to challenge the educational and practical value of manual training or to be dilatory in incorporating it into the curriculum.

The installation of manual training in Milwaukee's public schools, however, did not end there. Political mobilization in its behalf prepared the way for an even more drastic alteration in the way Milwaukee's schools functioned. Successes with respect to cooking and manual training inspired more ambitious changes. Not only did manual training continue to thrive in Milwaukee during the next decade, but an even bolder innovation, the creation of the Milwaukee Trade School, would soon make the city a leader in the next phase in the vocationalization of the American curriculum—direct trade training. In the course of the effort to create a coherent program of manual training, Milwaukee's business interests and citizens generally became convinced that the schools should become more directly attuned to the occupations being created in the workplace. With organization and experience, local interest groups were able to translate vague anxieties and ambitions into effective political action.

4

LET THE "GOOSE" WADDLE AND THE "EAGLE" SOAR

Vocational Training in Milwaukee, 1907–1917

Herbert M. Kliebard and Carol Judy Kean

Our public schools are planned for the average child. Who is the average child? Nobody can tell. Why not? Because he doesn't exist. Just try to strike an average between a goose and an eagle. Can you do it? Of course not. The thing is impossible. And even if you could, what becomes of the goose and the eagle? . . . When a pupil is found to be a goose, he should be carefully guided to waddle and to swim and become proficient in the things nature intended him to do and to avoid an attempt to soar and perch upon the mountain top, lest his lighting be as painful as that of Darius Green. A large proportion of true genius is lost to society because it is born among the children of the poor, where it perishes for want of opportunity, as we have had no plan for conserving the talents of the poor. It is a proper function of the school to discover, develop and guide this genius. If a pupil is found to be an eagle, he should be guided into the sphere nature intended him to occupy, to soar and to perch upon a mountain top, and to avoid the natural sphere of the goose, where he would have a constant struggle to 'keep his head above water.'

President's Annual Address,
Milwaukee Board of School Directors, 1913

Although the early impetus for the introduction of manual training into Milwaukee's schools derived about equally from the effort to rejuvenate the curriculum and from the need to train young people for the workforce, the vocational imperative began to assume much more prominence as the new century progressed. Milwaukee's industrial base was growing dramatically, and with it the need to supply factories with competent workers. As was the case nationally, that need brought with it the potential for a transformation in the way in which Milwaukee's schools functioned. One of the most significant signposts of that transformation was a bifurcation in the system of schooling, a bifurcation that in the colorful language of Milwaukee's school board president would create one curriculum that would train the "goose" to waddle and another that would teach the "eagle" to soar.

Milwaukee's rapid industrial expansion created a popular perception that a sharply increased number of skilled workers, such as carpenters, plumbers, pattern makers, tool makers, machinists, mechanics, was needed. Many skilled trade unions existed within the city at the time, but apprenticeships sponsored by these unions were limited, and the city's leaders believed that the needs of the growing manufacturing base were not being met. To many Milwaukeeans—manufacturers and workers alike—the traditional apprenticeship system was failing to train workers in sufficient numbers for the new industrial system. The reasons for the decline of apprenticeship were reasonably clear. Machines were not only replacing workers; they were changing the nature of workers' training. The skills needed to operate the new machines could be learned at the workplace often in a matter of days, and once a young worker learned how to tend a new machine, there was no reason to move the apprentice to another area of the plant to master different aspects of the trade. Mass production techniques obviated the need for a single worker to be skilled in all aspects of the manufacturing process; it was less costly and more efficient to train workers for one job and to keep them there. Unions were beginning to recognize this problem. As the secretary of the Machinists' Union, John Handley, explained it, "these apprentice courses [under contemporary factory conditions] are of little value as manufacturers cannot or do not change the student from one department to another. He becomes a specialist in one machine, but does not learn the trade."[1] Although the leadership of Milwaukee's trade unions realized that the factory apprenticeship system was failing, they, like national union leaders, were wary of placing such training in the hands of the manufacturers, fearing that they would flood the factories with partially trained workers who would be willing to work at lower wages. From the manufacturers' point of view, however, unions were artificially restricting the labor market. Milwaukee's manufacturing leaders, therefore, decided to press for a trade school which would offer the types of trade training deemed most critical to the city's expanding industrial base.

THE POLITICAL CONFIGURATION IN MILWAUKEE

Although Milwaukee's industrialists enjoyed considerable political power, a strong labor movement existed, as represented by the well-organized Federated Trades Council. The Federated Trades Council, joined by Milwaukee's socialists, formed the basis of the politically powerful Social Democratic Party, which acted as its political wing. Milwaukee socialists around the turn of the century and for years thereafter were led by Victor Berger, a former school teacher, who became the editor of the socialist *Wisconsin Vorwarts* in 1893. Socialism in Milwaukee was very much tied to a German ethnic identity, with much of the city's German population arriving after the failure of the European revolutions of 1848. As late as 1910, three German-language daily newspapers still operated in Milwaukee.

In 1898, a year after Berger and socialist leader Eugene Victor Debs formed the Social Democrats of America, the party won only 5 percent of the vote in Milwaukee, but their platform of reform soon proved popular with the voters, and in 1901, when Berger and Debs allied themselves with other socialists to form the Socialist Party, the party became a strong voice in Milwaukee politics. By 1910, socialists reached the peak of their political power. In that year, their candidate, Emile Seidel, was elected mayor, and socialists captured twenty-one of the thirty-five seats on the city council. In that election as well, Berger was elected to Congress.[2] While remaining committed to traditional socialist platforms such as the redistribution of wealth, Milwaukee socialists were particularly active in promoting social programs, including school reform, a stance that was sometimes referred to as "Sewer Socialism" by radical socialists in the East.[3] The implication, of course, was that Milwaukee Socialists were more concerned with amelioration of living conditions for workers and with civic improvement than with class conflict or revolution. Indeed, one reason for the political successes of Milwaukee's socialists was their ability to incorporate into their platform social welfare reforms enunciated by other groups such as the populists and women's volunteer organizations. The reform of schooling in Milwaukee was a persistent theme. Socialists, the *Social Democratic Herald* declared, "have a big stake in the public schools and are sufficiently awakening in Milwaukee to see from now on that the educational system is not abused and misdirected."[4] This interest in schooling extended to the establishment of a flourishing system of secular Sunday schools designed to convey the principles of socialism to socialist youth.[5]

In terms of school policy, Milwaukee's socialists were particularly active in trying to have the board of education elected by ward rather than at-large. At the time, business leaders were arguing that educational policy was too important to be subject to the vagaries of the polling booth. At one function organized by the Merchants' and Manufacturers' Association, William J.

Turner, a former school board president, declared that "We have many immigrant voters who do not understand the requirements of a school board, and they are not qualified to choose the men who are to direct our schools."[6] Representing the socialist position, Winfield R. Gaylord argued that "We are tired of being represented by members of the Merchants and Manufacturers' Association and similar gentlemen, because: THEY DO NOT REPRESENT US! Let us have some representatives of our own. We have men in the ranks of the working class movement whom we will match for intelligence and for understanding of the educational problems of our time with any of you more favored sons of the privileged classes."[7]

Even under the system of at-large representation, Meta Berger, a committed socialist and wife of Victor Berger, was elected to the school board in 1909 and remained there for thirty years. By 1915, five of the fifteen school board members were socialists. Throughout the first two decades of the twentieth century, socialists remained active in debates of such issues as teacher salaries as well as school governance, and they also achieved some success in their efforts to expand health services and recreational programs and to open evening programs for adults.[8] They took no strong positions, however, in the debates over manual training and vocational education. As a result, although opposition to trade training emerged, it was based mainly on practical and financial rather than political grounds. In due course, vocational education in Milwaukee manifested itself in four distinct ways: a new trade school for boys, a new trade school for girls, a major expansion of existing programs in manual training, and finally, a vocationally oriented continuation school along the German model for adolescents who had left school.

A TRADE SCHOOL FOR BOYS

As early as 1894, the Milwaukee Board of School Directors considered establishing an evening trade department in connection with the public schools. The board's Committee on Manual Training was asked to investigate this matter and make its recommendations to the school board. In the course of its investigation, the committee consulted nationally known leaders in the industrial education field, notably Calvin M. Woodward and Henry M. Belfield, director of the Chicago Manual Training School, but it came to the conclusion that "to add to the public schools the expense of establishing and maintaining an evening trade school would not prove acceptable to the tax payers at the present time."[9] As was often the case in the drive to install manual training, the desire to undertake vocational training was strong, but financial considerations stood in the way. As with the kindergartens, the cooking and sewing centers, and the manual training department, the impetus for the trade school came not from educators but from individuals and groups out-side the public schools, most conspicuously in this case the Milwaukee Mer-chants' and Manufacturers' Association.

Organized in 1861 through the leadership of John Nazro, a hardware jobber and one of Milwaukee's wealthiest citizens, the Merchants' and Man-ufacturers' Association engaged in the broad range of promotional endeavors that characterized such interest groups in the latter half of the nineteenth cen-tury. These organizations acted as promoters of civic pride and lobbyists for particular causes. One accomplishment of the Milwaukee association, for example, was to win advantageous transportation facilities and improved freight rates from the railroads when what they perceived as favoritism toward Chicago was also brought to the attention of the Interstate Commerce Com-mission. In 1896, the Merchants' and Manufacturers' Association was instru-mental in bringing the Baptist Young People's Convention to Milwaukee, and in the following year, the NEA followed suit. In 1897, the association began to organize excursions of county merchants to the city. By 1902, approx-imately 70,000 circulars describing these excursions had been distributed throughout the Northwest. Milwaukee merchants also conducted semiannual visits throughout the city's commercial hinterlands. These rail trips ranged as far east as Indiana, as far south as Iowa and Missouri, and as far west as South Dakota. Stops were made at all the sizable towns along the way. At each town, speakers extolled Milwaukee's trade advantages, and the Merchants' and Manufacturers' Octet literally sang the city's praises. These excursions were credited with producing an increase of almost 100 percent in the wholesale business of the city between 1900 and 1910. In addition, the association devoted time and effort to inducing manufacturers to locate in Milwaukee. In this venture, too, the association's efforts proved successful.

In 1903, Frederick W. Sivyer, a prominent Milwaukee industrialist and former school director (1894–99), who had been the school board's strongest enthusiast for manual training, called the attention of his associates in the Merchants' and Manufacturers' Association to the potential value of trade schools to manufacturing communities; at his urging, the association appointed a committee to consider the establishment of a trade school in Milwaukee. Sivyer himself chaired the committee, and, during the years 1904 and 1905, he called several meetings, corresponded with the directors of man-ual training, trade, and technical schools all over the country, and perhaps most important, solicited subscriptions from the businessmen of the city to support the school. When the association decided to establish its own trade school for boys, the administration of the school was placed in the hands of a separate body consisting of its leading members. Of the nineteen original members of the Merchants' and Manufacturers' Association who had charge of the trade school, at least eight were directly connected with the public schools, six as school directors, one as superintendent of schools, and one as a high school principal. The association provided the initial funding with its own resources and through the private subscription of many of its members, thus sidestepping what was a perennial obstacle in instituting school reform in Milwaukee.

Sivyer's trade school initiative was apparently well received by Milwaukee's business community. In 1906, he became president of the Merchants' and Manufacturers' Association, and in that same year, the Milwaukee School of Trades opened with an enrollment of fifty boys. In less than a month, enrollment increased to 117. With the issue of financial support for the school temporarily resolved, Sivyer turned to the very real problem of what should be taught in the new school. To address that problem, Professor Charles F. Perry, a mechanical engineer on the faculty of the University of Illinois, was hired as the Milwaukee Trade School's first director.[10]

Perry believed that the most prominent trades of the city should determine the curriculum to be offered. Milwaukee's principal manufacturing output in 1905 was in iron and steel and products made from them. It was on the metal trades, then, that Perry built the school's first curriculum. As Perry explained in an article for the Milwaukee Merchants' and Manufacturers' Association *Bulletin*, the manufacture of a high-grade steam engine or machine tool was both a professional undertaking and the product of skills entailed in three separate and costly trades. The professional aspects came in the designing and drafting of the product. The next three steps involved the most important trades from the viewpoint of manufacturing—the pattern making, molding, and machinist trades. Since these three trades formed a necessary and logical sequence of manufacture, it was obvious to Perry that they should constitute the core of the Milwaukee Trade School curriculum.

Perry went on to describe the courses of instruction being carried out in the trade school and the equipment found in the school's different shops or departments. The pattern shop had a capacity for twenty-five students at one time (twenty-five day and twenty-five evening students). It was equipped with the necessary tools for "first class pattern making." Practical work was begun at once, the first problem being to introduce the apprentice to the proper use and care of tools. Each student then had to master the molding process through which his pattern passed. For the first month, students made actual molds of all the patterns until they knew the necessity of draft, shrinkage, and the proper arrangement of core prints. Describing the course as arranged as "rigid and full of interest to the student," Perry noted that at least half of the craft of a pattern maker lay in his ability to correctly interpret the working drawing and plan the work. In this way, the trade school and this department provided thorough training in making and interpreting mechanical drawings. Workshop mathematics was taught as instrumental to learning the trade. It consisted of practical problems in arithmetic, algebra, geometry, and trigonometry and was taught to students when a mathematical solution was needed for the successful completion of the task at hand. Students also engaged in a series of "shop inspection trips." The students in pattern making, for example, were taken to the pattern storage departments and pattern shops of some of the city's largest plants. The patterns made in these plants were studied and discussed, and the processes of actual practice noted in the shops. Trips were also taken to foundries in order to study the application of the pattern maker's trade. Students were also encouraged to subscribe to a pattern-making journal to keep apprised of developing technology.

Instruction in molding and foundry practice was very similar to that of the pattern-making shop. Equipment was furnished for a day class of twenty-five apprentices, and lectures were given on all essential points in foundry practice. Visits to other foundries were arranged in order to compare methods. The machinist and toolmaking shop (also designed for twenty-five students each in the day and evening classes) was equipped with the large machinery necessary as well as the needed small tools and accessory supplies, and pupils were taught the use and care of each tool. This took a great deal more time than in pattern making. One of the aims in planning instruction in this area was to present problems which involved as many processes as possible so that when the task was completed, the quality of the work became self-evident to the student. Problems assigned in the machine tool class were designed to make the apprentice able to apply basic principles to future work. A course in tool making and tempering was included. Lectures were given on modern machine shop practices and, as with the other areas, shop inspection trips were liberally provided.

The Milwaukee School of Trades also incorporated a plumbing shop equipped for fifty-two students each in the day and evening classes. Plumbing varied from the other training in that the work was done wholly by hand and consisted of the mastery of a smaller number of essential principles. It was divided into two sections. First, pupils studied the specific conditions and environment of the location in which the plumbing was to be installed and determined the most efficient approach to installation. Second, the pupils learned how to install the plumbing apparatus. Lectures on plumbing practice were also part of the curriculum.

To be admitted to Boys' Trade, a boy had to be in good health and of "good moral character," at least sixteen years of age, and have a "natural aptitude for the trade he wishes to pursue." Preference was given to those boys who had completed the eighth grade in the Milwaukee city schools. A candidate who had not completed the eighth grade but who showed promise of ability to carry on the work in the trade school could be admitted on probation. Each student who completed the prescribed course in a satisfactory manner and passed the final examinations received a diploma.[11] The school year for day students was a full twelve months, from July 1 to June 30, eight hours per day. Evening instruction was conducted for seven months, from October 1 to April 30, four nights each week. Mechanical drawing and workshop mathematics were taught to the evening pupils as well as the day pupils. Tuition in the day class in pattern making, molding, and machinist and tool making was $90. Plumbing class tuition, covering only a five-month period, was $50. Night classes in pattern making, machinist, and tool making were $40 each and plumbing was $35. A careful record of the students' attendance and work habits was kept, particularly for day students. As Perry explained, "He is taught not only to be careful and accurate, but also to be a neat workman. The best possible influences which make for a thorough mechanic and for a worthy citizen surround him."[12]

In short order, Perry had constructed a workable curriculum, developed a school calendar, and set the terms of admission. Relatively absent from Perry's conception of Milwaukee's new trade school was the kind of pedagogical rhetoric that was so integral to the national movement for manual training and the arguments for its inclusion in the public school curriculum of Milwaukee a few years earlier. To be sure, the curriculum was integrated in one sense; the subjects of study were clearly related to the vocational skills being taught; but there was no longer a sense that industrial education would somehow "complete" a liberal education as had been argued by national leaders of the manual training movement such as Woodward. It was vocational skill training, pure and simple. Milwaukee's industries required an infusion of trained workers, and the new trade school, now under the auspices of the public school system, would provide it.

By 1907, Sivyer and the other members of the executive committee charged with overseeing the trade school decided that its usefulness would be widened considerably if its existence could be placed upon a more secure and permanent footing than private subscription. Accordingly, Sivyer, Albert J. Lindemann, and others drafted a legislative bill that would enable the trade school to become a part of the Milwaukee public school system. Prior to this time, the only visible source of opposition to the trade school idea had come from Milwaukee's labor unions in the form of a strongly worded editorial published in 1904 in the *Social Democratic Herald,* the official organ of both the Federated Trades Council and the Social Democratic Party. Describing the trade school as "the latest trump which the bread-masters hope to play in their game with the workers," the editorial declared that "it should be called a 'school to Graduate Strike Breakers.'"[13] At a time when the drive for open shops was developing in their city, Milwaukee's labor unions initially equated the trade school idea with anti-unionism. The Federated Trades Council, comprising skilled craft unions in the city, was an influential affiliate of the

American Federation of Labor. On the one hand, its leadership was well aware of the arguments being used by National Association of Manufacturers to persuade local manufacturing groups to sponsor trade schools. On the other hand, the council seemed genuinely concerned that young apprentices be given an adequate amount of time to learn a trade. This tension placed the trade unions' leadership in an uncomfortable situation. With the exception of the one condemnatory editorial, however, the trade school issue was not raised again in the *Social Democratic Herald* or, so far as can be ascertained, in the meetings of the Federated Trades Council. Sivyer and his colleagues eventually received the support of the council for the 1907 trade school bill.

Certain legal obstacles had to be overcome, but by 1907, the Wisconsin Legislature enacted Chapter 122, Laws of Wisconsin, which permitted public school boards to establish or take over and maintain trade schools, equip the school with the proper machinery and tools, employ competent instructors, and provide instruction in one or more of the common trades. With the passage of this law, the Milwaukee public schools assumed control of the trade school that had been established only two years before.[14] Once the trade school became part of the public school system, Milwaukee labor's suspicions that the school would be used to produce strikebreakers were mollified, and the *Social Democratic Herald* cautiously endorsed this addition to the public school system:

> The trade school under the public control is now in working shape and will probably prove an advantage to the cause of labor now that some objectionable features have been abolished. The school in the hands of, and under the control of, local manufacturers did not appeal to the labor organizations. The argument was advanced that the school might make use of its members to break strikes and otherwise assist interested concern in defeating labor.[15]

The trade school operating under public control had apparently allayed these fears.

Another union objection was also addressed. The trade school under the old ruling allowed students to graduate after only six months of instruction. Fearing a flooding of the job market, unions argued that this was not enough time to "perfect oneself in any trade." Ultimately, the courses were lengthened to two-year periods, and graduates were not considered journeymen, but merely as having served their apprenticeships and therefore entitled to a fair wage while perfecting their skills in the workplace.[16] From this time forward, as was the case with labor at the national level, Wisconsin's organized labor, both in Milwaukee and at the state level, supported the development and expansion of vocational education programs, but the support was somewhat equivocal.

An important provision of Chapter 122 was that a school board could choose to appoint a five-member committee of citizens with trade experience to oversee the work of the trade school.[17] At the September 24, 1907, meeting of the Statutory Committee on Trade Schools, Sivyer was elected chair, and Perry reported on the revised rules governing the Boys' Trade School. Again, boys had to be sixteen years of age and able to read, write, and do simple arithmetic; eighth-grade graduates were admitted without examination. The school was free to Milwaukee residents over age sixteen and under twenty. Residents over twenty years of age and nonresidents were charged $10 per month if day students, and $3 per month if evening students. Day students had to pay tuition for six months in advance, evening students for the entire term in advance, and a materials fee was charged to tuition-free students. The required term for the course in plumbing and gas fitting was six months; for pattern making and for machinists, it was two years. Mechanical drawing and "work shop mathematics" were taught to all students. The school made no claim to turn out journeymen mechanics. Its primary aim was "to thoroughly instruct each student in as short a time as possible, in all the fundamental principles of the trade in question, so that he may upon graduation possess ability and confidence and be of immediate practical value to his employer and receive a fair remuneration at once."[18] This aim addressed the concerns of both organized labor and Milwaukee's manufacturers. In effect, boys would serve partial apprenticeships through the trade school, thus acquiring a rudimentary knowledge of a trade. When they presented themselves at the factory gate for employment, they would therefore not be totally without training or skills. On the other hand, these young workers could not claim to be skilled in their trade. Some period of on-the-job training would still be necessary. The unions would thus retain some control over the requirements that needed to be met in order to achieve the status of journeyman.

Expansion of the Boys' Trade School curriculum began within a year of the school's opening. On February 4, 1908, the Statutory Committee on Trade Schools convened a special meeting at the request of the group of Milwaukee businessmen representing the woodworking and building trades. Approximately twenty-five businessmen appeared before the committee to argue their case for offering courses in carpentry, joinery, and interior woodwork. As a result, the trade school committee recommended the immediate installation and equipping of a complete woodworking department and the appointment of a suitable instructor.[19]

One of the most important changes was a program proposed by Superintendent Pearse and Professor Perry. In July 1909, they completed work on a two-year preparatory course to be added to the high school course of study. Boys of approximately fourteen years of age who planned to enter the trade school at age sixteen now had their own curriculum. Although academic studies such as English, mathematics, algebra and geometry, and general science were represented in this preparatory course, the adjectives attached to these studies—"constructive," "applied," "business," and "elementary"—implied that the content of these subjects would be different from those offered in the regular high school curriculum, reflecting the skill training orientation that Perry had instituted when the program was privately supported. As a result, curriculum differentiation now began in the ninth grade. With new vocational programs in place, students were needed to enroll in them, and it is likely that the preparatory program was a response to a fiscal imperative.

In August 1909, the Board of School Directors adopted a resolution establishing this special course and, at the same meeting, created the position of Supervisor of Industrial Education. As expected, Pearse recommended that Perry be appointed to that position. The school board created the position in order that various forms of industrial education—manual training, cooking, boys' trade programs, studies preparatory to boys' trade—be "so arranged that the parts may fit together into a systematic whole."[20] At the same time that coordination was being effected in the system as a whole, the curriculum of the Boys' Trade School continued to expand. The plumbing course was extended from six months to one year in 1908. In 1910, a course in architectural drawing was added, and in 1913, courses in mechanical and architectural draftsmanship were established. Requests were made by the Milwaukee Electric League and the Master Sheet Metal Contracting Association to establish courses in these areas, and indeed, they were added as resources became available. Once the first trade program was introduced, the way was eased, not only to expand that program, but to introduce other programs of similar character. Whereas the original manual training programs once represented an adjunct to general educational offerings, the new programs in trade training were beginning to assume much larger dimensions. An entirely distinct and separate system of high school education was beginning to emerge. Under the new system, traditional academic studies would be the fare for those who were destined to soar, while vocational training would be provided for those whose lot it was to waddle. For the waddlers, academic studies became an adjunct to vocational training and were modified to reflect the vocational orientation of the students.

The process by which such a division was created took time. In fact, the initial impulse of school officials was to avoid a clear dichotomy between academic and vocational education. In 1917, the name of the trade school was changed to Boys' Trade and Technical High School, a junior high technical department was created, and academic courses such as English, German, French, Spanish, civics, and history were added to the curriculum. In effect, the technical high school became a junior-senior high school division located within the trade school. This change was made without controversy upon the recommendation of Superintendent Potter. He had discovered that on the average, fifty eighth-grade graduates each year entered the trade school preparatory department, while 2,534 boys entered the high schools of the city. Potter believed that in a "great industrial center" such as Milwaukee, this disparity was too great. He suggested that either all efforts cease to secure eighth-grade graduates into the preparatory department or that its curriculum be restructured so that more boys would be attracted to it. The four-year technical course beyond the eighth grade would be directly related to shop experiences. One-half of the students' time every day would be devoted to actual shop work; the remaining half would be given to academic studies, their content being directly drawn from the shop experiences. This course of study reportedly would have greater flexibility of program and promotion than similar courses now being offered in the other high schools. It would presumably foster a genuine respect for shop and commercial processes because the students would enjoy a "shop atmosphere" rather than the atmosphere of the ordinary high school. This arrangement, Potter asserted, would result in "maximum efficiency for the pupil and maximum economy for the city."[21]

Potter's arguments for developing a technical high school course were presented largely in terms of cost-effectiveness. As a way of keeping per-pupil costs down, more students needed to be encouraged to take advantage of the trade school's offerings. Potter also appealed to civic pride:

> Milwaukee is in the twenty-first century in industrial education if those discussions at the convention of the National Society for the Promotion of Industrial Education are of the twentieth. . . . Wisconsin is showing the way to the country in this work. While the matters discussed were indications that most of the country is behind Wisconsin, they also indicated that there is a trend toward us. Real vocational training is being given in Milwaukee's training and continuation school. This city has gone further in elaboration and actualization of means for properly fitting children for industry.[22]

Potter's appeal was essentially threefold. Crafted first of all in terms of costs, it also invoked the desire of Milwaukeeans to be in the forefront of school reform. Finally, it held out the promise of supplying Milwaukee's industries with skilled workers.

The standard offerings for day students in the Boys' Trade and Technical High School were mechanical drafting, architectural drafting, pattern making, plumbing, woodworking, and courses for machinists and electricians. All preparatory department students were required to take mechanical drawing and the standard academic branches as modified. Those boys studying to become pattern makers, machinists, or electricians were required to take mechanical drawing and math, with science as an option. Would-be plumbers and woodworkers were to take architectural drawing and math. In the advanced plumbing section, lectures in physics were required. All high school students were required to attend classes in English. Students could elect to earn either a trade diploma or a high school diploma through the Boys' Trade and Technical High School. Telegraphy, radio, and army electrical work were added to both the day and evening curricula in 1917 in order to support the nation's war effort.[23] At the outset, boys' trade programs did not lack rigorous academic components, and efforts were being made to keep the curriculum of the Boys' Trade and Technical High School open enough so that students could avail themselves of higher education should their circumstances permit. Although these efforts appeared to be initially successful, the separation between academic and vocational education widened as vocational education became more entrenched in Milwaukee's schools.

A TRADE SCHOOL FOR GIRLS

While the creation of Milwaukee's trade school for boys was the culmination of the efforts of the Merchants' and Manufacturers' Association under the energetic leadership of Fred Sivyer, the impetus for the girls' trade school arose largely from charitable impulses and support by women activists and female school administrators in the city. In January 1909, Lizzie Black Kander, a school board director, philanthropist, and social worker who had earned a national reputation as the author of the *Settlement Cook Book,* proposed to the board that a trade school for girls be established as a part of the Milwaukee public schools. Her resolution was referred to the Joint Committee on Trade Schools and Course of Instruction and Textbooks. Within a month, twelve women principals sent a letter to the board offering their reasons for supporting a girls' trade school:

> Knowing that the desire to become a happy homemaker is innate in every woman, is [sic] seems only right and just to give her the opportunity to be trained to become what she was intended for. If fate has decreed that she be useful in some other field, she should be given the chance to develop into a happy independent woman instead of becoming a helpless, dependent one.
>
> To your honorable body is entrusted the responsibility of giving boys and girls the opportunity to gain the training necessary to become happy and useful men and women.
>
> In the working out of life's problems the woman is as essential a factor as the man and it seems a fair demand that she be given a chance to receive industrial training—not of the same kind—but upon a parallel basis with the boy.
>
> Realizing the enormous evil that results from the fact that so many girls are forced to work in the factory or thrust into a life of degradation, not hav-

ing been given the opportunity to become skilled in any line of work, and knowing the unhappiness that is brought about in the home where the wife and mother is ignorant of the duties devolving upon her, we respectfully request that you give the question of establishing a trade school for girls your serious consideration.[24]

The principals' letter reflects the humane impulses that led reformers to endorse a trade school for girls, and at the same time is illustrative of the ambiguity as to the status of women in the new industrial age. The principals assumed a woman's "innate" desire to become a "happy homemaker" but recognized that the new industrial economy required that women as well as men be offered the chance to achieve economic independence. Although the twelve school principals were careful not to suggest that girls be trained for the same jobs as boys, they argued that girls be offered the educational opportunities "upon a parallel basis." It seems clear that by the second decade of the twentieth century, vocational education was being perceived as a successful school reform and that its benefits should accrue to girls as well as boys, but the form it should take remained somewhat ambiguous.

The letter was referred to the Joint Committee on Trade Schools and Course of Instruction and Textbooks at the March meeting of the Board of School Directors, and within three months, the joint committee passed a resolution recommending the establishment of a trade school for girls. At its next meeting, the school board authorized Perry to visit as many girls' trade schools as he deemed necessary in order to make recommendations for a course of study.[25] Perry's trip was apparently very successful. Not only did he determine the initial studies which would be included in the curriculum of the Girls' Trade School—cooking, sewing, applied art and design—and hired a principal, but he was also able to recruit the school's first faculty members.

The school opened in the old normal school building on December 8, 1909. As Laura Tiefenthaler, one of the original faculty members of the Girls' Trade School, described it in retrospect,

> Four old rooms in the Normal School Building had been refreshed with clean paint . . . with Miss Donovan as principal, Miss Goold . . . as teacher of foods, Miss Copp . . . as art teacher, Miss Boice . . . as teacher of elementary sewing, and Miss Celestine Schmit from Milwaukee, a practical milliner, to teach her subject. Thirty-four girls enrolled,—but this number grew, so that . . . three months later, Miss Markwiese, a practical dressmaker, was appointed, and two weeks later I was asked to come to this school. . . . Two days after I came, Mrs. Mary Scott came to us as a teacher of spelling, arithmetic, English and physical training. There were eighty-nine girls enrolled then . . . by September our enrollment had grown considerably.[26]

Here, as was the case in the Boys' Trade School, when qualified teachers could not be found to teach a specific trade, someone experienced in the trade was hired and the instructional aspects of the subject were developed as the course proceeded. Tiefenthaler was responsible for the course of study in millinery and sewing.

The curriculum for the Girls' Trade School was designed to cover a two-year period, seven hours a day, five days per week, fifty weeks a year. All pupils followed a prescribed course of study: applied arts and designs, eight hours per week; cooking, three hours per week; academic work, two hours per week; gymnasium, one hour per week. The remaining hours (twenty-one) were devoted to the actual trade (sewing, dressmaking, hat making) the student was studying. Each pupil was charged five cents per day for the noon meal if she desired to take it, and the proceeds were used to purchase the supplies needed by the cooking classes to prepare the meals. Evening classes were offered from the outset, and nonresidents were charged a fee, as were girls over twenty years of age. A small materials fee was charged to all pupils.[27]

Enrollments in the Girls' Trade School grew rapidly, and by 1912, when it graduated its first students, approximately 300 pupils were enrolled in the day school and an almost equal number in the evening schools. As in the case of the Boys' Trade School, the curriculum was expanding. It was now arranged in terms of six divisions: sewing, dressmaking, millinery, cooking, applied art and design, and academic work.[28] The program mainly reflected the domestic arts usually associated with women's work in the home but showed some concern as well for their earning power. Girls were allowed, for example, to make hats and dresses for others who purchased the needed materials and to charge for their labor.[29] The curriculum exhibited an improvised quality. As Tiefenthaler described it: "We had no pattern for our school. We met the situations as they presented themselves. The number of branches being taught increased. All the teachers put their shoulders to the wheel, and with the principal leading us, we moved forward. It was a big task!"[30] In the summer of 1912, drafting was added to the curriculum of the Girls' Trade School, and by October 1, 124 girls enrolled in that program.[31] Between 1912 and 1917, the course of study remained unchanged while enrollments continued to climb steadily.

High enrollments were achieved quickly, increasing from 50 to 100 percent each year. By contrast, enrollments at the Boys' Trade School remained consistent but low between 1906 and 1917, the top figure being about 150–200 pupils at any one time. Some of the differences may have been the result of the way the two schools were administered and organized. A boy had to be sixteen to enter Boys' Trade, whereas a girl had to be only fourteen to enter Girls' Trade. Most eighth-grade graduates were approximately fourteen years of age. A girl could go directly into her trade school without a break, whereas the boy had to postpone his entrance for two years. Even though the schools developed several options to keep the boys occupied during those two years, including continuing in the "regular" high school or entering one of two prevocational two-year programs, quite often by the time he reached age sixteen, the boys' interests or commitments were elsewhere. Boys' Trade was somewhat more selective in its admissions policies, it cost more, and attendance regulations were more rigid than at Girls' Trade. Boys were expected to complete the course once started. If they did not, they forfeited tuition and fees, received no credentials, and most likely would be unable to reenter the program. Girls were allowed to leave their trade school whenever they needed to earn money, but they could then return to finish their studies. The substantial difference in enrollments for boys in their respective trade schools was probably also a reflection of the changing job market and that girls were availing themselves of secondary education in far greater numbers than boys.[32]

Milwaukee's Girls Trade School enjoyed the support of some of the city's leading activist women, who perceived that the home was no longer preparing young women to assume their traditional roles. The public schools were now offering occupational training for boys, and it seemed only right and proper that girls should also be given vocational training as well, although in the case of the girls, vocational preparation was intertwined with preparation for their prospective adult roles of wife and mother. Reflecting as they did the traditional feminine occupations, vocational programs such as dressmaking, millinery, and cooking may not have had the direct connection to the job market in Milwaukee as did the programs for boys, but they did provide a limited basis for entry into the job market for young women.

EXPANSION OF MILWAUKEE'S
MANUAL TRAINING PROGRAMS

Much time and energy were devoted to the establishment of both the Milwaukee trade schools, but the existing manual training component of the curriculum of Milwaukee's other schools was not neglected. In September 1910, Superintendent Potter and Professor Perry revised both the elementary and high school manual training courses. Manual training at the high school was now organized as shown in Figure 7. The academic side of the curriculum was losing ground. English now replaced American classics and grammar. Mechanical drawing replaced freehand drawing in the first semester, and physical geography and physiology were dropped as optional courses during the first year. In the second year, English replaced two semesters of rhetoric and composition, and German was dropped as an optional study. In year three, English history, American history, physics, and mechanical drawing were all

	FIRST SEMESTER	SECOND SEMESTER
I	English Algebra I Joinery 1/2 Mechanical Drawing 1/2	English Algebra II Turning 1/2 Mechanical Drawing 1/2
II	English Geometry I Pattern Making 1/2 Mechanical Drawing 1/2	English Geometry II Cabinet Making 1/2 Drawing 1/2
III	English or a Foreign Language Forging (double period)	English or a Foreign Language Machine Shop Practice (double period)
IV	English or a Foreign Language	English or a Foreign Language

FIGURE 7. Manual training course for high school. *Source:* Board of School Directors of the City of Milwaukee, *Proceedings*, 1910–11, 52.

dropped as required subjects. Prior to this revision, advanced algebra, zoology, chemistry, botany, trigonometry, English literature, American literature, and machine shop work had all been required in the fourth year, but these were now replaced with English or foreign language study.[33] This revised course of study allowed a student greater flexibility in determining what his individual manual training course would entail, but it did not systematically introduce students to the study of history, any of the sciences, or higher mathematics in the way the academic programs did. These subjects were, rather, options from which the individual student could choose. With the new revisions, the manual training program began to be more sharply distinguishable from the academic program.

To be graduated from a Milwaukee high school, pupils had to complete thirty credits, thirty-two credits if they took the elective course rather than one of the standard courses. The manual training course was twenty credits, leaving ten other credits to be selected by the pupil with the advice and consent of the principal. Pupils could select subjects from other courses of study or from those marked "elective studies" such as French, German, freehand drawing, advanced algebra, advanced geometry, astronomy, geology, trigonometry, and mechanical drawing.[34] Students were advised to select one of the regular courses and "persevere" in that one until graduation. With the exception again of the elective course, the manual training course allowed the most flexibility, having the fewest required credits. This meant that according to the desires of the individual students, the manual training course could be more or less academic, more or less trade oriented.[35]

Whether the Boys' Trade School or the manual training course of study in the high schools attracted more students at this time is difficult to establish. Since comparative enrollment data are no longer available, the actual extent to which the trade schools were affecting enrollments in other Milwaukee schools cannot be precisely established. The school board's *Proceedings*, however, did report lists of high school graduates by course of study during this period. In 1910, twenty-two boys graduated in manual training from the four high schools. Boys' Trade reported no graduates until 1911 when three boys received their diplomas. These data, however, give no indication as to the numbers of boys who may have dropped out before completing either program. It is also doubtful that the manual training course and Boys' Trade were in direct competition for the same students. Boys who were uncertain about their future careers but who could afford to remain in school for an additional four years beyond the eighth grade probably opted for the manual training course, which left open the possibility of enrolling in the engineering department of the University of Wisconsin. The changes made in the manual training course were made with this in mind. By contrast, boys who had little desire or hope either of higher education or even of completing high school probably selected the trade school as a way of preparing themselves directly for the workplace.

Both the manual training and cooking centers continued to flourish throughout the city. In August 1909, the Committee on Course of Instruction and Textbooks recommended that Milwaukee residents of legal school age attending private or parochial schools be provided instruction in cooking and manual training. Toward that end, instructors and classroom space would be provided free of charge by the public schools. By October 1909, ten special classes in cooking serving 224 girls in four different locations and six classes in manual training instruction enrolling 121 boys in four different locations were operating.[36] In March 1913, the twelve manual training and cooking centers were serving 2,939 public school pupils in cooking and 337 private and parochial students;[37] in the manual training program, 3,288 public school pupils and 274 private and parochial students were enrolled.

In the summer of 1914, the Committee on Course of Instruction and Textbooks made a series of recommendations to the school board designed to extend manual training shop facilities to all grammar school buildings in the city. Superintendent Potter recommended this change because, even though confining the shop centers to the larger school buildings had proven to be economical in terms of equipment and had kept the number of instructors low, too much of the children's time was wasted in the long trips to and from the centers. Henceforth, grammar schools were to be equipped with benches, tools, and a teacher as soon as possible. In addition, grade school teachers would teach sewing to the girls while the boys were in shop.[38] Gender segregation in Milwaukee's elementary schools was now beginning to sharpen as a byproduct of these arrangements to expand manual training in the lower grades.

VOCATIONAL TRAINING
IN CONTINUATION SCHOOLS

Enthusiasm for vocational education also extended to those who were no longer enrolled in school. To accommodate this group, one additional institution, the Milwaukee Vocational School (now the Milwaukee Area Technical College) was initiated during this period, especially for those fourteen to sixteen years of age. This was precisely the same group that the Douglas Commission had focussed attention on in Massachusetts in 1906. With respect to continuation schools, Milwaukee was not so much aligning itself with an established reform as it was actually leading the way. Again, the work of several prominent Milwaukeeans was vital, but the initiative for the 1911 legislation came from Madison in the person of Dr. Charles McCarthy, director of the Wisconsin Legislative Reference Library.[39] McCarthy, representing neither industry nor labor nor even professional educators, undertook a vigorous crusade to provide trade training for an overlooked segment of Wisconsin's youth. Motivated by what appears to be the simple conviction that trade training should be extended to youth who had left school, his almost single-minded campaign reflects the extent to which vocational training appealed to broad segments of Wisconsin's citizens.

Almost as soon as trade training became firmly entrenched in Milwaukee schools, it began to transcend its traditional boundaries and to reach beyond the typical school population. Continuation schools, of course, had been favored for years by the National Association of Manufacturers as a way of providing additional skill training for youth no longer in school. Now it was being promoted as a way of benefiting the working class. In April 1909, McCarthy drafted a planning resolution which was introduced into the state senate by Senator Edward Fairchild of Milwaukee. The resolution called for the organization of a committee to study the question of providing part-time schools for the working youth of the state.[40] This resolution was passed expeditiously in both houses. As special investigator, McCarthy visited at his own expense such cities in the East as New York, Lowell, Boston, and Pittsburgh where industrial education had been offered for some time, as well as major cities in Germany, Belgium, Great Britain, and Ireland.[41] The trip brought him into direct contact with the most advanced practices of industrial education in Europe,[42] and on the basis of his observations there, McCarthy refined his vision of an educational system that would increase educational opportunities for the working people of Wisconsin. The study commission's report, submitted to Governor Francis McGovern on January 10, 1911, dealt with industrial education and agricultural training and became the basis for the ardent promotion of continuation education at the state and even national levels.

McCarthy's report was premised on the three fundamental principles on which he believed effective part-time schooling for working people was to be constructed. First, parents and employers must be *required* to allow young workers to attend school in the daytime. Second, the state must provide adequate funding for these schools. Third, separate state and local administrative boards, comprising representative employers and employees, must be formed to organize and develop a part-time continuation school system. Attendance in the continuation schools would be compulsory for those of school age, a separate tax would be levied to support these schools, and local advisory boards would be established.

The question of charging tuition was discussed at some length in the commission report. McCarthy argued that a small tuition might be required of evening school students to induce them to complete the program, but that no tuition should be charged to continuation school students. When he considered the question of selling products made in the school, as was done by the Milwaukee School of Trades for a time, McCarthy was skeptical about such a policy, fearing that educational and social considerations might give way to economic ones. Experimental work was to be encouraged even though it could prove costly. By experimental work, McCarthy meant anything that could be done to encourage the originality, ingenuity, and creative invention of American workers. Instruction was to be carried on by the "task system." According to McCarthy, the task system offered incentives to the student because it made provisions for speed, energy, and ambition. The trade to be learned was broken down into a series of tasks, and each student could proceed at his own pace until the lessons were mastered, thus replacing what McCarthy called "time serving," where a period of time rather than mastery was specified in order to complete the course. In the context of a national mood favoring educational reform, this new system was seen as a way to take individual differences into account.

Considerable emphasis was placed throughout the report on the need for special training for a new type of teacher. The problem was that the ordinary school teacher did not know much about industry, and the skilled worker presumably did not know how to teach. McCarthy was not enthusiastic about the Fitchburg, Massachusetts, cooperative plan, which required students to spend one week in school and the next week in the factory, because the students were still being instructed by the traditional high school methods. He viewed most manual training programs as ineffective for the same reason.[43] Teachers, he thought, should be skilled workers who had taken a short course for teachers rather than enduring a long course of professional training. McCarthy believed along with Charles Prosser that if the industrial education movement were to be successful, it should follow the German example, and he insisted that vocational schools be administered by those familiar with industry rather than by impractical school administrators. H. E. Miles, at this time president of the Wisconsin State Board of Industrial Education and a member of the Vocational Education Committee of NAM, shared McCarthy's suspicion of educators. McCarthy and Miles were among those who lobbied successfully for a federal advisory board of vocational education representing capital, labor, and agriculture to oversee the work of school managers, a governance structure that was to become a crucial provision of the Smith-Hughes Act.

The energetic lobbying of McCarthy and the support of leading industrialists, influential state legislators, and representatives of the Wisconsin Federation of Labor led to the first statewide continuation school laws in the United States. Racine was the first city to establish a continuation school under the 1911 law. Milwaukee quickly followed suit. According to Dr. Edward A. Fitzpatrick, a contemporary of McCarthy and an activist in the Wisconsin vocational education movement, McCarthy drafted a number of provisions for the national legislation. He kept in close contact on this issue with Senators La Follette and Hasting and Wisconsin congressional representatives, particularly Irvin Lenroot, who was at this time a very influential member. McCarthy was also in touch with Earl H. Goodwin of the United States Chamber of Commerce, Alvin S. Dodd of the NSPIE, and of course, H. E. Miles, who represented NAM. He even persuaded John R. Commons, then a renowned labor history and economics professor at the University of Wisconsin, to take a two-year leave of absence in order to serve on the Wisconsin Industrial Commission. McCarthy also recruited Charles Van Hise, the president of the University of Wisconsin in Madison, to his cause. Van Hise, in turn, proved to be particularly influential with Senator Hoke Smith, a major force in southern politics and one of the chief sponsors of the Smith-Hughes Act. By enlisting prominent state and national leaders to his cause, McCarthy had a notable, if somewhat indirect, influence on the 1917 federal vocational education legislation.[44]

With the passage in 1911 of Chapter 616, Laws of Wisconsin, the Milwaukee Board of School Directors organized a special committee on industrial education in order to ascertain the obligations of the city under the new law. Milwaukee's Industrial Education Board held its first meeting on May 20, 1912, but not until September did it begin actively to carry out the provisions of the law by which it was created. Robert L. Cooley was appointed to take charge, and for the next quarter century, Milwaukee, under Cooley's direction, led the country in developing models for vocational education for youth (fourteen to sixteen years of age) and adult workers. Nationally recognized leaders in the movement, such as Charles Prosser and David Snedden, came to Milwaukee to visit the school and confer with its director. A reciprocal relationship apparently existed between educational reformers at the local level and national figures prominent in the movement for vocational education.

In a related development, an evening school was established by the industrial board in one of the elementary schools in October 1912, and by 1915, seven such schools were in operation outside of and in addition to those operated by the school board, with an attendance of over 3,000 pupils per week. Classes in cooking, sewing, mechanical drawing, elementary academic work, and English for immigrants were the best attended. The language classes were used as a vehicle for lessons in history, civics, hygiene, industrial geography, and the like. In the steam, internal combustion engine, and electrical courses, as well as in other areas, instruction was carried on by correspondence, supplemented by lectures, laboratory work, and quizzes which brought the students and their instructors into personal contact. Much of the work was done at home, and required attendance was kept to two evenings a week. Other subjects offered in the evening schools included: mathematics, estimating and contracting, gas, electric and steam, stationary engineering for those working in such positions, printing, architectural drawing, bookkeeping, stenography, and commercial law. No one under sixteen years of age was allowed to attend the evening schools.[45]

The most difficult task was developing the vocational school for the fourteen- to sixteen-year-old permit students (students who had left full-time school and enrolled in part-time vocational programs). That program had its inception on November 1, 1912, in a small room on the eighth floor of the Manufacturers' Home Building. Two hundred girls under sixteen years of age from the various department stores of the city were in attendance. The school grew rapidly, requiring the acquisition of additional space and a rapid expansion of the teaching corps. By 1914, approximately 1,600 permit girls and 2,000 permit boys attended school one half day a week (four hours each day while unemployed temporarily) in the Stroh Building and Manufacturer's Home. Thirty-one classrooms were in use, and seventeen women and twenty-one men made up the faculty for the day school. The hours of school attendance were from 8:00 A.M. to 12:00 P.M. and from 1:00 P.M. to 5:00 P.M.

The Milwaukee Vocational School offered studies which, as in the case of the two trade schools and the manual training programs before them, were gender specific. Girls were taught to prepare "tasty and economical dishes," what constituted good nutrition, and how to shop wisely. They were taught to sew, judge the quality of goods, acquire "good" taste in color and design, and select suitable goods in personal dress and in the furnishing and decorating of the home. Academic subjects usually encountered in the elementary school were also taught, as well as a short course in the purchase of beds and bedding, airing and making of beds, bedroom ventilation and arrangement, and the care of the sick. A direct effort was made to encourage each girl to use the public library and to direct her reading so that a taste for "good" books could be formed at "this critical time in a girl's life, when she is breaking away from school, also, in a measure, from home, and is entering upon a wage-earning career in shop or factory."[46] The only courses which appeared to cross gender lines and which would prepare girls for employment were typewriting and stenography. At the time, there was a strong demand for these skills in Milwaukee and nationally.

The vocational offerings directed to boys were much more mixed and were geared more directly to earning a livelihood. Those young men who clearly intended to take up commercial careers were permitted to stress academic work in connection with typewriting, stenography, bookkeeping, business practice, commercial law, and the like. Those who demonstrated a special talent such as freehand drawing, coupled with an eye for color and design, would be informed about the various occupations where such abilities would prove an asset.

The great majority of the 2,000 permit boys who attended the Milwaukee Vocational School during their early years did not work at jobs which would pay them a living wage as adult men; nor did these jobs teach them skills which could lead to better paying work. Reflecting a growing concern for vocational guidance, Cooley noted,

> Some of the boys have ill-formed ambitions to become one or another kind of journeyman, at some remote time. On the other hand, they have no idea of what is before them, are not thinking ahead, and had no conception of the various trades or occupations available in this community which might afford them a way up. They shift without thought or reason from one job to another, and frequently their latter condition is worse than the former.[47]

For these pupils, the best approach appeared to be a diversified shop experience including wood working, metal working, and simple work with electrical appliances. One and one-half hours each week (more if the boy were temporarily unemployed) were spent in small-group work in these shops. In addition, these young men spent one and one-half hours each week in mechanical drawing and one hour in academic work. Mechanical drawing was emphasized because it was seen to be the fundamental skill needed to become successful in any of the mechanical trades and industries. The maximum enrollment in all classes was kept at twenty or less.

Guidance in the selection of vocations was viewed as an integral part of the work of the vocational school. In 1914, Cooley was ready to offer the boys definite prevocational work along the lines shown in Figure 8. Cooley pro-

1. Carpentry	11. Concrete work
2. Cabinet making	12. Power plant operation
3. Pattern making	13. Drafting
4. Tinsmithing	14. Bookkeeping
5. Sheet metal work	15. Store clerking
6. Plumbing	16. Stenography
7. Steam fitting	17. Printing
8. Electric work	18. Baking
9. Masonry	19. Printing and decorating
10. Machine shop work	

FIGURE 8. Prevocational work for boys.

vided an illustration of how these prevocational opportunities would evolve. If a boy declared his intent to become a plumber, Cooley would respect that ambition. He would first teach the names and uses of all the plumbers' tools to the boy, as well as familiarize him with the prices of plumbing work and supplies. The boy would do simple shop work and would study the conditions of the trade. Cooley's first aim was "to get the boy to take seriously his own wish to be a plumber . . . to get (quickly) into the work he expects to follow . . . [and] to get the boy to value an apprenticeship contract and demand one." At the same time, he would try to broaden the boy's training by instructing him in mechanical drawing and providing simple lessons in architectural sheet metal and freehand drawing. Cooley recognized that although the boy might earnestly desire to become a plumber and work hard to achieve that goal, "chance . . . will be a large factor in determining where the boy will land in seeking a job."[48]

In work with permit pupils, especially the boys, Cooley and his faculty were interested in discovering and promoting career opportunities—not merely getting any job, but to "prepare to earn a livelihood in a man's job" (see Figure 9). To this end, he and his colleagues devoted many years to developing and writing a series of texts under the general heading *My Life Work*. These texts were organized into four subgroupings and sold separately: (1) *My Life Work: Building and Metal Trades*; (2) *My Life Work: Printing and Servicing Trades*; (3) *My Life Work: Store and Office Occupations*; (4) *My Life Work: Representative Industries*. Each of these texts was divided again into subparts and chapters, and each chapter focused on a specific occupation or industry. *Representative Industries*, for example, included chapters on the hosiery, baking, candy, shoe, electrical, automobile, and telephone industries. Within the discussion of each industry, such topics as entry-level requirements, conditions of the workplace, pay, acquisition of marketable skills, and potential for advancement were reviewed.[49]

FIGURE 9. Continuation School, Milwaukee, Wisconsin, 1915. Milwaukee's Continuation School was established in 1911 as a way of helping students who had left school to upgrade their vocational skills. *Courtesy State Historical Society of Washington.*

As in the case of the other successes involving vocational education in Milwaukee, the drive to create continuation schools was propelled from outside the educational establishment. Of the four major initiatives, McCarthy's crusade was probably the most high-minded. To be sure, the trade training that continuation schools provided was beneficial to business interests, but McCarthy's principal concern was for providing the population of young people no longer in school with some kind of useful education. Continuation school programs did not actually weaken existing academic programs; they were virtually the only educational option available to fourteen- to sixteen-year-olds, and it proved to be a reasonably popular one at the time.[50] In later years, their record was decidedly mixed, but to the extent that some of these schools evolved into postsecondary vocational and technical schools, they became the nucleus of a major alternative to vocational education at the high school level. Unlike vocational training in high schools, programs in vocational and technical schools serve neither to bifurcate the curriculum nor do they require long-range prognostications as to one's future occupational status. In the Wisconsin context, with its dual system of control, the connection between schooling and the work of these part-time students was kept reasonably taut, and this accounted for much of the success of these early continuation schools. Elsewhere, especially as continuation schools developed, that connection became quite remote.[51]

THE MILWAUKEE EXPERIENCE WITH VOCATIONAL TRAINING

An incredible transformation of Milwaukee's system of educating its young had taken place in little more than a decade. By 1917, Milwaukee's dual system of vocational schools was more or less in place—the long-standing academic program and a new fourfold alternative which included a trade school for boys, a trade school for girls, an expanded program of manual training in regular schools, and an extensive program of continuing education for boys and girls who had left school. For boys who continued their studies in the public schools after the eighth grade, several options were now available. They could select one of the six regular courses of study offered in the high school or they could choose to enter the Trade and Technical High School and there pursue either a high school diploma or a trade diploma. For girls, the options were somewhat more limited. Although they, too, could select from the regular courses of study offered at the high school or enter the Girls' Trade School, the trade school curriculum was narrowly focused on a few "women's occupations," and no diploma was awarded when a girl completed her training there. For boys and girls who left school soon after the age of fourteen, the part-time vocational school offered a fairly broad range of training designed to enable these students to upgrade their job skills.

As always, financing the programs was no small consideration. The question of the cost of the new vocational programs tended to be a more persistent concern at the local level than was evident when national leaders debated the merits of vocational education. For this reason, the most critical single event that led to the success of the drive for vocational education in Milwaukee was probably the establishment by the newly organized Merchants' and Manufacturers' Association of its own trade school. By financing the Milwaukee Trade School for Boys over the course of its first two years, the most ardent proponents of vocational education, the manufacturers of the city, substantially eased the way to public acceptance. After they could put their successes on display and demonstrate the popular appeal of vocational programs, political support was not far behind. The Wisconsin legislature quickly passed the legislation drafted by the manufacturers permitting the public schools to take over the trade school, and thereafter, vocational education was supported at public expense. The privately financed Milwaukee trade school posed a threat to public school educators; not only were powerful business interests behind it, but the possibility of a private alternative to public schooling was emerging. In effect, Milwaukee's school managers had to respond. As political scientist Paul E. Peterson interprets the extension of the reach of public schools into vocational education, "Curricular expansion in the public schools occurred in response to demands from different groups that had the political power to force such an expansion or that had the resources to set up competing systems unless their demands were met."[52] While modifications, particularly the expansion in the scope as well as the length of the programs of study, were instituted over time, the basic direction of the programs—direct trade training tied to the particular industrial needs of the city (at least for boys)—remained intact. Once vocational programs were in place, the original identification of the trade school with manufacturing interests seemed to evaporate in the enthusiasm of Milwaukee's citizens generally for the new reform.

Although the swiftness with which vocational options became available and the enthusiasm with which they were greeted on all sides are indeed remarkable, in certain respects, the Milwaukee experience with vocational education was not notably different from that of other major cities. In general, the same confluence of social, political, economic, and pedagogical ideas and events that shaped the national drive for vocational education at this time also shaped the direction that the curriculum of the Milwaukee public schools was to take. As was the case nationally, the concerns of the usual array of interest groups, including manufacturers and organized labor, seemed to coincide when it came to the introduction of vocational education as a public school function. The National Association of Manufacturers had a local counterpart in Milwaukee's Merchants' and Manufacturers' Association, and the voice of labor as represented by Samuel Gompers and the AFL at the national level found expression in Milwaukee's highly organized local unions.

Milwaukee was different from other major cities in certain respects. In terms of election victories, Milwaukee's socialists were able to exercise a political power that was probably unprecedented in any American city. After Seidel's election in 1910, Milwaukeeans continued to elect socialist mayors, and socialists succeeded not only in sending their longtime leader Victor Berger to Congress but elected his wife Meta Berger to the Milwaukee school board, a post in which she served actively for thirty years. While Meta Berger in later years took an active role in debates over ability grouping, led opposition to platoon schools on the Gary Plan, and even took a keen interest in the dissemination of the project method in Milwaukee schools, vocational education seemed to pose no threat to her abiding socialist convictions.[53] Apparently, Milwaukee socialists were persuaded that they could adopt the more beneficial aspects of the German educational model without sacrificing their ideals.

This absence of any real opposition by organized labor and socialists to the prospect of a dual school system, especially when seen in the light of the experience of other cities such as Chicago in the same period, remains somewhat puzzling. One possible explanation is Milwaukee's ethnic makeup. Milwaukee's distinctive ethnic identity made the influence of the "German model" especially powerful. Until the years just prior to America's entry into World War I, Germany had been held up in manufacturing, in labor, and in educational circles as the European country to emulate. Growing industries in the United States, and NAM in particular, saw themselves as competing with German enterprises for supremacy in the world marketplace. American labor organizations envied and admired the German programs of workmen's compensation and accident insurance and agitated for similar benefits at the national and state levels. Educators from kindergarten teachers to university professors flocked to Germany to study the pedagogical ideas being developed and taught there.

Although many Milwaukee citizens or their forebears had fled Germany because of political and religious persecution, it seems reasonable to assume that the Milwaukee German population had been acculturated to the German system of education and took pride in its accomplishments. To German immigrants and their descendants, the prospect of a distinct division in the way public education was conducted and administered seemed to pose no particular threat because Germany had a tradition of a school system organized in terms not only of different kinds of curricula but of different schools. To many Milwaukeeans, therefore, separate and distinct forms of education for different segments of the school population seemed normal and natural. What is more, technical education in Germany carried high status, making the prospect that working-class children would receive an inferior education only a remote possibility.

In 1910, the prominent German educational reformer, Georg Kerchensteiner, was brought to the United States by the National Society for the Promotion of Industrial Education for a lecture tour, during which he argued that the primary duty of education was developing skills needed for industry, a duty he believed to be more important than even moral training. In fact, reflecting the beliefs of many of the early promoters of manual training, he held that the most effective moral training was a byproduct of industrial training.[54] These sentiments must have resonated with the ethnic Germans of Milwaukee across the spectrum of political affiliation. Kerchensteiner, after all, was widely regarded as a progressive reformer and had become something of a culture hero in Germany. His program, entailing as it did a bifurcated school system, received strong support from business interests in nearby Chicago and was translated into a bill formally proposing a dual school system drafted by Edwin G. Cooley, a former school superintendent. The Cooley Bill was vigorously supported by the Commercial Club of Chicago, which was joined by such interest groups as the Chicago Association of Commerce and the Illinois Manufacturers Association. In contrast to Milwaukee labor's quiescence in this matter, however, organized labor in nearby Chicago strenuously opposed the Cooley Bill, rejecting the idea that the German educational system ought to be held up as a model.[55] They were joined by an outraged John Dewey, who argued that the German school system, being "frankly nationalistic," was not anything American schools ought to emulate.[56] The bifurcation, he went on to argue, would not only deprive vocational students of the intellectual education they should receive but would also lead to an arid academic education for the rest.[57]

The contrast between the position of organized labor in Milwaukee and Chicago on the pending division of the school system into academic and vocational components makes the ethnic explanation for Milwaukee labor's muted reaction to the prospect of a transformation of their school system seem much more plausible. As Ira Katznelson and Margaret Weir have observed in their treatment of organized labor's position on educational policy, differences between workers organized along ethnic lines (as in San Francisco) as distinct from workers organized as labor (as in Chicago) served to define the positions of the respective groups with respect to school policy and resulted in notable differences in terms of militancy. "Where workers mobilized as labor," they say, "our Chicago case suggests they were able to impose compromises more effectively than when they based their actions mainly on ethnic and religious identities."[58] The absence of class-based opposition by the ethnically oriented labor movement in Milwaukee in the face of the business community's initiatives with respect to trade training lends support to Katznelson and Weir's contention. That Milwaukee's socialists were so ethnically dominated may also have been one factor in their reputation as "Sewer Socialists."

Milwaukeeans generally, not just labor and socialists, viewed themselves ideologically as "progressive," and indeed the Progressive Party under Senator Robert La Follette Sr. achieved notable political victories in the state of Wisconsin. Whether they labeled themselves socialist, progressive, Democrat, or Republican, the citizens of Milwaukee stood together in the belief that their city was in the vanguard of reform during this era, and whatever the political configuration in support of vocational education, it was unquestionably perceived by Milwaukeeans as a progressive reform, as was the case nationally. If leading cities across the nation were offering their children the opportunity to benefit from trade training, then Milwaukee schools would make it available as well.

The political configuration in Milwaukee, its ethnic identity, the need to overcome the very real problem of paying for the new programs, and civic pride were unquestionably significant factors in the way vocational education was instituted in Milwaukee. An array of inducements made vocational education a reform that appealed to a wide spectrum of constituencies. Manufacturing interests nationally and locally wanted a steady supply of skilled workers for their factories and shops; organized labor wanted to restrain the manufacturers from creating their own labor market and perceived vocational education under public control as the best option available to them; volunteer groups and social reformers pressed for schools to respond to changing human needs; professional educators needed to attune the curriculum to an ever growing school population; and parents needed reassurance that the new industrial order's cycles of prosperity and depression and the uncertainties of the job market would not disenfranchise their children.

The undeniable transformation in the nature of work and the workplace created a new imperative. New jobs were being created by the development of new technologies and new forms of cooperate management; the sheer range of occupations requiring some manual skills was expanding enormously (even though the number of skills required of any single worker was declining). Milwaukeeans, like Americans generally, were bewildered, even frightened, by these changes and what they portended in terms of their economic security and that of their children. With apprenticeship in steep decline as a source of training, it seemed obvious to educators, parents, social reformers, business and industrial leaders, and labor alike that education tied to the new workplace was required. The family alone could no longer mediate between the world of childhood and the new and puzzling world of work. A social agency had to intervene, and schools were the logical choice.

The image of the "young Vulcan," with its symbolic evocation of an earlier world of work, had opened the way for a restructuring of the American curriculum through the incorporation of manual training, but perceived economic imperatives ultimately worked to recast manual training along with its promise of moral rehabilitation and pedagogical renewal into a straightforward economic response to the vagaries of the new workplace. That response would acquire its own symbolic overtones, but for the time being, a further restructuring of the traditional American curriculum in order to accommodate vocational education seemed not only a practical solution to an array of urgent problems, but a miraculous elixir that would assuage ill-defined, nagging anxieties about the effects of the Industrial Revolution.

 5

A CURRICULUM ATTUNED TO "PROBABLE FUTURE NEEDS"

Vocationalism as an Educational Ideal, 1908–1919

Present educational practice differentiates between boys and girls in the provision of manual and domestic work in view of their different educational destinations. In a few cities special high-school preparatory classes exist for children who, at the age of twelve, obviously are qualified and intended for high-school work. In reform schools and various other types of special schools, children at the age of twelve or later receive a kind of education suited to their probable future needs. In American secondary schools as now organized some opportunities for specialization are offered to those who wish to take up commercial work, to prepare for college, etc. But in the main, American education, unlike that of Europe, refuses largely to take account of the probable educational destination of its pupils, especially those under sixteen years of age. The reason for this exists in the general tradition of the democratic character of American education but it actually operates, as we believe, to render such education undemocratic. At first it would appear that differentiation of education according to an educational destination could only affect vocational training; but a study of the conditions of life will show that the cultural and social needs of varying groups must make different demands upon the kind of cultural and social training given.

David Snedden, 1908[1]

The dramatic rise to prominence of trade training in Milwaukee schools during the first two decades of the twentieth century was not an isolated phenomenon. Milwaukee was one of many places where vocational education was increasingly being viewed as a response to the transformation of the workplace and a way of providing an appropriate education for certain classes of students. In his study of secondary education in suburban Somerville, Massachusetts, for example, Reed Ueda reports that in 1910 a new boys' vocational school was opened, and in 1911 a girls' vocational school as well. By offering metalwork and woodwork for the boys and millinery and dressmaking for the girls, Somerville's vocational programs followed a familiar gender-based pattern. In addition, as in Milwaukee, practices associated with manual training were giving way to explicit trade training. As Ueda puts it, "Vocational schools supplied a completely different set of courses from manual training of the last century, which had been subservient to cognitive development. Instead, the vocational program was a practical end in itself, a simple and plain preparation for industrial work."[2] As the new century progressed, manual training with its elaborate rationales framed in terms of pedagogical and moral reform lost considerable ground to courses designed frankly to teach the skills required by the new industrial order.

Beyond the vocational courses themselves, however, was vocationalism.[3] The term "vocationalism" usually refers to advocacy in behalf of a program of studies designed to teach job skills, but as used here, it also refers to the educational ideal that stems from the application of the precepts and demands of business and industry to the curriculum as a whole. Beyond the teaching of vocational skills in schools, vocationalism embodies a vision of what education is for. Vocational education exists alongside general education; vocationalism as an educational ideal subsumes general education. While vocational education, the creation of a separate and distinct program of studies attuned to the work requirements of the new industrial order, presents one set of crucial issues, vocationalization, the transformation of the curriculum as a whole in line with the criteria and protocols of the workplace, invokes an array of issues that are even more profound.

Besides vocationalism, however, the new industrial order gave rise to another powerful ideology, social efficiency. At certain significant points, social efficiency and vocationalism obviously converge. Both doctrines, for example, accept at least implicitly, but more often explicitly, the notion that education is above all a process of getting ready for adulthood. According to the doctrine of social efficiency, competent performance in a variety of adult social roles would become subject to the predictability, order, and scientific precision that were increasingly becoming the hallmarks of the modern factory. The same principles, such as specialization of function, that made the modern factory a model of productivity are adapted to create an orderly and smoothly running society. A transformed curriculum has a vital role to play in the realization of that social vision by training the next generation directly in the efficient performance of the activities that define their social role. Although vocationalism and social efficiency both draw their inspiration from the new industrial workplace, social efficiency expresses a broad social vision, whereas vocationalism represents an educational ideal tied particularly to occupational competence.

In this regard, some differences can be established, although they are differences in degree rather than in kind. Vocationalism's point of departure, like that of social efficiency, is the perceived needs of modern industrial society, but under vocationalism, other activities are subservient to those that bear on the efficient operation of the workplace and the need to get and hold a job. Citizenship activities, health activities, leisure activities—all of which, according to social efficiency, need to be anticipated as much as work-related activities—become secondary. Under vocationalism, academic subjects of study are reconstructed or adapted in order to meet the demands of the labor market. The subject of English becomes infused with writing job applications and preparing resumes; mathematics becomes business arithmetic. When literature, physics, geometry, or a foreign language cannot demonstrate its relationship to the demands of commerce and industry, it is relegated to a kind of ritual status, with its value seen almost entirely in terms of admission to college. In that case, direct preparation for work is merely postponed, since attending college quite as much as elementary and secondary schools is for the purpose of earning a living. Although under vocationalism the needs of commerce and industry are the principal driving force, the rhetoric is more often than not couched in terms of individual needs. In the end, however, vocationalism makes economic well-being the all-consuming purpose of education.

Vocationalism also has a subtler side. By borrowing the language of the workplace, vocationalism applies the conceptual apparatus associated with business and industry to the enterprise of schooling. The content of school subjects is not simply oriented to the workplace; schooling is actually conceived and understood in terms of raw material and finished products, gains and losses, inputs and outputs, productive and unproductive labor, elimination of waste, return on investment, precise production goals, and of course, the bottom line. These concepts do not apply simply to budgetary considerations or to the management of schools; they are what schools are fundamentally about. The ideals and criteria that govern industrial production are transferred metaphorically to schooling, and they become the way in which teaching and learning, the curriculum, and the process of education generally are conceived. To the extent that vocationalism becomes the controlling purpose of schooling, our sense of what constitutes pedagogical success and failure is governed by its strictures.

DAVID SNEDDEN: VOCATIONALISM AND
SOCIAL EFFICIENCY IN TANDEM

Beyond the conceptual distinctions and definitions that can be established in relation to vocationalism and social efficiency, there are specific policies to formulate and curricular practices to implement. No single person better personifies these doctrines and the effort to translate them into a practical reality than David Snedden. In a sense, the career of both these ideals can be traced through his work. Although his vision of a reconstructed curriculum attuned to a supremely efficient social order and of vocationalism as the controlling ideal of education was never fully realized, both American education and American society moved substantially in those directions. Relentlessly, Snedden pursued to their most far-reaching conclusions the doctrine of social efficiency and the extension of principles of vocational education to the curriculum as a whole. The question of his actual influence is moot; what his work illustrates is his ability not to transform or transcend the direction the curriculum was taking in his time but to articulate and epitomize it.

The outlines of Snedden's social vision were already being expressed while he was still a junior faculty member at Stanford University. A popular speaker before teachers' groups, he was described by one local newspaper as "magnetic," "forceful," and "eloquent." As early as 1903, he was, like Bobbitt, beginning to see the curriculum as governed by precise objectives and explicitly stated purposes, and he was unequivocal in asserting the primacy of the criterion of efficiency.[4] "Education," he said, "is to make men efficient," declaring this to be "the fundamental idea of education."[5] In 1905, Snedden took leave from Stanford to seek a doctorate at Teachers College, Columbia University. His Ph.D. dissertation, "Administration and Educational Work of American Juvenile Reform Schools," advanced the idea that reform schools were institutions that should be emulated in certain respects since they were in a position to exercise nearly complete social control over the inmates and thereby achieve supreme efficiency. (As residential institutions, reform schools presumably would not have to cope with the ill effects of "street and alley time" as Bobbitt had complained was the case with public schools.) Not the least of their advantages was that only four hours a day were allotted for the conventional school subjects, leaving plenty of time for vocational education.

Upon completion of his dissertation, Snedden was invited to remain at Teachers College as an adjunct professor. Soon he was arguing that traditional elementary and secondary subjects, such as history, must "pass in review" to determine whether they actually serve to realize the social purposes of education, thereby seeking to apply to them the efficiency standards that were at the heart of the new industrial society.[6] Increasingly as well, Snedden called for differentiated programs of study, arguing that age twelve would be the best time for that differentiation to begin. He proposed that with the end of sixth grade should come the end of a common curriculum and that secondary education should be defined in terms of curricular differentiation. Snedden was even suspicious of providing manual training for all pupils in elementary schools, implying that curricular differentiation was appropriate in that case as well. "No more fundamental mistake," he said, "has been made in the elementary school than in prescribing manual training for all." It would be better, he went on to say, to provide such training "for those who especially cared for that work,[7] thus rejecting some of the claims made by early proponents of manual training as to its universal benefits.

In 1909, Snedden assumed the powerful post of Commissioner of Education for the Commonwealth of Massachusetts, and this put him in a commanding position to bring to fruition the ideas that had been developing. In one of his first important decisions, Snedden brought his close friend and fellow graduate student at Teachers College, Charles Prosser, to be his Deputy Commissioner for Industrial Education. Together, they labored to institute what Snedden liked to call "real vocational education," that is, education directed toward specific skills needed in the workplace rather than general vocational training. In one of the commissioner's reports, skills such as "blueprint reading for plumbers," "applied design for granite workers," and "sleeve making for dress makers" were cited as examples.[8]

It was not simply vocational education, however, that needed a much higher degree of specialization. Just as the modern factory thrived because of specialization of function, so would society generally be improved by each individual efficiently performing the specialized tasks that society demanded. Rejecting the idea of a uniform curriculum or uniform methods, Snedden proposed a conception of civilization as "a thing of 'standardized parts'—preparation for which can be achieved by 'quality production.'" To this end, Snedden employed the appealing metaphor of teamwork. Schools, he said, should "be guided chiefly by the purpose of enabling each person, with his personal equipment and in the light of his probable part in the games of life, to make himself as a contributor to the success of the many teams—from family to nation—in which he must play his part."[9] The "great community," as he liked to call it, could be achieved by "division of function" and "specialization of service."[10] The specialized skills that each worker brought to the process of production, the particular contributions that each player made to the success of the team, and the distinctive functions that each individual performed in the interest of a placid social order were all of one piece.

The curriculum as Snedden saw it would not completely expunge subjects such as literature on the grounds of their inability to contribute to efficient functioning generally or the vocational function in particular; such subjects, however, would be reserved for those who were in a position to use them. "Some of us," he said, "find the novels of Henry James, Conrad and Meredith perpetual sources of satisfaction, but, clearly, only Utopians (or aspirationists) can expect the rank and file of people to have similar interests. "Aspirationists" is the term Snedden liked to use for leaders in education, like Dewey, who did not fully appreciate the crucial differences within the human species and therefore quixotically aspired to bring the benefits of intellectual culture to the "rank and file." Aspirationists also failed to realize that just as fine music, art, and literature were out of the reach of the common person, so were "leadership, planning, management, protracted responsibility [and] innovation."[11] By failing to recognize these crucial differences in terms of social role, aspirationists were cruelly inflicting the wrong kind of education on "the common person."

Although liberal education was one thing and vocational education clearly another, Snedden argued that liberal education ought to be subject to the same strictures and exacting standards as vocational education:

> Efficiency in education, as elsewhere in the regions of conscious effort, involves on one hand a fairly clear conception of goals to be reached, and on the other a degree of certitude as to the probable functioning of the means and methods employed. Our institutions devoted to liberal education are not able to apply themselves along these lines; they have no acceptable formulations of their purposes, and equally (and partly as a consequence) they have no evidence as to the efficacy of the procedures they use.[12]

Vocational education, then, was to provide the model for liberal education of clearly stated goals, along with efficient means to achieve them. This transference of the assumptions and conventions of vocational education to the rest of the curriculum defines vocationalism as an educational ideal. If vocational education required a forecast of one's role in the job market, then liberal education needed to anticipate adult functioning in other areas. In both vocational and general education, probable destinations of students had to be taken into account. "What . . . ," he asked, "has the obligatory study of algebra and geometry on the part of ninety-five per cent of the more than half million high-school girls in America to do with their liberal education?"[13] If girls were not destined to use those subjects, there was no point in teaching them either under the rubric of liberal education or vocational education.

A distinction of sorts, however, was to be made between the two. For Snedden, liberal education was to be defined in terms of its relationship to vocational education "in the same way that production and consumption (or utilization) are contrasted in social and economic life." Simply put, "vocational education may be designed to make of a person an efficient producer; liberal education may be designed to make him an effective consumer or user."

Thus, someone who is liberally educated "uses good literature rather than bad." In what may have been an implied criticism of the claims being made by advocates of manual training, Snedden went on to argue that, given this crucial difference, these different forms of education cannot be carried forward within the same organizational structure. Although liberal education needed to be subject to the same principles as vocational education, each form of education must be administratively independent of the other.[14]

VOICES OF DISSENT

Snedden's producer-consumer analogy did not go unchallenged. William C. Bagley, who was to become Snedden's colleague at Teachers College, thought the line between producer and consumer had been overdrawn, and in any case, "it is a mistake to think that all education which cannot be justified upon the basis of its specific vocational value must either seek justification as a preparation for leisure or surrender its place in our schools." Bagley's criticism went to the heart of the emerging new doctrine of vocationalism. Just because vocational education was a direct preparation for an anticipated adult activity, this did not mean that all education was. What was being called liberal education, he was saying, did not need to follow the same strictures as vocational education. In the same address, Bagley raised the issue of "the dangers of social stratification" that attend the creation of separate programs of vocational education. "A stratified society and a permanent proletariat," he argued, "are undoubtedly the prime conditions of a certain type of national efficiency. But whenever our people have been intelligently informed regarding what this type of efficiency costs, they have been fairly unanimous in declaring that the price is too high."[15] That conflict between a socially efficient and a democratic society, however, was only infrequently raised as the vocationalization of the American curriculum proceeded.

Other objections were voiced every now and then. One complaint was that industry was simply transferring the cost of training its workers to the public schools. In his autobiography in 1912, William Maxwell, the longtime superintendent of schools of New York City, warned that "Manufacturers who up to fifty years ago felt themselves responsible the world over for training of their workers must not be permitted, under any pretext, to shift the burden entirely to the public schools."[16] Maxwell's reservation was even more sharply expressed by Owen Lovejoy, general secretary of the Child Labor Committee. Speaking to a meeting of the Vocational Guidance Association, he said:

> The employers have a very definite program. They know what they want
> and are going after it. Let us not delude ourselves by thinking that they are

actuated by philanthropy. It is simply good business. They want a crop of fresh, young labor furnished them every year that can make fewer mistakes and more profits.[17]

Indeed, as the effort to adjust to the decline of apprenticeship by providing vocational training in schools proceeded, it was often forgotten that this shift represented a radical change in the cost and responsibility for such training from the private sector to the public.

From a pedagogical perspective, another problem was the actual extent to which the curriculum ought to be differentiated according to the characteristics of school children and their probable destinations. As indicated by the Milwaukee experience, the creation of vocational training courses had the effect in practice of creating not just a bifurcated curriculum but a bifurcated school system. Wisconsin was the first state to formalize that split by creating a dual system of control. By the second decade of the twentieth century, efforts were being made, with Snedden in the forefront, to create separate governing structures for general education on one side and vocational education on the other. The proposed creation of separate administrative structures for vocational and general education brought Snedden into a spirited debate with John Dewey. Snedden's exchange with Dewey had its inception in an article by Dewey which drew attention to the fact that the newly formed Commission on National Aid to Vocational Education included not a single professional educator. The responsibility for formulating and implementing educational policy in vocational education, it appeared, was now being transferred to interest groups outside of education. Apparently, Dewey sensed that a new educational ideal was being fashioned by these groups and tried to indicate the ways in which the interests of such groups might come into conflict with his cherished notions of the relationship of the school to society. The aim of schooling in a democracy, he said, "must be to keep youth under educative influence for a longer time" rather than to induct them prematurely into the demands of the workplace. Dewey feared that the emergence of industrial education not as part of general education but as an alternative to it and under separate administrative control would serve to deprive much of America's youth of the educative influences they need by substituting specific skill training for general education at an early age. Industrial education, he went on to say, should be in the interest of developing "industrial intelligence" rather than "technical trade efficiency."[18]

In his reply, Snedden sounded almost betrayed. He had become accustomed, he said, to "the antipathy of educated men toward the common callings, 'menial' pursuits and 'dirty' trades," but to find "Dr. Dewey giving aid and comfort to the opponents of a broader, richer and more effective program of education ... is discouraging." This symbolic identification of vocational education with ordinary Americans was one of the most powerful weapons in the hands of vocationalists. To raise questions as to the appropriateness of vocational education was associated not merely with hidebound tradition but elitist and hence antidemocratic sentiments. As to Dewey's call for industrial education in the interest of promoting industrial intelligence, Snedden declared simply, "vocational education is, irreducibly and without unnecessary mystification, education for the pursuit of an occupation." The question of dual control, with vocational education on one side and general education on the other, he argued, "is merely one of securing the greatest efficiency." Businessmen, he pointed out, have good reason to be suspicious of the "academic mind," and therefore, it seems reasonable to extricate the control of vocational education from its influence.[19]

Dewey's rejoinder took exception to Snedden's charge of "giving aid and comfort to the opponents of a broader and richer program of education," and he went on to reject trade training for anyone below the age of "eighteen or twenty." "I object," Dewey went on to say, "to regarding as vocational education any training which does not have as its supreme regard the development of such intelligence, initiative, ingenuity and executive capacity as shall make workers, as far as may be, the masters of their own industrial fate." As Dewey saw it, the kind of vocational education that Snedden supported gave "the power of social predestination, by means of narrow trade-training, to . . . fallible men no matter how well-intentioned they may be." The strict separation of general education from vocational education would only serve to make vocational education all the more constricted and reinforce that process. Sensing that Snedden's social vision required a one-sided adjustment of the individual to the demands of the society, Dewey concluded his response by asserting that his differences with Snedden were "not so much narrowly educational as . . . political and social." Vocationalists, like Snedden, were interested mainly in serving the needs of the existing "industrial regime."[20] Dewey was seeking to change it.

Within three months of Dewey's reply to Snedden, the debate over both the structure of vocational education and its positioning vis-á-vis general education spilled over into the annual meeting of the National Education Association. The attack on vocational education as it was being formulated was led by the superintendent of schools in Chicago, Ella Flagg Young, the woman Dewey once described as "the wisest person in school matters" that he had ever known.[21] One part of her address challenged the way in which work had been "divided into exceedingly small parts," and the effect that this had on the well-being of adolescents subjected to that kind of training. "It is not necessary for me before an audience of teachers," Young said, "to enlarge upon the effect, mental and physical, of limiting boys and girls between fourteen and eighteen years of age to moments which day after day have no aim excepting duplication of a few particular movements, without variation, in order to feed or take from a machine." She appealed to teachers and the American public to "see to it that the early education of... children and their vocational training shall not be a preparation for life which reduces the human being to the level of an automatic mechanism."[22]

In the second part of her address, Young specifically criticized what then passed for the vocational education of girls. "What seemed to get lost in much of the discussion on that subject," she said, was that "the great mass of women must do some industrial work." Undoubtedly referring to the concerted attention then being given to home economics, she objected strongly to the fact that "industrial training of girls is limited almost entirely to cooking and sewing." Girls are taught to serve in the dining room of homes but not in hotels and restaurants. Girls are taught to sew but not to earn a living as a tailor. Young concluded her address by asking rhetorically, "after the children are reared what are our girls who have become middle-aged women to do?"[23] She was calling attention, of course, to the gender-based division that had emerged in the drive for vocational education. Vocational education for boys was being aimed specifically and directly at the job market; vocational education for girls was being geared largely to nonremunerative work in the home. Young was one of a number of women who were deeply suspicious of the emphasis being given to home economics rather than trade training for girls. That group included Susan Kingsbury, the principal investigator of the Douglas Commission report, who in 1913 coauthored a government report documenting the need for industrial training for women.[24]

At the same NEA conference, equally sharp criticism of the new industrial education was voiced by Frederick W. Roman, a professor of economics at Syracuse University. Roman was particularly critical of the dual system of control that had been initiated in Wisconsin and now was being promoted in other states. Arguing that the dual-control idea was based on an assumption that "the boy is to be trained to be a high-class machine," he went on to say that advocates of dual control, "are anxious to establish an independent school system so that the large number of boys and girls, or the so-called waste product of our public-school system, may find their true function in society." Education, he insisted, "must include much more than the mere making of skilled tools out of our children." To Roman, this was not education but exploitation. "Our capitalists have already robbed our forests and our mines and the natural resources of our country generally," he added acidly, "and now we are asked to accept a system of education which looks to the exploiting of our children."[25]

The remarks by Young and Roman at the Oakland, California, conference did not go unnoticed in the press. The *Bulletin* of the National Association of Corporation Schools reported that, in an interview following her address, Young expressed the view that there is "a conflict coming between the rich and the teaching fraternity in regard to the education of the poor. . . . They want us to turn out the kind of labor that they have been importing from Europe." The report went on to describe Young as "jealous of her authority," and "unwilling to concede anything to industrial education."[26] An editorial in the *San Francisco Chronicle* was critical but not quite as acerbic:

> Mrs. Young is perhaps wide of the mark in saying that there is a move-ment on foot on the part of big interests to control the education of schools. . . . Rather it is the work of meddlesome and muddlesome politicians and misguided educators, who probably have the very best intentions, but who certainly have lost sight of the democratic ideal in education.[27]

Despite the efforts of the likes of Bagley, Young, and Dewey to show other-wise, the association of vocational education with democracy remained strongly entrenched.

The *Chronicle* was even more critical of Roman's address than Young's:

> It is difficult to write with patience about the foolish babble on vocational training that is set free by schoolmasters and schoolmarms. And with every desire to be polite to the great educational gathering which is honoring this State with its presence, we are compelled to say that some of the worst of such stuff which has come under our notice has been delivered at sessions of that meeting.[28]

Commenting on Roman's contention that the selection of a vocation should never be final, the editorial went on to say that "if there is anything that a boy needs . . . it is . . . the habit of submission to authority."[29] Whatever the merits of their criticisms of the way industrial education was going forward, clearly Young and Roman had expressed some very unpopular views. Criti-cism of vocational education as usually practiced was not reaching a wide audience.

COALITION BUILDING: THE ROAD TO THE SMITH-HUGHES ACT

Even with objections being voiced every now and then, the time seemed ripe to mount a concerted drive to gain federal support for vocational education. As early as 1910, leaders in vocational education of the stature of David Sned-den were openly calling for such support. "The National Government itself," Snedden argued, "could legitimately be called upon to aid this form of education, since the general migratory tendency of laborers carries them constantly beyond State bounds."[30] By 1912 or so, the main outlines of the new industrial education were in place, although a few issues remained to be ironed out. NAM still favored a dual system of trade and academic schools but was willing to accept joint representation of business and labor on a federal board for vocational education. Labor still opposed the dual system and was suspicious that anti-unionism might creep into public sponsorship but was nevertheless ready to support some form of trade training if labor was represented on its governing bodies. The role of NSPIE was critical in reconciling remaining differences between management and labor and in resolving inconsistencies. Opposition to a dual system of vocational and academic schools, for example, was too strong, but some form of clear differentiation short of institutional separation was still possible. At its meetings, the question of a dual system along the lines of the much admired German system would sometimes emerge, but the main direction of NSPIE's efforts was elsewhere.

To bring about the industrial education it was established to promote, NSPIE needed somehow to resolve, or at least to paper over, the diversity that various interest groups had brought to the cause of vocational education. Without a viable political coalition, industrial education would remain a vague ideal lacking the unified support or financial wherewithal to make a lasting impact on the American curriculum. Several historians of what is commonly called the Progressive Era have called attention to the crucial role that coalition building played in what is usually regarded as progressive reform. Some of them even believe that social and political progressivism can be defined not by a coherent and consistent philosophy, or for that matter by stable characteristics of any sort, but by what Peter Filene refers to as "shifting coalitions around different issues."[31] The same may be said about educational progressivism, since no single ideology or coherent array of practices defines it. Reforms governed by the criterion of efficiency, efforts to base teaching and learning on the child's developmental growth, and the impulse to use the schools in order to achieve a harmonious social order all existed side by side, and only temporarily did the proponents of these movements coalesce around a single issue.

The coalition that formed around the drive for vocational education provides an ideal example of what these historians of the period use as their touchstone for defining the nature of progressivism. The alliances that NSPIE needed to forge in order to obtain the necessary political support to create a truly national movement, however, had to extend beyond their main thrust in industrial education and the supplemental effort in the area of home economics. Apart from mediating NAM and AFL differences over industrial education, NSPIE needed to form alliances with such organizations as the National Education Association and the American Association of Home Economics, and especially agricultural interests. Accordingly, NSPIE began to reach out to such other politically potent groups as the National Farmer's Congress and the Southern Commercial Congress.

As early as 1907, when Representative Charles R. Davis of Minnesota introduced his bill, federal aid for industrial education, home economics, and vocational agriculture were already joined together. Even with the active support of the AFL, however, what became known as the Davis-Dolliver Bill failed, largely because land grant college administrators opposed linking vocational education with agricultural extension. In the ensuing year or two, however, NSPIE was able to consolidate its forces. In return for backing a new agricultural extension bill introduced by Senator Hoke Smith of Georgia in 1913, for example, NSPIE earned the enduring loyalty of a powerful force in southern politics. By incorporating agricultural interests into a cross-class coalition that included not only NAM and AFL but the American Bankers Association, the United States Chamber of Commerce, the National Metal Trade Association as well as local unions, NSPIE was now poised for a major breakthrough in their campaign in behalf of vocational education.[32] These groups had different stakes in the outcome, but in one way or another, they all saw federal support as critical to the realization of their aspirations, and they put their differences aside in order to join in the campaign for federal financing of vocational education.

New public criticism of the way schools were functioning also served to prompt NSPIE to intensify its efforts in the direction of state and federal legislation supporting vocational education. By 1912, NSPIE's leaders could view with some satisfaction the legislative gains in such states as Connecticut, Indiana, Massachusetts, New York, Ohio, and Wisconsin, but the wide diversity of vocational programs and the unevenness of financial support remained a source of considerable concern. In the interest of focusing their efforts at the national level, NSPIE decided to hire a full-time executive secretary, and the appointment of Charles Prosser to that post in 1912 was an inspired choice. Prosser not only faced the daunting task of bringing organized labor into line but disgruntled farmers' groups and the still suspicious educational establishment as well. After five years of intensive lobbying, he succeeded in forging the necessary coalition. Prosser himself drafted the key provisions of the Smith-Hughes Act and was chiefly responsible for their implementation. Manufacturing and business groups eagerly lent their endorsement. At their annual meeting in 1912, NAM overcame its traditional opposition to government spending and approved of the efforts to gain federal support for vocational education. The United States Chamber of Commerce followed suit in 1913 and again in 1916.

Given the strong tradition of local financing and control of public schooling in the United States, efforts to involve the federal government in the conduct of vocational education were sure to meet with political opposition.

Critical to overcoming that opposition was obtaining the support of southern politicians. That the South had a meager economic base for the support of schools made southern congressmen amenable to suspending their traditional suspicions of the centralized control in order to benefit from the kind of financial support that the federal government could provide. Moreover, maintaining two separate systems of schooling, one white and the other black, was very costly, with low levels of spending on education in the South being particularly debilitating to African Americans. A year before the passage of Smith-Hughes, a government report indicated that the cost of educating whites stood at $22.22 per student while for African Americans it was $1.78.[33] By taking the lead in framing federal legislation in the area of education, southern congressmen could minimize its effects on the segregated system while at the same time bringing needed financial support. It should not be surprising, therefore, that the National Act for Vocational Education was sponsored by two southern congressmen, Senator Hoke Smith and Representative Dudley Hughes, both of the state of Georgia.[34]

The Smith-Hughes Act, as it came it be called, was first introduced in 1914, but Congress took no action on the bill, and it was reintroduced in 1915. When amendments to the bill delayed approval because the different versions passed in the House of Representatives and the Senate could not be reconciled, President Woodrow Wilson himself appealed to the joint conference committee for speedy action. American entry into World War One was imminent, and increased industrial productivity as a result of vocational training in schools was an alluring prospect. The actual signing of the bill on February 23, 1917, by President Wilson coincided with the meeting of the NSPIE in Philadelphia. When news of the signing was announced at the meeting, the assembled members erupted into cheering and applause. Dewey, however, was anything but sanguine about the new legislation. Speaking to the Public Education Association just a month after the signing of Smith-Hughes into law, he told his audience that "It settles no problem; it merely symbolizes the inauguration of a conflict between irreconcilably opposed educational and industrial ideals."[35] Indeed, Smith-Hughes marks the point when vocationalism began to gain ascendancy over rival educational ideals. With the passage of the act, the National Society for the Promotion of Industrial Education changed its name to the National Society for Vocational Education, reasoning that vocational education no longer required "promotion."[36]

By skillfully resolving or in some cases sidestepping the most controversial of the issues that still beset the drive for industrial education, the framers of the Smith-Hughes Act provided enduring federal aid to vocational training in secondary schools. The reservations of organized labor, for example, were substantially overcome by vesting the administration of vocational education in the hands of vocational educators rather than manufacturers. Labor was at least as wary of the competence of professional educators to administer such a program as were the manufacturers, but from their point of view, public schools as the site of vocational education did not pose nearly as strong a threat to flooding the labor market as would be vocational education controlled by the manufacturers. In addition, with programs under the aegis of the public schools, the National Education Association saw the legislation as enhancing their growing professional standing. Perhaps the most critical opposition came in the form of "states rights," including the long-standing belief in local control of education. By placing the control of the programs in the states and localities subject only to rather loose federal guidelines, however, that objection was mitigated. In addition, rural constituencies were appeased by the inclusion of agricultural programs of study. Although agricultural education had not been of interest to NAM and was only belatedly incorporated into NSPIE's political agenda, important precedents existed for federal support of scientific farming and the development of agricultural stations to aid farmers, and this made the inclusion of vocational agriculture in the provisions seem part of an ongoing program of support. The Smith-Lever Act of 1914, for example, made agricultural education a prime beneficiary of federal largesse. There was not only precedent for federal support of agriculture but a politically powerful reason for including it. Support just for industrial education (with some supplementary funding for home economics) could be interpreted as favoring industrial states in the North, although certain southern interests found the idea of building an industrial base an inviting prospect as well.

As finally enacted, the Smith-Hughes Act incorporated support for vocational agriculture as well as trade and industrial education and home economics. Specifically, the Smith-Hughes Act provided support in the form of federal matching funds for the salaries of teachers in those subjects, and $1 million was appropriated for teacher training in vocational education. Backing for supervisory personnel was later incorporated. Commercial subjects, however, such as typewriting, bookkeeping, and stenography, were excluded. Congress may have been reluctant to antagonize the burgeoning private secretarial and commercial schools by supporting clerical education in the public schools, but the omission is still glaring in the face of the extraordinarily rapid growth in office work.

The Smith-Hughes Act specified that before a state could receive funds, it must establish a responsible vocational board whose job it would be to develop a state plan that would indicate precisely how the funds would be used. Strict guidelines were put into place in terms of the beneficiaries of the legislation, the instructional time devoted to vocational training, and the actual content in order to insure that the money could not be expended for general education purposes. For example, under the provisions, federal money would be available only for schools "of less than college grade and shall be designed to meet the needs of persons over fourteen years of age who are preparing for a trade or industrial pursuit or who have entered upon the work of a trade and industrial pursuit," and "at least half the time of . . . instruction [must] be given to practical work on a useful or productive basis, such instruction to extend over not less than nine months per year and not less than thirty hours per week." To further ensure that financing would not be provided for educational purposes unrelated to work, evening industrial schools were required to "confine instruction to that which is supplemental to daily employment."[37] In effect, the plans the states submitted under such guidelines would become legal contracts between them and the federal government, but these contracts allowed local officials to retain their basic educational structure. With congressional supporters from the South suspicious of those federal initiatives in education that would intrude upon the system of segregated schools, the inclusion of provisions for local administration of the funds once the guidelines were met was critical. Local control was also a major issue outside the South, with state and local school officials carefully guarding their prerogatives and privileges.

A highly significant but sometimes overlooked consequence of the terms of Smith-Hughes was the creation of a cadre of committed supporters of vocational education whose status and careers were tied to its promotion. Much of the aid provided through Smith-Hughes went for salaries of teachers, supervisors, and directors of the school programs being supported. Between 1917–18 and 1925–26 alone, appropriations for salaries of school personnel in agriculture rose from $548,000 to $3,027,000 and in home economics and industrial trades from $566,000 to $3,050,000.[38] The burgeoning contingent of teachers, supervisors, and teacher educators of vocational subjects supported by the new legislation, as well as the members of state vocational boards, now constituted a potent new interest group that could be relied on to provide dedicated support for the extension and expansion of vocational education at both the state and federal levels. The renamed National Society for Vocational Education (later the American Vocational Association) forged these vocational educators into an aggressive and highly effective political lobby.

As part of the effort to create a distance from policies and practices in general education, the Smith-Hughes Act created a Federal Board of Vocational Education that included the secretaries of commerce, agriculture, and labor along with the commissioner of education and three citizen members. A six-member executive staff was also appointed. Conspicuously, seven of the thirteen members of the board and its staff had been committed members of NSPIE. The functioning of the board as an independent agency served to shield vocational education from U.S. Office of Education oversight in the administration of Smith-Hughes's provisions. Some of the chief lobbyists for the legislation were now in charge of administering it. Prosser, for example, was the natural choice as staff director, and in that role, he continued to perform as a highly effective advocate for vocational education. By 1919, all forty-eight states had instituted courses under the provisions of the Smith-Hughes Act.[39]

SMITH-HUGHES AND THE EDUCATION OF WOMEN

The Smith-Hughes Act was to affect the course of American education at least until the end of the twentieth century, but given the mystique that has emerged around vocational education, many of the actual effects of the bill's provisions still are clouded. A few of those effects as well as the miscalculations that surrounded Smith-Hughes, however, began to manifest themselves within a few years. One thing is certain: The symbolic as well as the material changes attributable to Smith-Hughes affected different segments of the school population in different ways.

Unexpectedly, the education of women was the most profoundly affected of the changes in the years immediately following Smith-Hughes. The clear impetus for the legislation was industrial education for the factory floor, and with few women being trained for such work, this left home economics as the most obvious alternative for the vocational education of women. Actually, the two women members of a Commission on National Aid to Education appointed in 1914 to help frame the bill, Florence Marshall, director of the Manhattan Trade School for Girls, and Agnes Nestor, president of the International Glove Worker's Union, were eager to include industrial trade training for women in the new legislation. In fact, their appointment to the commission, something that Prosser had urged, was tied to their known advocacy in behalf of trade training for women as opposed to home economics. The General Federation of Women's Clubs, however, lobbied vigorously in behalf of home economics, and the House education committee finally added it to the bill in preference to supporting industrial education for women.[40] In her autobiography, Nestor recalled: "We felt that if domestic science were allowed the greater appropriation, it would be too easy to push all the girls into that field and not given them the technical training they were likely to find themselves in need of."[41] The fears of Marshall and Nestor proved to be substantially justified.

That the inclusion of home economics in the provisions of the Smith-Hughes Act was somewhat belated did not dilute its impact. A 1932 study indicated that, whereas the number of high schools offering home economics stood at 53 percent in 1915–17, that percentage had risen to 95 percent in 1930–31.[42] In California in 1922, ninth-grade enrollments in home economics were more than double that of industrial education.[43] Although home economics was hardly the trade training that was uppermost in the minds of the chief promoters of vocational education, its new prominence was of some practical import and very considerable symbolic significance. In the practical sense, it presumably reduced inefficiency in the curriculum by preparing girls directly for their destiny as homemakers; in the symbolic sense, home economics performed the critical function of responding to vague but deeply troubling anxieties that the new industrial age would somehow undermine traditional values. Although obvious uncertainty existed as to what the eventual role of women would be, particularly in the light of a shifting job market, the education of girls was being directed to what was assumed to be their probable social role. Some vocational education for women was provided, but for the most part, it was considered to be only temporarily useful. As Snedden put it, women "must be prepared, as it were, for two careers, the first of which will continue for a few years only; the other of which must be prolonged and for which a proper education is highly desirable."[44] The effect of embodying those predictions into Smith-Hughes, of course, was to accelerate gender-based curricular differentiation.[45]

Data collected by George S. Counts in his 1922 study of what he called "the selective character of secondary education" provide some evidence that the study of home economics was attuned to racial considerations. Although blacks and whites enrolled in the four-year general program of studies in almost equal percentages (43.4 to 44.1 percent), the home economics program was a source of wide enrollment differences. In St. Louis high schools, 9.5 percent of white high school students were enrolled in four-year home economics programs, whereas among African Americans that percentage was 30.4, more than three times the enrollment of white girls.[46] For black, immigrant, and Hispanic girls, home economics was not so much an avenue to refined domestic skills or "scientific" management of the home as it was a way to enter "the service" or menial jobs, such as laundry work.[47] In 1924, the supervisor of home economics in Texas, for example, described the program for Mexican girls leading to domestic service as one of the "best examples of training" that she knew of.[48] One study reported in 1931 that in twelve southern states, 85 percent of black high schools required home economics of their girls, whereas only 30 percent of the white high schools did.[49] Home economics was also considered to be particularly desirable for girls in rural areas. For those young women, home economics commonly included such activities as raising poultry and vegetable gardening, although in the 1920s only 6 percent of young women were enrolled in vocational agriculture *per se*. Despite the prevailing notion that the study of home economics would somehow keep women "down on the farm," home economics enrollments in rural areas were similar to those in urban schools. The aspirations of rural girls, not unlike their urban counterparts, were in the direction of clerical work, teaching, and nursing.[50]

Home economics enrollments not only surged after Smith-Hughes; home economics as a program of studies accelerated racial, ethnic, and class differentiation as well as differentiation by gender. This should not be surprising. If the curriculum was to be based on a prediction as to a student's adult social and occupational role, then it should be expected that the variables of gender, race, ethnicity, and class would be given considerable weight. A pervasive pattern of discrimination, limited English proficiency in some cases, and restricted educational opportunity may have made home economics one of very few available educational options for these girls. Nevertheless, it is in this sense that Dewey's warning of the potential for predication to eventuate in "social predestination" seems especially apropos.

CONFUSIONS AND MISCALCULATIONS: THE CASE OF CLERICAL EDUCATION

The new federal legislation did not create the idea that education was primarily a preparation for an adult role, but it did put the imprimatur of the federal government on an emerging educational ideal that made it the school's most urgent task. What is somewhat surprising about the immediate aftermath of the Smith-Hughes Act is the extent to which the promoters of vocational education and the framers of the legislation miscalculated. Little evidence exists that the immediate purposes of the act were realized. Industrial trade training experienced a slight boost in enrollments after Smith-Hughes, but the effect on home economics was far greater. If the central thrust of Smith-Hughes was to prepare youth for their roles as industrial workers, there is little credible evidence that it did. The United States emerged as the world's most powerful industrial nation and became a leading competitor in world markets as NAM so fervently desired, but these developments can hardly be attributed to the modest skill training that American schools provided to such a small minority of its youth. If anything, promoters of vocational education seem to have seriously underestimated the swiftness of technological advance and the changing nature of the labor market, as well as the effects of division of labor on work itself. Even before Smith-Hughes, increasing specialization in industrial labor and the assembly line had had a major de-skilling effect in the workplace, and this reduced sharply the need for extensive vocational training.

In 1921, Paul H. Douglas (later Senator Douglas of Illinois) in his now classic examination of apprenticeship and industrial education noted that the craft-based skills that were central to Smith-Hughes were already passé. His study of the Emergency Fleet Corporation, which undertook to train workers in the shipyard trades, for example, found that "the average training period for all men in the seventy-one yards for which statistics were available, was only nineteen days!"[51] The work requiring a high level of skill was repair of malfunctioning machinery, not just in shipbuilding but in industry generally. As Douglas pointed out, however, "repair work claims but a small proportion of the laboring force."[52] The institution of apprenticeship was moribund, but it was dying for good reason. An extended period of apprenticeship training was no longer needed to enter the industrial workforce; providing extended vocational training in schools was just as pointless. "Learning a trade," Douglas found, "was no longer a difficult affair."[53] As he put it, "leaders in the vocational education movement have been . . . reluctant to face the facts of modern large-scale production with its specialization of labor. They have been trying to equip the boy with an education that he does not need and cannot utilize."[54] The provisions of the Smith-Hughes Act reflected that failure to appreciate the new industrial facts of life.

If anything, the most significant of the concrete changes in job training after Smith-Hughes were the effects that were, if not exactly unanticipated, at least incidental to the main thrust of the legislation. Commercial education is a case in point. Like home economics, commercial education was not associated with the kind of industrial labor that was central to the drive for vocational education, but unlike home economics, commercial subjects were conspicuously absent from the provisions of Smith-Hughes. The shift in the nature of labor markets, however, made commercial employment and commercial courses of study an ever more popular option for high school students, particularly girls. In 1870, 97.5 percent of the clerical workforce was men. In 1880, the percentage of women in commercial work had climbed to only 6 percent, but by 1910, women constituted 35 percent of the clerical workforce.[55] In 1900, the number of girls enrolled in commercial courses in public high schools stood at 35,757. By 1917, the year the Smith-Hughes Act went into law, that enrollment had almost quadrupled to 138,043. While office work was overwhelmingly male-dominated in the nineteenth century as was commercial education, the rapid expansion of office jobs as well as specialization in the early twentieth-century workplace opened up new opportunities for women.[56] As a result, private commercial and business schools were booming. In 1900, enrollments in such schools were 68,890. By 1918, a year after Congress passed the Smith-Hughes Act, private school enrollments reached 243,185, of which 138,043 were women.[57] One study indicated that in Boston in 1913, over 63 percent of girls in public high schools were taking at least one commercial course.[58] In 1915, two years before Smith-Hughes funding was available, female student enrollments in commercial subjects in the public schools of California had already reached 52 percent.[59] When it became evident that women—and men as well—were flocking to private commercial schools in such large numbers, public schools found it necessary to expand their commercial course offerings even without Smith-Hughes funding.[60]

When Counts surveyed the high schools of Bridgeport, Connecticut; Mt. Vernon, New York; St. Louis, Missouri; and Seattle, Washington, he discovered that a full 24.9 percent of the girls expected to pursue a clerical career after graduation, second only to college entrance (36.5 percent) in terms of aspirations. An additional 5.7 percent of girls expressed their intention to go to a business college.[61] Apparently, this was not because vocationalists had consciously worked to promote commercial education for girls. According to historian Harvey Kantor, the initiative for what he calls "the sexual transformation of commercial education" came not from educators but "from the girls themselves."[62] U.S. Office of Education data indicate that, overall, 11 percent of high school students were enrolled in what was called business education in 1910; in 1922, the next year that data were collected and five years after Smith-Hughes, enrollments had skyrocketed to 42.1 percent. Enrollments in all business subjects rose from roughly 739,000 public high school students in 1910 to 2,155,000 in 1922.[63] In little more than a decade, enrollments in business subjects had nearly tripled.

Although the leading proponents of Smith-Hughes were nearly silent on the question of commercial education, young women were unquestionably shifting their aspirations from the shop floor or from domestic employment to office work (see Figure 10). For obvious reasons, these dramatic changes cannot be attributed to Smith-Hughes; they are instead mainly a function of changes in the labor market and particularly the changing role of women in the workplace. If Smith-Hughes actually was meant to tie school job training to the workplace, then in the case of women at least, the legislation was bungled. By emphasizing industrial training in manufacturing and vocational agriculture rather than in commercial subjects, the framers of Smith-Hughes were firing at the wrong target with regard to the education of women—and probably men as well.

Despite the miscalculations and confusions that beset the actual legislation and the surprisingly paltry results when measured in terms of changes that were being most actively sought, the victory represented by Smith-Hughes was a mighty one when viewed in terms of its symbolic significance. The victory of the forces aligned in support of Smith-Hughes marked the triumph of the image of the sweaty, muscular "young Vulcan" over the prissy, bookish "penny-a-liner," and with that victory came the entitlement for an educational ideal that was ultimately to transform the American curriculum. Although Americans had always thought of themselves as a "can-do" people, the Industrial Revolution had made the remote intellectual values presumably being advanced by their schools seem all the more irrelevant. In a curriculum that still emphasized academic subjects, as the Committee of Ten report had so

FIGURE 10. Class in business machines operation, Seattle, Washington. Demand for clerical education was so great that school districts found it necessary to expand their offerings even without support from the Smith-Hughes Act. *Courtesy Seattle Public Schools.*

140

ardently championed in 1893, Americans were being presented with an education that was at odds with their own image of themselves. In this sense, whether vocational education actually provided the skill training that modern industrial society required or even whether students were enrolling in subjects supported by Smith-Hughes hardly mattered. What mattered a great deal was the symbolic repudiation of what was regarded as the traditional elitist curriculum and a simultaneous validation of the values of the hardworking laborer, honest tiller of the soil, and devoted helpmate. The image of the office worker replete with sleeve garter and green eyeshade just did not carry the same emotional loading. Some opponents of vocationalism like Charles W. Eliot, the venerated president of Harvard University and architect of the Committee of Ten report, were drawn into an abject recantation. Remaining defenders of an academic education like William Torrey Harris and W. E. B. Du Bois were outnumbered and outflanked.

It was not simply a case of the nineteenth-century symbol of the noble artisan re-emerging in the twentieth. The Industrial Revolution and the triumph of corporate capitalism could not be denied. If the ideal advanced by the manual training movement was a version of Woodward's "young Vulcans," then the ideal of the new vocational education became the efficient producer of goods, as Snedden had urged. While these two ideals are not quite the same, they manifestly complement each other. One symbolizes the moral imperative; the other the economic one. The dignity of work becomes inexorably intertwined with tangible rewards in the workplace; merged into a single ideal—a symbolic affirmation of work as noble, even heroic, combined with the promise of economic gain and an efficient social order—they become the basis for how the schools were to be seen by most Americans.

Crucial to the ascendance of the new educational ideal was the strong perception that American education was failing. By the turn of the century, a number of reforms were being advocated that would address that failure, but most of them, such as the reforms introduced by John Dewey through his Laboratory School at the University of Chicago, lacked the support of potent political interest groups and, in the end, the public appeal to make much of an impact. His reforms had no NSPIE behind them and no NAM. Among the various reform initiatives emerging at the turn of the century, success was bestowed not on those reforms that were most intellectually satisfying or most socially responsible, or even that offered the best chance of addressing the genuine needs of the burgeoning school population, but on those reforms that attracted the most powerful actors in the political arena. The appeal of an educational reform that on the one hand promised direct and immediate economic benefits, as the NAM so insistently argued, and on the other offered to make American schools more satisfying or at least more tolerable to the swelling school population, as the Douglas Commission so earnestly sought, proved too alluring to the American public to be denied. In short order, principles of the new vocationalism became incorporated into what was in effect a new national education policy.

CARDINAL PRINCIPLES: ARTICULATION OF A NATIONAL POLICY

A public expression of new national policy on education was not long in coming. At the center of that effort was Clarence Kingsley. In 1912, in another of his fateful moves, Snedden brought Kingsley to Massachusetts as a supervisor of secondary education. From a rather obscure position as a mathematics teacher at Manual Training High School in Brooklyn, New York, Kingsley had already begun to achieve national prominence as chair of the NEA's Committee of Nine on the Articulation of High School and College (1911), and his new position as one of Snedden's trusted assistants cemented his growing stature as an educational reformer.

In the summer of 1913, the president of the National Education Association (NEA) appointed Kingsley to chair of the Commission for the Reorganization of Secondary Education. Around that time, Kingsley presented a portent of his ideas on the purposes of education at the NEA national convention, arguing that "The school must assist in the whole process of adjusting the pupil to life." As he saw it, the near collapse of the theory of mental discipline as a justification for academic subjects, along with the dramatic rise in secondary school enrollments over the previous two decades, lent credence to a reconsideration of the functions of schooling and a broadening of the curriculum beyond the traditional subject boundaries. "When . . . [the] discipline theory was questioned and abandoned," Kingsley declared, "the way was opened for the next step, vocational training, which means specialized training, training for industries, for commerce, and for agriculture, as well as for the professions."[64] By implying that the study of academic subjects was simply a form of specialized preparation "for the professions," Kingsley was in effect arguing that other forms of training—for factory labor, for example— had the same status and should occupy an equally important place in the school curriculum. In that regard, Kingsley expressed high praise for the work of the Vocation Bureau of Boston in their efforts to provide vocational guidance for the youth of the city and to the Middletown, Connecticut, schools for offering a course in which information is provided on fifty vocations.

Less than a year later, Kingsley reported to the High School Masters' Club of Massachusetts on the progress that had been made by the Commission on the Reorganization of Secondary Education. Once again, he struck the theme of an institution that needed to free itself from what he regarded as elitist traditions. Schools, he insisted, must train not only the leaders of the coming generation but the "rank and file as well." The criterion in this reorganization would be the needs of society. "I believe," he said, "we should say that the controlling aims of the modern high school must be stated in terms of the kind of boys and girls of eighteen who are needed by society rather than in terms of the subjects to be mastered."[65] In expressing such ideas, Kingsley was taking a position fundamentally consistent with that of his mentor Snedden, extending even to the use of Snedden's term "rank and file" to denote students whose needs were presumably not being met by the academic curriculum. That these ideas were expressed in terms of a rejection of an elitist tradition in favor of a democratic one made his arguments all the more persuasive.

When the Commission on the Reorganization of Secondary Education issued its much admired *Cardinal Principles of Secondary Education* in 1918, the conjunction of social efficiency and vocationalism was brought to a national audience. The message, however, was delivered in a diluted form, and this may account in part for its overwhelmingly favorable reception. The report is not so much a straightforward expression of a single ideology as it is a medley of the reform creeds that were then competing for dominance. The report, says historian Edward A. Krug, "was a masterly summary of doctrines current at that time, and it worked them out in a somewhat original combination."[66] The dominant refrain, however, as he also indicates, is clearly social efficiency.

As would be expected from Kingsley's earlier statements, *Cardinal Principles* is saturated with the language of democracy, and this served to mute its underlying social efficiency orientation. Some accounts attribute the emphasis on democracy to Dewey's influence on the commission.[67] To be sure, John Dewey had published his *Democracy and Education* two years before the report was issued, but there is no direct or even indirect reference to Dewey's work in the report. As would be expected, there is a condemnation of the school subjects as they were conventionally taught, but criticism of the traditional curriculum had become extremely common by the time the report was issued, and the tenor of the reforms that the report embodies is manifestly reflective of the criticisms of the likes of Bobbitt, Charters, and Snedden rather than of Dewey. Neither is the report's repeated references to democracy evidence that Kingsley was reflecting Deweyan ideas in contradistinction to those of his mentor, Snedden. If there is a direct influence behind the oft repeated references to democracy (and there might not be), it is likely to be the wave of patriotism engendered by American participation in World War One rather than Dewey's book. More particularly, as historian Jurgen Herbst has pointed out, the report might have been influenced by a statement issued by the Creel Committee on Public Information in 1917 declaring that the Great War was being fought "to make the world safe for democracy."[68]

Although there is no reason to question the sincerity of Kingsley's commitment to democracy, his somewhat subdued but nevertheless discernible dedication to social efficiency colored his sense of how democracy was to be defined. The democratic ideal, the report asserts, "demands that human activities be placed upon a high level of efficiency; that to this efficiency be added an appreciation of the significance of these activities and loyalty to the best ideals involved; and that the individual choose that vocation and those forms of social service in which his personality may develop and become most effective."[69] For Kingsley, democracy required the highest order of efficiency on the part of its citizens, and therefore, the adult role of a citizen in a democracy needed to be anticipated. The curriculum could then be attuned to that specific role, and waste would thereby be kept to a minimum.

Prediction in the case of women took the form of acknowledging that while many girls may "enter wage-earning occupations directly from the high school [they] remain in them for only a few years, after which home making becomes their lifelong occupation."[70] This is precisely the position that Snedden had advanced in 1910.[71] In this regard, *Cardinal Principles* was especially critical of academic requirements for young women, blaming, of course, the colleges. "[T]raditional ideals of preparation for higher institutions," the report declared, " are particularly incongruous with the actual needs and future responsibilities of girls."[72] In general, the emphasis of the *Cardinal Principles* on education as direct preparation for one's social and vocational destiny is virtually the antithesis of what Dewey saw as the role of education in a democracy.

The centerpiece of Kingsley's report was the seven aims: "health, command of fundamental processes, vocation, worthy use of leisure, worthy home membership, citizenship, and ethical character."[73] Education would become the instrument for achieving those aims. The inclusion of "worthy use of leisure" as one of the seven aims probably derives, oddly enough, from the transformation of the workplace. For Americans, idleness had long been, in Benjamin Franklin's characterization, "the devil's workshop"; but with the coming of industrialization, leisure became a tantalizing prize dangled before the worker as reward for labor that was increasingly routine. As relief from monotonous work, leisure was now serious business, and with scientific management came the idea of structured leisure.[74] No longer conceived of as simply idleness, leisure, like everything else on Kingsley's list of aims, had to be conscientiously prepared for as a school function. In general, the achievement of externally supplied aims to whose achievement education was somehow to contribute was foreign to Dewey's way of thinking. "[T]he educational process," he said in *Democracy and Education*, "has no end beyond itself; it is its own end." Aims for Dewey were never something supplied through "external dictation," whether the source be the federal government, state departments of education, prestigious individuals, or commissions of the National Education Association. "In our search for aims in education," Dewey emphasized, "we are not concerned, therefore, with finding an end outside of the education process to which education is subordinate. Our whole conception forbids."[75]

With the exception of "command of fundamental processes" (reading, writing, and arithmetic), all the aims proposed in *Cardinal Principles* represent categories of life activities, precisely as Bobbitt and other efficiency oriented educators were urging at the time. The function of secondary education as the report saw it was nothing less than getting youth ready to perform in the most efficient manner possible in their health activities, leisure activities, ethical behavior, as members of families, as citizens, and of course, as workers. In short order, these aims became widely accepted as the supreme wisdom on the question of what secondary education was all about. Snedden's earlier proclamation that the academic subjects be made to "pass in review" became one of the report's most important recommendations. Subjects like history, physics, mathematics, music, and English were called upon to reorganize themselves so as to demonstrate their functional efficiency in terms of meeting one or more of those seven aims. If they could not, they faced the prospect of being expunged. In line with Snedden's conception of a liberally educated person as an efficient consumer, the subjects identified with liberal education, as much as vocational subjects, had to be governed by the criterion of potential adult use.

In a singular departure from Snedden's long-standing position, Kingsley's report strongly endorsed the comprehensive high school, thus largely settling the debate over dual control and the large-scale creation of specialized vocational high schools. In effect, Kingsley was rejecting the German system so long admired by the National Association of Manufacturers and the institutionally bifurcated system of secondary education that Snedden endorsed. Instead, he was recommending a form of secondary education where students, regardless of anticipated social role, would rub shoulders in the same institution, the comprehensive high school. Kingsley's compromise, nevertheless, strongly encouraged curricular differentiation within that institution. A central recommendation in his report was that, "The work of the senior high school should be organized into differentiated curriculums," and furthermore, that "the basis of differentiation should be, in the broad sense of the term, vocational, thus justifying the names commonly given, such as agricultural, business, clerical, industrial, fine-arts, and household arts curriculums."[76] Within the confines of the same institution and under the same administrative control, groups of adolescents at a relatively early age were to be routed in relation to their prospective social and occupational roles, and the curriculum for each of these groups was to be adjusted in keeping with the imperatives of an education governed by their probable destination.

Although Snedden and Kingsley shared a commitment to vocationalism as well as to social efficiency, Snedden expressed disappointment as to the extent to which his educational vision had been reflected in Kingsley's report. While commending Kingsley for his "quiet persistence, patience and insight," Snedden thought that the seven aims were in danger of becoming what he called "mystic principles" because they lacked "visible or demonstrable connections with specific subjects."[77] He wanted, in other words, an even more explicit and direct connection between the subjects of study and functional aims. Moreover, to him, only health and vocation met the sociological test of representing a natural grouping of activities, and in the case of vocation, "the report almost completely misses the significance of the extension of vocational education through schools." Particularly irksome to Snedden was the support being given to the comprehensive high school. As he saw it,

> there is not the slightest reason why suitable qualified persons should not through special schools, be trained as effectively as persons are now trained for dentistry, nursing and pattern-making, for such other vocations as tailoring, jewelry salesmanship, poultry farming, coal cutting, stationary engine firing, waiting on table (hotel), cutting (in shoe factory), automobile repair, teaching of French in secondary school, mule spinning, power machine operating (for readymade clothing), raisin grape growing, general farming suited to Minnesota, linotype composition, railway telegraphy, autogenous welding, and street car motor driving.[78]

Although Snedden expressed approval of the statement of the purpose of vocational education—"vocational education should equip the individual to secure a livelihood"—he objected to the idea that such training could be carried forward effectively in the context of the comprehensive high school. Declaring Kingsley's report "almost hopelessly academic in the unfavorable sense,"[79] Snedden considered it just too tame.

WINNERS AND LOSERS

The particular issue of a dual system of education which had initially stirred up so much heat in the debate over vocationalism in the second decade of the twentieth century was resolved as Kingsley, not Snedden, had proposed. Vocational education, for the most part, became a program of studies in comprehensive high schools, although large city school districts did create separate vocational high schools along the lines of Snedden's recommendations. Rather than a system of specialized high schools along the German model, the comprehensive high school became the dominant form of secondary education in the United States. Although Snedden may have lost the battle over a dual system of schools, he won the larger victory in his contretemps with Dewey. Vocational and general education were now separated by a widening curricular chasm. Under the provisions of the Smith-Hughes Act, for example, the critical control of vocational education at the federal level was lodged in a separate agency, the Federal Board for Vocational Education, which was administratively independent of the U.S. Office of Education. In secondary schools, students were now labeled in terms of their educational and social destinies, and their program of studies was largely determined by those prognostications, as *Cardinal Principles* had advocated. In the matter of how education came to be viewed in relation to the larger social order, Snedden more accurately reflected the sentiments of the majority of Americans, while Dewey articulated the aspirations of a small minority. Rather than supporting an educational system that sought to address social injustice by creating an idealized social community in school and installing a curriculum designed to promote critical intelligence to the fullest extent possible, as Dewey fervently desired, Americans had reached a consensus, as articulated in *Cardinal Principles*, that secondary students would attend the same institution but follow separate curricular paths in the interest of social and occupational adjustment.

The language of *Cardinal Principles* is studiously balanced, but the social ideal that ultimately emerges is one in which the adjustment of the individual to existing social conditions takes precedent over the reconstruction of both the social order and the workplace. Although references to democracy permeate the report, and although Kingsley's basic moderation eventually comes through, his democracy is, in the end, one that emphasizes the preservation of order and stability over change and social renewal. Dewey's conception of democracy, by contrast, emphasized the adjustment of society to the individual at least as much as the individual to society, with social change being continually effected through intelligent social action. In Dewey's democracy, the accent was always on change rather than stability. In marked contrast to the continuously renewing democracy that Dewey envisioned, the kind of democracy that Snedden sought and that *Cardinal Principles* substantially endorsed was simply a more efficient version of what existed already. It was a democracy where American citizens were trained directly to perform their specialized functions as the doctrine of social efficiency demanded and especially in the workplace as reflected in the emerging ideal of vocationalism. A school's success would be gauged in terms of its demonstrated proficiency in training its students for their anticipated tasks. Dewey's opposition to such a conception of democracy was unequivocal. "We lose rather than gain in the change from serfdom to free citizenship," he says in *Democracy and Education*, "if the most prized result of the change is simply an increase in the mechanical efficiency of the human tools of production."[80] This, however, was the direction in which American vocational education and, indeed, much of national as well as state educational policy was headed.

 6

ADJUSTING THE INDIVIDUAL TO A "PARTICULAR FORM OF SOCIETY"

Vocationalism Ascendant in a Business Culture, 1920–1929

Education means many things to many men. To the classicist, it is the ability to derive enjoyment from the study of the ancient philosophers, poets and writers. To the culturalist, it is the ability to enjoy the finer things of life. To the scientist, it often means a command of the special knowledge that goes with his specialty.

Lying back of all these conceptions, and of many more that have been held during the history of civilized mankind, has run an underlying idea, often obscured in educational controversy, but persisting nevertheless. The underlying idea may be expressed somewhat as follows: Education is the result of experiences whereby we become more or less able to adjust ourselves to the demands of the particular form of society in which we live and work.

Charles A. Prosser and Charles R. Allen, 1925[1]

World War One not only marked what Henry May called "the end of American innocence" but the conclusion of the era of political and social reform that had characterized the administrations of presidents Theodore Roosevelt and Woodrow Wilson.[2] What was emerging was a period of complacency at home and growing dominance abroad. In the 1920s, the status of industry reached new heights, and the needs and requirements of business and manufacturing moved even closer to the forefront of public consciousness. A new level of prosperity was bringing something close to veneration for the new corporate economy and a celebration of the benefits that

148

it had brought. The real income of workers remained fundamentally static from 1890 to 1918 but rose dramatically in the 1920s. A remarkable increase in productivity led to a general prosperity heretofore unknown in the United States or, for that matter, anywhere else. The sources of this prosperity seemed evident. There was the kind of technological innovation that Henry Ford had introduced in 1914 in Highland Park, Michigan, the continuous assembly line; there were new inventions, such as the electric motor, which by the 1920s had virtually replaced the steam engine; and, of course, there was scientific research into new methods of production which, according to some accounts, had produced large gains in productivity with no increase in the labor force.[3]

THE PERVASIVENESS OF THE BUSINESS CULTURE

Calvin Coolidge, who succeeded Warren Harding as president in 1923, unabashedly equated business enterprise with America itself. In 1925, he summed up the prevailing American creed in a single pithy remark. "The business of America," he said, "is business"[4] As the decade drew to a close, even the muckraking journalist Lincoln Steffens was caught up in the new enthusiasm for the success of corporate capitalism, proclaiming, "Big business in America is producing what the Socialists hold up as their goal: food, shelter, and clothing for all."[5]

The new reverence being accorded business was also reflected in the best-selling book of 1925 and 1926, a biography of Jesus entitled *The Man Nobody Knows*. The author, advertising executive Bruce Barton, depicted Jesus as a forerunner of the modern business executive whose organizational skills are reflected in his shrewd personnel decisions, including his choice of disciples. In a chapter entitled "The Founder of Modern Business," Barton reports on how the twelve-year-old Jesus became temporarily lost as he was being taken by his parents to the feast at Jerusalem. When Jesus is found, Mary asks, "Son why hast thou dealt thus with us?" For Barton, Jesus' reply provides an early indication of his proclivities in business:

> [W]hat interests us most in this one recorded incident of his boyhood is that fact that for the first time he defined the purpose of his career. He did not say, "Wist ye not that I must get ready to meet the arguments of men like these?" The language was quite different, and well worth remembering. "Wist ye not that I must be about my father's *business?*" he said. He thought of his life as *business*.[6]

Jesus was, according to Barton, not only the precursor of the modern businessman, but of the modern advertising executive, whose parables represented advertising at its best. Above and beyond the gaiety that is our abiding image of the "roaring twenties," there was business.

It was not simply that businesses themselves were now a prominent feature on the American landscape; the canons and codes of business had recast America's social institutions in powerful but sometimes unobtrusive ways. In the course of that process, the ethos of schooling was being radically altered. While vocational education existed alongside general education as a kind of alternative to it, vocationalism was now becoming established as an all-consuming educational ideal. Modern vocational education was born in the desire to meet the job requirements that accompanied industrialization, but that once limited function was now reaching far beyond trade training. School subjects generally were now being judged by the extent to which they met the demands of the workplace and reflected the prevailing business culture.

To a certain extent, the successes of vocationalism in the 1920s are reflected in cold data. In 1918, just a year after the passage of the Smith-Hughes Act, there were 5,257 teachers of vocational subjects in the United States, 3,236 of them males and 2,021 females. By 1930, that number had reached an astounding 24,876. Of these, 17,222 were males and 7,654 were females. In just twelve years, the male vocational teaching force had grown by about fivefold and the female force more than threefold.[7] At the least, the massive funding provided by Smith-Hughes for industrial education, vocational agriculture, and home economics was having the effect of exponentially increasing the number of teachers in those subjects. Evidently, the states had been committing resources to vocational education which, under the provisions of Smith-Hughes, would be matched by the federal government, and this permitted school districts to hire vocational teachers and supervisors in large numbers.

Whatever satisfaction the vocationalists derived from this success must have been tempered, however, by at least one sobering fact. Enrollments in the programs supported by Smith-Hughes were anything but electrifying. In 1915, two years prior to the passage of Smith-Hughes, enrollments in industrial subjects as a percentage of total enrollment in secondary schools stood at 12.9; in 1922, five years after passage, enrollment had risen only to a paltry 13.7, and by 1928, enrollments in industrial subjects actually slipped slightly to 13.5. In 1915, enrollments in vocational agriculture as a percentage of secondary school enrollments were 7.2; by 1922, that percentage had slipped significantly to 5.1, and by 1928, the enrollment percentage for vocational agriculture stood at only 3.7. Of the triumvirate of subjects supported by Smith-Hughes, only home economics showed a marked gain. Actually, the most dramatic rise in enrollments for home economics occurred between 1910 and 1915 when the percentage of secondary school students enrolled in that subject climbed from 3.8 to 12.9. Between 1915 and 1928, enrollments continued to rise modestly, reaching 14.3 in 1922 and 16.5 in 1928.[8] Only in home economics enrollments could the vocationalists really claim some success in terms of rising enrollments, and the virtues of home economics lay primarily in the symbolic message it sent as to the continued value school placed on domesticity. Few vocationalists were willing to make the argument that home economics was a bridge to the world of work. Even more significant than the matter of enrollments, however, was whether students taught vocational subjects actually benefited from such training in terms of their ability to obtain and hold a job or, for that matter, in any other respect. Data on that subject are notably lacking.

The failure of vocational education to demonstrate its efficacy did not deter school districts from extolling its virtues and embracing its claims. During the 1920s, the unnamed president of the school board in Middletown (actually Muncie, Indiana) proclaimed the triumph of vocationalism over other educational ideals that had presumably once guided the course of American schooling: "For a long time all boys were trained to be President. Then for a while we trained them all to be professional men. Now we are training boys to get jobs." This was not an inconsequential expression of abstract policy. It was reflected in the day-to-day school life that the children of Middletown experienced:

> Actual conditions of work in the city's factories are imported into the school shops; boys bring repair work from their homes; they study auto mechanics by working on an old Ford car; they design, draft, and make patterns for lathes and drill presses, the actual casting being done by a Middletown factory.

These activities were no longer considered to be on the periphery of the curriculum. Although Middletown's citizens complained here and there of a lowering of academic standards, "these vocational courses," the Lynds assert, "have caught the imagination of the mass of male tax-payers." One indication of this new status, they report, was that vocational supervisors were more highly paid than others in similar capacities, a consequence, in all likelihood, of the Smith-Hughes Act of 1917.

Nor did the change in the perception of the Middletown curriculum affect only the boys. For girls, programs in such areas as bookkeeping, stenography, and home economics were initiated or expanded. Homemaking as a school subject, for example, had been introduced only recently in Middletown's schools (1921–22) in the seventh and eighth grades. In line with the new emphasis being given to probable destination, home economics was designed "to meet the functional needs of the major group of the girls, who will be home-makers." The vocational education of girls in Middletown did not emphasize skills necessary to enter the workforce; the focus was on activities centered around "traditional household productive skills such as canning, baking, and sewing, rather than the rapidly growing battery of skills involved in the effective buying of ready-made articles."[9] Although boys and girls were being exposed to what were advertised as vocational studies by the 1920s, nostalgia seemed an element in the vocational courses designed for girls. The emphasis given to household activities rather than to job skills in vocational education of girls was precisely what Ella Flagg Young had been critical of at the NEA convention of 1915. Girls were being trained in traditional occupations associated with the home, while boys putatively were being given the skills needed to enter the workforce. This almost contradictory blending of romantic nostalgia with a desire to respond effectively to the new industrial economy was a central feature of vocationalism, as it had been in the case of manual training.

Robert and Helen Lynd, of course, chose Middletown as the subject of their classic sociological study because it was supposed to represent the typical American small city. There is reason to believe, therefore, that what Middletown's unidentified school board president proclaimed in mid 1920s was reasonably representative of new American attitudes toward schooling across the country. The decade of the 1920s was the period when the academic ideal of schooling, although retaining a few staunch defenders, was clearly in decline, while the criterion of direct utility in the American curriculum not just in the work arena but everywhere was reaching its zenith. The newly dominant ideal did not simply affect the content of the curriculum that the children and the youth of the nation were studying; it also was dramatically reflected in the ways in which a curriculum was to be fashioned.

A new technique of curriculum-making was also drawing its inspiration from the way vocational education was responding to the demands of the new industrial society. That new technique, usually called activity analysis or job analysis, was modeled after Gilbreth's painstaking analysis of the work of bricklayers and was widely employed in the construction of curricula. The logic was clear. If the ancient art of bricklaying could be scientifically disassembled and then reassembled according to the principles of scientific management, so could other kinds of work activity, and if work could be analyzed in this manner, so could other kinds of human activity. Once broken down into its component parts, all human activity could then become standardized, and idealized criteria could then be applied to the efficient performance of those activities. The way to improve the performance of bricklayers became the way to improve the performance not only of secretaries,[10] teachers,[11] and other occupations but of citizens and consumers. One simply had to isolate the characteristics that made for efficient performance of the activities that comprise those roles and prescribe the most efficient means for instilling them. The instrument for instilling them was, of course, a reconstructed curriculum.

SCHOOL SURVEYS AS A MECHANISM OF
CHANGING THE CURRICULUM

One relatively untapped source of evidence as to the extent that schools were changing in the first half of the twentieth century lies imbedded in school surveys, a popular educational practice that emerged in the late nineteenth century and reached its peak in the 1920s. As it evolved, a typical school survey would be initiated by a local administrator or school board and entailed bringing a national leader or leaders in education (usually with a team of data collectors) to report on the state of schooling in a particular school district. Although local school administrators initially were suspicious of outsiders intruding on their domain, in time, they came to view the practice as an effective vehicle for bringing about needed reforms. By the 1920s, it had become a widespread mechanism for reshaping school studies. David Tyack and Elizabeth Hansot describe the school survey as a practice "that would sweep the nation as a kind of crusade."[12]

As indicated by the Milwaukee experience in institutionalizing manual and vocational training, the most formidable obstacle to change was probably the public's reluctance to pay the bill for school reform. If, however, prominent national leaders with the status of George Strayer or Franklin Bobbitt could put their imprimatur on the need for change, then perhaps crucial public support could be marshaled. Since, by and large, these surveys were conducted by educational leaders who were considered "scientific" in outlook, practices associated with that approach tended to be promoted in those surveys. In this sense, school surveys became a potent vehicle for spreading a particular educational ideology and translating that ideology into scientifically efficient school practice. As historian Ellen Condliffe Lagemann puts it, "The school survey movement would not have been possible without tests and statistical devices that allowed researchers to measure the achievement of students and the costs of instruction and, then, through comparative statistical analysis, to determine which practices were apparently most effective, least costly, and therefore most efficient."[13] From the turn of the century until the 1960s, hundreds of such surveys were conducted.

Surveys are also invaluable sources of data. A typical comprehensive survey would include reports on the state of the physical facilities, the organization of the school system, the nature of the student body, the extent of equipment available, the administration, library resources, the competence and training of the teachers, and not least, the course of study. One of the most celebrated and comprehensive of these surveys examined the schools of Baltimore, Maryland, a school system which at the time was racially segregated. The survey was completed in 1921 under the direction of George D. Strayer of Teachers College, Columbia University, one of the most prolific of the school surveyors. The overall tone of the report was decidedly negative, with the special report on the secondary schools of Baltimore, directed by Thomas H. Briggs also of Teachers College, especially critical of Baltimore's high schools for not adjusting their predominantly academic curriculum to the demands of the new industrial society. School surveyors like Strayer and Briggs, of course, were not simply providing a dispassionate analysis of the problems of Baltimore's schools. They were bringing to that task their own strong convictions as to the problems of schools and of society. In an address delivered shortly after the Baltimore survey was completed, Briggs, for example, expressed in unequivocal terms what he believed to be the failure of American public education. The failure, he asserted, lies in the inability of the curriculum to adapt to social conditions and the new population of students entering secondary education as the *Cardinal Principles* report had so insistently urged. "The only justification for free public education," according to Briggs, "is that thereby the state intends to perpetuate itself and to promote its own interests." For him, this justification meant a more explicit commitment to what he regarded as the "basis of free public education," which he stated was "to fit each person to contribute better to the state." In a concise but fitting expression of social efficiency ideology, Briggs asserted that "the primary purpose of the school is to teach its pupils to do better the desirable things that they are most likely to do anyway."[14] Had the expression of this ideal been voiced only at an obscure meeting of education professionals, its significance, obviously, would have been limited; but it was the ideal that lay behind the curricular changes that Briggs brought to Baltimore and was reflected in scores of other surveys.

In the climate of the 1920s, the key to reforming Baltimore's schools was adapting the curriculum to the presumed needs of the new population of secondary school students by anticipating their future contributions to the wellbeing of the social order. Of understandable concern to the survey team was the low proportion of adolescents enrolled in the secondary schools of Baltimore. The report lists forty-one major cities for which data on enrollments in relation to various population indicators are given. Ranking first on the list was Portland, Oregon, where 3.06 percent of the city's population was enrolled in high school, whereas Baltimore, ranking forty-first, enrolled only 1.03 percent. The problem as they saw it was that "The curricula of Baltimore high schools are traditional and patched." Their recommendation was nothing less than the curriculum "be scrapped and remade in accordance with the needs of the youth of the city."[15] The remedy, in other words, for the failure of Baltimore's secondary schools to attract and hold a larger percentage of the teen-age population was to restructure the curriculum in line with the demands of modern life. Those demands, for the most part, entailed not a critical understanding of what it meant to live in a modern industrial society as a way of gaining a measure of control over one's life, as Dewey advocated, but in adjusting to the conditions that prevailed, as social efficiency doctrine dictated and as the *Cardinal Principles* reflected.

Once again, college entrance requirements represented a major obstacle to the realization of functional change. As the survey team saw it, no longer could Baltimore's high schools be controlled by the colleges. Their first recommendation was unequivocal: "The academic and college preparatory curriculum should be fearlessly reorganized in view of the actual needs of larger numbers of pupils, independent of specific college requirements." Moreover, students preparing for admission to Goucher College, the recommendation stated, "should not be obliged to take courses necessary to meet the requirements of Smith or Bryn Mawr," thus implying that even the college entrance function should be differentiated according to the demands of particular colleges.[16] As was becoming increasingly common, academic study was being seen as having little value other than preparation for admission to college.

Once freed of the curse of academic requirements, the program of studies would then bear a close resemblance to the kind of curriculum the *Cardinal Principles* recommended, a fact that the report, and Briggs in particular, explicitly acknowledged. The report, for example, lists the seven aims that Baltimore schools should follow:

Personal and community health
Ability in oral and silent reading, oral and written expression
Better home membership
Preparation for a vocation
Effective habits and ideals of citizenship
Worthy use of leisure
Standards of ethical character[17]

These are, of course, the seven aims of the *Cardinal Principles* with only minor changes in wording. Far from being a remote expression of educational policy, the recommendations of the *Cardinal Principles* committee were now becoming the yardstick for educational reform in school districts across the country.

For the Baltimore survey, separate reports were written in the areas of home economics and vocational education. In the home economics report, special attention was given to the effect that a properly conceived home economics course would have on the health of the community (the first of the seven aims). "What a waste it is," the report declared, "to feed patients into a great hospital system to be cured because lack of knowledge has prevented them from safeguarding health when information given in a home economics course might serve as a protection."[18] Recommendations, of course, centered on expanding offerings in home economics that not only emphasized meal preparation and household sanitation but the selection of fabrics for making clothing and the repair of clothing.

The report on vocational education began with a listing of the fifty-three principal occupations in the city of Baltimore, indicating the approximate number of workers in each of the occupations.[19] Included in the recommendations was an expansion of vocational education into eight new areas of skilled trades, including printing, shipbuilding, truck gardening, and "Trades and Occupations of Girls and Women."[20] Meeting the needs of the boys and girls in Baltimore's schools meant providing them with the occupational training that the industries of Baltimore required. But the report on vocational education did not neglect the other subjects of study. Mathematics was singled out for special criticism since the mathematics curriculum seemed to be based on "the idea of study for study's sake, with a resultant lack of practical value."[21] The survey team noted with satisfaction that the Massachusetts Institute of Technology and the University of Wisconsin were in the process of constructing a two-year course that would replace the traditional mathematics sequence. While the details of such a course were necessarily left out, the report indicated that the aim of the course should be clear: "It should be to give a command of those sections of mathematics needed as a working tool in industry and as part of a man's equipment to meet opportunities for promotion and the changing requirements of production."[22] Whatever had once been the lofty status accorded to mathematics in the school curriculum as a powerful intellectual tool, the study of mathematics was now being subordinated to the demands of industry and the workplace.

In a separate report on commercial education, the report declared, "Geometry, like algebra, cannot be justified as a required subject."[23] As to the subject of English, the report on commercial education complained that "No emphasis is placed on such business English as is required in business reports, accounting explanations, bookkeeping entries, catalog descriptions, credits and collection letters, sales letters, form letters, etc."[24] The survey team strongly endorsed a differentiated program of studies in English as a way of ameliorating these problems. The report also took issue with the claim that Spanish would be of practical value in office work. Their survey of businesses in Baltimore indicated "no appreciable demand for those who speak and write Spanish." In unequivocal terms, the report concluded that "Spanish as a required subject for all commercial students cannot be justified on any ground whatsoever."[25] It is evident that the vocationalization of the curriculum had by now reached far beyond specific courses in trade and commercial skills and was affecting the academic side of the curriculum.

The Baltimore survey that Strayer directed was not simply filed and forgotten. For years after it was issued, reports of the Baltimore Board of School

Commissioners continually referred to the recommendations of the report, even listing certain specific recommendations and then indicating progress made in relation to them. A decade after the survey had been completed, for example, the commissioners' report specifically undertook to review "what has been accomplished during the decade in carrying out the recommendations which Dr. Strayer's group made." As they saw it, that decade should be characterized as nothing less than "Baltimore's educational renaissance."[26] In a section entitled "Giving Effect to the Strayer Recommendations," the report systematically listed sixteen major recommendations along with a progress report in each case.[27] Clearly, the school survey had emerged as a major tool for getting recalcitrant school systems not only to abandon antiquated practices but to adopt the prevailing educational ideology.

Other school surveys in the 1920s and later followed a similar pattern in terms of organization and in the tenor of their recommendations. Many of them penetrated not simply the large urban centers but small towns and rural communities. In 1924, the survey of the town of Chanute, Kansas, for example, took the form of "running commentary" on the curriculum of elementary schools; for the curriculum of the junior and senior high schools, it consisted mainly of "constructive recommendations, based upon sound theories of curriculum construction."[28] These sound theories, it turned out, were avowedly those of Franklin Bobbitt, who had only two years before published a major survey in monograph form, *Curriculum Making in Los Angeles*.[29] The Chanute survey team criticized the senior high school's General Course (unlike the College Preparatory Course, the Commercial Course, and the Normal Training Course) for an absence of "certain outstanding social objectives." The objectives cited and recommended were exactly those of Bobbitt. Moreover, when objectives were enumerated, they tended to follow the pattern of numerous and highly explicit objectives that Bobbitt continually urged and had incorporated into his Los Angeles survey. Apart from recommending a wide range of clearly vocational and commercial subjects such as bookkeeping, stenography, building trades, vocational agriculture, and vocational homemaking, attention was also given to reconstructing the academic subjects. In first- and second-year English, for example, the surveyors indicated that "the subject *should be limited* to constructive English needed in speaking and writing" (emphasis added), and then went on to list twenty-seven explicit objectives for English, presumably reflecting that overall purpose.

A similar pattern appeared in the survey team's review of Chanute's junior high school curriculum. The "general objective" of third-year arithmetic, for example, was vocational guidance. Various kinds of occupations were listed, with the recommendation that each vocation be studied "from its mathematic aspect," such as "the mathematics of the vocation itself."[30] What was called "prevocational experience" was also recommended in the form of free electives including commercial subjects, industrial art, woodwork and drawing, printing, agriculture, sheet metal work, practical electricity, mechanical drawing, and applied design.[31]

Attention to vocational guidance was encouraged even in the elementary schools of Chanute. The report states unequivocally that "Vocational guidance should not be an after thought of the elementary school but should be consciously built for and carried through the elementary schools in an organized way and furnish a foundation for prevocational activities of the junior high school." In fourth grade, for example, the recommended curriculum calls for study of certain "fundamental occupations." While the idea of engaging young children in fundamental occupations like gardening or preparation of food is not necessarily vocational or even prevocational in nature, and was absolutely central to the curriculum of Dewey's Laboratory School, the specific emphasis in this version was explicitly to "furnish activities that gradually pyramid in directing [the child's] mind in vocational guidance thinking,"[32] whereas occupations in the Deweyan sense had a far different, virtually antithetical, purpose in mind.[33] From the elementary school on, the process of vocationalization of the curriculum was being endorsed and recommended in Chanute's schools.

Representative of the small rural communities is the survey of the Stanford, Illinois, schools. Much less grandiose in scope and more restricted in its recommendations than those of larger cities, the survey of this tiny community was actually conducted and written not by a nationally prominent educator such as Strayer but by John C. Chiddix, a graduate student at Illinois State Normal University working under the direction of one of its professors, M. R. Starker. At the time of the survey, the village of Stanford had a "static population" of only 600. Even including surrounding villages, such as Covel, which had no high school, the population of the Stanford community was no larger than 1,200. Much of this modest survey consisted of reporting on the educational achievement in various subjects as measured by widely used standardized tests. The results of the administration of the Thorndike-McCall Reading Scale, for example, revealed mixed results, with grades three and eight being "above standard" and grades four and six as well as all the high school grades being "below standard."[34] As an indication of the extent to which standardized testing had become common practice even in small towns and villages by the 1920s, Stanford pupils were tested in handwriting using the Ayres Handwriting Scale, in arithmetic using the Monroe Survey Arithmetic Test, in spelling using the Ayres Spelling Scale, in English using the Charters Diagnostic Language Test, in history using the Presseys Richards Test in American History, and in algebra using the Illinois Standardized Algebra Test. Scores in these areas were by and large disappointing. In no case were the scores on these tests unequivocally at or above the statistical standard, and in each case limited recommendations were made as to how the performance of the pupils could be raised.

Perhaps the most dramatic data to emerge from the survey of the Stanford schools relates to the extent to which courses in manual training, vocational education, and home economics were not only offered in this small community school district but required of all students. In 1923–24, when the survey was conducted, three years of vocational agriculture were required, with a fourth year optional. In addition, two years of manual training were required of all boys in the sophomore and junior years. For girls, a three-year sequence in home economics was required, with a concentration on cooking in the first year, sewing in the second, and the home in the third. The survey reports that the Styles Show staged by the girls at the end of each school year is "a community event of much interest."[35] The high school course of study also included commercial law, commercial geography, shorthand, typing, and bookkeeping. A year after the survey was conducted, in the 1925–26 school year, new required courses were added, including more agriculture, manual training, and domestic science. Chemistry was discontinued.

The emphasis on requiring vocational courses and home economics for girls in Stanford, Illinois, is one indication of what may have been a limited range of curricular options, particularly academic options, for rural school youth. A small school population practically dictated a restricted curriculum, and instituting requirements was one way to ensure enrollments in courses that might otherwise be poorly attended. In all likelihood, offering, even requiring, vocational subjects and home economics reflected popular sentiment in the community, but generous support by Smith-Hughes must have had something to do with the ability of the Stanford schools to offer them. Chemistry, of course, received no such support. Commenting on her education in rural Illinois in the early 1930s, one woman recalled: "I wanted to take world history, but the principal said there wasn't enough kids for it so I had to take shorthand. And I wanted to take sociology and economics, but there wasn't enough kids for them either so I had to take home ec."[36]

Another survey, not of a specific school system but of a large cross-section of secondary school principals, is especially revealing as to the extent to which industrial education and home economics actually were making inroads into the school curriculum during the 1920s. The study had its inception in an address by Frank Boynton of the NEA Department of Superintendence in which he raised questions as to whether, as he saw it, the "college entrance" function ought to continue to dominate the secondary school curriculum. That academic subjects such as algebra, chemistry, and foreign languages were now being seen merely as serving the purpose of admission to college was consistent with the idea that all subjects were inevitably preparatory for something off in the future, and that such subjects came to be called college entrance subjects is perfectly consistent with "probable destination" as the key criterion in the design of a curriculum. The problem as many school administrators saw it was that the requirements imposed by the colleges were exercising a greatly disproportionate and even pernicious influence on the secondary school curriculum. At the conclusion of Boynton's remarks, the Department of Superintendence passed a resolution requesting the Research Division of the NEA "to prepare a study on the problems presented in [the] address."[37]

With college entrance requirements increasingly seen as the chief obstacle to a thorough reordering of the secondary school curriculum, the NEA Department of Superintendence was charged with collecting data in order to confirm that contention. A focal point of the study were the recommendations of *Cardinal Principles*, which in the decade following its appearance had become a call to arms for functionally oriented educators. Of some 21,000 high school principals in the United States at the time, 5,000 were sent detailed questionnaires, and 1,352 replies were received from all forty-eight states. When asked whether they had actually "undertaken a reorganization of the high-school programs of studies . . . in line with the Cardinal Principles of Secondary Education," 689 or 56.1 percent of the principals replied in the affirmative. Since many more principals of larger high schools (defined as having an enrollment of 1,000 or more) as compared to principals of high schools with 100 or fewer students reported such a reorganization, 74 percent to 46.3 percent, the actual number of students affected by these curricular changes was probably much larger. When asked which subjects had been added to the curriculum within the last five years, 417 principals reported that they had added commercial subjects, 256 had added industrial arts, 124 had added home economics, and 100 had added counseling, guidance, morals, and manners (see Figure 11). By contrast, only 176 had added biological and physical science, 61 had added foreign languages, and 46 had added mathematics. Heading the list of subjects dropped from programs of study was science at 102. Last was home economics with 2.[38] If the results of the survey are to be believed, the direction that the curriculum was taking was clearly away from the academic, so-called college preparatory subjects and toward the presumably functional subjects that vocationalists demanded.

When the principals were asked how they would *like* to change their curricula, the results are even more startling, and it is here that the triumph of vocationalism is most evident. Whatever may have been the reluctance of students to enroll in vocational courses, they were clearly being encouraged to do so. Principals of both large and small high schools gave the highest priority to adding more vocational, commercial, and home economics courses. Of the three changes most frequently mentioned by principals of small high schools, for example, the first category included "Would give manual train-

FIGURE 11. Automobile mechanics class, Seattle, Washington. The success of Ford's Model A introduced in 1928 helped make automobile mechanics a relatively popular vocational course in many high schools. *Courtesy Seattle Public Schools.*

ing; add vocational work; introduce manual arts and vocational work for both boys and girls; give semi-vocational courses to eighth and ninth grade pupils; and introduce courses in vocational mathematics and English." Second in order of the most desired changes was adding home economics, and the third was to "establish a junior high school for grades 7, 8, and 9 introducing vocational subjects." For grades 10, 11, and 12, principals of small high schools, if "entirely free to organize the work of their school with no restriction from any source," put "less academic and more vocational work" in the highest category, followed by "offer more commercial work" and "make commercial arithmetic compulsory." The third category of desired changes was in the area of vocational agriculture, and the fourth in home economics.[39]

What these data indicate is that if colleges were not imposing their requirements on the high school curriculum, principals would go even further than they already had in the direction of vocationalizing the curriculum. "The data show," the report concluded, "that if high-school principals were completely free to organize their curriculums to their own liking, they would increase the number of vocational, commercial, and home economics courses offered; modify the present courses in social studies, mathematics, and foreign languages; and differentiate work to fit the needs of individual pupils."[40] Principals reported that they had already taken major steps in that direction, but, the report strongly implied, college entrance requirements had kept them from an even more comprehensive reorganization of the curriculum. In the years ahead, the notion that the heavy hand of college requirements represented a major obstacle to reform of the secondary school curriculum became a familiar cry among many school reformers.

One of the report's major conclusions was that *Cardinal Principles* "have been one of the fundamental guides in secondary education since their publication in 1918."[41] This is at least partially accurate. The recommendations of *Cardinal Principles* were undoubtedly reflected in the data both in terms of actual changes in the school curriculum and in terms of the declared commitments of school administrators. The American curriculum was unquestionably reflecting the central ideology of *Cardinal Principles*. What the survey does not indicate, however, is the extent to which students were actually enrolled in these new courses. Even to say that *Cardinal Principles* greatly influenced the course of curricular change is to exaggerate its impact. Rather, the issuance of the report under the auspices of the NEA gave quasi-official sanction to both social efficiency as a social ideal (in a more subdued form than had been commonly expressed by its major proponents) and to the ongoing process of vocationalization. A key symbolic message was being conveyed. Henceforth, American schools would renounce their elitist biases and undertake a program of studies that would address common people's concerns and desires.

VOCATIONAL GUIDANCE IN THE INTEREST OF INDUSTRIAL AND SOCIAL EFFICIENCY

Beyond the main report of the *Cardinal Principles* commission, several sub-committee reports addressed particular issues. One subcommittee of the *Cardinal Principles* commission, the Committee on Vocational Guidance, devoted itself not so much to restructuring the American curriculum but to the task of providing a vital support service. Under the leadership of Frank Leavitt, associate superintendent of schools in Pittsburgh, Pennsylvania, the report of the subcommittee expressed the humane concerns in which this emerging field was born. Issued in 1918, the same year as the main report, the subcommittee report reflected not only an early tradition of altruistic impulses in the evolution of vocational guidance but also anticipated what for members of the subcommittee seemed clearly undesirable directions. The report argued, for example, that "It is not the purpose of vocational guidance to decide for young people in advance what occupation they should follow, nor to project them into life's work at the earliest possible moment, nor to classify them prematurely by any system of analysis, either psychological, physiological, social or economic."[42] There was even a strong hint of an objection to an overemphasis on adjusting the individual to the demands of the social order, a contradiction of the kind of social efficiency doctrine that Briggs and others were promulgating. "The school must teach the youth not only how to adjust himself to his environment," the report cautioned, "but also how to change the environment when the need arises."[43] As a reflection of the previous decade or two of activity in the developing vocational guidance field, the tone of the report was remarkably accurate; but as an anticipation of the direction that vocational guidance would take in the years ahead, it was off the mark. In the 1920s, the demands for a truly efficient curriculum that would serve the interests of the job market and of the social status quo were too strong to be denied.

To be truly efficient meant not merely eliminating a few wasted motions here and there. It meant as well a close correspondence between individual capacities and job requirements, since a worker unsuited to the demands of a given occupational role was a source of great waste. This meant that schools had to undertake the responsibility for matching individual capacities with ultimate social roles and for the differentiated training that would be required to perform successfully in those roles. If children were indeed to be regarded as "raw material," as Bobbitt and other leaders in education metaphorically contended, then it made perfect sense to determine as scientifically as possible exactly what the raw material was good for. To address the wide differences that were to be found in that raw material initially in the context of work but ultimately in a much broader context, a new professional field, vocational guidance, began to achieve national prominence. In effect, the growing emphasis on individual differences, along with the criterion of probable destination in the design of the curriculum, demanded it. Vocational guidance not only filled that need but served to extend the reach of vocational education beyond the confines of job skills into human functioning generally.

Without question, the early founders of the vocational guidance movement were prompted by humanitarian impulses. The most revered of these early leaders of the movement was undoubtedly Frank Parsons. Born in 1854 and trained as an engineer, Parsons at first found work as a civil engineer with a railway company, but when the panic of 1873 put him out of work, he drifted into manual labor in a rolling mill, and then to teaching in Southbridge, Massachusetts, a small industrial city. While teaching, he studied law in the office of a local attorney and passed the bar examination in 1881. After a severe illness, which required a three-year recuperation in New Mexico, Parsons accepted a position as the chief clerk for a Boston law firm. He began to publish legal works and, in 1891, was offered a faculty position at Boston University Law School, where he became a widely admired lecturer, specializing in railroad law. In 1895, Parsons ran for mayor of Boston supported by the Populist, Socialist, and Prohibitionist parties. He lost by less than 1 percent of the vote. In time, his advocacy of liberal causes such as public ownership of monopolies, women's suffrage, and proportional representation led to the loss of his lectureship at Boston University in 1899.[44]

Parsons's dedication to civic reform prompted him to join the Civic Service House of Boston, which had been founded in 1901 with the financial support of Pauline Agassiz Shaw, a widely respected philanthropist. There, Parsons joined with two other emerging leaders in the vocational guidance movement, Meyer Bloomfield and Philip Davis. As part of his continuing concern for the well-being of the poor, he took the initiative in founding Breadwinners' College, an institution where workers could take courses in such subjects as literature and economics during the evening or on Sundays. Parsons's interactions with working people at the college led to an interest in helping youth choose a vocation, and from there, he began to develop his plans for a systematic approach to vocational guidance. He submitted those plans to Shaw, who provided the funding to launch the Vocation Bureau of Boston as part of Civic Service House in 1908. In time, branches were founded in other parts of the city.

In 1908, Parsons presented his first report to the executive committee and trustees of the Vocation Bureau. He died that same year at the age of fifty-four. Portions of Parson's report were incorporated into what is probably the first book published on the subject of vocational guidance, *Choosing a Vocation*, which had been in preparation at the time of his death. Like so many other successful school innovations, vocational guidance had its inception in private philanthropic initiatives, but Parsons, at the time of his death, was already entertaining the hope that one day vocational guidance would become a standard feature of American schooling. In his book, Parsons outlined the kinds of procedures he envisioned for vocational guidance and thereby anticipated many of the features that became part of its credo. Through a combination of serious self-examination, knowledge of job requirements, and wise decision making, appropriate matches would be created between the aptitudes of individuals and the needs of the workplace. Perhaps drawing on his own life experiences, Parsons deplored "the haphazard way in which young men and women drift into employments, with little or no regard to adaptability and without adequate preparation, or any definite aim or well-conceived plan to insure success."[45]

Within a year or two after the publication of Parsons's book, vocational guidance became established in the public schools of Boston, as were training courses for teachers. A few months after Parsons's death, Bloomfield became director of the Vocation Bureau and served in that capacity until 1918. A master publicist, Bloomfield was largely responsible not just for expanding the scope of the Vocation Bureau's activities but for transforming what had been essentially a local initiative into a national movement. Just as Susan Kingsbury's concern for the well-being of the fourteen-year-olds cast adrift in the commonwealth of Massachusetts was manifest in the Douglas Commission report only a few years earlier, so was Bloomfield's sympathy for the plight of youth who leave school around the age of fourteen conspicuous in his early writing. He continually emphasized that not only were children dropping out of school in large numbers at that age, but without the benefit of vocational counseling, they tended to drift from one menial job to another. As Bloomfield put it, "They become job hoboes."[46] To reformers like Bloomfield, the answer lay in the schools' undertaking vocational counseling as a social necessity and as a humanitarian enterprise. "The right of every child to the best possible chance in life," he said, "makes necessary the public control of vocational training."[47] With the advent of the 1920s, vocational guidance began to undergo a significant shift not only in leadership but in direction. One change was the new emphasis on professionalization; a second was the significance now attached to scientific testing; and finally, there was the beginning of a shift from strictly vocational guidance to guidance of all sorts.

With professionalization in the budding field of vocational guidance came, naturally, the strengthening of its organizational apparatus. John Brewer, one of the new generation of leaders, reported some years later, for example, that "1920 marks a turning point in the history of the movement." In that year a conference was held in New York City that adopted a new statement of principles and proposed a new organization to take the place of the National Vocational Guidance Association, with Brewer as president.[48] In 1921, a new journal, the *National Vocational Guidance Bulletin* (changed in 1924 to the *Vocational Guidance Magazine*) began publication. As a sense of a profession developed, several of the early articles in that journal made the case for certification of vocational guidance personnel and college professional training. What had begun as a humanitarian campaign to alleviate the deploring conditions that awaited school dropouts in the workplace was evolving in the 1920s into a national movement replete with a formal organizational structure, a professional journal, a prescribed course of training, and professional certification. The philanthropic tradition as embodied in the work of Parsons and Bloomfield was being superseded by a new professionalism propelled by its own priorities.

One of the most important of those priorities entailed invoking the authority of science in behalf of the guidance function. The 1920s was a period when the scientific measurement of human capacities was being felt in American life generally and in the world of professional education in particular. Although the modern mental measurement movement is usually associated with the publication of the Binet-Simon scales in 1904 and the subsequent refinements and extensions by American psychologists such as H. H. Goddard and Lewis M. Terman in the first fifteen years or so of the twentieth century, mass administration of intelligence tests did not take place until America's entry into World War One when Robert M. Yerkes was assigned the task of classifying army recruits according to their mental capacities. The administration of the Army Alpha and Beta tests to approximately 1.7 million inductees in 1917 and 1918 brought the whole issue of allegedly wide variation in human mental capacity to the forefront of public consciousness. Some of the published results emphasized the differences in intelligence levels according to occupation, and this lent scientific credence to the idea that certain kinds of work required certain identifiable mental abilities.[49] Particularly intriguing to guidance counselors was the intelligence range in each of the occupations. For the emerging profession of vocational guidance, this meant that success and failure in vocational roles could be accurately predicted. With mass testing now possible, this could be done relatively cheaply in schools.

Much of the impetus for aptitude testing came as well from the emergence of a new subfield within psychology, industrial psychology. The German-born professor of psychology at Harvard University, Hugo Munsterberg, who is the generally acknowledged founder of that field, was an ardent admirer of Frederick Winslow Taylor, and Munsterberg's ground-breaking textbook, *Psychology and Industrial Efficiency*, is studded with examples of Taylor's efficiency techniques.[50] Rather than concentrating on clinical matters or the general question of human mental capacities, industrial psychologists studied actual performance on the job in relation to the job requirements that were allegedly derived from scientific studies of work. In 1924, for example, Morris S. Viteles reported on his studies designed to test the aptitudes of department store cashiers. Using three classifications of cashiers (very satisfactory, satisfactory, and barely satisfactory), he was able to identify what he called a critical score which would serve to guide the hiring process. By plotting the scores his subjects achieved on his test, he determined the scores that would predict what he called "satisfactoriness" on the job.[51] "Job analysis," as this process came to be called, was already being adopted by curriculum designers as the technique of choice by which the subject matter of study would be determined.

By the early 1920s, guidance professionals were adopting mass testing with great enthusiasm. New group intelligence tests were making their way into schools, and with them aptitude tests such as the Seashore Measures of Musical Talents, developed in 1919. In 1925, the MacQuarrie Test for Mechanical Aptitude was introduced, and the O'Rourke Mechanical Aptitude Test made its appearance in 1926. At the same time, the guidance function was expanding beyond vocational guidance into academic counseling. Between 1923 and 1927, Dean J. B. Johnston produced tables of probabilities which combined scholastic aptitude test scores with high school rank in class.[52] As a result, the kind of probability tables that were being developed in the military and in industry were now being made available to admissions officers in colleges and to high school guidance counselors. Whereas the earlier generation of vocational guidance leaders had to rely on instinct and insight, the generation emerging in the 1920s had an array of scientific tests at their disposal. The idea that the administration and interpretation of these tests required a high degree of professional expertise only served to solidify the new status being accorded to guidance counselors. As one historical account of the vocational guidance movement put it, "Without a scientific means to justify the first step of individual assessment, it is unlikely that vocational guidance would have been received so widely."[53] Some early testers urged caution. H. D. Kitson, for example, reminded counselors that they are "dealing with probabilities and not with certainties,"[54] but uncertainty was out of keeping with the culture of the 1920s.

As testing took hold, prominent psychologists such as Clark L. Hull began to refine statistical techniques that could be used in predicting vocational destinies. In his book, *Aptitude Testing*, Hull traces the concept of individual aptitudes and the impulse to determine them back to Plato. He quotes Plato as saying in *The Republic* that "no two persons are born exactly alike, but each differs from each in natural endowments, one being suited for one occupation and another for another." From this simple fact, according to Hull, Plato deduced that "all things will be produced in superior quantity and quality, and with greater ease, when each man works at a single occupation in accordance with his natural gifts."[55] In support of Plato's contention, Hull then cited a series of studies indicating the wide variation that exists between the poorest performance at a given task and the best. In trimming the heels of shoes, for example, the number of pairs daily is represented by a ratio of 1:1.4 while the ratio of elementary school teachers rated by their superiors is recorded as 1:2.5.[56] In an autobiographical account, Hull recalled that while at the University of Wisconsin, he "worked very hard trying to develop a scientific basis for vocational guidance." In that regard, he developed a machine that would actually perform the product-moments correlation computations that would be necessary in order to create the batteries of tests that were needed. In the end, however, he reported that "The survey leading to the publication of *Aptitude Testing* left me with a fairly pessimistic view as to the future of tests in this field, and I abandoned it permanently."[57] Hull's personal disappointment notwithstanding, the field of vocational guidance embraced the aptitude testing enthusiastically. It was, after all, a key element in the professionalization of the field.

One byproduct of the professional status being accorded to guidance counselors was the further extension of the guidance function beyond vocational counseling not only into academic counseling but psychological counseling in its several forms. In this respect, the evolution of the field of guidance parallels developments generally in the vocationalization of the curriculum. What had once been specifically job-related guidance now began to entail the broader sphere of vocationalization. In one unalloyed expression of vocationalism, for example, a leader of the vocational guidance movement urged that traditional academic subjects such as English, modern languages, mathematics, science, and history ought to "be taught with the object of use; that is, the commercial slant."[58]

To some extent, this expansion of professional responsibilities beyond strictly vocational guidance also may have stemmed from the events relating to World War One. The appearance, for example, of a new mental illness, "shell shock," as well as other psychological problems related to combat led to the creation of a division of neurology and psychiatry in the Surgeon General's office, and the National Committee for Mental Hygiene was given the task of defining the responsibilities of the new division. In the 1920s, the National Committee conducted a series of studies indicating that mental defects were a far more widespread phenomenon among schoolchildren than had been previously imagined. Such reports of rampant emotional disturbance among schoolchildren provided impetus for the mental hygiene movement, which had run parallel to vocational counseling since its inception around 1908.[59] In time, school counseling expanded to include many of the causes that mental hygienists had espoused. Not only did school guidance counselors undertake to address the emotional needs of schoolchildren, but schoolteachers, particularly at the elementary school level, were encouraged to address problems of social adjustment and emotional development in the classroom. Particularly in the early years, the Progressive Education Association (which had been founded in 1919) incorporated the mental health of schoolchildren as an important part of its platform. What had begun as a way of addressing the vocational needs of adolescents and young adults now began to flourish in a much wider arena affecting not simply the transition from school to work but the very heart of classroom practice.

The emergence and development of the guidance function in American schools followed a now familiar pattern. First, a genuine problem is identified by dedicated and humane individuals who commit themselves to address it, usually under philanthropic auspices. When the undertaking achieves some success, it begins to assume the trappings of a profession, and in time, the practice becomes an officially recognized component of school practice. Once installed in schools, the enterprise not only expands in scope but begins to incorporate the dominant ideological strains that are prevalent in society generally.

In the case of vocational guidance, the shocking neglect of youth who leave school and become "job hoboes" is identified by sensitive and dedicated social reformers such as Parsons and Bloomfield, and with philanthropic support, a handful of like-minded reformers begins to address the problem on a small scale. When vocational guidance becomes installed in schools, it develops organizationally and bureaucratically. Patterns of training are prescribed and certification requirements adopted. Perhaps more important, it begins to incorporate elements of prevailing social doctrines, and what was once almost a purely humanitarian effort incorporates the ideals that define those doctrines. In the context of the 1920s, those ideals include the notion of scientific predictability, and with the sanction of science came the inclination to forecast the future with ever increasing confidence. While never quite losing its humanitarian underpinnings, especially in its rhetoric, vocational guidance now becomes oriented to adapting individuals to the requirements of the prevailing social order. In a sense, the status of guidance counselors becomes dependent on their perceived or actual contributions not only to the dominant social ideology but to prevailing social trends. Other social and professional movements, such as mental measurement, with its aura of scientific precision and its widespread public acceptance, have their impact as well and lend credence to the identification of guidance counselors as possessing a level of technical expertise not only invaluable in preserving social stability but unavailable to those outside the profession. Similarly, a new awareness and public concern for emotional well-being becomes part of the professional configuration.

On balance, the emergence of a professional cadre of guidance counselors in America's schools was probably beneficial to schoolchildren. To the extent that school counselors provided reliable knowledge of the vagaries of the job market and a realistic assessment of job prospects, they surely served the best interests of their clientele. To the extent that they also offered emotional support for children and youth in times of crisis or mental turmoil, they undoubtedly performed a noble service. A darker side to the establishment of a profession of school counseling, however, relates particularly to their role as prognosticators. As Julia Wrigley reports, that darker side did not go unrecognized in labor circles in Chicago of the 1920s. "Vocational guidance programs," she says, "increasingly came under fire as a means of shunting working-class children into dead-end jobs. The intelligence tests were likely to provide only a means of adding a scientific gloss to a class-based process." As the Chicago Federation of Labor newspaper, *New Majority*, reported in 1922, vocational guidance departments were developing into "human feeders for factories and manufacturing establishments."[60] In this regard, under the guise of guiding youth in terms of their natural capabilities, guidance counselors were actually just serving the interests of the dominant business class.

Vocational guidance practices also had important educational consequences. Whatever may have been the scientific validity of their new instruments in making their predictions, vocational counselors in many cases were presuming a knowledge they just did not have.[61] In the case of many children and youth, they presumed to know what the future held in terms of their individual social and occupational role and even in terms of the direction of society and the workplace. If their efforts had merely resulted in an incorrect guess as to an individual's eventual adult activities, then the consequences would have been relatively innocuous. To the extent, however, that important educational decisions were based on erroneous prognostications, serious, even dire, consequences could ensue. When a curriculum is prescribed in relation to a prediction of a given child's future occupational or social role and that prediction is wrong or the definition of that role undergoes a significant change, then it becomes a very grave mistake indeed. Specific training is provided that is believed to be supremely utilitarian in both an occupational and social sense but turns out in the end to be of no use at all. What is more, the opportunity cost entailed in substituting an education tied to a spurious utility for a general education is immense. In a system of education tied above all to the elimination of waste, that cost, ironically, becomes the biggest waste of all. Children are induced to squander their best opportunity to cultivate those intellectual resources that allow them to take some control of their lives both in the present and in a remote and essentially unknowable future.

There is also a significant social dimension to the work of school counselors as prognosticators. As they undertook on an ever expanding scale the responsibility for predicting the eventual occupational and social roles of their clients, guidance counselors also began inadvertently to *determine* their futures.

That some boys who trained as mechanics actually became mechanics, that some girls for whom a home economics program was prescribed actually became homemakers, or that so-called "non-college-bound" students never actually were admitted to college does not so much provide evidence of the accuracy of the forecasts as it lends credibility to the suspicion voiced by Dewey and others that what was really afoot was a self-fulfilling prophecy. In this sense, counselors may not have simply matched abilities and propensities to eventual social and occupational roles but actually may have inadvertently shaped the destinies of their clientele.

WHAT VOCATIONALISM WROUGHT IN THE 1920s

By the end of the 1920s, the key elements in the vocationalization of the American curriculum were in place. The supreme criterion of efficiency in curriculum matters had led to the need to make fateful decisions as to each student's eventual occupational and social role. Only in this way could the curriculum be differentiated "to meet the needs" of a diverse school population. To do otherwise meant risking a dreadful waste. Algebra, literature, and history would be taught to large numbers of students who simply had no use for those subjects in terms of their adult functioning. Although the rhetoric in behalf of vocationalism was framed in terms of the best interests of students who were presumably being mistreated by exposure to those studies, students were in large measure expected to adjust to the dictates of the new industrial society. Vocational guidance, for example, had its origins in genuine concern for the well-being of youth but, by the 1920s, had been transformed almost inadvertently into an instrument for serving the needs of the workplace and of a socially efficient society. Increasingly, however, the demands of the workplace and the well-being of society were being regarded as all of one piece. What had been the governing principles of vocational education were now being seen as the governing principles of all of education.

This is not to say, of course, that the vocationalizers achieved total victory. The curriculum is inevitably a site of struggle and contestation, but none of the contending parties ever wins a complete victory.[62] At the same time that vocationalism was gaining ground in schools across the nation, opposition, or perhaps just inertia, served to retain significant elements of the traditional academic curriculum. Perhaps the single most important factor in that regard was the existence of college entrance requirements. Vocationalized subjects were unquestionably being added to the curriculum on a large scale, but academic subjects were not expunged. The labels used to designate the conventional school subjects, however, tell only part of the story. At the same time that traditional English was being supplemented here and there by the likes of business English, English even under its familiar subject label was quietly being transmuted. The "novels of Henry James, Conrad and Meredith," as Snedden characterized traditional English, may have retained their place in the curriculum of English for the "book-minded," but English, even when it was still called English, took on another character entirely for the students Snedden liked to call the "rank and file."

Given the prevailing social milieu in the 1920s, disapproval of this turn of events was muted. To some extent, opposition was reflected in an undercurrent of dissatisfaction with what Dewey once called "the religion of 'prosperity.'"[63] As the decade ended, he ruefully concluded, "we are living in a money culture. Its cult and rites dominate."[64] Nowhere is that "money culture" more mordantly depicted than in the novels of Sinclair Lewis. Of the books he published in the 1920s, *Main Street* and especially *Babbitt* portray life in middle America as culturally impoverished and individually confining. George F. Babbitt, a pillar of Zenith's business community, leads an outwardly contented life and delights in the wonders of the new technological America. His is a life of getting and spending. When his daughter, Verona, a recent graduate of Bryn Mawr, confides in him that she would like "to be doing something worth while" like working for Associated Charities, Babbitt admonishes her: "What do you mean 'worth while'? If you get to be Gruensberg's secretary—and maybe you would, if you kept up your shorthand and didn't go sneaking off to concerts and talk-fests every evening—I guess you'll find thirty-five or forty bones a week worth while!"[65]

When Babbitt's seventeen-year-old son Ted (Theodore Roosevelt Babbitt) complains that "I don't see why they give us this old-fashioned junk by Milton and Shakespeare and Wordsworth and all these has-beens," Babbitt looks up from reading the comic strips and delivers a stern lecture to his son:

> I'll tell you why you have to study Shakespeare and those. It's because they're required for college-entrance, and that's all there is to it! Personally, I don't see myself why they stuck 'em into an up-to-date high-school system like we have in this state. Be a good deal better if you took Business English, and learned to write an ad, or letter that would pull.[66]

In Babbitt's admonition, Lewis acidly captures the "money culture" attitude toward schooling. School is for achieving success in the world of jobs and business. Everything else in the curriculum is simply a consequence of those inexplicable college entrance requirements. This is vocationalism pure and simple.

But there is more to George Babbitt than Babbittry. His outward conformity notwithstanding, Babbitt harbors largely unarticulated yearnings for something that lies beyond his day-to-day existence as a successful real estate broker and model citizen. To one of his sons he reveals, "Practically, I've never done a single thing I've wanted to in my whole life. I don't know's I've accomplished anything except just get along."[67] Babbitt is no mere caricature of an American businessman in the 1920s; Lewis makes him a symbol of individual impotence in the face of overwhelming technological achievement and an overpowering industrial landscape. For all his love for Zenith's skyline and the prosperity it symbolizes, for all the good fellowship he enjoys at Boosters' Club meetings, and for all the commercial vigor of his beloved city, Babbitt still yearns for an organic relationship to his work and ultimately for some control over it. Work in the new industrial society was now clearly something different from what it had been in the days of the noble artisan. Although there remained a romantic nostalgia for that bygone era and a continuing symbolic adherence to the Protestant work ethic, work was now what you did in order to consume. For most Americans, work had become detached from the rest of life.

That rupture in the relationship between the individual and work not only was reflected in the content of the curriculum but in the way the curriculum was actually constructed. Efficiency became a nearly universal watchword, and the dissection of the activities that comprise human life became a familiar first step in the construction of courses of study. The standardization of highly specific activities that seemed so appealing in the case of bricklaying and later in a variety of other vocational settings now was being carried over to the tasks of being a citizen or a member of a family. Creating a curriculum became a process of discovering the activities that people performed, converting those activities into precise curricular objectives, setting those objectives down in unequivocal terms, and then proceeding to find the most efficient methods for achieving them. Success of the venture would depend on the extent to which the objectives that were stipulated at the outset were realized in the end. The hyper-rationality that scientific management brought to the world of production had taken hold not simply in the content of the curriculum but in the way the curriculum was now understood and constructed.

Vocationalism as promulgated by the new leaders of the curricular world was never fully realized, but by the 1920s, it became difficult for most Americans, like Babbitt, to see any other point to a system of public schooling besides success in the workplace. With the timely support of the burgeoning guidance movement in the period after 1920, the prognostications required by such an ideal began to seem all the more plausible, and "meeting the individual needs of students" became an ever-present slogan that lent further credence to the idea that a common curriculum was not only socially inefficient but a psychological impossibility. To most Americans, whatever the curriculum was, it needed to address the differences that batteries of aptitude tests were documenting and to train the young for the destinies that those tests foretold. This could be accomplished not by recognizing the distinctive individuality of each student but by neatly classifying children and youth in terms of their predicted social and occupational roles and then training them directly for successful performance in those roles. Objections along the lines of what Dewey called "the feudal dogma of social predestination" were heard here and there,[68] but these voices were muffled. The supreme differentiation of function that had become a hallmark of the modern factory was now mirrored in a self-conscious differentiation of function in society and given critical support by a curriculum deliberately designed to facilitate it. What had begun as a metaphor became a reality.

7

THE NEW DEAL LAUNCHES "A GREAT NATIONAL YOUTH MOVEMENT"

Vocationalists under Siege, 1929–1946

[W]e are somewhat perplexed over the fact that the new national youth movement, a movement that should be of great significance to the present and future social and economic stability of our people, has been planned without the advice and assistance of our educational leadership. If there is one place above all others in the activity of our National Government where our educational leadership is qualified and ready to render service, it is in dealing with the problems of youth. Our responsible educational representatives in the National Government had made a careful survey of the plight of American Youth in these difficult days. Definite plans and recommendations for dealing with the youth situation had been prepared. The educational world was, therefore, quite startled, amazed and even indignant to find that our educational leadership was ignored when plans were promulgated for a great national youth movement.

L. H. Dennis, Executive Secretary,
American Vocational Association, 1935[1]

On August 12, 1928, with optimism still the order of the day, presidential candidate Herbert Hoover was able to proclaim in his speech accepting the nomination of the Republican Party that "we will soon with the help of God be within sight of the day when poverty will be banished from the nation."[2] His nomination seemed to signal a course of continued prosperity for the nation, symbolically marking a reaffirmation of the reverence for business and industry and reasserting the primacy of the ideal of efficiency that had been a familiar refrain over the previous quarter century. Hoover, who had been trained as a mining engineer, had prepared an influential report in 1921 on "Waste in Industry," and as Secretary of Commerce under presidents Harding and Coolidge between 1921 and 1928, he had earned a reputation as an astute and efficient administrator. His overwhelming election victory in November 1928 epitomized the rise to prominence of the engineering profession, not simply as builders of bridges, tunnels, and dams, but as the efficiency experts and scientific managers of the new industrial age. Historian Robert Kanigel even interprets Hoover's election as bringing "scientific management into the White House itself."[3]

THE CRASH

Between January 1928 and February 1929, Hoover headed a commission on unemployment charged with conducting a study of the state of the economy. Leaders in finance, education, labor, and science joined Hoover in predicting abiding prosperity. America simply had to continue pursuing the economic path that it had been following. The opening sentence of the committee's report set the tone: "Acceleration rather than structural change is the key to understanding our recent economic developments." The report went on to mention some technological unemployment here and there, but stressed the themes of "dynamic equilibrium" and "economic balance."[4] A year after Hoover's election, the stock market collapsed and with it the American economy. The 1920s, the decade generally associated with exuberance and confidence—with flappers, Lindbergh's transatlantic flight, dance marathons. speakeasies, and jazz—ended in a calamity.

Just up to the collapse, federal support for vocational education continued to flow. On February 5, 1929, the George-Reed Act went into effect. The new law extended the benefits to territories not covered by Smith-Hughes and granted an additional $500,000 each year for home economics and vocational agriculture. In a sense, Smith-Hughes had set a pattern by providing federal matching funds for state vocational initiatives, and vocationalists seemed satisfied with that pattern. An ominous sign insofar as the vocationalists were concerned was that, unlike Smith-Hughes, the new funding was actually due to expire in five years. Despite their continuing support for legislation in behalf of vocational education, members of Congress may have already begun to be apprehensive about the state of the economy and wary about long-term spending commitments.

By 1929, at least some business and industry leaders were beginning to accept cycles of prosperity and economic crisis as an inevitable byproduct of industrial capitalism. Major depressions, for example, struck in 1819, 1837,

1857, 1873, and 1893. Another one was imminent in 1914 but was averted by the outbreak of World War One. A severe economic recession struck in 1921–23. Nothing, however, had prepared business leaders—or the American people—for the disaster that struck in the stock market in the fall of 1929 and for the economic collapse that followed. When it came, the stock market crash was not as sudden as is sometimes believed. While the devastating sell-offs that occurred on Black Thursday (October 24, 1929) and Black Tuesday (October 29, 1929) have come to represent the end of the era of prosperity associated with the 1920s, the decline in fact continued over the course of several weeks, roughly from September 3 through November 13. For the most part, this downturn was greeted almost with disbelief, but on October 23, the day before Black Thursday, stocks lost twenty-one points within an hour, and the rush to sell was on. The *New York Times* account of Black Thursday was still cautiously optimistic, leading with the headline, "Worst Stock Crash Stemmed by Banks," followed with the caption, "Leaders, Confer, Find Conditions Sound." The *Times* reported that executives of the National City Bank, Chase National Bank, Guaranty Trust Company, and Bankers Trust Company had met with Thomas W. Lamont of the House of Morgan after the close of the stock exchange and declared that "There has been a little distress selling on the Stock Exchange." Merrill, Lynch and Company recommended that its customers keep their accounts "well margined" and advised investors "with available funds [to] take advantage of this break to buy good securities," as did other brokerage houses.[5]

The *Times* report on Black Tuesday a few days later also found room for hope. The headline captured the tone of the report: "Stocks Collapse in 16,410,030 Share Day, but Rally at Close Cheers Brokers." Although the *Times* story saw some promise in "an impressive rally just at the close," it acknowledged that the pressure to liquidate securities, "which had to be sold at any price," had brought about "the most disastrous trading day in the stock market's history." At one point, the *Times* story struck a poignant note:

> The crowds about the ticker tape, like friends around the bedside of a stricken friend, reflected in their faces the story the tape was telling. There were no smiles. There were no tears either. Just the camaraderie of fellow-sufferers. Everybody wanted to tell his neighbor how much he had lost. Nobody wanted to listen. It was too repetitious a tale.[6]

By the end of 1929, 50 percent of the value of stocks had evaporated.[7]

The economic collapse associated with these events extended far beyond unprecedented losses in the stock market. Along with disintegration in stock prices came a sharp decline in confidence in investment generally, and economic repercussions were felt throughout the entire economy. Unemployment began to rise almost immediately. In March 1930, an estimated 3,250,000 to

4,000,000 workers were unemployed. Within a year, estimates of unemployment had doubled to between 7,000,000 and 8,000,000, and by March of 1932, unemployment reached an astounding 11,250,000 to 12,500,000.[8] Hoover appealed to businesses to hold the line on salaries, and indeed, wages were slower to be affected, but in time, they too began a steady decline. In the last quarter of 1930, manufacturing wages dropped one cent from the average of 59 cents an hour in 1929, but in August of 1931, United States Steel cut salaries by 10 to 15 percent, and by another 10 per cent in September. The steel industry generally followed suit, and then other corporations as well. By the end of 1931, hourly wages dropped three more cents. Weekly wages were also hard hit. The National Industrial Conference Board reported that industrial wages were $28.50 in 1929, $25.74 in 1930, and $22.64 in 1931.[9] By the fall of 1931, effects of what came to be known the Great Depression were being felt everywhere.

Schools remained relatively unaffected at the outset of the depression, but salaries of teachers were soon being cut and school services sharply curtailed. By the spring of 1932, Chicago's teachers had experienced several "payless pay-days," and each of Chicago's approximately 14,000 teachers was owed $1,400, representing about six months of unpaid salaries.[10] Here and there, a profound disillusionment with the reigning business culture began to set in. In florid prose, an editorial in *School Life*, the official journal of the Office of Education, renounced the effort on the part of education to ally itself with business:

> By borrowing the terms of the market place we tried to borrow from the temporary glory of the market place. We tried to improve education's estate by clothing her in scraps of royal purple snipped from the hem of the new king of America. Business was the undisputed monarch of America during the last decade.
>
> Let us talk no more of education as a business. Let us divest education of its unseemly costume, not merely because the king is deposed but because education should never be false to its high purpose. To abandon the symbol of the lighted lamp for a bag of gold is a poor exchange.[11]

The tone of the editorial was a dramatic departure from close alliance with business that was so central to education policy in the 1920s and even in the early days of the depression, but professional educators, on the whole, were strangely quiet on the subject. As Tyack et al. characterized their early reaction to the Great Depression, "Anyone glancing through the articles in the American School Board journal, or listening to the speeches at the NEA's Department of Superintendence (the meeting place of the mighty), or looking over the agenda of meetings of the prestigious Cleveland conference during the first two years of the depression would hardly have known that the maelstrom had begun."[12] By 1932, such complacency began to dissipate.

With the continuing disintegration of the economy, schools were now experiencing hard times. School closings became quite common in the 1932–33 school year, with southern states being the hardest hit. In Alabama, 81 percent of white children in rural schools were on a forced vacation. In Arkansas, more than 300 schools were open for just sixty days or less. In Georgia, 1,318 schools actually closed. As revenue from the tax rolls dropped, many schools across the country drastically shortened the school year and cut programs.[13] Even before effects of the crash were being felt, half of all black children in the South were not in school, and of those who were, three-quarters had not reached the fifth grade.[14] When farm prices collapsed and mortgages were being foreclosed at an unprecedented rate, the situation became even more desperate.

The severity of the economic crisis makes the relative silence on the subject by vocational educators in the first years of the depression rather puzzling. Their stock in trade, after all, had been providing job training for America's workplace, and now that workplace was clearly in disarray. Somehow, though, the Great Depression seemed to have escaped the notice of the *American Vocational Association Journal and News Bulletin* until its August 1931 issue, where it was mentioned in a single article.[15] In 1930 and 1931, the American Vocational Association (AVA) seemed preoccupied with lobbying once again for increased federal support, mainly in the form of what came to be known as the Capper-Reed bill, which contained a few provisions that at least on the surface seemed to address the crisis. Drafted and heavily promoted by the AVA, the new bill, for example, would expand vocational education by extending its benefits to employed workers. The bill also attempted to address problems of technological unemployment.[16] The president of the AVA, C. M. Miller, was particularly concerned that the new bill not be considered emergency legislation without the permanent funding that vocationalists had grown used to. So far as he was concerned, Smith-Hughes was to set the pattern.[17] Ominously in terms of the interests of the vocationalists, however, the Capper-Reed bill never was passed. In time, of course, vocationalists sought to make their presence felt as a force to counteract some of the most devastating effects of the depression, but although some concessions were made here and there, they found it difficult to relinquish the established pattern of vocational education that had been in effect since the days of Smith-Hughes.

THE BATTLE FOR CONTROL OF
VOCATIONAL EDUCATION BEGINS

In the spring of 1929, even before the economic crisis had become apparent, Hoover appointed a National Advisory Committee on Education to which he assigned the task of reviewing federal education policies. Since vocational education had enjoyed a clearly favored position in terms of federal aid to education, any potential revamping of federal aid to education raised alarm among the leadership in vocational education. In an urgent letter addressed to the American Vocational Association, C. M. Miller, the chairman of its legislative committee, warned the membership that "some of the members of the National Advisory Committee at least are not in sympathy with vocational education." He exhorted the membership to attend the Atlantic City meeting of the organization in February, since, as he put it, "the cause of vocational education is being weighed in the balance." In that regard, he outlined a strategy: "it is our plan to be on the offensive, playing the defensive game only when it becomes necessary." A copy of Miller's letter was sent to all state directors of vocational education and all state supervisors of trade and industrial education.[18] Apparently outraged, Charles Hubbard Judd, a member of the committee and head of the Department of Education at the University of Chicago, asserted that, contrary to Miller's allegation, "there is not a single member of the National Advisory Council of Education who is 'not in sympathy with vocational education'" and declared that Miller's effort "to stir up partisan feeling is a form of disloyalty to American education which ought to be sharply reproved."[19]

In 1931, when the final report was published, no overt hostility to vocational education was evident, but it did contain recommendations that were potentially devastating to interests of the vocationalists. In general, the advisory committee took a strong stand against federal control of education, recommending that federal grants for particular purposes such as vocational education be continued for only five years, since such grants represented a form of policy-making at the national level. Fearing that the use of matching funds in particular might eventuate in an indirect form of federal control, the report further declared that "The matching of federal money grants, with state or local funds, whether their use is for general or special educational purposes is a policy not to be favored in the field of education." Rather than aid to vocational education in particular, the report recommended federal promotion of education research with aid to the states taking the form of "intellectual assistance . . . through scientific research, and the collection and dissemination of reliable information." Also potentially disastrous to the vocationalists was the recommendation that Congress, "enact no additional laws that grant federal financial aid to the States in support of special types of education or that increase existing federal grants for such special purposes as already aided." Rather than the federal government matching designated expenditures by the states, the report recommended that "all future grants [be made] to States as grants in aid of education in general, expendable by each State for any or all educational purposes as the State itself may direct."[20] As a way of avoiding federal intrusion into educational policy-making, the advisory committee recommended a pattern of general aid to education that did not single out any special area to be supported and instead provided aid in terms of very general criteria.

There were two minority reports. Catholic representatives on the advisory committee went even further than the main report in opposing federal control of education by objecting narrowly to a provision that would establish a federal department of education headed by a secretary of education. In their view, such a step could bring about unneeded and unwarranted centralization of educational policy-making. Black members of the advisory board, on the other hand, took exception to the position of the majority against aid for particular purposes, arguing in their minority report that the federal government was obliged "to exercise special solicitude" for the education of African Americans in view of the seriousness of the problem of unequal education.[21] Obviously concerned about the serious gap that existed in the financing of black education in the segregated South, their minority report recommended that aid for those segregated schools "be conditioned upon some definite increase in the per capita amounts and in the percentages of State support made available for Negro education."[22] Although framed as a modest dissent, the three black college presidents, John W. Davis, Mordecai W. Johnson, and R. R. Moton, who wrote the minority report were advancing a rather startling proposal in its time. Aid would be directed in terms of the actual recipients rather than to the various states. Obviously, however, federal aid if provided in this form would further undermine the enviable position that vocational education had enjoyed, since such aid would be provided for the overall education of African Americans, and not for the specific support of industrial education, vocational agriculture, and home economics as the Smith-Hughes Act stipulated. Aid in that form would also have undermined the pattern of unequal financing of education in the racially segregated schools of the South.

A seemingly bureaucratic but nevertheless serious problem for the vocationalists was the argument advanced by the advisory committee to eliminate the Federal Board for Vocational Education (FBVE). Provisions incorporated into the Smith-Hughes Act had had the effect of establishing a system of vocational education that was administratively independent of the U.S. Office of Education (later to become the Department of Education). From its beginning, the FBVE had among its membership and especially among its staff a strong contingent of committed warriors in the cause of vocationalism, and this virtually insured favorable oversight of vocational programs supported by the federal government. The independent vocational board, after all, had been the brainchild of the National Society for the Promotion of Industrial Education (predecessor of the American Vocational Association), and that separate board represented a symbolic declaration of independence from the rest of education. There were also some practical benefits. When FBVE was formed, Charles A. Prosser, the doyen of American vocational education, assumed the powerful post of chief executive officer, and although his own reign was rather brief, he and other officials of the FBVE, such as Charles R. Allen, were able to establish a course for vocational education that emphasized as much as possible separate vocational schools and virtually autonomous programs within comprehensive high schools, generously supported, of course, with Smith-Hughes appropriations. With virtually the only surveillance coming from FBVE, vocationalists were relatively untrammeled in the administration of many millions of dollars in federal aid and in creating what was in effect a separate and distinct educational policy for the nation.

The advisory committee's recommendation now threatened to subvert that independence. The report put the matter squarely: "Certainly it is an unsound policy to make grants for one type of education, such as vocational training, in such a way as to induce States with relatively low economic ability to withdraw support from their already too meager programs of general education in order to maintain the services which the Federal Government desires to stimulate."[23] The creation of the vocational board, in other words, had served to establish a distinct bias in educational programs toward vocational education, and this had had a detrimental effect on other educational endeavors. Depending on the outcome of the recommendations, the favored position that vocationalists had enjoyed since 1917 in terms of generous federal financial aid and relative freedom from critical surveillance "hung in the balance," as Miller had feared.

There was another potentially catastrophic turn of events. Perhaps influenced by the advisory committee's recommendations, Hoover, in an economy move undertaken in the last days of his administration, sought to eliminate federal aid to vocational education entirely by reducing financial aid by 10 percent over the course of ten years. When he informed the FBVE in September 1932 that he intended to cut $500 million from the budget of the FBVE for the 1933 fiscal year, it came as a stunning surprise. As Secretary of Commerce, Hoover had been a strong supporter of vocational education, and there was no advance warning of this new move. Acting to forestall deeper reductions, the FBVE presented a budget for 1934 that cut 6.5 percent from administrative costs, but when Hoover submitted his budget for the 1934 fiscal year, funds for vocational education were reduced by another 10 percent. Hoover's appropriations bill also provided for the annual review of permanent appropriations. This meant that the provisions of the Smith-Hughes Act would actually be subject to review by agencies independent of FBVE. Members of Congress, however, particularly the longtime allies of the AVA from the South and states with high rural populations, vigorously opposed any reduction. When Representative Clarence Cannon of Missouri and Senator Warren Austin of Vermont introduced amendments that would eliminate cuts in vocational education, only 10 percent of the House of Representatives voted against it, and the Austin amendment in the Senate passed as well. Eventually, all provisions in the bill intended to eliminate permanent appropriations were struck down.[24] For a time at least, disaster had been averted.

THE CHALLENGE OF THE NEW DEAL

The most visible reaction on the part of Americans to the economic crisis was to elect Franklin Delano Roosevelt, the governor of New York, as president in November 1932. When Roosevelt assumed the office on March 4, 1933, the American economy was near collapse, with businesses failing, farms being foreclosed, and an estimated 12 million Americans out of work. Almost immediately after assuming his duties, Roosevelt sought further budget reductions, including reductions in the level of funding for vocational education. This time, however, vocationalists were ready. J. C. Wright, the director of FBVE, sent letters to state vocational directors warning that further reductions would be introduced in the 1934 special session and that these cuts might have the effect of eliminating or sharply reducing certain vocational programs. The cuts effected in 1933, he pointed out, already had seriously damaging effects, and he further advised the directors to write their members of Congress to protest additional cuts. Although there is some evidence that vocational directors responded to Wright's call, Roosevelt remained adamant, and he signed the budget reduction bill in June 1933. Appropriations were reduced from $6,450,300 in Smith-Hughes to $5,940,000, and from $1,500,000 in George-Reed to $1,275,000. On top of the previous reductions for fiscal 1933, this represented a reduction of 17 percent from Smith-Hughes and a 49 percent reduction from George-Reed over a two-year period.[25]

Further trouble was brewing for the vocationalists. With Roosevelt determined to economize through the consolidation of federal agencies, the independent status of the Federal Board for Vocational Education that had been called into question by Hoover's advisory committee was now being seriously reconsidered. By April 1933, Roosevelt's budget director, Lewis W. Douglas, announced a plan to effect budget reductions through the reorganization of federal agencies, including the reallocation of the functions of the FBVE to the Office of Education, which was then under the Department of the Interior. In certain respects, that transfer of power represented a more dangerous situation for vocational educators. As the official historian for the American Vocational Association put it years later, "Tampering with the Federal Board for Vocational Education was looked upon by industrial educators as only slightly short of a major crisis."[26] Roosevelt, moreover, was keen on the idea. In one memorandum to Douglas, he inquired whether he could simply accomplish the transfer by special executive order. In that same memorandum, FDR endorsed the position taken by Arnold B. Hall, the director of the Brookings Institution, that the power of the vocational educators was growing, and this was inhibiting efforts to reduce or eliminate governmental support for vocational education and the transfer of the FBVE functions to the Office of Education. With respect to the latter, Hall had stated in his memorandum that "If not done now the political power of the vocational board will be invincible." In his own handwritten commentary on the memo to Douglas, Roosevelt endorsed the move and added a marginal comment: "Let's do it now—I understand the Board is an 'independent office.'" Douglas, however, still mindful of the extraordinary political strength of the vocationalists, replied that, "In view of the power of the proponents of independence for vocational education I would not advise giving prominence by special executive order, but would recommend its incorporation in the general order." Indeed, one item in FDR's general executive order called for the transfer of the functions of the FBVE to the Office of Education, and another item reduced programs in cooperative vocational education, agricultural extension, and agricultural experiment stations by 25 percent.[27]

Various influential senators sought to intervene in favor of an independent FBVE, but FDR stood firm and refused to suspend the general executive order that would eliminate the agency. Finally, on October 1, 1933, the functions of the FBVE were transferred to the Office of Education. When it came, however, the elimination of FBVE was not as devastating as first seemed. A new Vocational Division within the Office of Education was created, with the head of FBVE, J. C. Wright, becoming the Assistant Commissioner for Vocational Education and all the employees of the old FBVE reappointed. Partly as a result, only $20,000 in administrative costs were saved in the year of the merger. A year later, in 1934, appropriations returned to their former level and continued to rise after that.[28]

The impact of the elimination of FBVE in terms of actually reducing the power and influence of the vocationalists appears to be minimal. Berenice Fisher concludes that by 1933, FBVE had been "reduced to a mere advisory board,"[29] and in the decade or so preceding its abolition, the vocational board met infrequently and seemed to be functioning largely to ratify the policy initiatives of the FBVE staff. Larry Cuban contends that although there was some loss of authority and influence as a result of the shift to the Office of Education, the transfer of personnel, if anything, reinforced existing administrative patterns. Despite a somewhat less determined championing of vocational education causes, critical oversight of federally sponsored vocational programs remained notably weak. "Monitoring, inspection and tough-minded reviews of State Plans," Cuban concludes, "were foreign to OE (Office of Education) officials at this time."[30]

The most significant impact of the elimination of FBVE as an independent agency seems to have been the symbolic one. If nothing else, FBVE epitomized the autonomy that vocationalists had enjoyed since Smith-Hughes, and the absorption of its functions into the Office of Education meant at least a nominal connection with the rest of public education, something many vocationalists considered inimical to their best interests. If vocational education were perceived to be tied to general education, then the special status that vocational education had enjoyed with the American public and with Congress would be undermined. Vocationalists and their allies were forced to surrender important symbolic ground, but they managed to avert disaster in terms of the actual administration and control of vocational programs.

As FDR mobilized his New Deal, one factor could hardly be overlooked: Of all the sectors of the American population, youth was the most severely hit by unemployment, and early in his first administration, Roosevelt undertook dramatic steps to address the problem of unemployment generally and youth unemployment in particular. Accurate unemployment data for this period are difficult to establish, but statistics compiled by George P. Rawick indicate that of the total of 3,187,647 unemployed in 1930, 878,562 were between the ages of fifteen and twenty-four. Of all youth between fifteen and twenty-four, 28 percent were unemployed, and of African American youth, 37.8 percent were without jobs. Some 36 percent of youth had been unemployed between eight and twenty-six weeks, and an additional 9 percent had not been working for more than twenty-six weeks. Of working youth, 39 percent of whites and 85 percent of African Americans were earning less than $1,000.[31] Whatever may have been the merits of vocational training in the past in preparing youth for the job market, it did not seem to address that very immediate and pressing problem.

The first of FDR's measures directed to the problem of youth unemployment was the Civilian Conservation Corps (CCC). The idea of connecting the unemployment problem with conservation had its inception during Roosevelt's last term as governor of New York, and in his acceptance speech at the Democratic convention he indicated that up to a million men could be employed in public works in such areas as soil erosion and reforestation. Shortly after he took office, Roosevelt began to compile data on how many workers could be usefully employed in such work. After consulting with his "brain trust" early in the Spring of 1932, Roosevelt, in a message accompanying the introduction of the CCC bill in Congress, argued that the measure would bring unemployed youth "into healthful surroundings" which would have the effect not only of reducing the vast numbers of unemployed, but of bringing "spiritual and moral stability." Some objections were voiced. The

AFL was troubled by the $30 per month salary being offered to workers for conservation work, fearing that it would only depress the wage scale further; reservations were also expressed about the Army being involved in running CCC camps and that the CCC represented a drafting of the unemployed into work camps.[32] In the light of the seriousness of the youth unemployment problem, however, these objections were quickly overcome. In its final version, the bill provided for "subsistence, clothing, housing, medical attendance and hospitalization and cash allowances as may be necessary."[33] At one and the same time, the bill was aimed at reducing the army of unemployed youth, bringing them into healthful surroundings under beneficent supervision, and providing a needed public service in the area of conservation. Interestingly, in the whole course of the congressional debate on CCC, the issue of that bill being an extension of federal involvement in education never arose.[34]

In its early stages at least, CCC enjoyed considerable success. Various government agencies were almost immediately deluged with inquiries by applicants, and by July, 1,330 camps had been established, averaging about 200 workers. For the most part, those enrolled were between the ages of eighteen and twenty-five, but in time the age range expanded to sixteen to twenty-eight. Various agencies of government were assigned important responsibilities. The Labor Department made the selections; the War Department built and administered the camps; the departments of Agriculture and the Interior planned the projects.[35] Missing from this virtually unprecedented collaboration was the U.S. Office of Education. Actually, as initially envisioned, the CCC had no relation to education. Much of the work of the CCC workers was in reforestation, leading to their designation as "Roosevelt's tree army."

By 1933, however, considerable sentiment had built to create an educational component to the CCC, although some suspicion remained in governmental circles as to what practical effect such measures would have. Apparently convinced that conventional schooling was neglecting a major portion of the youth population, George F. Zook, the Commissioner of Education at the time, took the lead in lobbying in favor of such programs. General Douglas MacArthur, however, was unconvinced that such programs would be worthwhile and wanted Roosevelt's personal approval before he would accede to initiating educational programs. Roosevelt explicitly endorsed the programs, and a CCC Education Advisory Commission was established by the end of 1933. MacArthur, however, continued to be deeply suspicious of the education side of the undertaking. Nevertheless, by the spring of 1934, educational programs began to take shape. For the most part, the educational program was characterized by loose organization, voluntary participation, and broad curricular offerings which included not only vocational training but some academic study and recreational activities. In many cases, the teaching staff lacked the customary professional credentials, and this was the subject of some criticism. By 1934, Clarence S. Marsh, the newly appointed National Educational Director of the CCC, had produced a handbook for what were then being called "educational advisors," and by the summer of 1934, approximately 40 percent of the CCC force was participating in the educational programs. In a burst of enthusiasm, Marsh described them as comprising "a great American folk-school movement." Ominously, in terms of the established interests of the vocationalists, he also declared that the CCC educational programs presented "new ways of bridging the gap between school and job."[36] A federally sponsored and controlled rival to school-based vocational education seemed to be emerging. Strategically, it was in the best interest of professional educators to gain some measure of control over these federal programs.

One of the key issues was whether the educational programs in CCC camps should be a military operation or under USOE control. In the first few years of CCC's existence, educational advisors were required to report to the camp commander and remained under his jurisdiction. The Office of Education, however, continued to maneuver for control of the education side of the operation and in 1936 developed a plan to extricate educational programs from military supervision. When CCC was reauthorized in 1937, ten hours a week were set aside for vocational training. After that, educational programs continued to grow, and by July 1938, 249 vocational subjects were being taught in CCC camps. One advantage of these programs was that, unlike programs in school-based vocational training, considerable opportunity existed for the enrollees to practice their skills in the field. Surveys of the boys enrolled indicated that only 6 percent of the CCC trainees had had any vocational training in public schools,[37] a fact which should not be surprising since, on average, CCC recruits had attained only the ninth grade. When asked whether "The courses I had in school were very good," a full 77 percent agreed, while only 14 percent disagreed, and 9 percent were uncertain. When prompted further with the statement "Most of my teachers were terrible," only 17 percent agreed and 76 percent disagreed, with 7 percent uncertain. Despite the fact that CCC enrollees were overwhelmingly high school dropouts, they seemed to come away with a favorable impression of the schooling they had received. The authors of the American Council of Education report on the CCC, however, interpreted these data to mean that "The favorable answers probably express in part a lack of imagination about other kinds of schooling that might have been offered,"[38] indicating perhaps that criticism of existing school practices was so fashionable as not to be denied. In the climate of the times, it seems as if the long-standing criticism by the vocationalists as to academic schooling and the New Deal's distrust of the education establishment were somehow coinciding. Under these circumstances, it seemed prudent for vocationalists to refrain from opposing CCC initiatives, and in 1935, the AVA urged support of CCC's vocational programs.[39]

After 1935, however, tension began to develop as to who would control those vocational programs. As Harry Zeitlin has indicated, "educators seem to have missed entirely the educational implications involved in the initiation of the CCC program,"[40] but with the educational component of the CCC growing, and in some respects flourishing, educators became divided as to whether CCC represented a fresh opportunity for youth training and therefore was worth backing, or whether it threatened the established order sufficiently to warrant challenging its existence. Zook's successor, Commissioner of Education John W. Studebaker, after an initially positive reaction to CCC, seemed persuaded of the latter course and took the leadership in undermining its programs, although this was often done covertly in private memoranda rather than in open confrontation. Zook had been a professor of European history before becoming head of USOE's Division of Higher Education and then Commissioner of Education and was not really part of the professional education establishment. Studebaker, by contrast, was a former state superintendent in Iowa and was especially wary of federal intervention into state and local officials' traditional prerogatives. The military's involvement in the administration of CCC camps provided an opening wedge for the critics, and much was said about the inappropriateness of the military being involved so heavily in an educational undertaking. In fact, CCC camps were run much like military units, with recruits subject to rigid discipline and required to wear military-style uniforms. There was also a rather high rate of "desertion." Rawick reports that approximately 20 percent of the young men enrolled in CCC either deserted or were discharged for infractions of discipline.[41] These problems notwithstanding, CCC continued to serve an educational function. By 1938–39, more than 90 percent of CCC recruits were engaged in educational programs involving an average of four hours per week, two-thirds of which were vocational in nature.[42]

Despite the declarations by government officials that the CCC really posed no threat to state and local control of education, many professional educators became deeply suspicious of an undertaking that in effect created a rival agency for the training of youth. Protestations to the contrary, the appearance of federal agencies like the CCC under federal control threatened the independence and standing that professional educators had long cherished. What emerged in the 1930s was what Edward A. Krug characterized as a struggle "for the control of youth" between Roosevelt's New Deal and professional educators.[43] The issue that Roosevelt raised only very gingerly in public but which he gave voice to in private was the extent to which educators could be entrusted with important policy decisions. From the perspective of a president wrestling with a monumental economic crisis, it was anything but self-evident that professional educators generally and vocationalists in particular were equal to the task or even whether they were more interested in enhancing their professional status and expanding their domain than in the welfare of youth and the health of the economy.

Vocationalists were not simply protective of their independence and sources of funding. They were also concerned that the part-time and rather loosely organized vocational training that was emerging in the CCC threatened the pattern of extensive training that had become established since Smith-Hughes and which served their own interests best. Short-term training programs with limited objectives simply did not entail the professional status that vocationalists had long sought and, to a large extent, had achieved. For the most part, for example, the short and relatively informal courses common in CCC camps did not require extensively trained teachers or, for that matter, as large a contingent of teachers. Tension between professional educators and New Dealers over the issue of the control of youth continued until CCC was abandoned in 1942.

CCC provided a significant opening wedge in the New Deal's challenge to state and local school vocational programs, but as a way of actually addressing the youth unemployment problem, it was limited in scope. Given the millions of unemployed youth, CCC programs accounted only for something less than one million of them. Around 1933, sentiment began to build among certain New Deal officials for a more ambitious program to address the problem. Although Roosevelt was very reluctant to enunciate a long-range federal education policy, he felt deeply that the schools had failed a large population of youth, many having already left school. In his view, only by major federal involvement in education could that neglected segment of the youth population be reached.[44] In pursuing that course, Roosevelt earned the often submerged but at times overt enmity of professional education groups such as the National Education Association and the American Vocational Association, who saw his New Deal programs as a threat to their established professional interests. On their side, New Dealers, according to Tyack et al., "chafed at the turf-protection of organized groups that opposed them."[45] New Dealers were primarily concerned with direct and immediate action to alleviate the devastating unemployment and the social disorganization created by the Great Depression, and they were being continually frustrated by the reluctance of many leaders in professional education to depart from established practices, especially if that meant potential loss of status and territory.

THE NATIONAL YOUTH ADMINISTRATION TAKES SHAPE

In short order, another major New Deal relief initiative, the Federal Emergency Relief Administration (FERA), designed to coordinate and administer relief programs, was hatched. A cooperative program between the federal government and the states, it was authorized by Congress in 1933 with an initial appropriation of $500,000,000. Under the plan, half of the money would be provided in grants-in-aid to the states, with states contributing three dollars for every one provided by FERA. The other half was retained in a discretionary fund to be used where states were not in a position to provide funds. FERA had a large measure of control over state relief activities, and to head the powerful new agency, Roosevelt appointed one of his most trusted aides, Harry L. Hopkins, a former social worker. Between 1933 and 1938 (when he became Secretary of Commerce), Hopkins administered an estimated $8–10 billion in connection with a variety of New Deal relief programs. Among FERA's work relief projects were several that included educational components, and in the early stages of those programs, the new agency sought to cooperate in their establishment and implementation. One program, for example, was designed to provide vocational training for workers who would be employed for construction and other jobs, with the federal government paying the salaries of vocational teachers. Both general and vocational teachers were employed under the plan, and FERA served at one and the same time to provide work for unemployed teachers and to make other workers more employable. In a kind of compromise between New Dealers and professional educators, the teachers of vocational subjects had to meet state requirements but did not need to have the actual certificate. Ray Fife, the president of the AVA, supported those cooperative efforts, and in fact, an arrangement was agreed upon in which FBVE would review the state plans, and FERA would provide the funds based on those recommendations. Over the first two years of its existence, FERA provided local school districts with $26,000,000, enabling many of them to stay open. About 10 percent of that amount was for vocational education.[46]

In 1935, these FERA activities culminated in the Works Progress Administration (WPA). WPA, like other New Deal programs, was primarily a work relief agency, but it sponsored some activities in adult education, created nursery schools, and helped repair and restore school buildings. Some vocational programs also were initiated, such as those involved in training hospital aides for work in health projects, and some vocational education was connected with preparing workers for construction jobs. In all, approximately 15 percent of WPA's educational programs were vocational in nature. Signs of strain began to emerge between federal relief administrators and the leadership of the AVA. One source of difficulty was that, beginning in July 1934, FERA ceased requiring that teachers in their programs meet the standard licensing requirements of the states. State vocational leaders began criticizing FERA programs for hiring unqualified teachers and duplicating state programs.

Complaints were also being voiced that FERA programs were not selective enough in admitting students to their programs. Referring to the now venerated Smith-Hughes Act, one editorial in the AVA *Journal* reminded the membership that steps were taken at that time "to prevent the dumping of imbeciles, low-grade morons, and other social misfits into vocational classes,...and now those safeguards were being let down." An analysis of FERA's vocational education activities, the editorial continued, "shows that classes are thrown open to all comers regardless of their ability to profit by the instruction."[47] Similar sentiments had been voiced earlier by Charles Prosser. In an article written in 1932, when the full effects of the Great Depression were being felt, Prosser called attention to the very real issue of technological unemployment, a problem he believed was affecting the less skilled workers disproportionately. Insofar as the implications for industrial and trade schools were concerned, Prosser thought it imperative that vocational educators "resist the studied effort to use such schools as a dumping ground for the regular schools," and not only to "set high standards for students" but to "drop those who fail to meet the requirements."[48] By contrast, WPA administrators gave little attention to the niceties of eligibility and high standards. Their social concern encompassed a wider arena and gave much more concerted attention to the poor and to educationally deprived minorities. It is estimated, for example, that 100,000 African American adults learned to read and write under the aegis of the WPA.[49] One great source of friction between vocational educators and the New Deal was becoming clear. While New Deal programs for youth were designed almost single-mindedly to put young people to work and to alleviate the conditions of the poor generally, these programs were threatening established systems of teacher certification as well as admission and retention standards in vocational programs of study, and thereby jeopardizing the professional status of vocational educators. Although vocational educators were generally slow to respond to federal initiatives, their guards went up once WPA was established and the full extent and nature of federal education programs became evident.

Soon there were stirrings in New Deal circles for an even grander federal initiative designed to address specific problems of youth unemployment. Among the social and economic advisors who were urging FDR to embark on a major coordinated educational program was Charles W. Taussig. As chairman of the board of the American Molasses Company, Taussig did not have the academic background typical of Roosevelt's "brain trust," but he had made the education of youth his special concern, and his ideas found an influential ally in Eleanor Roosevelt. Taussig was profoundly disillusioned by the state of American education and was particularly alarmed by reports of Hitler Youth and the growing attraction of socialism and communism to youth in the United States as well as in Europe. He attributed these tendencies to an alienation of youth prompted by unemployment and the failure of American education to address the needs of large numbers of Americans. Through a combination of federal job training and a revivified education in democracy, Taussig sought to neutralize the attraction that such radical causes presented. By redefining the mission of relief agencies in the New Deal, he hoped that American education could become a more effective force in promoting democratic commitments and increasing participation in civic affairs.[50]

Although Roosevelt never formally approved Taussig's ambitious plans for the education of American youth, he was generally sympathetic to his ideas and remained profoundly skeptical about the extent to which professional educators were capable of addressing the economic emergency. As a result, he was extremely reluctant to appropriate federal funds simply to support education administered by the states along established lines. Educators had long sought increased federal aid to education while at the same time condemning federal control. This, for example, had been the major theme of Hoover's Advisory Committee on Education, but with FDR so dubious of the motives of professional educators and even their competence, he was much more inclined to support his own programs. Nevertheless, the idea that the federal government ought to provide general aid to education while at the same time repudiating federal control remained a strong but chimerical article of faith among professional educators in the ensuing years.[51]

With the New Deal's deep-seated suspicions of professional education organizations still festering in 1935, an ambitious federally sponsored program for youth under the auspices of Hopkins's FERA began to gain favor. Within a month or two of being assigned the task of developing preliminary plans for such a program, Aubrey Williams, deputy FERA administrator, developed a plan to coordinate local youth activities at the federal level. Shortly thereafter, FDR asked Eleanor Roosevelt, Secretary of Labor Frances Perkins, and Taussig to draft legislation for a coordinated federal program for youth. Although previous New Deal ventures into education had been largely incidental to the task of providing unemployment relief, the National Youth Administration (NYA) from the outset threatened to become a rival to the state-controlled education system.

To head the new agency, Roosevelt appointed Williams, who had been primarily responsible for developing the plans. Like Hopkins, with whom he was closely allied, Aubrey Williams had been a professional social worker and shared his deep concern for the poor and underprivileged. An Alabaman by birth, he was especially sensitive to the effects of racism on blacks and whites alike. As NYA administrator, for example, he insisted that NYA's social functions in Alabama be racially integrated. A former college student pastor, Williams served in the American army in World War One and the French Foreign Legion before becoming executive secretary of Wisconsin's program for aid to dependent children and working for the American Public Welfare Association. His commitment to creating jobs for youth was unequivocal, and according to Richard A. Reiman, "Without question, he was the leader of the group of New Dealers who discovered almost immediately that training for youth could be secured only at the cost of alienating one of the most vocal factions within American education."[52] In effect, Williams personified the threat that the New Deal posed to the vocationalists.

Williams's plans for the new agency, which called for combining job training with actual work experience under the general control of the public schools, was the subject of much discussion within the Roosevelt administration. One friendly critic was Fred J. Kelly, head of the Division of Higher Education in USOE, whose ideas on job training seemed to be at odds with those of Studebaker, his chief. Kelly was very supportive of Williams's efforts to combine school work with actual job experience, but he believed that the plan relied much too heavily on the ingenuity of public school officials. Public schools, he believed, would be "none too quick to visualize the greatly enriched and varied program" that Williams had in mind.[53] More studies were conducted, with Secretary of Labor Perkins having a strong hand in the development of the program, and she, more than most other New Deal insiders, was particularly wary of professional educators. As would be expected, Hopkins and Studebaker vied for control of the new agency, and although Roosevelt was reluctant to take a public stand on that issue, he worked behind the scenes to minimize Studebaker's influence.[54] Alarmed by this turn of events, Studebaker submitted a program of his own. His plan would set up regional "guidance and adjustment" centers to be funded by the federal government but which would be controlled by state and local agencies. (Studebaker later became a strong advocate of life-adjustment education after it was proposed by Charles Prosser in 1945.) In effect, his competing proposal represented a public eruption of the fierce behind-the-scenes struggle taking place within the Roosevelt administration for the control of youth. Roosevelt, however, did not really trust Studebaker, and his plan was never considered seriously. According to syndicated columnists Drew Pearson and Robert S. Allen, FDR's distrust of Studebaker stemmed from derogatory comments Studebaker reportedly had made about the CCC.[55] Studebaker's alternative proposal and his public campaign in its behalf may even have had the effect of hardening the position of the New Dealers in terms of who should control the new agency. FDR, of course, chose to pursue the direction provided by his close New Deal associates.

On June 26, 1935, by executive order, President Roosevelt created the National Youth Administration as a special federal agency under the WPA. With the help of Roosevelt's direct intervention, the educational side of the new agency would include not simply job training but elements of the political education that Taussig and Eleanor Roosevelt had been supporting. In fact, the NYA as finally realized was very similar to the proposals that Taussig and Williams had developed. Not surprisingly, Williams was appointed executive director, and Taussig became chair of the National Advisory Committee. Administrators of the NYA working at the local level would coordinate job training for unemployed youth with work projects outside of school. The bypassing of the educational establishment outraged many of it members. Speaking before the National Education Association, for example, George Strayer of Teachers College declared that "The President has not only deliberately ignored the Office of Education, . . . but he has gone against the best interests of the young people involved."[56] In short order, the NEA formally requested FDR to put the NYA under the Office of Education. In an unusually harsh criticism of WPA's failure to require teaching certificates for its instructors, Willard E. Givens, NEA executive secretary, told NEA membership that "once again the schools have been repudiated and their officers and their teachers placed among the untouchables of the present depression." Alluding to NEA's long-standing position of federal aid to education without federal control, Givens went on to say that the NEA takes the position that "preparation of young people for the duties of citizenship, reading, writing, and arithmetic should take precedence over harmonica blowing, lariat throwing, and boondoggling."[57] So annoyed were New Dealers at Givens's charges that they asked Commissioner Studebaker to respond. The draft of Studebaker's letter to Givens was so conciliatory, however, that it was rejected, and no reply was ever sent.[58]

VOCATIONALISTS RENEW THE DRIVE FOR FEDERAL AID

With appropriations from the George-Reed Act due to expire, the AVA launched a major campaign to continue the flow of federal dollars for vocational education. In 1934, four bills were introduced in Congress within a two-week period, all designed to maintain appropriations for vocational education. In such a cause, the members of the coalition that had long supported vocational education could be relied on. Interest groups, such as the American Home Economics Association, the Future Farmers of America, the National Grange, and the American Farm Bureau Federation sent representatives to testify in behalf of continuing appropriations. The AVA was represented by Charles Prosser and L. H. Dennis, who testified that unemployment was indeed being alleviated by vocational programs designed to train skilled workers. In the end, the George-Ellzey Act, replacing the George-Reed Act, was passed in May 1934. For the years 1935 to 1937, it provided an additional

$3 million annually beyond Smith-Hughes for vocational agriculture, vocational trade training, and home economics apportioned equally, and it included Alaska in the provisions. Roosevelt delayed signing the bill, which raised concern that he was considering a veto. He did finally sign, but in letters to Hopkins, Secretary of Labor Perkins, and Secretary of the Interior Harold Ickes, FDR explained that he had done so "after some hesitation," basing his decision, he said, on the assumption that the expenditures would be "primarily for relief of unemployment."[59]

With some signs of an economic recovery beginning to emerge in the mid-1930s, the AVA embarked on an even more ambitious campaign to obtain further federal support. Partly as a result of the increased appropriations for vocational education provided by the George-Ellzey Act (which helped reopen previously closed programs), enrollments in vocational education began to rise after a steady decline since 1933, with enrollments in vocational agriculture and home economics increasing more than in industrial education. To some extent, however, the additional appropriations for vocational education created a dilemma for the states. With states unable to maintain their general education expenditures, and with future federal support for vocational education uncertain, states were reluctant to expend further money for vocational programs. Partly as a result, nearly half of the additional federal funds provided under the George-Ellzey Act went unused in fiscal 1934 and 1935. In an urgent message, AVA president Ray Fife reminded vocational educators that "Unless these funds are used and used wisely in the extension of our program of vocational education, it will be difficult if not impossible to secure the enactment of a similar measure in 1937."[60] In addition, Roosevelt had taken note of those unexpended funds and remained concerned that what was being spent was not really aiding the unemployed. Rather than focusing on short intensive training, vocational educators tended to follow their traditional practice of focusing on long-term training for the often distant future. In general, it proved difficult for vocational educators to abandon the patterns that had been established around the time of the Smith-Hughes Act, and its fixed provisions, as Fife seemed to recognize, made it particularly difficult for vocational educators to respond effectively to new conditions.

Within a year after the passage of George-Ellzey in 1934, a major campaign was launched for a new and grander vocational education bill. Since George-Ellzey was due to expire on June 30, 1937, vocationalists wanted to insure continued federal funding after that date. Accordingly, the AVA drafted a bill in May 1935 which would provide $12 million annually, distributed equally among the old standbys, industrial education, vocational agriculture, and home economics, with states again providing matching funds. Walter George of Georgia was in the forefront of the campaign and introduced the bill in the Senate later that month. When his bill was not taken up in that session, AVA mounted a concerted lobbying campaign, with Dennis leading the charge. "It will be necessary," he reported to the membership of AVA, "to plan very definitely and systematically to inform their senators and representatives in congress concerning our legislation and the effect it will have on their respective states."[61] The Vocational Division of the Office of Education contributed to the campaign by sending copies of two of their pamphlets to senators and congressmen. Although publicly the Office of Education pursued a neutral stance on the bill, they quietly helped publicize its presumed benefits.[62]

The bill that Congressman Braswell Deen of Georgia introduced in the House of Representatives in January 1936 was identical to the one that George had introduced in the Senate a year before, but when the Senate Committee on Education and Labor reviewed it, they interjected a new $1.2 million authorization for vocational training in the distributive trades, both wholesale and retail. Although enrollments in courses for so-called "white-collar" occupations had been growing steadily without the support of Smith-Hughes, most vocational educators seemed reluctant to depart from their traditional emphasis on industrial education, along with aid to agricultural education and home economics as needed in order to build a political coalition. In effect, the Senate committee's amendment to AVA's drafted bill forced them to expand beyond that limited base. Since Roosevelt had recommended that only $3 million be appropriated, AVA undertook an intense lobbying campaign to insure that the full $14 million be authorized. Near the close of the Senate debate, Senator James F. Byrnes of South Carolina took the floor in June to complain that members of Congress had been deluged with virtually identical telegrams signed by Dennis, AVA executive secretary, supporting the full appropriation. "A few moments ago," he said, "I was advised that 73 telegrams had been received in my office during the last 3 hours. They read alike, and that they are inspired is evident. Somebody has been spending 60 to 75 cents per telegram to wire me to vote for the proposed increase in the appropriation."[63]

When the George-Deen Act reached the floor of Congress, support was overwhelming, although organized labor, concerned that extensive vocational training was creating a glut in the job market, opposed it. Efforts on the part of the administration to reduce the appropriation failed, and in the end, the measure passed on a voice vote in both the House and the Senate. Including the $1.2 million for distributive education, the new appropriation amounted to approximately $14 million. The funds available for distributive education meant that federal support now extended to such classes as advertising, store management, merchandizing, and store display. The act more than doubled the amount of federal funds available for vocational education, and, for the first time, the District of Columbia was allowed to participate. Coming at a time of continuing economic crisis, congressional passage of the bill represented a major victory for AVA over its New Deal adversaries.

Roosevelt, however, expressed "much reluctance" upon signing the George-Deen Act. In one of his few public expressions of dissatisfaction with vocational education as usually practiced, FDR alluded to a recent committee finding that "the basis for the distinction of funds among the States as provided in the vocational education statutes, including the George-Deen Act, tends in many cases to increase rather than decrease inequalities in educational opportunity." These inequalities, FDR went on to point out, arose because of minimum allotments and matching provisions which had the effect of denying funds to areas most in need of aid, such as small rural high schools. In an unusually candid declaration of his deep suspicion as to the motives of the vocationalists, particularly on the eve of a presidential election, Roosevelt attributed "the apparent demand for the immediate extension of the vocational education program under the George-Deen Act [to] an active lobby of vocational teachers, supervisors and administrative officers in the field of vocational education, who are interested in the emoluments paid in part from Federal funds." He further noted that "members of both houses of the Congress referred to the pressure exerted upon them by groups actively lobbying in behalf of the full appropriation." The impetus for the passage, Roosevelt added pointedly, "emanated from a single interested source."[64]

Despite his obvious reluctance to sign, Roosevelt could not risk a veto of the appropriation. That action would have jeopardized the delicate political coalition he had forged between northern liberals and southern conservatives. For all intents and purposes, a one-party system existed in southern states, which had the effect of extending the seniority of southern Democrats, thereby making them eligible for key leadership posts in Congress. Moreover, their solidarity on the question of racial segregation through a policy of "states rights" seemed to carry over to cohesiveness on other issues.[65] With the crucial support of southern congressmen, vocationalists won the battle over increased appropriations in the form of the George-Deen Act. That victory, however, came at the cost of invoking the open enmity of the President of the United States.

Although Roosevelt was unquestionably reluctant to alienate his southern allies, members of his administration, and particularly Eleanor Roosevelt, worked behind the scenes to extend the benefits of New Deal programs to African Americans. The work of Mary McLeod Bethune in connection with NYA is illustrative in this regard. Although initially appointed only as an advisor for black affairs, Bethune soon became a force within the agency for reshaping youth policy. After she impressed Roosevelt at a White House meeting, he appointed her to head the NYA Office for Negro Affairs in June 1936, just a year after NYA was born.[66] In 1937, her efforts to promote a more inclusive NYA policy in terms of black youth participation culminated in FDR's executive order 8802, which sought to establish an antidiscrimination policy. NYA's chief administrator, Aubrey Williams, immediately endorsed the policy. Although equality of expenditure in terms of black and white youth in NYA projects was never fully realized, Bethune was able to achieve substantial gains in that regard, as well as to increase participation of blacks in training programs. She was able to establish model training programs for black youth, for example, and worked to shift programs for African Americans away from service jobs toward industrial work.[67] Although the record of the New Deal in matters of civil rights and in creating equality of opportunity is somewhat mixed by present standards, its policies in terms of providing for America's underclass in such areas of job training were much in advance of what in that time had become standard practice.

THE RUSSELL REPORT: VOCATIONALISM ON TRIAL

The animosity between vocationalists and the New Deal took a new turn with the issuance of a report by a committee FDR had appointed upon signing the George-Deen Act in 1937. Roosevelt expressly hoped that their recommendations would bring about changes in the legislation. John D. Russell, a professor of education at the University of Chicago but with no specific association with vocational education, was appointed chair, and the other members were also from outside the vocational education establishment. The committee gathered testimony from various individuals and groups and conducted a number of staff studies in the spring of 1937. By 1938, the report, entitled *Vocational Education*, was ready.

Several of the Russell committee's findings were damaging to the cause of vocationalism. "In many respects," the report declared in its summary, "the general operation of the program of vocational education is unsatisfactory."[68] At least some of the progress that had been made in the area, the report contended, would have taken place without federal support. "Education for office occupations," the report pointed out, "has been extended greatly in the secondary school, of the United States," without the benefit of federal aid. The report was especially critical of the lack of available data on nonreimbursed vocational education, estimating that such aid is "possibly in excess of that which goes into the federally reimbursed program." While praising federally supported vocational programs for "the rapid extension and improvement of instruction,"[69] the report was nevertheless critical of several aspects of the way vocational education had developed in the United States since the Smith-Hughes Act. Among the specific criticisms was that a limited conception of vocational education was being promoted. Although the Smith-Hughes left open the possibility of broader training, the actual federal programs were based on the assumption that "to be effective, [it] must be very specific and narrowly related to the occupational skills it seeks to develop." The report especially deplored the "vigorous promotion of the idea that vocational education and general education are two entirely distinct and separate things" and was unqualified in its insistence that such an emphasis had served to limit the effectiveness of vocational education. Even more significantly, however, the requirement that states match federal funding for vocational education had served to divert "funds to vocational education that otherwise would have been available for general education."[70]

The Russell report also took particular issue with the vocationalists' advancement of a dual system of schools, arguing that American democracy stands in contrast to the European ideas that gave rise to such a system. "Stated in the plainest terms," the report declared, "the concept behind the program of vocational education would segregate the young people who are to become industrial workers from those who are to go into the professions and other scholarly pursuits, and would provide separate school facilities for those two groups." This criticism was extended to regular high schools where "there seems to be a deliberate attempt to keep the vocational work as separate as possible from the other phases of the educational program."[71] In general, referring to the "separate administration of vocational education which shields the programs from much careful assessment," the report further observed that "there appears to be an increasing tendency among many of those engaged in the federal program of vocational education to consider themselves a separate educational group and to do everything to restrict positions of administrative authority to those who have come up through the program." Specifications in state plans for vocational education are so drawn, the report found, as virtually to exclude those who are not part of the vocational education establishment from any administrative post.[72]

As a result of this closed system, reporting on the expenditure of federal vocational funds had been limited largely to favorable interpretations. In an unusually strong indictment of oversight procedures, the report stated that "one cannot avoid the conclusion that the published reports tend to emphasize the favorable aspects of the program and to minimize the unfavorable aspects. The reports seem to be conceived of as propaganda for the program rather than a dispassionate and scientific analysis of the results accomplished."[73] In fact, much of the data that are reported are so restricted, they cannot be easily interpreted. Such open, semiofficial criticism of vocational education practices had been virtually unprecedented.

When the committee report turned to specific programs sponsored by the federal government, they had favorable things to say about home economics and vocational agriculture. In the area of industrial and trade education, however, the report was much less positive. For one thing, evaluative reports that would shed light on this aspect of federally sponsored programs were distinctly absent. In the more than twenty years since Smith-Hughes, publications on the subject were numerous, but "relatively few of the published studies could be classified as research by any strict definition of the term."[74] Although reports had been issued which provided accounts of various programs, "little or no evidence has been gathered regarding the results or effectiveness of the instruction given."[75] No evidence was available, for example, on the number of students who drop out of vocational programs. On the other hand, reports from both labor and industry sources constituted "a substantial body of evidence to the effect that in general the highly specific training in the all-day program of vocational schools has been of little value to boys intending to enter trades and industrial occupations."[76] A staff study conducted by Katherine Lenroot, "Relation of Vocational Education to Jobs Held by Workers under 18 Years of Age," indicated that only 18 percent of sixteen- and seventeen-year-old youths were actually employed in the occupations for which they had been trained.[77]

Moreover, representatives of labor complained that vocational educators failed to seek their advice in providing for vocational education and that "the program of instruction has ignored the necessity of providing thorough training in social and economic studies of value to workers entering industry."[78] Of particular concern to labor was the tendency for vocational programs to prepare workers for specific trades without reference to the question of whether they could be absorbed into the job pool. The Russell report also alluded to the failure of vocational educators to recruit and train an adequate teaching force for their programs. Such open criticism of their programs posed a formidable challenge to vocationalists. The Russell report's reservations as to their established policies and practices made the threat of a rival federally sponsored system along the lines of the CCC and the NYA all the more plausible.

VOCATIONALISM REDEEMED: JOB TRAINING FOR NATIONAL DEFENSE

Events on the world stage soon turned FDR's attention away from domestic policy. The Munich Pact, signed on September 30, 1935, surrendered the Sudetenland (which had been part of Czechoslovakia) to the Germans. By 1938, German troops had occupied Austria. It became clear to Roosevelt that war loomed in Europe and that the United States needed to undertake a major reconstruction and acceleration of its industrial capacities in the event that the United States was drawn into that conflict. That reconstruction required new and extensive industrial training, and the vocationalists were well positioned to seize the opportunity. When German troops invaded Poland on September 1, 1939, the war in Europe became a reality, and the race to rearm achieved a new urgency.

The intense effort to convert to military preparedness in terms of industrial strength in the years leading up to World War Two put the vocationalists in a commanding position vis-à-vis their New Deal enemies. By 1938, Roosevelt had decided that a major defense initiative was needed; he ordered that an air force of 10,000 planes be established and an additional 10,000 planes be built each year. Foreseeing that industrial production would be vital to an all-out war effort, in his January 4, 1939, message to Congress, Roosevelt called for a defense budget of nearly $2 billion, with the greatest part of that money going to build new ships and airplanes. Such massive government expenditures not only brought an end to the depression but to the New Deal. "As 1939 drew to a close," says Robert McElvaine, "the New Deal as a continuing source of innovation was through."[79] By the end of that year, employment in industry had already risen by 10 percent, and salaries had increased by 16 percent.[80] The end of the economic crisis was in sight.

Training workers for new defense industries soon became an urgent national priority. By 1938, 1,682 full-time students were in aviation training classes, along with an additional 3,242 part-time students,[81] but these programs still needed to be expanded. In 1938, Roosevelt ordered the Vocational Division of the U.S. Office of Education to undertake a study of the training of aircraft workers. The Vocational Division recommended that an interdepartmental committee be set up for the purpose of developing a specific plan, and in May 1939, the committee recommended that public vocational schools be enlisted in the training of workers in aeronautical industries.[82] Highly skilled jobs would be broken down into semiskilled operations so that a minimum of training would be entailed. State and local supervisors of vocational education were encouraged to provide instruction to NYA youth. The Vocational Division enlisted the cooperation of aircraft manufacturers, and with further redefinition of skilled jobs, training periods were reduced.

In the context of war preparedness, Bethune, still functioning as an official of the NYA, accelerated her efforts to provide job training for black youth. One of her projects, the War Production Training Project in Wilberforce, Ohio, for example, proved to be very successful in terms of the participation of black youth in defense industries. She also directed her efforts toward providing guidance and placement services for black youth through the NYA. As Elaine M. Smith summarized the work of the NYA in this regard, "the NYA provided the 'crack in the door' which led to the employment of Negroes on assembly lines in plants such a Bell Aircraft, Buffalo, New York; Sun Shipbuilding in Chester, Pennsylvania; Radio Corporation of

America in Camden, New Jersey; and Kane Manufacturing Company in Louisville, Kentucky."[83] The pressures of the defense buildup would almost surely have served to create new job opportunities for blacks in any case, but the NYA had paved the way for that shift in terms of providing industrial job training that had previously been available to blacks only on a very limited basis, particularly in the South. The opening up of opportunity in industrial work for African Americans contributed to a substantial migration of blacks from the rural South to northern cities where relatively high-paying industrial work could be found. This was already pronounced in the 1920s, but with new opportunities in defense industries opening up, black migration accelerated. By 1940 or so, as Nicholas Lemann, describes it, "There wasn't really any young black person in Clarkstown (Mississippi) who wasn't thinking about Chicago."[84] Between 1940 and 1944, one million black workers were employed in civilian occupations. By 1944, the workforce included more than double the number of skilled black workers than had existed a few years earlier.[85] In obvious ways, the defense buildup had the effect of challenging a pattern of discrimination in the industrial sector.

Job training in public schools was also flourishing. By 1940, with the passage of the massive Vocational Education for National Defense Act, vocational education was on sound financial footing for at least the duration of the war. With the Office of Education disbursing money to states and local school districts under provisions similar to the Smith-Hughes Act, vocationalists now had the financing and status they had long dreamed of attaining. Perhaps the only significant change from their long-standing position was that training programs could not exceed three months. During wartime, the highest priority was given to training as many semiskilled workers as possible in the shortest amount of time, so training periods lasting years were at least temporarily abandoned.

With industrial production a pressing national concern, vocationalists were now in a commanding position to reassert their prerogatives and demonstrate their value in terms of the national interest. Industrial production, after all, had long been the centerpiece of their efforts; with many industries converting to defense work and semiskilled workers in much demand, vocationalists were prepared to step into the breach. Along the way, however, were some scores to be settled with their New Deal enemies. Roosevelt's effort to extend defense training funds to the NYA in 1940 was successfully thwarted in Congress, and newly passed legislation put the Office of Education in charge of all defense training while providing an additional $6.5 million for further training in defense industries. In 1941, an additional $116 million was appropriated. Support for training programs for shipyard work, machine shops, sheet metal, electricity, telephone installation, and automobile and truck repair was added. By 1941, some vocational schools were operating twenty-four hours a day. Between July 1940 and June 1941 alone, 420,000 potential workers received training, and by June 1942, an additional 1,051,346 were trained. By the end of the war in 1945, some 7.5 million workers had been trained under the Vocational Education for National Defense Act at a cost of $326,900,000.[86]

Their position solidified, vocationalists decided to deliver a death blow. With the war consuming the president's time and attention, and the New Deal largely a thing of the past, the AVA undertook a campaign to insure the quick demise of the NYA. (The CCC had already been discontinued in 1942.) Their key arguments were that the NYA was duplicating vocational training provided by other agencies such as the War Manpower Commission and was lowering standards. Walter Dexter, the Superintendent of Public Instruction in California, for example, wrote to Studebaker complaining that NYA officials lacked the necessary experience and a sound philosophy of vocational education.[87] Aware of these allegations, NYA director Aubrey Williams moved to blunt the criticisms. In a message sent to the 1939 AVA convention in St. Louis, he professed his "earnest desire to cooperate fully with the established educational institutions which you represent."[88] Vocationalists, however, would not be denied. In March 1943, a questionnaire was sent to AVA members, urging them to report infractions by the NYA such as duplication of programs and misuse of funds. Having received a copy of the questionnaire, which was sent to him anonymously, Williams wrote to the president, accusing the AVA of directing its members to unearth even minor problems with the operation of NYA and reporting them to members of Congress.[89] The questionnaire sent to the membership did not bear any identification as to its source, and the AVA actually denied distributing it, but one of the extant copies in U.S. Office of Education files is specifically identified as coming from the AVA.[90] Vocationalists were now adversaries to be reckoned with, and the days of the NYA were numbered. "The NYA," as Rawick expressed it, "died a hard death." The vote on June 14, 1943, in the House Appropriations Committee was 17 to 16 in favor of abolition, and although Senator Harry S. Truman's motion to continue the funding for the agency narrowly passed in the Senate, it failed in the House.[91] The New Deal's threat to the vocationalists was now officially over.

Vocationalists still faced some difficulties here and there. With much of vocational training directed toward special programs tied to the war effort, for example, enrollments in regular vocational programs began to drop in 1942. For one thing, the availability of high-paying jobs in defense industries was an inducement for youth to leave school. The same applied to teachers, and as a result, some vocational classes were being canceled. On the whole, though, vocational education had demonstrated its worth in terms of the national interest. Those vocational classes that continued to exist overwhelmingly stressed defense training. In vocational agriculture and home economics classes, increased food production and food conservation were emphasized.[92] The building of model airplanes by vocational students for identification purposes became a commonplace activity.[93] In 1943, the high school program in Detroit was entirely reconstructed in order to contribute to the war effort. Along with efforts to tie the education program to potential induction into the armed forces and toward civilian support for the military effort, schools were, according to historian Jeffrey Mirel, being directed to "demonstrate their validity in terms of . . . pre-employment preparation for employment in war industries."[94] Vocational education's contributions to the war effort were real and widely admired. Their most worrisome tribulations behind them, vocationalists could now look forward to a bright postwar future, assuming, of course, that the federal government would continue underwriting much of the cost.

ON TO GEORGE-BARDEN AND VICTORY!

In January 1944, as part of the effort to set vocational education policy in the postwar years, Commissioner of Education Studebaker authorized a study called *Vocational Education in the Years Ahead*, and a year and a half later, the report was ready. Once more, there was common agreement that the high school was failing a large proportion of America's youth. At the conference at which the report was presented, Charles Prosser, as would be expected, was called upon to summarize the conference's major recommendation:

> It is the belief of this conference, that with the aid of this report in final form, the vocational school of a community will be able better to prepare 20 percent of youth of secondary school age for entrance upon desirable skill occupations; and that the high school will continue to prepare 20 percent of its students for entrance to college. We do not believe that the remaining 60 percent of our youth of secondary school age will receive the life adjustment training to which they are entitled as American citizens—unless and until the administrators of public education with the assistance of vocational education leaders formulate a comparable program for this group.[95]

Thus was born the ill-fated life adjustment movement, which enjoyed the active support of Commissioner Studebaker and the U.S. Office of Education until the movement collapsed in the late 1950s. Although life adjustment as an educational ideology was difficult to define even by its proponents, it took its cue from the belief that schools should address the full range of activities that youth engage in as part of the effort to "adjust" them to the kind of soci-

ety in which they found themselves. Academic study, by and large, was dis-
dained as irrelevant to the lives of youth. While life adjustment education as
a specific movement had a short lifespan, its basic precepts had a long history. Life adjustment education was the logical extension of the social efficiency ideals and the anti-academic tendencies that were imbedded in the now
revered *Cardinal Principles*. As Dorothy Broder has indicated, "Apologists for
Life Adjustment Education ritually cited the *Cardinal Principles* as the touchstone of their inspiration and guidance."[96]

As educational ideals, vocationalism and social efficiency had always
been inexorably linked, but they were now becoming almost indistinguishable. The effort to prepare workers for the demands of the workplace had
become intertwined with the effort to adjust future citizens to social conditions generally. On September 20, 1945, less than three months after delivering his stirring new challenge to the nation's schools, Charles Prosser, the
leading architect of the Smith-Hughes Act and long-standing knight-errant
in the cause of vocationalism, retired. He was leaving vocational education
on solid ground. The Smith-Hughes Act, along with various extensions, continued to provide generous federal support for vocational agriculture, home
economics, and industrial training; moreover, a strong movement was afoot
to extend and liberalize those provisions. Prosser had reason to be proud of
his accomplishments. "During its first 23 years," he said at his retirement din-
ner, "the national system of vocational schools, departments, and other classes
gave training to more than 20,000,000 youths and adults."[97] What is more,
vocational schools, he said, had been instrumental in the overthrow of Hitler.
He then went on to outline the direction that vocational education needed
to take in the postwar period.

At the occasion of his retirement, Prosser repeated the same message
he had delivered a few weeks earlier, using the same percentages in terms
of high school youth, but implicitly at least, he changed the nature of the
program he envisioned for the 60 percent presumably not being served by
the educational system. Life adjustment education *per se* for that group was
not mentioned. Instead, Prosser declared that "The remaining 60 percent
are not reached and prepared successfully *to earn a living in any employment*"
(emphasis added).[98] The implication, of course, was that with the exception of the 20 percent presumed to be college bound, all high school students should be directed toward vocational training. Prosser's declaration
was a concrete expression of the emerging educational ideal. With the
exception of the college entrance function, most Americans were finding
it difficult to visualize any other purpose to secondary education besides
getting ready for work.

In the last months of World War Two, vocationalists undertook a campaign for yet another federal bill to support vocational education. With the

country yearning for normalcy, and their old nemesis, FDR, ailing and pre-occupied with the final military campaign, vocationalists sought, once and for all, to put their depression-related problems behind them. The additional funding provided by the George-Deen Act of 1936 and various bills designed to promote defense production was certainly welcome, but vocationalists were now looking ahead to the postwar period. Less than five years after George-Deen, they embarked on a drive for an ambitious new piece of leg-islation. Once more, the American Vocational Association undertook the task of crafting the legislation, and that stalwart backer of vocational edu-cation causes, Walter F. George of Georgia, who had lent his name to the George-Reed Act of 1929, the George-Ellzey Act of 1934, and the George-Deen Act of 1936, led the charge in the Senate. Graham A. Barden, as cosponsor, introduced the bill in the House of Representatives on October 16, 1945.

Roosevelt was not happy with this turn of events. Even before the bill was formally introduced, he sent letters to Senator George and Congressman Barden, seeking to head off the new legislation at least until the end of the war,[99] and no action was taken on the measure in 1944. By 1945, however, the AVA would not be denied, taking the position that the existing voca-tional education system was not large enough to accommodate the need for retraining after the war.[100] The George-Barden Act not only provided new funds for vocational programs but authorized additional reimbursement for the salaries of vocational administrators and supervisory personnel. Provisions for their travel were even included. As was the case with previous legisla-tion, George-Barden provided for federal matching aid for states on a dol-lar-for-dollar basis, but this time with fewer restrictions on how the money could be used. Vocational guidance stood to gain under its liberal provisions, since George-Barden funds could be directed for that purpose as well. The fiscal effect was to double the appropriations for vocational education pro-vided by George-Deen. Both houses of Congress passed the bill on nearly unanimous votes, and on August 1, 1946, less than four months after assum-ing the presidency upon Roosevelt's death, Harry S. Truman signed it into law.

The American public's growing commitment to vocationalism as the pri-mary purpose of schooling was backed once again by solid congressional sup-port. The passage of the George-Barden Act, so soon after the tribulations vocationalists endured at the hands of the New Deal, signaled a major expan-sion of vocational education in the postwar years, marked a renewed promi-nence for vocationalism as an educational ideal, and presaged an enduring commitment on the part of Congress to its cause. After George-Barden, voca-tionalists were virtually invincible in terms of consolidating and extending their dominion.

THE NEW DEAL VERSUS THE VOCATIONALISTS

Some accounts of the New Deal period and of the FDR presidency convey the impression, perhaps inadvertently, that an otherwise great president somehow had a blind spot when it came to education policy. As seen from the perspective of professional educators, a good president is supposed to be a champion of America's schools, and this is usually measured by the willingness of the president to support federal aid to education. By that standard, Roosevelt was clearly lacking. He resisted the role of federal government as mere financier of schools, mainly because he and many of his closest associates were suspicious of the motives and even the competence of professional educators. This was reflected in a clear aversion to providing federal funds for their use, and more important, in a concerted effort to develop youth programs that amounted to creating a federal rival to state-run vocational education. From his point of view, the professional educational establishment, their own protestations notwithstanding, had failed America's underclass.

When seen against the record of the vocationalists, Roosevelt's stance in education matters becomes more understandable and his suspicions as to the ability of vocational educators to address the economic crisis more plausible. Roosevelt's domestic priorities lay with creating jobs and putting the unemployed, particularly youth, to work without delay. A long-standing tradition in vocational education entailed long periods of training, close attention to the qualifications and credentials of vocational teachers and their supervisors, and very considerable leeway for local school authorities to shape the programs. Roosevelt's New Deal allies surely realized that these cornerstones of vocational education policy were inimical to their approach to the economic crisis. New Deal priorities lay in putting even minimally trained youth to work as soon as possible, keeping the period of training as unencumbered as possible by bureaucratic regulations, and centralizing authority in order to carry those programs forward expeditiously. Given a strong president, accustomed to getting his policies implemented, a clash with the vocationalists (as well as professional educators generally) was almost inevitable.

While federal programs such as CCC and NYA were surely deficient in many respects, they were focused on the problem of unemployment in a way conventional vocational programs were not. By 1935, with suspicion of the vocationalists growing, those relief agencies evolved quite deliberately into educational institutions. Vocationalists were simply not as nimble in responding to the economic emergency as were their New Deal adversaries. Improvisation was not the vocationalists' strong point. In a sense, their professionalism got in their way. So far as vocationalists were concerned, established procedures relating to admission and retention as well as professional niceties

FIGURE 12. The Allis-Chalmers plant, Milwaukee, Wisconsin. President Franklin
D. Roosevelt visited the Allis-Chalmers plant, which employed women defense work-
ers, on September 19, 1942. Official U.S. Navy Photograph. *Courtesy State Historical
Society of Wisconsin.*

such as credentialing and the prerogatives of local administrators needed to
be honored. After all, their own professional status and ability to control
polices and programs rested on those structures. As the Great Depression

wore on, it was not at all clear whether the edifice they had built and that had been preserved and strengthened since Smith-Hughes would endure.

World War Two, with all its tragic loss of life and grim destruction, proved to be a blessing to the vocationalists. Two factors were critical. First, Roosevelt's attention was drawn away from domestic policy toward military preparedness and foreign policy. In the context of a pending world conflagration, his quarrels with professional educators seemed petty. Secondly, defense industries served to resolve the unemployment problem and even mitigated the problem of a segregated workforce. Women were also being employed in industrial work on a scale never before realized (see Figure 12). "Rosie the Riveter" was not just a popular song of this period; it reflected a new ideal of women in the workforce. At the peak of wartime production, in July 1944, 19 million women were employed, representing an increase of 47 percent over the level of female employment in March 1940.[101] Although long-standing vocational education policy had not emphasized industrial training for women, concentrating instead on home economics, that pattern was now being broken, at least temporarily.

The employment situation that had existed since the early days of the depression was essentially reversed. The problem now was not finding work for an unemployed army; it was training large numbers of men and women for plentiful and relatively high-paying jobs. In that context, vocationalists reasserted themselves. They worked effectively to undermine and even destroy the federal agencies that were threatening to usurp their power and prerogatives, while at the same time enthusiastically undertaking the task of vocational training for defense industries. The expertise and experience of the vocationalists was now in great demand, while the Roosevelt administration lacked the time and inclination to develop an independent system of vocational education, especially since vocational educators were undertaking their wartime tasks with great ardor and some willingness to compromise. What remained in some doubt was the fate of vocationalism in a peacetime economy, and the passage of the George-Barden Act in 1946 went a long way toward putting those fears to rest.

 8

"THE DOMINANT VOCATION OF ALL HUMAN BEINGS"

The Successes and Failures of Vocationalism

The principle . . . that the educative process is its own end, and that the only sufficient preparation for later responsibilities comes by making the most of immediately present life, applies full force to the vocational phases of education. The dominant vocation of all human beings at all times is living—intellectual and moral growth. In childhood and youth with their relative freedom from economic stress, this fact is naked and unconcealed. To predetermine some future occupation for which education is to be a strict preparation is to injure the possibilities of present development and thereby to reduce the adequacy of preparation for a future right employment. . . . Such training may develop a machine-like skill in routine lines (it is far from being sure to do so since it may develop distaste, aversion, and carelessness), but it will be at the expense of those qualities of alert observation and coherent and ingenious planning which make an occupation intellectually rewarding.

John Dewey, 1916[1]

The remarkable success that vocational education enjoyed in the period 1917 to 1946 in terms of marshaling governmental as well as popular support was achieved despite a paucity of evidence in support of its efficacy. The question of whether vocational education actually provides the skills needed in the modern workplace remains unresolved even today. A full-blown assessment of the successes and failures of vocationalism in American education is surely outside the scope of this study, but some effort to draw implications from the historical record of vocationalism is irresistible. Even a modest and selective review of its record of accomplishments and disappointments, however, is no easy task. As labor historian Walter Licht put it,

> The historian does not have at his or her command easy means to assess accurately the actual value of schooling in occupational achievement—to go beyond the question of intentions. Assembling sufficiently large, representative samples ... from different eras, gathering social and demographic background information for those elected, and tracing their ensuing educational and job histories presents formidable obstacles to the researcher. Relating levels of education to vocational attainments in a general and certain way is simply not possible. From a historical standpoint, the question can only be approached in a composite fashion.[2]

In assembling a composite picture of the record of vocational education, no single factor will be decisive in drawing a conclusion, but the various component parts may come together to provide an overall impression and direction.

VOCATIONAL EDUCATION EVALUATED: THE MENEFEE REPORT

Formal evaluations of the concrete effects of vocational education between 1917 and 1946 came late and remained sparse. In part at least, this is attributable to the ability of the vocationalists to avoid oversight by any but the most favorably disposed to their massive enterprise. Apart from the question of the extent to which secondary school students actually enrolled in the vocational courses that were being offered, for which some data are available, the far more complex issue remains of whether those who did enroll actually benefited from their training. Understandably, no study definitively answers a question of such complexity, but one effort to evaluate vocational education during the period under study provides some telling indications of its relative success and failures in this regard.

By far the most comprehensive and most carefully designed evaluation up to World War Two was conducted by a staff member in the Labor Market Research Section of the WPA, Selden C. Menefee. Menefee's study appeared in 1942, although the data refer to the year 1938. In a sense this is fortuitous, since the 1938 data would not be materially affected by the intense buildup in defense industries that occurred shortly thereafter. Designed primarily to examine the work histories of youths trained under the Smith-Hughes Act, the study was based on interviews with 3,042 youths in four cities: St. Louis,

Birmingham, Denver, and Seattle. The work histories of vocationally trained youth were then compared to untrained youth in those cities, with a view to determining some of the effects of their vocational training. The study focuses principally on the extent to which youth trained under provisions of the Smith-Hughes Act benefited from their training in terms of participation in the job market and increased income, but Menefee also addressed similar issues involving state-supported and private vocational education.

Although Menefee's report balances the predominantly negative findings with some positive outcomes, it is clear that youths receiving Smith-Hughes vocational training did not enjoy a material advantage over their untrained counterparts in terms of the criteria employed. On the positive side, the trained youth maintained a small advantage in terms of entry into the workforce—94 percent, compared with 85 percent without training. In addition, 81 percent of the trained workers were still in the labor market as of July 1, 1938, whereas only 67 percent of the untrained were still employed. Unfortunately, these particular data are not analyzed in terms of gender, although Menefee reports that the trained group included "a greater preponderance of young women."[3] Since women historically have benefited more than men from vocational training, their presence in the data affected the results. The relationship between school training and clerical occupations in which women predominated, for example, had always been much stronger than in the case of industrial occupations.[4] Additionally, there were no consistent differences in terms of total time spent in the labor market. In Birmingham and Denver, trained youth spent more total time in the labor force, whereas in St. Louis and Seattle, untrained youth had the edge. As would be expected, black youth, whether trained or untrained, were unemployed or employed only part-time to a much greater extent than white youth. Whereas only one in six white youths was unemployed, four in ten black youths were without work. These latter data, however, are reflective of a racially biased job market rather than attributable to presence or absence of vocational training.

Many of Menefee's findings showed small or inconsistent differences. There were, for example, some differences in terms of weekly salary between youths who had completed their vocational training and those who had not, although these differences were not particularly striking. The earnings differential in Denver and Seattle was only 7 and 8 percent, while in St. Louis, the percentages were roughly the same. When those who had completed training were compared with those who had not in terms of weekly earnings, the salaries were again very close. In St. Louis, both groups were earning $14.70; Birmingham had the largest differential, $16 to $15; in Denver, the difference was only 20 cents; and in Seattle, youth who had not competed their training were actually earning more than their fully trained counterparts,

TABLE 1. Percentage of youth in full-time jobs

	With Smith-Hughes Training	Without Training
St. Louis	76	74
Birmingham	73	61
Denver	78	78
Seattle	67	70

$15.30 to $15,[5] indicating perhaps that time spent on the job there was more remunerative than time spent in training.

Surely troubling to supporters of vocational education were the findings that showed no consistent advantage for trained youth over untrained youth in terms of participation in the labor force. A table in Menefee's report (see Table 1 herein) shows the percentage of youth in full-time jobs (averaging 30 hours or more per week) of both male and female youths with Smith-Hughes training and those without in the four cities used in the study. Birmingham, Alabama, was racially segregated at the time, and that was reflected in the employment data. The advantage shown by the trained youth there is attributable to the fact that all the trained youth in that city were white, while many of the youths in the untrained group were African Americans. Average weekly earnings of all white youth in Birmingham in 1938 were $17.20, while the average weekly earnings of black youth were $8.50. Taking all four cities together, the Smith-Hughes trained group had only a 4 percent better chance of being employed full-time than the untrained youth.[6] Leaving Birmingham aside, the trained group had no advantage over the untrained group in terms of full-time employment.

The data on average weekly earnings for the trained and untrained groups were about as disappointing, although the data are again difficult to interpret because of the differences in racial and gender composition between the trained and untrained groups. Birmingham showed the clearest advantage for the trained youth, $18.20 per week compared to $15.20, but again, the higher earnings of the Smith-Hughes trained group there reflected that the trained group included only white youth, while a substantial proportion of the untrained youths were black. When African Americans were removed from the samples of untrained youth in the four cities, the average earnings of the remaining untrained whites rose to $17.10, or within a dollar of the weekly salaries of trained youth. A similar pattern existed in terms of gender. In Denver, for example, Smith-Hughes trained youth earned $18.90, while the untrained youth earned $16.80. All of the trained youth, however, were young men, and when young women were eliminated from the untrained group, the earnings for the remaining men were about the same as the average for the trained youth.[7]

TABLE 2. Average wages for young men and women with and without Smith-Hughes training

	With Smith-Hughes Training	Without Training
Young Men		
St. Louis	$18.40	$18.60
Birmingham	19.00	18.00
Denver	18.90	19.00
Seattle	20.20	23.40
Young Women		
St. Louis	$15.00	$14.40
Birmingham	13.10	12.30
Seattle	15.60	16.40

Gender differences in terms of average wages in general were quite substantial, as would be expected (see Table 2), but there was also a clear indication that fully employed young women benefited more from their training than the fully employed men. For young men, the strongest advantage in the four cities in terms of average income was for Seattle's *untrained* men. Taking the city of St. Louis as an example, young men there had only a 20-cent advantage over the untrained in average weekly earnings, and young women had a 60-cent advantage. If both gender and amount of education are taken into account, young women with training had a slight advantage over untrained girls who left school after completing the eighth grade, but it is not clear whether this advantage is attributable to the additional years of schooling, to the high school diploma itself, to age, or to specific vocational training. Female workers with training and a full twelve years of education averaged $15.40 per week, whereas young women with ten or eleven years of education were earning $14.60. In the case of young men, however, this advantage was dissipated if not reversed. Young men with Smith-Hughes training and twelve years of schooling earned $18.10 per week, while those without training and ten or eleven years of schooling earned an average of $18.40, and those who left school before completing the ninth grade earned an average of $19.60 per week.[8] For young men in St. Louis at least, it seems as if the additional years in the workforce as a result of quitting school proved to be a greater advantage in weekly earnings than completing their vocational training in a school setting. Another factor seemed to be age. Among both trained and untrained youth, four years of additional age resulted in a substantial $6 per week advantage.

Apart from entry into the workforce and weekly salaries, Menefee also considered the relationship between specific job training and finding work in the particular area of training. In this regard, he classified each job as having (1) a primary or direct relationship to the job, (2) a secondary relationship, or (3) no relationship at all. Taking St. Louis as a special case study, Menefee found distinct differences between commercial and industrial training in terms of leading to employment related to the training. Of 1,338 youths in the clerical labor market (85 percent of whom were women), 50 percent had jobs closely related to their training, and another 13 percent were employed in jobs having a secondary relationship to their training. Of the remaining 38 percent, 29 percent had jobs in unrelated areas and 9 percent were unemployed. Completion of commercial training was quite important in securing clerical employment. Specific industrial training, however, was not as clearly related to the jobs youth actually had in St. Louis. Of 699 youth in the labor market, 40 percent had jobs directly related to their training and another 14 percent had jobs indirectly related. In particular jobs, machine shop work, printing, and electricity were roughly at or above the 50 percent level, but in such areas as aeronautical and auto mechanics, only 28 percent were in jobs directly related to their training. For woodworking and sheet-metal work, the percentages fell to 19 and 14. Among young women, training in cosmetology was remarkably successful, with 83 percent holding jobs directly related to their training, 46 percent in industrial sewing, and 30 percent in cafeteria-tearoom work.[9]

The bright spot in Menefee's report was clerical education. Taking St. Louis again as his example, Menefee reported that of 1,348 youth in the labor market who had been trained in commercial programs, 63 percent had jobs related to their training, and 50 percent had jobs closely related to their training. A full 85 percent of those trained in the commercial subjects were young women. Significantly, what he calls special commercial training, which is of short duration (a year or less), was the most successful. The courses entailed in such training mainly involved various forms of business-machine operations and general office procedure, but they also included accounting and secretarial studies.[10] Moreover, unlike industrial training, completion of a program of commercial education was an important factor in terms of obtaining related work, as was the case with young women generally (e.g., cosmetology).[11]

Race differences were also significant in the St. Louis sample. Only about a third of African Americans had obtained employment in jobs specifically related to their training, compared to about half of the white youth. This disadvantage was also evident in clerical employment. Only 20 percent of black youth found work related to clerical training, while the comparable figure for whites was 51 percent. In general, racial barriers to employment tended to negate even extensive training for black youth. One black youth who took the full course in printing at Booker T. Washington High School and received his high school diploma reported:

I couldn't get a steady job in printing or in any other kind of work. The teachers try to place boys, but there are never many requests for printers. They did get me a job at Goodwill Industries. For a while I worked there 1 or 2 days a week, setting up and printing letterheads and cards, but that gave out. I put in applications at the State employment office and the Urban League, the only places where colored folks can get jobs. But nothing happened so about a year ago I went up to the NYA people and they put me on. I make about $25 a month working on a project at the "Y," and I've saved up $40.[12]

Although anecdotal in nature, that youth's experience may indicate that New Deal work programs, such as NYA, may have been critical in putting black youth to work, even those with extensive vocational training at the secondary school level. Put another way, completion of vocational training in itself did not seem to affect employment possibilities for African Americans materially.

Vocational guidance in the four cities that Menefee studied was notably ineffective or simply absent. Taking all four cities together, only one in six Smith-Hughes trained youths received *any* advice in relation to enrolling in vocational programs, although in Seattle a third of the trained group received some guidance. Much of the problem lay simply in the paucity of guidance counselors. In St. Louis, for example, a city with a population of 1 million at the time, three full-time counselors were added to the Division of Vocational Counseling in 1925, but they were dropped during the depression. The largest high school in Birmingham had two guidance counselors for boys and one for girls. There were 13 counselors in the entire white system, and none at all in the black system. Of the employed youths interviewed in the four cities, the vast majority reported that they were helped to find jobs primarily by friends, through their own initiative in filing applications, and through previous employers and relatives. The percentages in this regard were roughly the same for Smith-Hughes trained youth as for the untrained. Only 8 percent of the trained youth and 4 percent of the untrained reported getting help from their schools. Menefee reported that none of the vocational schools in the four cities had adequate placement services.[13] Whatever may have been the high hopes of the early leaders of the vocational guidance movement, little assistance in terms of vocational choice or in job placement was actually being felt by the youth themselves in 1938.

Menefee's remarkable study, *Vocational Training and Employment of Youth,* did not appear until a quarter century had elapsed after the passage of the Smith-Hughes Act. As the Russell report indicated in 1938, no serious effort had been made to assess the effects of vocational training since it had become law in 1917. When Menefee's study was released in 1942, six years after the Russell report, its central conclusion was surely contrary to the hopes and expectations not only of vocationalists but of Americans generally:

Youth without any Smith-Hughes training fared almost as well in terms of total employment as did trained youth. This suggests that nonvocational education had about as much value as vocational training for the youth interviewed in these four cities.[14]

Menefee sought to account for this failure. One common explanation, for example, was that youth enrolled in vocational training programs were somehow inferior to other youth in terms of ability or social status. Menefee, however, found no significant differences in this regard, and he concluded that this explanation had no merit. The absence of adequate guidance, however, was more plausible. Five-sixths of the youths with training had not had any vocational counseling. Menefee also considered the complaints often voiced by employers and unions that the vocational training itself was inadequate, and indeed, he found this to be the case in some instances. Equipment was outmoded, as was the teaching of the skills required. Black youths were particularly affected in this regard. Vocationalists consistently sought longer and more comprehensive programs of industrial training, but only about 20 percent of the youth who had completed programs offered any criticisms as to the comprehensiveness of the training. Precise data with respect to the question of whether the training was actually related to labor-market requirements were simply unavailable, but Menefee found "some evidence that the types of training offered in the Smith-Hughes schools did not always correspond closely with labor-market needs."[15] Labor unions, for example, complained that too many workers were being trained in certain occupations while others were being ignored. By Menefee's own account, however, the largest single factor was probably the depression itself, which had the effect of forcing youth to seek jobs outside their chosen field. In this regard, Menefee pointed out, such work programs as the CCC, NYA, and WPA needed to be supported. "Vocational education," he concluded, "is no cure for unemployment."[16]

While the effects of the depression certainly affected the results of Menefee's study, certain findings point to difficulties with vocational training that may transcend that economic crisis. While the problem of outmoded machinery in such fields as automobile mechanics or printing in schools was exacerbated by the extreme budgetary problems that schools faced, it is nevertheless difficult to imagine public schools even in the best of times keeping up with the rapid technological change that occurs in a modern industrial society. Apart from outmoded equipment and machinery, the problem of obsolescence may also manifest itself in the ability of teachers in vocational programs, who are themselves often removed from the workplace, to keep abreast of the shifting skills that a given job requires. Moreover, the problem of matching specific training to jobs surely transcends the depression era. In the normal course of events, the sheer number of industrial as well as clerical occupations in a complex industrial society is enormous, compared with the few occupations that schools can reasonably be expected to incorporate into their curriculum. A public high school, even one dedicated to vocational training, simply cannot train students specifically for more than a tiny fraction of the occupations that exist in the labor market. The widespread claim that general vocational education may carry with it some advantages in terms of developing desirable attitudes toward work irrespective of specific job training is highly questionable and would in any case hardly justify the extensive skill training that is often entailed. In addition, the depression-related phenomenon of youth with fairly extended training failing to find related work suggests that the widespread and politically popular assumption that in vocational training lies the solution to structural problems in the economy needs to be seriously reexamined. It is no longer clear that employers are seeking highly developed vocational skills in entry-level jobs.

TEACHING VOCATIONAL SKILLS

In choosing public schools as the site for industrial training, vocationalists were undertaking to accomplish a deceptively complex and difficult task. Skills that would presumably find their expression on a factory floor were taught in schools and classrooms that were both geographically and conceptually removed from the scene of action. A substantial part of the failure of vocational education in the instrumental sense stemmed from the fact that the kind of knowledge vocational teachers sought to instill cannot readily be conveyed in a school setting. Schools have a demonstrated ability (although far from an unbroken record of success) in teaching the young to manipulate symbols and in explaining how things work, ranging from the machinery of government to the production of chlorophyll in plants to the structure of a novel. Coming to an understanding of the principles of such complex phenomena, however, is not particularly relevant to what Michael Polanyi calls "skilful performance," and it is skillful performance that the job market requires. Rather than a knowledge of principles, "*skilful performance is achieved by the observance of a set of rules which are not known as such by the person following them*" (original emphasis).[17] Polanyi then proceeds to illustrate his point with a now famous example:

> [F]rom my interrogations of physicists, engineers and bicycle manufacturers, I have come to the conclusion that the principle by which a cyclist keeps his balance is not generally known. The rule observed by the cyclist is this: When he starts falling to the right he turns the handlebars to the right, so that the course of the bicycle is deflected along a curve towards the right. This results

in a centrifugal force pushing the cyclist to the left and offsets the gravitational force dragging him down to the right. The manoeuvre presently throws the cycle out of balance to the left, which he counteracts by turning the handlebars to the left; and so he continues to keep himself in balance by winding along a series of appropriate curvatures. A simple analysis shows that for a given angle of unbalance the curvature of each winding is inversely proportional to the square of the speed at which the cyclist is proceeding.[18]

When Polanyi then raises the question of whether this explanation tells us how to ride a bicycle, his answer is a flat *No*. It is remotely conceivable that a knowledge of the physics of bicycle riding could be of some use to the novice bicycle rider, but in no sense does that knowledge in itself translate into the ability to ride a bicycle. Polanyi concludes, "Rules of art can be useful, but they do not determine the practice of an art; they are maxims, which can serve as a guide to an art only if they are integrated into the practical knowledge of the art. They cannot replace this knowledge."[19] By implication, schools can explain quite successfully the physical principles behind the operation of machines like lathes and printing presses that the operators are required to use, but that knowledge is no substitute for the actual skill in how to use them. That latter kind of knowledge is more likely to be conveyed not by teaching in the sense of explaining basic principles or structures but by guiding the novice in the actual performance of the task. Rather than teaching in the ordinary sense, it is more like running along the side of the bicycle and coaching the novice until the task is mastered. This is just the kind of knowledge that schools are structurally ill-equipped to provide.

Running alongside the bicycle need not be regarded as a trivial activity. It requires patience, persistence, the requisite experience with the task at hand, and a certain amount of caring. The purpose is to transmit to the novice something of the expertise of the master. In highly skilled vocations, such as electrical work and furnace installation and repair, such expertise is considerable, and "running alongside" usually takes years. This is the case with modern apprenticeships in those fields, and they may be supplemented, here and there, with a modicum of formal instruction. As in the case of bicycle riding, however, in no case is the formal instruction even remotely adequate as a means of acquiring the skill needed to perform the job successfully. If relevant at all, it is strictly supplementary to on-the-job training.

"The public school," Dewey observed in 1916, "is the willing pack-horse of our social system; it is the true hero of the refrain: Let George do it."[20] Schools in America take on important responsibilities, ranging from safe driving to safe sex, and their decidedly mixed record in these undertakings has not deterred lawmakers, state departments of education, and the public alike from heaping new responsibilities on schools and teachers. On their side, educators themselves in many cases assume these responsibilities with great eagerness. More often than not, these efforts are sustained not by real prospects of success but by the extraordinary faith that Americans have in the power of schools to address matters of urgent necessity. That faith can sometimes be comforting, but it also results in the substitution of symbolic action for instrumental action. Under those circumstances, compelling social concerns are not so much addressed as placated. In an insightful analysis of the relationship of education to the labor market, W. Norton Grubb and Marvin Lazerson concluded that "the attractiveness of the educational solution has . . . been a block to formulating other kinds of reforms; policy makers have consistently reasserted the potential of schooling, rather than face its limitations."[21] The idea that schools can successfully convey the skills necessary for survival in the industrial workplace is one such instance, and it is the result not of the demonstrated success that schools have achieved in teaching those skills but of the fact that vocationalists were effective in shaping the way Americans thought of the purposes of schooling. Whether such skills need to be conveyed is not the issue. The real issue is whether those skills could be more adequately imparted in a setting other than the public school, such as the workplace itself. Self-reporting in this matter, beginning with Du Bois and Dill's *The Negro American Artisan*, indicates that to an overwhelming extent learning the skills of a trade takes place on the job.[22]

In certain instances of vocational education, the structural limitations of the school site were minimal or reasonably well overcome. Agricultural education is a case in point. Industrial education dealt with a world that was remote not only in terms of time but in terms of the experience of the youth presumably being served. By contrast, agricultural education, for the most part, dealt with the world that the students actually inhabited outside of school. Their work site was as proximate as their own homes. Under those circumstances, the vocational agriculture that was taught in schools bore an immediate relevance to the work on the farm that students were experiencing on a daily basis. This feature of vocational agriculture was a critical factor in leading William Heard Kilpatrick to propose a revolutionary reform of the curriculum generally. What he called the "project method" had actually taken shape as "home projects" in the context of the teaching of agricultural subjects.[23] Industrial education, on the other hand, was based on what the future presumably held rather than the students' own experience. As Dewey consistently argued, when education is tied above all to one's predicted occupational or social role as distinct from one's present reality, the remoteness of school from life is accentuated rather than diminished. If Dewey is right in his condemnation of education as preparation, then the emphasis on the here and now in the interest of creating a realized present may turn out to be the best preparation for what lies ahead. Indeed, vocational agriculture, unlike industrial education, was able to incorporate some elements of a Deweyan approach to education. In a 1984 article addressing key differences between vocational agriculture and industrial education, Stuart A. Rosenfeld points out that "Vocational agriculture was never intended to meet occupational demand."[24] Instead, it emphasized problem solving and initiative, something that industrial education, he goes on to argue, would do well to emulate. In his time, Kilpatrick, it seems, was able to recognize these Deweyan features of vocational agriculture as it was then practiced, and this led to his ambitious effort to reconstruct the curriculum along those lines.

Another aspect of the problem of teaching industrial skills in a school setting is illustrated by the relative success of clerical education, despite its lack of financial support from the federal government or the political support of the AVA. Something of that success can be seen in extant statistical data from the period. Although precise estimates as to enrollments are difficult to establish because U.S. Office of Education publications are framed in terms of the relevant individual subjects, such as stenography and bookkeeping, rather than course of study, it is virtually certain that clerical courses of study enrolled more students than the combined total of all other vocational programs.[25] Counts's 1922 study of the high school, for example, indicated that in the cities he studied, enrollment figures in vocational programs other than commercial education were between 2 and 34 percent, while in commercial education the range was 19 to 34 percent.[26]

The evidence also indicates that the clerical skills students learned in school did translate into better job prospects and, so far as we know, considerably greater success on the job than in the case of industrial education. It is not, then, that schools cannot teach skills; they have for centuries. It is that certain skills lend themselves to teaching in a school setting and others do not (see Figure 13). Alongside the creation of programs of study in commercial education in the public schools, for example, existed a flourishing industry of singularly successful private schools (sometimes called colleges), such as the Katherine Gibbs schools, which trained large numbers of students, mostly women, for clerical occupations. In one relevant study, Olivier Zunz tracked twenty-two men and forty-three women who graduated in 1910 from Goldey College in Wilmington, Delaware, and in the course of his account presents a revealing picture of what private clerical education was like.[27] By 1910, more women than men were entering the clerical field, and specialized "colleges" like Goldey were quick to see the commercial possibilities. In 1910, twenty-four years after it had been founded, Goldey's enrollment had reached 700 in day and evening classes. While some of the students were high school graduates, the majority were not, and so Goldey College was effectively competing with public secondary education. By 1910, 150 Goldey graduates had been hired by the Du Pont Corporation, and in that year alone, when

FIGURE 13. High school typing class, Watertown, Wisconsin. Conditions of the office workplace were more easily reproduced in classrooms than were conditions in factories. *Courtesy State Historical Society of Wisconsin.*

Du Pont's new office building had been completed, twenty-seven men and thirty-six women, were hired. An important factor in the success of Goldey in moving students from school to work was its well-established employment bureau. Goldey College's very survival depended on its ability to find jobs for its graduates, and its employment bureau established and maintained the necessary connections with the chief employer in the state. This permitted many Goldey graduates to move seamlessly into jobs. The public schools in the four large cities Menefee studied had nothing of the sort. While it is remotely conceivable that public schools could also establish job bureaus, and they may have in a handful of cases, public schools never formed the relationship with business and industry that private schools did. Moreover, it is possible that a close relationship between public schools and industry would have evolved into the schools' becoming subservient to industrial interests. What was good for Goldey College may not be good for the public school system as a whole.

Furthermore, pivotal differences existed between clerical and industrial studies in terms of the kinds of skills being imparted. The curriculum at Goldey College included courses in arithmetic, bookkeeping, commercial law, composition and rhetoric, English grammar, spelling, and stenography. Zunz reports that these courses were designed to simulate actual office conditions as much as possible, and in all likelihood, these courses were successful in that regard. One factor in making this possible was that such courses, not just as offered in Goldey College and other private institutions but in commercial courses in public schools as well,[28] were, pedagogically speaking, much more like the symbolic and cultural studies that characterize the standard curriculum than were industrial courses. Teaching stenography, for example, is not much different from teaching reading, spelling, and penmanship. For the most part, it entails the encoding and transcribing of language. In addition, typewriters, Dictaphones, adding machines, and so forth could be introduced into the classroom much more easily than lathes and milling machines. To be sure, industrial machinery was introduced into school shops but on a necessarily much more limited scale than the business machines needed for clerical training. As a result, commercial education was in a far better position to reproduce the conditions of the workplace and therefore to transmit relevant skills than was industrial education. The relative success of clerical education vis-à-vis industrial education may be attributable, then, to at least two key advantages it enjoyed. First, what was being taught did not entail a drastic reordering of the structure of the conventional classroom or of established teaching patterns; commercial subjects could be taught much like traditional subjects. Secondly, the actual conditions of the office as a workplace could be more easily approximated in the classroom. Reproducing the factory floor, on the other hand, presented a far more formidable obstacle.

VOCATIONAL EDUCATION, EQUALITY OF
OPPORTUNITY, AND SOCIAL CHANGE

One of the greatest sources of friction between the New Deal and the vocationalists was their apparent neglect of the most disadvantaged segments of
American society. For the most part, the grooves of vocational policy that had
been dug in the battle for Smith-Hughes continued to guide their policy initiatives in the 1930s and beyond. The professional interests of vocationalists
were served by long periods of training conducted by teachers who themselves had been fully qualified rather than by intensive short courses designed
to put youth to work as expeditiously as possible. Also, with remarkably few
exceptions, vocationalists set their priorities in terms of keeping the industrial process running smoothly, with little concern for the injustices that
existed in the occupational structure or on the factory floor. That failure is
no more evident than in their implicit support for a pattern of segregation
and restriction of educational opportunity in southern states.

In a study of an American town in the 1930s, John Dollard focuses on
the persistence of a caste system along racial lines and, along the way, docu-
ments the role that the education system generally and vocational education
in particular played in the perpetuation of that caste system. In the little city
Dollard calls Southerntown, the education of African Americans was instrumental in that regard. Schools, he says, were used "to educate the Negro in
order to fit him for place first as a slave and then as a caste man in society."[29]
Alluding to a tradition going back to Booker T. Washington, Dollard points
out that much of this form of education for blacks was necessary in order to
appease the white power structure. In 1935–36, when he was conducting his
research, the subordination of African Americans was effected not so much
through their exclusion from the educative process as by providing an inferior system of education. For Dollard, the caste principle functions in education in this way: "It stresses especially craft and vocational training for
Negroes, a type of training which would prepare him for, but not beyond, the
opportunities of lower-class status." For black women, restriction on opportunities took the particular form of training in home economics. "From the
caste standpoint," he found, "it was self-evident that 'domestic science' was
the training needed by Negro women."[30]

In Dollard's findings are echoes of Du Bois's warnings as to the education of African Americans for manual labor and menial pursuits. The shunting of black youth into an education leading to manual labor preserved the
caste system not only by training them explicitly for such work but by effectively denying them the opportunity for a strong general education. There was,
in other words, a significant opportunity cost. Although Southerntown maintained a "colored" high school, it offered a three-year rather than a four-year

program of studies, thus effectively precluding blacks from entering college unless they were somehow able to add the other year in a high school away from home. The ability of African Americans to transcend the town's caste system was being severely impeded both by a systematic differentiation of the curriculum and by meager financing of black education. The city of Atlanta, for example, did not have a single black high school until the 1920s.

It seems evident that in Southerntown of the 1930s, at least some of the early fears expressed by critics of vocationalism, such as W. E. B. Du Bois, William Bagley, Ella Flagg Young, and John Dewey, were being realized. By flying the banner of providing for the "needs" of certain student populations, educators were effectively restricting educational opportunity. African Americans in particular were not only being denied a general education but were being trained in a very limited range of vocational skills. Vocationalism, of course, did not create what Dollard calls the caste system, but it does appear that the vocationalization of the curriculum was functioning at least here and there and perhaps generally as an instrument for perpetuating and reinforcing race, gender, and class lines.

Dollard's interpretations are supported by some solid empirical evidence. In a detailed study of the effects of vocational legislation in the states of Mississippi, Georgia, and North Carolina between 1917 and 1936, Regina E. Werum concludes that "Elite actors in the South were largely successful in reproducing a racial caste system in vocational education."[31] The picture she paints is one of vocationalists forging a powerful alliance with northern industrialists and with agricultural interests in southern states. The most important pieces of federal legislation in behalf of vocational education not only included major funding for agricultural occupations but allowed state boards of vocational education the latitude to structure vocational education in line with established patterns of racial segregation, and thereby to maintain an inequitable pattern of support for black schools. Because elite interests in the South dominated the political process more than in other regions of the country, they were able to use the latitude that federal legislation allowed in order to reinforce established patterns in terms of social class, gender, and especially racial lines. It is likely that those elite interests were able to use federally supported vocational education for similar purposes in other regions as well but to a somewhat lesser extent.

Dominant elites focused most directly on vocational training for males except in the area of home economics, which was not particularly related to remunerative work. Employment in domestic service was the only real exception. Through their home economics courses, young women received instruction in household maintenance and work related to food such as cooking, canning, and pickling—training with almost no implications for the job market. This was in keeping with the dominant ideology with respect to home economics. As Rury has indicated, "The term 'vocation' when employed in reference to home economics was meant to convey a sense of women's calling rather than the more modern notion of a particular occupation."[32] Werum's analysis of how federal money was used in support of vocational education in Georgia, Mississippi, and North Carolina indicates that vocational courses for whites as well as blacks were male dominated. Since agricultural education was central in those states, very few women benefited, but male vocational training was not much better in terms of its relationship to the job market. Between 1917 and 1936, instruction in male trades remained virtually unchanged, giving little indication that vocational education was responding to a shifting job structure, with the exception of North Carolina. The occupational picture there made it important for blacks as well as whites to be trained for work in textile mills and lumber production.

Generally, insofar as opening up educational opportunity for African Americans is concerned, the record of vocational education in the South and elsewhere is decidedly mixed. On the one hand, opportunities for African Americans in secondary education in the South and to a lesser extent in other parts of the country were limited. The support that vocational legislation such as the Smith-Hughes Act provided made some form of secondary education available to some of those who were being denied that opportunity. On the other hand, the range of opportunities made available was extremely limited in scope. In 1916, of the forty-nine black high schools in the South, fully half were manual training schools, all offering woodworking and a handful of other trades such as shoe repair.[33] Vocational education under Smith-Hughes did virtually nothing to change that pattern. Black female education was even more severely restricted. Black female enrollments in *all-day* home economics courses in the twenty years or so after Smith-Hughes was sometimes greater than those of white women, largely because black women had few other opportunities to receive a secondary education in the South,[34] and if their place in the workforce was considered, it lay in domestic service. In general, federal legislation, by providing aid for vocational education and not for general education, reinforced the pattern of excluding blacks, male and female, from an academic education, and therefore denied access to educational opportunity beyond high school. In addition, the requirement that states match federal dollars for vocational education undoubtedly reduced state money that would otherwise be available for general education. Even the range of *vocational* options for blacks, especially women, remained very narrow.

A national survey on black vocational education in 1936 supports the contention that the range of vocational choices for African Americans was severely restricted. Undertaken under federal auspices, the study, conducted by Ambrose Caliver and employing 500 black field workers, was based on data collected from 27,366 black high school and college students in eighteen states. Including all-day, evening, and extension programs, white students were registered in ninety-three different trade programs, while blacks were registered in thirty-four. African Americans were excluded entirely from such occupations as boiler installation and maintenance, general mechanics, ship building, pulp and paper making, steel manufacture, and sign painting. In certain other relatively high-status trade training, participation by blacks was extremely meager. Only one black student out of 878, for example, was being trained in welding and twenty-eight out of 1,805 in printing.[35] After reviewing a series of studies conducted in the 1930s involving black vocational education, historian James D. Anderson concluded that "Schooling as it existed was not part of the solution, it was part of the problem."[36]

It could be argued, of course, that the failures of vocational education in terms of extending educational opportunity in the South and elsewhere were simply part of a pervasive pattern of discrimination. That such a pattern of discrimination existed can hardly be disputed, but the record of the New Deal in this regard stands in sharp contrast to that of the vocationalists. New Deal programs were surely affected by existing discriminatory structures with respect to race, class, and gender, but they also presented a formidable challenge to those structures. CCC, for example, maintained racially segregated camps, but as New Deal education policies evolved, programs such as the NYA made substantial efforts to redress educational inequities. As a result of a policy of equitable distribution of funds by the NYA, black schools actually received a higher per capita allocation of funds than white schools. Between 1933 and 1937 alone, the number of African Americans receiving some form of NYA assistance increased from 5,000 a month to 28,500.[37] Moreover, NYA support was not restricted to narrow trade training. In 1937, NYA, in an effort to increase black graduation rates in high school generally, supported some 180,000 black students. In the 1939–40 fiscal year, 113 black colleges received some form of aid, with students at those schools receiving 11.1 percent of the college program funds that NYA expended.[38] The contrast with the pre–New Deal years is dramatic. In states with segregated school systems, the difference in per capita expenditures between white and black schools in 1900 was 48 percent. By 1930, the difference ballooned to 252.5 percent.

Whatever may have been the beneficial effects of the federal vocational legislation in those years, it did not address the rapidly deteriorating position of black vis-á-vis white schools in the South.[39] With state vocational boards administering the funding that flowed from the Smith-Hughes Act and supplementary legislation, black schools in the South were systematically denied a fair proportion. "The New Deal programs," Paula Fass concludes, "were at once an implicit criticism of established educational offerings and a demonstration that the federal government could do what established agencies failed to do."[40] Social concern was not the inevitable by-product of an economic disaster; it was the expression of a particular human sensibility that the Roosevelt administration brought to the situation. Quintessential New Dealers such as Mary McLeod Bethune and Aubrey Williams brought to their work a moral passion that the vocationalists lacked.

In some sense, vocationalists were reformers. They challenged existing school practices and worked to change them, but from a social perspective, their reforms were limited to the achievement of order, efficiency, productivity, and stability, and even those ideals were marred by an overweening and largely self-serving professionalism. Above all, vocationalism suffered from a cramped social vision. In his examination of the social positions of key figures in the vocationalist movement, such as Charles Prosser and David Snedden, the distinguished historian Merle Curti concluded that they "held that vocational schools must avoid the discussion of all social and economic questions. . . . The practical effect of this position was to align them with the *status quo*."[41] One of their greatest failures in this regard was their systematic neglect of the grueling conditions of the workplace. Even more than the issue of dual control, the vocationalists' acceptance of existing work structures was the pivotal point of contention between Dewey and Snedden in their debate on the subject of vocational education. By and large, vocationalists simply took the conditions of the workplace for granted. When Prosser, for example, addressed the question of "deplorable industrial conditions,"[42] he tended to treat it as a thing of the past. Despite the concerns that vocationalists publicly expressed for the conditions of the workplace or for a neglected segment of the population, their policies and the legislation that emerged from those policies were monumentally silent on the wretched conditions that the working poor had to endure.[43] Vocationalists directed their criticisms not at the way workers were being made appendages to their machines and at inequality of opportunity in the job market, but at schools for being inadequately attuned to the workplace.[44] This was just what Dewey was afraid of.

VOCATIONALISM'S SYMBOLIC TRIUMPH

Although the *promise* of a direct payoff both to the individual and to society is an ever-present expectation, vocationalism as an instrument for achieving economic prosperity either in the individual or social sense has never been adequately documented. Nor was the expectation that vocationalization would provide for segments of the school population previously neglected actually realized. Yet from one point of view, vocationalism was supremely successful. The appeal—the triumph—of vocationalism does not stem from its realized economic benefits. Instead, the success of vocationalism can be seen largely in terms of the abiding place it has earned in American consciousness, something which derives in large measure from the symbolic meaning that Americans attach to work as central to their identities. As Rodgers and Tyack put it, "the deeper question is why the appeal to education, and to vocational education in particular, has endured despite so much evidence of inability of education to work a significant change on the structures of jobs and opportunities facing young workers." The success of vocational education, in other words, cannot be attributed to its record of accomplishment either in training skilled workers for future occupations or in keeping America's economy competitive with those of other industrialized nations. If an answer is to be found to its success, it will lie, say Rodgers and Tyack, "in a deeper recognition of the symbolic function education serves in American political life."[45]

That symbolism derives in part from Americans' image of themselves. For much of their history, Americans have thought of themselves as the people of rolled-up sleeves and sweaty brows. This is the land of can-do citizens. Our heroes are the rugged athletes, the tough-talking captains of industry, the self-made entrepreneurs. The most common visual cliche of a candidate for public office is the suit jacket slung over one shoulder. Symbolically, that image presents the candidate as shucking off the effete trappings of formality and ceremonial correctness and assuming the identity of the brawny, down-to-earth practical man of affairs. Beyond the very alluring promise of economic security, vocationalism as an educational ideal is buttressed by the popular image of the American as figuratively grease-stained and relatively unrefined in language and deportment.

It is tempting to dismiss such matters as "mere symbolism," but much of what actually passes for educational policy is only marginally an effort actually to reform or preserve curricular practices in the interest of materially affecting the educational experiences of children and youth. The principal effect of much of what passes for policy-making generally and educational policy-making in particular lies in its connection to the status interests of various constituent groups. Embedded in policy statements are expressions of regard and messages of status. Many policy initiatives and curricular changes are signals to certain groups that their values and vital concerns have been officially sanctioned and, at least nominally, are being addressed. Perhaps more than anything, a curricular policy is a signal not just of respect for the interests of one group but of the dominance of one group over the other. In many policy pronouncements, the deeply felt convictions of one group are implicitly declared to be superior to those of another. As sociologist Joseph Gusfield expressed this point:

> Psychologists may show that the pledge of allegiance every morning has no discernible effect upon patriotic feeling, but this is not the issue as status elements are involved. What such curricular changes "bear witness" to is the

domination of one cultural group and the subordination of another. As most educators know, schools are run for adults, not for children. There is more than expression of feeling in such demands. There is an effort to dominate the rituals by which status is determined.[46]

What applies to the daily pledge of allegiance, or proposed prayer in the public schools, also is relevant to interpreting the appeal of vocational education. With the victory of vocational education came the vindication of the traditional work ethic in the face of a new workplace determinedly inimical to it. Symbolically speaking, whether vocational education is actually instrumental in getting youth ready for the workplace is really beside the point.

David K. Cohen and Bella H. Rosenberg have suggested that reading the past is something like prose or poetry. "The meaning," they say, "lies in what the texts express, not in their function or what they are caused by."[47] Viewed from this perspective, the statements of leaders in a field such as vocational education *as well as the actual incorporation of vocational programs of study in schools and classrooms* can be interpreted in terms of what they "broadcast" to a designated audience. According to Cohen and Rosenberg, battles over what should be taught in schools took place "on a great social proscenium, a stage on which terrific struggles over the content and character of the culture were played out."[48] With the schools as their stage, vocationalists depicted their cause as liberating the curriculum from its elitist, academic traditions, usually expressed in terms of the heavy hand of college entrance requirements. The heroes in this drama were the common laborers and their children, whose concerns had for so long been spurned by the public schools. Their interests, according to the convolutions of the plot, lay in the ties between schooling and the workplace and not in intellectual pursuits or other purposes of education. Although it has never been clear that the protagonists in this morality play actually benefited materially from that message, the effect on the audience was powerful and enduring.

This symbolic side of vocational education has led a large majority of the American public, most members of Congress, many educational leaders, and politicians everywhere, including a succession of recent presidents, to conclude that schooling finds its ultimate justification in its connection to the workplace. For many Americans, it is the only justification. Whether the work entailed is manual labor, skilled trades, business management, highly skilled and technical labor, or the professions, getting ready for work occupies center stage wherever educational policy is considered. In the popular acceptance of that educational ideal, vocationalists achieved by far their most important success.

Although the symbolic triumph of vocationalism was well nigh complete by the time of the George-Barden Act in 1946, developments since that time have served to cement and extend that victory. What in the 1930s and 1940s was a dedicated and effective lobby became in later years a nearly irresistible force. A few years after returning to Harvard University, Francis Keppel, President John F. Kennedy's Commissioner of Education, confided in one of his graduate students that, despite his earnest attempt to reform vocational education during his tenure of office, that effort proved futile. He found the vocationalists' lobby too powerful to overcome.[49] A succession of federal acts in the years following George-Barden, along with massive state efforts in behalf of vocational education, is testimony to the power of vocationalists to gain support for their interests. The fragile presence that intellectual virtues maintain in the American curriculum has correspondingly become eroded. The recent high status accorded to subjects like mathematics and science is not so much an indication of their role in gaining a command of the intellectual resources of our culture or in the demands and responsibilities of citizenship as it is a recognition that jobs in the new American workplace and economic considerations generally entail the skills that presumably accrue from the successful study of those subjects. Subjects like history and literature have not been widely recognized as contributing to getting and holding a job or in enhancing the country's competitiveness in world markets. Controversies surrounding those subjects center not on national interest but on which groups are honored and which neglected. In any case, vocationalism has served to relegate their function to the curriculum's purgatory, college entrance requirements. A sign of vocationalism's sovereignty as an educational ideal is that leaders in those subjects have tried mightily to establish them as in fact contributing to the vocational imperative. Whatever the instrumental failure of vocationalism, its achievements are striking when seen in terms of the extent to which it emerged as the controlling purpose of American schooling.[50]

A DEWEYAN CRITIQUE OF VOCATIONALISM

The events that frame the emergence, maturity, and ultimate triumph of vocationalism as an educational ideal occurred during John Dewey's lifetime. When Calvin Woodward first set eyes on the Russian exhibit at the Philadelphia Centennial, sometime between April 19 and October 19, 1876, the president of the United States was Ulysses S. Grant, and Dewey was a sixteen-year-old freshman at the University of Vermont. When President Woodrow Wilson signed the Smith-Hughes Act into law on February 23, 1917, Dewey, at fifty-seven, had achieved world renown. On February 23, 1946, when President Truman signed the George-Barden Act, Dewey, now eighty-six, was still an active scholar. Over the course of his lifetime, a powerful educational ideal had materialized from a medley of competing influences and established its dominance. This did not escape his notice. Dewey's reactions to the emergence of vocationalism, however, are scattered over many of his writings, and this, combined with the subtlety of his position on the subject, has led to some confusion as to how he regarded the construction of a newly dominant educational ideal for America's schools. Dewey never outlined an explicit plan for vocational education, nor did he write extensively on the subject, but from the scattered criticisms he directed at the way vocationalism was developing, it may be possible to limn the contours of what a Deweyan critique might look like.

Surely, there is some irony in the fact that John Dewey, the apostle of active engagement and of the centrality of what he called "occupations" in the school curriculum, should emerge as one of the most vociferous opponents of industrial education as it is usually practiced, if not its most astute critic. Dewey's criticisms actually began just before the turn of the century with reservations he expressed about what was surely the most benign of the three stages that led to the vocationalization of the American curriculum, manual training. In addressing the question of how to capitalize on children's instincts and impulses in an educational setting, Dewey argued against the then widespread idea that the student's constructive impulse needs to be marshaled in order to create useful things. He attributed that belief to "some of the manual training high schools whose main object is preparation for trades."[51] In *School and Society* and other writings during the period of the Laboratory School at the University of Chicago, Dewey took pains to disabuse his readers from believing that the primary purpose of introducing active occupations into the curriculum of the school was anything but educational and social.[52] The "occupations" that became such a crucial part of the curriculum of the Laboratory School were not occupations that in any sense prepared students for earning a living. Typical "occupations" included raising a pair of sheep, building a clubhouse, and growing and preparing food. Dewey was not preparing children to become shepherds in the middle of Chicago or, for that matter, woodworkers or farmers or chefs. There were several reasons behind the introduction of these "occupations," such as the interest that the children found in them, but the primary educational reason was that the "occupations" provided an excellent vehicle for demonstrating the vital connection between knowledge and the realization of human purpose, thereby bridging the gap that typically separates knowledge from action in schools. Through participation in fundamental social occupations, human beings learned to use their intelligence in order to gain mastery over their lives and fortunes. Dewey did not oppose the idea that every system of schooling "should result in the possession of power on the part of [students] to earn their own living in an intelligent, orderly and effective way."[53] The problem as he saw it was that this one purpose should not be emphasized to the point where it begins to undermine the most important function of education, the fostering of intellectual and moral growth.

That overemphasis amounting to the subordination of other purposes to the vocational function is the essence of vocationalism as an educational ideal, and Dewey's opposition to the supremacy of that conception of education was unequivocal. Referring to the vocational function of schooling, Dewey observed that "that factor of the educational process cannot be emphasized, cannot be exaggerated so as to regard it as the chief or predominating aim of any one group of studies, like the manual training studies, without resulting in the introduction of a somewhat illiberal spirit, and forcing the studies themselves into a one-sided position."[54] The point, as Dewey reminded his students at the University of Chicago, was that "an over-utilitarian point of view defeats itself."[55] Because it is restricted to what seems to be immediately practical, such an exaggerated emphasis on the one purpose undermines the possibility of intellectual and moral growth and, thereby, the kind of education that is, in the long run, the most durable and functional of all.

Despite his reputation as a philosopher of the practical and that his educational theories are commonly encapsulated as "learning by doing,"[56] Dewey emerged as a potent critic of the kind of vocationalism that over the course of seventy years became a curricular reality; however, he was also a vocal critic of the sterility of the academic side of the curriculum. Over the course of his career, he consistently attacked the puerile forms of academic knowledge that had become standard curricular fare in schools across the country (what is now rather contemptuously called "school knowledge"). For Dewey, the source of the problem was the wall that had been erected between academic and vocational studies, between the theoretical and the practical, between thinking and doing. He objected to curricular bifurcation not simply because many vocational students were being denied reasonable access to the intellectual resources of their culture, but because students on the academic side of the curriculum, and perhaps students generally, were being denied the opportunity to experience the integral connection between thought and action.

This bifurcation of the curriculum and its resulting negative consequences in terms of intellectual development, according to Dewey, had their origins not in modern vocational education but in ancient Greece. Aristotle was "permanently right," Dewey said, "in assuming the inferiority and subordination of mere skill in performance and mere accumulation of external products to understanding, sympathy of appreciation, and the free play of ideas." He erred, however, in assuming the inevitable separation of the intellectual and the practical. This Aristotelian conception of a "natural divorce" between "significant knowledge and practical achievement" has led to an unwarranted and ruinous bifurcation in the curriculum. When academic and practical or vocational subjects are not somehow harmonized in the curriculum, "the result," Dewey observed, "is a system in which both 'cultural' and 'utilitarian' subjects exist in an inorganic composite where the former is not by dominant purpose socially serviceable and the latter are not liberative of imagination or thinking power."[57] Vocational education is stripped of its potential role in intellectual development, and general education becomes needlessly disconnected from the familiar world of affairs.

Dewey held out the hope that vocational education, properly conceived, had the potential for alleviating that problem, although his hopes in that regard failed to materialize. It is in this sense that vocationalists, with all their intense lobbying and exaggerated claims as to its material benefits, missed a historic opportunity. Although Woodward held out that promise of integrating the mind and hand in his campaign for manual training, that noble ideal was abandoned in favor of a straightforward economic payoff. In Deweyan terms, vocational education could serve to make the school curriculum less remote and less disengaged from the lives of the students who were supposed to master it. Conceived and implemented as it was, however, vocational education offered only a dubious expectation of rewards to be collected in a faraway and often unattainable future. The benefits of integrating vocational and general education extend, then, not simply to the revitalization of academic education by connecting knowledge with action but to the infusion into vocational education of an intellectual substance that it has traditionally lacked.[58]

To complete the revitalization of both academic and vocational education, a crucial defect that afflicts both of them needs to be addressed: the nearly universal conviction that the benefits derived from education can only be collected at a remote time in the future. Although education has always been assumed with some justification to have some relevance to future activities, with the ascendance of vocationalism and the allied doctrine of social efficiency, education was now seen as little more than a process of getting ready for what presumably lies ahead. Under those circumstances, students became progressively more alienated from an education where present satisfactions are limited, and rewards are to be attained only in a prophesied hereafter. Dewey once called this "a preparatory probation for 'another life.'"[59] Although vocational education was commonly justified as making school relevant to the real world, that promise was projected into a distant and often illusory future. As a result, industrial education no more successfully reflects the world that children and youth inhabit than does academic education, and this emphasis on what may some day be realized is the source of much of the alienation and disaffection that modern schooling has bred among children and youth. Mathematics, science, and language, which have a vitality and a potency outside of school, typically take the form in the school curriculum of artificial and inert bodies of skills and knowledge, but their relevance to students' lives is sacrificed to a promise of future reward, which in the case of academic subjects is usually college entrance. Vocational subjects, while advertised as eminently functional, also require a suspension of disbelief which children and adolescents, for the most part, find understandably difficult to sustain. They are asked to prepare for a world of jobs that is constantly shifting and where existing skills are continually being replaced by new ones. The subjects comprising the academic and vocational curricula embody knowledge and skills that presumably need to be learned, but their value is projected into an allegedly predictable but fundamentally impenetrable future.

This greatly exaggerated emphasis on education not simply as getting ready generally but as direct and explicit preparation for what lies ahead is perhaps the cruelest of the legacies of vocationalism. It afflicts vocational and academic education alike. "Preparation," Dewey declared in his last book on education, "is a treacherous idea," stemming from the assumption that the mere acquisition of knowledge and skills constitutes "preparation for right and effective use under conditions very unlike those in which they were acquired." Dewey regarded the idea that a person learns only one particular thing at a time as "perhaps the greatest of all pedagogical fallacies." At the same time that children may be learning discrete knowledge and skills allegedly for use off in the future, they are also forming "enduring attitudes, of likes and dislikes," and it is the potential suppression of the desire to go on learning that may be the most destructive consequence of the overwhelming emphasis on education as preparation. "When preparation is made the controlling end," he said, "then the potentialities of the present are sacrificed to a supposititious future." That situation, however, is not immutable. Besides the kind of integration that can be achieved between the academic and the vocational, there is also the integration that is possible between the present and the future. Dewey rejected the idea that an education for the present and an education for the future are somehow irreconcilable. This is not, he said, "an *Either-Or* affair. The present affects the future anyway."[60] By concentrating on human efficacy in the world of the here and now, we provide the best kind of preparation for a future that is, for all practical purposes, unfathomable.

If vocational education is to build on its symbolic success and help redress the injustices inflicted on a neglected segment of the school population as well as revivifying education for all, it will not be by concentrating obsessively on rewards to be reaped at some indeterminate point in the future, or by isolating itself from the rest of education, and certainly not by converting the entire educational system to the narrow end of economic gain, as important as that may be. It can succeed only by extending its reach beyond the promise of distant monetary benefits. As Dewey once put it, vocational education can be part of "a plan for an educational system by which all education shall be relevant to a life remunerative to the individual in happiness, in intellectual progress, as well as in material rewards."[61] Recent years have seen some movement in this regard,[62] but if that Deweyan vision is to be realized, vocational education needs to repudiate a good part of its history and ally itself with "intellectual progress" in its most liberal and humane sense.

Dewey's critique of vocationalism, however, extended past the question of the efficacy of its practices in the school and in the workplace. In a stunningly penetrating passage in *Democracy and Education*, he reflected upon the broad social impact of a system of vocational education that is directed merely toward "securing technical efficiency." Under those circumstances, education becomes "an instrument of perpetuating unchanged the existing order of society instead of operating as a means of its transformation." In place of "a society in which every person shall be occupied in something which makes the lives of others better worth living, and which, accordingly, makes the ties which bind persons together more perceptible,"[63] we are left with a society in which work structures serve not only to perpetuate but to magnify alienation, dislocation, and invidious distinctions.

Work—its stresses and constraints as well as its compensations—shapes lives and destinies, and contrary to much current thinking on the subject, its relevance to schooling is not limited to securing a smooth transition to the workplace. As a vital ingredient of living, work needs to manifest itself in the curriculum, not simply in terms of securing job skills, even assuming that is possible, but principally in terms of its human dimensions and its social bearings. Perhaps, under those circumstances, some of the most egregious injustices of the workplace can be modified. For Dewey, schools and classrooms did not simply reflect the world outside of school, as many vocationalists assumed; rather, schools had a responsibility to create an *idealized* social community. He was not so naive as to think that "we can change character and mind by direct instruction," but he did hold out the possibility that "we may produce in schools a projection in type of the society we should like to realize, and by forming minds in accord with it gradually modify the larger and more recalcitrant features of adult society."[64] It is that kind of social vision that vocationalists failed to articulate and act upon.

 NOTES

PREFACE

1. Stanley E. Elam, Lowell C. Rose, and Alec M. Gallup, "The 28th Annual Phi Delta Kappa/Gallup Poll of the Public's Attitudes toward the Public Schools," *Phi Delta Kappan* 78 (September 1996): 55–56.

2. Richard Craig, "Don't Know Much about History," *New York Times,* 8 December 1997, A23.

3. E. D. Hirsch, Jr., *Cultural Literacy: What Every American Needs to Know* (Boston: Houghton Mifflin, 1987). E. D. Hirsch, Jr., *The Schools We Need: Why We Don't Have Them* (New York: Doubleday, 1996).

4. Carol Judy Kean, "The Origins of Vocational Education in the Milwaukee Public Schools, 1870–1917: A Case Study in Curricular Change" (Ph.D. diss., University of Wisconsin, Madison, 1983).

CHAPTER 1

1. Calvin M. Woodward, "Manual Training in General Education," *Education* 5 (July 1885): 621–22.

2. Samuel P. Hays, *The Response to Industrialism: 1885–1914* (Chicago: University of Chicago Press, 1957), 4–7.

3. Daniel T. Rodgers, *The Work Ethic in Industrial America, 1850–1920* (Chicago: University of Chicago Press, 1978), xi.

4. Ibid., 26.

5. Berenice M. Fisher, *Industrial Education: American Ideals and Institutions* (Madison: University of Wisconsin Press, 1967), 14–49.

6. Charles H. Ham, *Manual Training, the Solution of Social and Industrial Problems* (New York: Harper and Brothers, 1886), 332.

7. John R. Pannabecker, "Industrial Education and the Russian System: A Study in Economic, Social, and Technical Change," *Journal of Industrial Teacher Education* 24 (1986): 19–31.

8. Kathryn D. O'Connell, "Industrial Education in Boston, 1870–1890: A Case Study in Curricular Change" (Ph.D. diss., University of Wisconsin, Madison, 1975), 76.

9. Rodgers, *The Work Ethic in Industrial America,* 19.

10. John D. Runkle, "The Manual Element in Education," Forty-first Annual Report to the Board of Education, State of Massachusetts, 1867–1877. Reprinted in Charles Alpheus Bennett, *History of Manual and Industrial Education, 1870–1917* (Peoria, Ill.: Chas. A. Bennett, 1926), 340–41.

11. Ibid., 345.

12. Woodward, "Manual Training in General Education," 622.

13. Calvin M. Woodward, *Manual Education* (St. Louis: G. I. Jones, 1878), 3–4.

14. Ibid., 9.

15. Ibid.

16. Ibid., 16.

17. Ibid., 20.

18. Calvin M. Woodward, *The Manual Training School* (Boston: D. C. Heath & Co., 1887), 256–57.

19. Ibid.

20. Ibid., 245–52, 261–68.

21. Calvin M. Woodward, "Manual Training," National Education Association *Addresses and Proceedings* (1883): 87.

22. Bennett, *History of Manual and Industrial Education*, 373–89.

23. Calvin M. Woodward, "The Results of the St. Louis Manual Training School, National Education Association *Addresses and Proceedings* (1889): 73–74.

24. William Torrey Harris, "Report of the Committee on Pedagogics," National Education Association *Addresses and Proceedings* (1889): 417.

25. Ibid., 418–19.

26. Ibid., 419–20.

27. William Torrey Harris, "The Intellectual Value of Tool-Work," National Education Association *Addresses and Proceedings* (1889): 97–98.

28. Gilbert B. Morrison, "A Critical Review of the Report of the Committee on Pedagogics," in *The Educational Value of Manual Training*, ed. Calvin M. Woodward (Boston, New York, and Chicago: D. C. Heath, 1890), 62.

29. Woodward, *Educational Value of Manual Training*, 6.

30. Ibid., 9–10.

31. Ibid., 15.

32. Ibid., 19.

33. Calvin M. Woodward, "The Rise and Progress of Manual Training," *Report of the U.S. Commissioner of Education*, part 1 (1893–1894): 877.

34. Joseph Lee, *Constructive and Preventive Philanthropy* (New York: Macmillan Company, 1902), 204. Quoted in Marvin Lazerson, *Origins of the Urban School: Public Education in Massachusetts, 1870–1915* (Cambridge, Mass.: Harvard University Press, 1971), 76.

35. Benjamin Brawley, *Early Efforts for Industrial Education*, Occasional Papers no. 22 (Charlottesville, Va.: John F. Slater Fund, 1923), 1–3.

36. James D. Anderson, "The Historical Development of Black Vocational Education," in *Work, Youth, and Schooling: Historical Perspectives in American Education*, eds. Harvey Kantor and David B. Tyack (Stanford: Stanford University Press, 1982), 184.

37. Samuel Chapman Armstrong, "Address at the Anniversary Meeting of the American Missionary Association, October 24, 1877," *Southern Workman and Hampton School Record* 6 (December 1877): 94.

38. General Samuel Chapman Armstrong, "Lessons from the Hawaiian Islands," *Journal of Christian Philosophy* 3 (1883–1884): 213.

39. David Wallace Adams, *Education for Extinction: American Indians and the Boarding School Experience, 1875–1928* (Lawrence: University Press of Kansas, 1995), 45. Adams's book is easily the best history of American Indian education.

40. Samuel Chapman Armstrong, *Indian Education in the East: At Hampton, Va., and Carlisle, Penna.* (Hampton, Va.: Normal School Steam Press, 1880), 3.

41. Ibid., 4.

42. Susan De Lancey Van Rensselaer, "Review of Normal School Class Work," *Southern Workman and Hampton School Record* 21 (June 1892): 96.

43. Ibid., 95.

44. Ibid., 98.

45. Booker T. Washington, "Industrial Education for the Negro," in *The Negro Problem*, ed. Booker T. Washington et al. (New York: Arno Press, 1903/1969), 9–11.

46. Booker T. Washington, *The Story of My Life and Work* (Atlanta: J. L. Nichols, 1901), 117–18.

47. Booker T. Washington, *The Future of the American Negro* (New York: Haskell House, 1899/1968), 69.

48. Washington, *Story of My Life and Work*, 301.

49. For a highly perceptive analysis of how problems can be defined by those in power in relation to those they are "helping," see Murray Edelman, *Political Language: Words That Succeed and Policies That Fail* (New York: Academic Press, 1977).

50. W. E. B. Du Bois, "The Talented Tenth," in *The Negro Problem: A Series of Articles by Representative American Negroes of Today* (New York: James Potts, 1903): 33–75.

51. W. E. B. Du Bois, "The Hampton Idea," in *The Education of Black People: Ten Critiques 1906–1960*, ed. Herbert Aptheker (Amherst: University of Massachusetts Press, 1973), 9.

52. Ibid., 11.

53. W. E. B. Du Bois and Augustus Granville Dill, *The Negro American Artisan*, Atlanta University Publications no. 17 (Atlanta: Atlanta University Press, 1912), 37.

54. Ibid., 121.

55. Ibid., 122

56. Ibid., 115.

57. Ibid., 127.

58. Walter Licht, *Getting Work: Philadelphia, 1840–1950* (Cambridge, Mass.: Harvard University Press, 1992), 44–45.

59. Paul H. Douglas, *American Apprenticeship and Industrial Education* (New York: Columbia University, 1921), 182–83.

60. *Report of the Commissioner of Education* (Washington, D.C.: U.S. Government Printing Office, 1906), 1043.

61. Christine A. Ogren, "Education for Women in the United States" (Ph.D. diss., University of Wisconsin, Madison, 1996), 277–330.

62. Wellford Addis, "Manual and Industrial Training," *Report of the U.S. Commissioner of Education*, vol. 1 (1888–89): 411.

63. Frederick G. Bonser, "The Industrial Arts in the Elementary School," *School Arts Magazine* 13 (November 1913): 183–84.

64. Ibid., 184.

65. Calvin M. Woodward, "The Rise and Progress of Manual Training," *Report of the U.S. Commissioner of Education*, vol. 1 (1906): 903–04.

66. Licht, *Getting Work*, 67.

CHAPTER 2

1. Charles A. Prosser, "Discussion," National Education Association, *Proceedings and Addresses* (1912): 928.

2. For an excellent treatment of the crisis in the apprenticeship system, see Daniel Nelson, *Managers and Workers: Origins of the New Factory System in the United States, 1880–1920* (Madison: University of Wisconsin Press, 1975), 95–99, from which much of the foregoing was drawn.

3. National Association of Manufacturers, "Annual Report," *Proceedings* (1898): 22.

4. National Association of Manufacturers, "Annual Report of the President," *Proceedings* (1903): 20.

5. Ibid., 20.

6. National Association of Manufacturers, *Proceedings* (1905): 142–43.

7. National Association of Manufacturers, *Proceedings* (1906): 49–65.

8. Ibid., 55–56.

9. National Association of Manufacturers, "Report of the Committee on Industrial Education," *Proceedings* (1907): 114.

10. Ibid., 117.

11. National Association of Manufacturers, *Proceedings* (1911): 192.

12. National Association of Manufacturers, "Report of the Committee on Industrial Education," *Proceedings* (1911): 187.

13. National Association of Manufacturers, "Report of the Committee on Industrial Education," *Proceedings* (1912):156–57.

14. Ibid., 160.

15. Ibid.

16. Ibid., 168–69.

17. Ibid., 176.

18. *Report of the Massachusetts Commission on Industrial and Technical Education* (Boston: Massachusetts Commission on Industrial and Technical Education, 1906), 1.

19. Ibid., 6.

20. Ibid., 7.

21. Ibid., 30–31.

22. Ibid., 44, 86–87.

23. Ibid., 77–79.

24. Fisher, *Industrial Education*, 123–24.

25. John B. Lennon, "Four Alleged Crimes of Trade Unions," *American Federationist* 7 (September 1900): 273.

26. American Federation of Labor, *Proceedings* (1907): 319.

27. American Federation of Labor, *Proceedings* (1909): p. 103.

28. Samuel Gompers, "President Gompers' Report," *American Federationist* 16 (December 1909): 1075.

29. American Federation of Labor, *Proceedings* (1912): 275.

30. American Federation of Labor, *Proceedings* (1911): 136, 270.

31. American Federation of Labor, *Proceedings* (1915): 321.

32. Ibid., 16.

33. Samuel Gompers, "Editorial," *American Federationist* 20 (January 1913): 48–52.

34. Arthur G. Wirth, *Education in the Technological Society: The Vocational-Liberal Studies Controversy in the Early Twentieth Century.* (Scranton, Pa.: Intext Educational Publishers, 1972), 79–80.

35. National Society for the Promotion of Industrial Education, *Bulletin No. 1* (1907): 39–40.

36. Ibid., 17–19.

37. National Society for the Promotion of Industrial Education, *Bulletin No. 4* (1907): 7.

38. Geraldine Joncich Clifford, "'Marry, Stitch, Die, or Do Worse': Educating Women for Work," in *Work, Youth, and Schooling*, ed. Kantor and Tyack, 242. Clifford also provides excellent accounts of women's experiences with vocational education and work generally drawn from their life histories.

39. John L. Rury, *Education and Women's Work: Female Schooling and the Division of Labor in Urban America, 1870–1930*. (Albany: State University of New York Press, 1991), 135.

40. National Society for the Promotion of Industrial Education, *Bulletin No. 5* (1908): 23.

41. National Education Association, *Report of the Committee on Secondary School Studies*. (Washington, D.C.: Government Printing Office), 1893.

42. Charles W. Eliot, "Industrial Education as an Essential Factor in Our National Prosperity," National Society for the Promotion of Industrial Education, *Bulletin No. 2* (1908): 12–13.

43. Charles W. Eliot, "The Fundamental Assumptions in the Report of the Committee of Ten," *Educational Review* 30 (November 1905): 325–43.

44. Ibid., 13.

45. National Association of Manufacturers, "Report of the Committee on Industrial Education," *Proceedings* (1909): 2.

46. "Declaration of Principles," National Education Association, *Proceedings* (1907): 29.

47. U.S. Congress, *Senate Document*, no. 36, no. 40, 62d Congress, 2d Session (1911–1912): 21–22.

48. Nelson, *Managers and Workers*, 3–5.

49. David F. Noble, *America by Design: Science, Technology, and the Rise of Corporate Capitalism* (New York: Oxford University Press, 1977), xxiv.

50. Nelson, *Managers and Workers*, 48–54.

51. Frederick Winslow Taylor, "A Piece-Rate System, Being a Step Toward Partial Solution of the Labor Problem." *Transactions of the American Society of Mechanical Engineers* 16 (1895): 856.

52. The term "soldiering" probably derives from the fact that soldiers, when being transported by sea, were exempt from seaman's duties.

53. Quoted in Frank Barkley Copley, *Frederick Winslow Taylor: Father of Scientific Management*, vol. 1 (New York: American Society of Mechanical Engineers, 1923), 183.

54. Frank B. Gilbreth, *Bricklaying System*, in *The Writings of the Gilbreths*, ed. William R. Spriegel and Clark E. Meyers (Homewood, Ill.: Richard D. Irwin, 1953) 46. Originally published in 1909 by the Myron C. Clark Publishing Co.

55. Ibid., 53.

56. Ibid., 64. I had an opportunity recently to observe modern-day bricklayers in action. I am happy to report that they tapped bricks after laying them not once but as many as six or eight times. Moreover, after laying three bricks, they used a three-foot level to insure that the bricks lay evenly, tapping the level repeatedly when they did not.

57. Nelson, *Managers and Workers*, 57.

58. Frederick Winslow Taylor, *Scientific Management Comprising Shop Management, The Principles of Scientific Management, Testimony Before the Special House Committee* (New York: Harper and Brothers, 1911), 57–58.

59. Taylor, *Scientific Management*, 10.

60. Nelson, *Managers and Workers*, 60–61.

61. Taylor, *Scientific Management*, 77–85.

62. Ibid., 46.

63. Robert Kanigel, *The One Best Way: Frederick Winslow Taylor and the Enigma of Efficiency* (New York: Viking, 1997), 316–23.

64. Ibid., 70.

65. Samuel Haber, *Efficiency and Uplift: Scientific Management in the Progressive Era, 1890–1920* (Chicago: University of Chicago Press, 1964), 75–98.

66. Peter Drucker, *Post-Capitalist Society* (New York: Harper Business, 1993), 39.

67. Christopher Lasch, *The True and Only Heaven* (New York: W. W. Norton, 1991), 224.

68. Sean Wilentz, "Speedy Fred's Revolution," review of *The One Best Way*, by Robert Kanigel, *New York Review of Books* 44 (20 October 1997), 32.

69. Taylor, *Scientific Management*, 69.

70. Leonard P. Ayres, *Laggards in Our Schools* (New York: Charities Publication Committee, 1909).

71. Ibid., 5.

72. Ibid., 175.

73. Ibid., 176.

74. The schools of Gary, Indiana, in this period were the subject of much discussion, including John Dewey and Evelyn Dewey's *Schools of Tomorrow* (New York: E. P. Dutton, 1915). For a comprehensive study of the Gary schools, see Ronald D. Cohen, *Children of the Mill: Schooling and Society in Gary, 1906–1960* (Bloomington: Indiana University Press, 1990).

75. John Franklin Bobbitt, "The Elimination of Waste in Education," *Elementary School Teacher* 12 (February 1912): 260.

76. Ibid., 264.

77. Ibid., 269.

78. Ibid., 270–71.

79. Franklin Bobbitt, *The Curriculum* (New York: Houghton Mifflin, 1918).

80. Franklin Bobbitt, *How to Make a Curriculum* (New York: Houghton Mifflin, 1924), 8.

CHAPTER 3

1. Board of School Directors of the City of Milwaukee, *Proceedings* (1898–99): 248. Hereafter cited as *Proceedings*.

2. Quoted in Bayard Still, *Milwaukee: The History of a City* (Madison, Wis.: State Historical Society, 1948), 323.

3. Ibid., 324–25.

4. Ibid., 328–35.

5. *Twenty-fourth Annual Report of the School Board for the City of Milwaukee for the Year Ending August 31, 1883*, 56. Hereafter cited as *Annual Report*.

6. Ibid., 56–63.

7. Ibid., 64.

8. Ibid., 68.

9. Ibid., 69.

10. Ibid., 56–59.

11. *Annual Report*, 1884, 47–48.

12. *Annual Report*, 1885, 68.

13. Ibid., 68–70.

14. *Annual Report*, 1907, 43.

15. *Proceedings*, 1888–89, 93.

16. *Wisconsin Journal of Education* 18 (December 1888): 536.

17. *Proceedings*, 1888–89, 174, 208, 249, 256.

18. Ibid., 257.

19. Ibid., 258–59.

20. Ibid., 259–60.

21. *Annual Report*, 1889, 27, 59–61.

22. *Proceedings*, 1889–90, 62.

23. *Annual Report*, 1891, 69.

24. *Proceedings*, 1890–91, 75

25. Ibid., 56, 87, 136. *Annual Report*, 1891, 24–25; *Proceedings*, 1891–92, 124–125.

26. *Proceedings*, 1892–1893, 115, 169–170.

27. Ibid., 232.

28. See, for example, *Proceedings*, 1892–93, 66; *Proceedings*, 1899–1900, 136, 211, 239–43; *Annual Report*, 1900, 41; *Proceedings*, 1902–03, 149, 217, 337–38.

29. *Proceedings*, 1894–95, 117, 164, 204–05, 213.

30. Ibid., 164. See *Wisconsin Journal of Education* 14 (January 1888): 37–39; *Wisconsin Journal of Education* 18 (April 1888): 37–39. On the Chicago Manual Training School, see *Wisconsin Journal of Education* 18 (April 1888): 186–88.

31. *Annual Report*, 1897, 29–31. On the Stout Manual Training School, see *Wisconsin Journal of Education* 27 (September 1897): 195.

32. *Proceedings*, 1897–98, 45.

33. Ibid., 107.

34. Ibid., 266–67.

35. *Proceedings*, 1897–98, 381–85. On the theory and practice of sloyd as understood in the late-nineteenth century, see *Wisconsin Journal of Education* 18 (April 1888): 171–77, and *Report of the Commissioner Appointed by the Legislature in 1899* (Madison, Wis.: Democratic Printing Company, State Printer, 1901), 53–55.

36. *Proceedings*, 1898–99, 220.

37. Ibid., 218–22, 246, 275–76; *Proceedings*, 1899–1900, 25–26, 81.

38. *Proceedings*, 1898–99, 113.

39. *Proceedings*, 1898–99, 248.

40. Ibid., 284–88; *Annual Report*, 1899, 65–69.

41. *Annual Report*, 1900, 30–31.

42. William M. Lamers, *Our Roots Grow Deep, 1837–1967*, 2d ed. (Milwaukee: Milwaukee Public Schools, 1974), 40.

43. *Proceedings*, 1898–99, 298; *Proceedings*, 1899–1900, 20.

44. *Proceedings*, 1899–1900, 113.

45. Ibid.

46. Ibid.

47. Ibid.

48. Ibid., 177–97.

49. Ibid., 172–73.

50. Ibid., 263–73.

51. Ibid., 323.

52. *Proceedings*, 1902–03, 216–17.

53. Ibid., 1901–02, 185–86.

54. *Annual Report*, 1903, 33–34.

55. *Proceedings*, 1902–03, 337–38. On problems which arose when private philanthropists purchased manual training equipment for use in public schools, see *Proceedings*, 1899–1900, 239–43, 257–92. On requests to initiate sewing classes, see *Proceedings*, 1899–1900, 136, 211, and *Proceedings*, 1902–03, 189–217.

56. *Proceedings*, 1903–04, 309–10.

57. *Annual Report*, 1905, 32–33.

CHAPTER 4

1. *Social Democratic Herald*, 5 October 1907, 5.

2. David Levine, "Milwaukee Socialists and the Struggle for Democratic Schools, 1916–1930" (M.A. paper, University of Wisconsin, Madison, 1995), 16.

3. William J. Reese, *Power and the Promise of School Reform: Grass-Roots Movements during the Progressive Era* (Boston: Routledge & Kegan Paul, 1986), 127–28. Reese's is the best treatment of the political processes in Milwaukee as related to school reform during this period. Much of the discussion on the influence of the socialist tradition in Milwaukee is drawn from his work.

4. *Social Democratic Herald*, 1 July 1905. Quoted in Reese, *Power and the Promise*, 128.

5. Kenneth Teitelbaum, *Schooling for 'Good Rebels'; Socialist Education in the United States, 1900–1920* (Philadelphia: Temple University Press, 1993), 81–89.

6. *Milwaukee Free Press*, "Should Be Small: Members Should Be Appointed," 20 March 1907, 3. Cited in Levine, "Milwaukee Socialists," 17.

7. *Social Democratic Herald*, "Give the People a Voice in Their Schools!" 30 March 1907, 1–3. Quoted in Levine, "Milwaukee Socialists," 17.

8. Levine, "Milwaukee Socialists," 23.

9. Board of School Directors of the City of Milwaukee, *Proceedings* (1894–95): 278. Hereafter cited as *Proceedings*.

10. Milwaukee Merchants' and Manufacturers' Association *Bulletin* (May 1906): 8.

11. William Lamers, *Our Roots Grow Deep, 1836–1967*, 2d ed. (Milwaukee: Milwaukee Public Schools, 1974), 41.

12. Charles F. Perry, "The Milwaukee School of Trades: Founded by and Conducted under the Patronage of the Merchants' and Manufacturers' Association of Milwaukee," Merchants' and Manufacturers' Association *Bulletin* (November 1906): 10–15.

13. *Social Democratic Herald*, 10 December 1904, 4.

14. *Social Democratic Herald*, 2 February 1907, 5; Chapter 122, Laws of Wisconsin, 1907, 218–21.

15. *Social Democratic Herald*, 5 October 1907, 5.

16. Ibid.

17. Chapter 122, Laws of Wisconsin, 1907, Sections 926-22 to 926-30; *Proceedings*, 1907–08, 3–8. In the case of Milwaukee, a tax levy of one-half mill produced about $100,000 annually to support the trade school.

18. Statutory Committee on Trade Schools, *Minutes*, 24 September 1907.

19. Statutory Committee on Trade Schools, *Minutes*, 14 February 1908. *Proceedings*, 1907–08, 316–17.

20. *Proceedings*, 1909–10, 26–27.

21. Committee on Course of Instruction and Textbooks, *Minutes*, 17 May 1915.

22. Milwaukee *Free Press*, 24 January 1916.

23. Statutory Committee on Trade Schools, *Minutes*, 29 October 1917, 24 June 1918.

24. *Proceedings*, 1908–09, 319.

25. *Proceedings*, 1908–09, 424–25, 539.

26. Laura Tiefenthaler Papers, Milwaukee County Historical Society, "Miss Ora S. Blanker, Principal, Girls Trade and Technical High School—1910–1935" (typewritten copy of a talk given 29 May 1945), 2. See also *Proceedings*, 1909–10, 329, for the appointment of Tiefenthaler.

27. *Proceedings*, 1909–10, 328, 303–31.

28. *Proceedings*, 1911–12, 314–15.

29. Statutory Committee on Trade Schools, *Minutes*, 21 February 1910.

30. Laura Tiefenthaler Papers, 2.

31. *Proceedings*, 1912–13, 89.

32. Rury, *Education and Women's Work*, 11–48.

33. *Proceedings*, 1910–11, 52.

34. Ibid., 50–52.

35. Ibid., 53.

36. *Proceedings*, 1909–10, 64–65.

37. *Proceedings*, 1912–13, 315.

38. Committee on Course of Instruction and Textbooks, *Minutes*, 29 July 1914; *Proceedings*, 1914–15, 29; *Industrial Arts Magazine* 11 (October 1914): 185.

39. On vocational education at the state level see Edward A. Fitzpatrick, *McCarthy of Wisconsin* (New York: Columbia University Press, 1944); Joseph H. McGiveny, "The Politics of Vocational Education in Wisconsin, 1909–1967" (Ph.D. diss., University of Wisconsin, Madison, 1967); Robert J. Spinti, "The Development of Trade and Industrial Education in Wisconsin" (Ph.D. diss., University of Missouri, 1968).

40. Wisconsin Senate, Joint Resolution No. 53 (1909).

41. *Report of the Commission on Industrial and Agricultural Training* (Madison, Wis.: Democrat Printing Company, 1911), p.7. Hereafter *Report of Commission*.

42. Frank J. Woerdehoff, "Dr. Charles McCarthy's Role in Revitalizing the University Extension Division," *Wisconsin Magazine of History* 40 (Autumn 1956): 13–18; Frank J. Woerdehoff, "Dr. Charles McCarthy: Planner of the Wisconsin System of Vocational and Adult Education," *Wisconsin Magazine of History* 41 (Summer 1958): 270–74.

43. *Report of Commission*, 26–29, 79–80, 90–96, 101–02.

44. John R. Commons, *Myself: The Autobiography of John R. Commons* (Madison: University of Wisconsin Press, 1964), 107–11, 153–65.

45. Ibid. See also Robert L. Cooley, "Schools and Continuation Schools," *Industrial Arts Magazine* 11 (August 1914): 49–54; Robert L. Cooley, "The Apprenticeship and Continuation Schools of Milwaukee, Wisconsin," National Education Association *Addresses and Proceedings* (1914): 617.

46. Robert L. Cooley, "The Apprenticeship and Continuation Schools," 615.

47. Ibid.

48. Ibid., 616–17.

49. Robert L. Cooley et al., *My Life Work* (New York: McGraw-Hill, 1930).

50. Wisconsin State Board of Vocational Education, "Coordination in Part-Time Education, *Administrative Series Circular* 8 (Madison: Wisconsin State Board of Vocational Education, 1924).

51. By the time I taught in a continuation school in New York City in the early 1950s, the separation between the work the students did on their jobs and their school studies was nearly complete.

52. Paul E. Peterson, *The Politics of School Reform, 1870–1940* (Chicago: University of Chicago Press, 1985), 70.

53. Levine, "Milwaukee Socialists," 39–68.

54. Julia Wrigley, *Class Politics and Public Schools: Chicago, 1900–1950* (New Brunswick: Rutgers University Press, 1982), 70–75.

55. Ibid., 78–90.

56. John Dewey, "A Policy of Industrial Education," *New Republic* (19 December 1912): 11.

57. John Dewey, "Splitting up the School System," *New Republic* (17 April 1915): 283–84; John Dewey, "Education vs. Trade Training—Dr. Dewey's Reply," *New Republic* (15 May 1915): 42–43.

58. Ira Katznelson and Margaret Weir, *Schooling for All: Class, Race, and the Decline of the Democratic Ideal* (Berkeley: University of California Press, 1988), 92.

CHAPTER 5

1. David S. Snedden, "Differences Among Varying Groups of Children Should Be Recognized; and the Period at Which this Recognition Takes Place May Rationally Constitute the Beginnings of Secondary Education," National Education Association *Addresses and Proceedings* (July 1908): 754–55.

2. Reed Ueda, *Avenues to Adulthood: The Origins of the High School and Social Mobility in an American Suburb* (Cambridge, Mass.: Cambridge University Press, 1987), 198.

3. The earliest use of the term *vocationalism* (as distinct from vocational education) that I know of appears in Marvin Lazerson's *Origins of the Urban School: Public Education in Massachusetts, 1870–1915* (Cambridge, Mass.: Harvard University Press, 1971). It surfaces again in *American Education and Vocationalism: A Documentary History, 1870–1970*, ed. Marvin Lazerson and

W. Norton Grubb (New York: Teachers College Press, 1974) and in the superb collection of essays edited by Kantor and Tyack, *Work, Youth, and Schooling*. Rury's *Education and Women's Work* also uses the term. The particular definition of vocationalism offered here, however, is my own.

4. Walter H. Drost, *David Snedden and Education for Social Efficiency* (Madison: University of Wisconsin Press, 1967), 63.

5. Ibid., 67–68.

6. David Snedden, "History Study as an Instrument in the Social Education of Children," *Journal of Pedagogy* 19 (June 1907): 259–68.

7. Snedden, "Differences Among Varying Groups," 756.

8. Drost, *David Snedden*, 112.

9. David Snedden, "Education for a World of Team-Players and Team Workers," *School and Society* 20 (1 November 1924): 553.

10. Ibid., 554.

11. Ibid.

12. David Snedden, "What of Liberal Education?" *Atlantic Monthly* 109 (January 1912): 111–12.

13. Ibid., 114.

14. David Snedden, "Practical Arts in Liberal Education," *Educational Review* 43 (April 1912): 379.

15. William C. Bagley, "Fundamental Distinctions between Liberal and Vocational Education," National Education Association *Addresses and Proceedings* (1914): 169–70.

16. William H. Maxwell, *A Quarter Century of Public School Development* (New York: American Book, 1912), 123.

17. Owen Lovejoy, "Vocational Guidance and Child Labor," in *Vocational Guidance, Papers Presented at the Organizational Meeting of the Vocational Guidance Association*, Bureau of Education Bulletin no. 14, (Washington, D.C.: Government Printing Office, 1914):13.

18. John Dewey, "Policy of Industrial Education," *New Republic* 1 (19 December 1914): 11–12.

19. David Snedden, "Vocational Education," *New Republic* 3 (15 May 1915): 40–42.

20. John Dewey, "Education vs. Trade Training—Dr. Dewey's Reply," *New Republic* 3 (15 May 1915): 42–43.

21. Jane Dewey, ed., "Biography of John Dewey," in *The Philosophy of John Dewey*, ed. Paul Schilpp (Evanston, Ill.: Northwestern University, 1939), 29.

22. Ella Flagg Young, "Industrial Training," National Education Association *Addresses and Proceedings* (1915): 125–26.

23. Ibid., 126–27.

24. May Allison and Susan Kingsbury, *A Trade School for Girls, A Preliminary Investigation in a Typical Manufacturing City, Worcester, Mass.*, U.S.

Bureau of Education bulletin no. 17 (Washington, D.C.: Government Printing Office, 1913).

25. Frederick W. Roman, "Vocational Education—Its Dependence upon Elementary Cultural Training," National Education Association *Addresses and Proceedings* (1915): 1174–75.

26. "Professor Roman Attacks Vocational Training," *National Association of Corporation Schools Bulletin* 2 (October 1915): 24–25.

27. Ibid., 25.

28. Ibid.

29. Ibid., 26.

30. David Snedden, *The Problem of Vocational Education* (Boston: Houghton Mifflin, 1910), 67.

31. Peter G. Filene, "An Obituary for the 'Progressive Movement,'" *American Quarterly* 22 (1970): 33. See also, Daniel T. Rodgers, "In Search of Progressivism," *Reviews in American History"* 10 (December 1982): 113–32; David P. Thelen, "Social Tensions and the Origins of Progressivism," *Journal of American History* 55 (September 1969): 523–41; John D. Buenker, "The Progressive Era: A Search for a Synthesis," *Mid-America* 51 (July 1969): 175–93. Coalitions among interest groups play an important role in Reese's *Power and the Promise*, and in Julia Wrigley's *Class, Politics and the Public Schools: Chicago, 1900–1950* (New Brunswick: Rutgers University Press, 1982).

32. Elizabeth Fones-Wolf, "The Politics of Vocationalism: Coalitions and Industrial Education in the Progressive Era," *The Historian* 46 (November 1983): 39–55.

33. Thomas Jesse Jones, *Negro Education: A Study of the Private and Higher Schools for Colored People in the United States*, U.S. Office of Education, bulletin 36 (Washington, D.C.: Government Printing Office, 1917): 7.

34. Smith was an unusually astute politician. See Dewey Grantham, *Hoke Smith and the Politics of the New South* (Baton Rouge: Louisiana State University Press, 1958). See also Wayne Urban, "Educational Reform in a New South City: Atlanta 1890–1925," in *Education and the Rise of the New South*, ed. Ronald K. Goodnow and Arthur G. White (Austin: G. K. Hall, 1981): 114–30.

35. John Dewey, "Learning to Earn: The Place of Vocational Education in a Comprehensive Scheme of Public Education," *School and Society* 5 (24 March 1917): 335.

36. Robert Ripley Clough, "The National Society for the Promotion of Industrial Education: Case Study of a Reform Organization, 1906–1917" (M.A. thesis, University of Wisconsin, Madison, 1957), 63–65.

37. National Vocational Education Act, S703, Public 347, Sixty-fourth Congress.

38. Douglas, *American Apprenticeship*, 294.

39. Clough, "National Society," 72.

40. Harvey A. Kantor, *Learning to Earn: School, Work, and Vocational Reform in California, 1880–1930* (Madison: University of Wisconsin Press, 1988), 42.

41. Agnes Nestor, *Woman's Labor Leader, An Autobiography* (Rockford, Ill.: Bellevue Books, 1954), 151.

42. U.S. Department of Interior, Office of Education, The *Program of Studies Bulletin*, no. 17 (Washington, D.C.: Government Printing Office, 1933), 128.

43. California High School Teachers' Association, *Report of the Committee of Fifteen on Secondary Education in California*, 1923 (San Francisco: California High School Teachers' Association, 1924), 43–44. Cited in Kantor, *Learning to Earn*, 134.

44. Snedden, *The Problem of Vocational Education*, 52.

45. National enrollment figures by gender are not available. It is a safe assumption, however, that girls overwhelmingly predominated.

46. George S. Counts, *The Selective Character of American Secondary Education* (Chicago: University of Chicago Press, 1922), 119.

47. Jane Bernard Powers, "The 'Girl Question' in Education: Vocational Training for Young Women in the Progressive Era." (Ph.D. diss., Stanford University, 1986), 156–66.

48. Laura Murray, "Training of Mexican Women in Household Service," *Vocational Education Magazine* 2 (December 1924): 1120–21.

49. Ruth Aline Patton, "A Survey of Home Economics in Some Negro Schools," (M.A. thesis, George Peabody College for Teachers, 1931).

50. Powers, "Girl Question," 166–70.

51. Douglas, *American Apprenticeship*, 116.

52. Ibid., 119.

53. Ibid., 124.

54. Ibid., 123.

55. Marvin Lazerson, "'Choosing Our Roles': American Youth Guidance in Historical Perspective," paper prepared for the Organization of Economic Cooperation and Development (March 1981): 30–31.

56. Rury, *Education and Women's Work*, 93–96.

57. U.S. Commissioner of Education Annual Reports. Table prepared by Jurgen Herbst, *The Once and Future School* (New York: Routledge, 1996), 138.

58. Women's Educational and Industrial Union, Department of Research, *The Public Schools and Women in Office Service* (Boston, WEIU, 1914), 5–11.

59. Kantor, *Learning to Earn*, 63.

60. Janice Weiss, "Educating for Clerical Work: A History of Commercial Education in the United States Since 1850," (Ed.D. diss., Harvard Graduate School of Education, 1978).

61. Counts, *Selective Character*, 76.

62. Kantor, *Learning to Earn*, 63.

63. John Francis Latimer, *What's Happened to Our High Schools?* (Washington, D.C.: Public Affairs Press, 1958), 36, 61.

64. Clarence D. Kingsley, "The High School as a Testing-Time," National Education Association *Addresses and Proceedings* (1913): 49.

65. Clarence D. Kingsley, "The Reorganization of Secondary Education (VI)," *Journal of Education* 79 (23 April 1914): 48.

66. Edward A. Krug, *The Shaping of the American High School*, vol. 1 (New York: Harper & Row, 1964), 36.

67. See, for example, Henry F. May, *The End of American Innocence: The First Years of Our Own Time, 1912–1917* (New York: Oxford University Press, 1959), 152; Daniel Tanner and Laurel Tanner, *History of the School Curriculum* (New York: Macmillan, 1990), 363–64; William G. Wraga, *Democracy's High School: The Comprehensive High School and Educational Reform in the United States* (Lanham, Md.: University Press of America, 1994), 26–28. The issue of Dewey's influence on *Cardinal Principles* is of considerable historical and theoretical importance since any actual association could serve to link Dewey to social efficiency as well as to related doctrines and practices he opposed, thereby obfuscating important distinctions among the various kinds of education reform that were being advanced at the time.

68. Herbst, *Once and Future School*, 144.

69. National Education Association, *Cardinal Principles of Secondary Education: A Report of the Commission on the Reorganization of Secondary Education* (Washington, D.C.: Government Printing Office, 1918), 9.

70. Ibid.

71. Snedden, *Problem of Vocational Education*, 52.

72. *Cardinal Principles*, 12.

73. Ibid., 6–7.

74. Robert Goldman and John Wilson, "The Rationalization of Leisure," *Politics and Society*, 7 (1977): 157–87.

75. Dewey, *Democracy and Education*, 117.

76. *Cardinal Principles*, 22.

77. David Snedden, "Cardinal Principles of Secondary Education," *School and Society*, 9 (3 May 1919): 519.

78. Ibid., 227.

79. Ibid., 522.

80. Dewey, *Democracy and Education*, 300.

CHAPTER 6

1. Charles A. Prosser and Charles R. Allen, *Vocational Education in a Democracy* (New York: Century, 1925), 3.

2. May, *End of American Innocence*, 393–98.

3. William E. Leuchtenburg, *The Perils of Prosperity, 1914–1932* (Chicago: University of Chicago Press, 1958), 178–203.

4. Calvin Coolidge, Speech to the Society of American Newspaper Editors, 17 January 1925.

5. Quoted in Robert S. McElvaine, *The Great Depression: America, 1929–1941*, 2d ed. (New York: Times Books, 1993), 16.

6. Bruce Barton, *The Man Nobody Knows: A Discovery of the Real Jesus* (New York: Bobbs-Merrill, 1925), 162. (Original emphasis)

7. National Advisory Committee on Education, *Federal Relations to Education, Part 2: Basic Facts* (Washington, D.C.: National Capital Press, 1931), 222.

8. Data derived from *Historical Statistics of the United States, Supplement* (Washington, D.C.: Bureau of Census, 1957), H 262–326. Compiled by Jurgen Herbst, *Once and Future School*, 136. Since secondary school enrollments were rising dramatically during this period, vocational enrollments expressed in terms of numbers are misleading. Percentages are more revealing.

9. Robert Lynd and Helen Lynd, *Middletown: A Study in Contemporary American Culture* (New York: Harcourt, Brace, 1929), 194–96.

10. W. W. Charters and Isadore B. Whitley, *Analysis of Secretarial Duties and Traits* (Baltimore: Williams & Wilkins, 1924).

11. W. W. Charters and Douglas Waples, *The Commonwealth Teacher-Training Study* (Chicago: University of Chicago Press, 1929).

12. David Tyack and Elizabeth Hansot, *Managers of Virtue: Public School Leadership in America, 1820–1980* (New York: Basic Books, 1982), 161.

13. Ellen Condliffe Lagemann, "Contested Terrain: A History of Education Research in the United States, 1890–1990," *Educational Researcher* 26 (December 1997): 6.

14. Thomas H. Briggs, "What Next in Secondary Education?" *School Review* 30 (September 1922): 524–25, 529.

15. Thomas H. Briggs, Elbert K. Fretwell, and Romiett Stevens, "The Secondary Schools of Baltimore," in *Report of the Survey of the Public School System of Baltimore Maryland, School Year 1920–1921*, ed. George D. Strayer (Baltimore: Board of School Commissioners, 1921), 65.

16. Briggs, "Secondary Schools," 69.

17. Ibid., 73.

18. Anna M. Cooley, "Home Economics in the Schools of Baltimore," in Strayer, *Report of the Survey*, 157.

19. Arthur D. Dean, "Vocational Education," in Strayer, *Report of the Survey*, 205.

20. Ibid., 213.

21. Ibid., 293.

22. Ibid., 294.

23. F. G. Nichols, "Commercial Education," in Strayer, *Report of the Survey*, 324.

24. Ibid., 321.

25. Ibid., 320.

26. Baltimore Board of School Commissioners, *School Report* (Annapolis, Md.: Capital-Gazette Press, 1929–30), 34.

27. Ibid., 21–28.

28. F. P. O'Brien, *Survey Report of the Chanute, Kansas, School System* (Lawrence: Bureau of School Service, University of Kansas, 1924), 42.

29. Franklin Bobbitt, *Curriculum-Making in Los Angeles* (Chicago: University of Chicago, 1922).

30. Ibid., 58.

31. Ibid., 58–60.

32. Ibid., 80–81.

33. Herbert M. Kliebard, "Curriculum Theory: Give Me a 'For Instance,'" in *Forging the American Curriculum: Essays in Curriculum History and Theory*, ed. Herbert M. Kliebard (New York: Routledge, 1992), 180–81.

34. John C. Chiddix, "School Surveys in the Smaller Communities Illustrated by a Survey of the Stanford (Ill.) Schools," *Normal School Quarterly* 23 (July/October, 1925): 9–10.

35. Ibid., 18.

36. Alan Peshkin, *Growing Up American: Schooling and the Survival of a Community* (Chicago: University of Chicago Press, 1978), 200. Quoted in Clifford, "'Marry, Stitch, Die,'" in Kantor and Tyack, *Work, Youth, and Schooling*, 241.

37. William Martin Proctor and Edward J. Brown, "College Admission Requirements in Relation to Curriculum Revision in Secondary Schools," in *The Development of the High School Curriculum*, Department of Superintendence, Sixth Yearbook (Washington, D.C.: Department of Superintendence, 1928), 159.

38. Ibid., 174–75.

39. Ibid., 178–79.

40. Ibid., 187.

41. Ibid., 186.

42. Committee on Vocational Guidance, *Vocational Guidance in Secondary Education*, bulletin no. 19 (Washington, D.C.: Government Printing Office, 1918), 9.

43. Ibid., 10.

44. Anthony Paul Picchioni, "History of Guidance in the United States,"(Ph.D. diss., North Texas State University, 1980), 60.

45. Frank Parsons, *Choosing a Vocation* (Boston: Houghton Mifflin, 1909), 4.

46. Meyer Bloomfield, *Youth, School, and Vocation* (Boston: Houghton Mifflin, 1915), 20.

47. Ibid., 23.

48. John M. Brewer, *History of Vocational Guidance* (New York: Harper and Brothers, 1942), 148–49.

49. See, for example, C. S. Yoakum and Robert M. Yerkes, *Army Mental Testing* (New York: Holt, 1920) and Robert M. Yerkes, "Psychological Examining in the United States Army, *Memoirs of the National Academy of Sciences* 15, (1921).

50. Hugo Munsterberg, *Psychology and Industrial Efficiency* (Boston: Houghton Mifflin, 1913).

51. Morris S. Viteles, "Selecting Cashiers and Predicting Length of Service," *Journal of Personnel Research* 2 (April 1924): 467–73.

52. Dean J. B. Johnston, *Who Should Go to College?* (Minneapolis: University of Minnesota Press, 1930).

53. Roger F. Aubrey, "Historical Developments of Guidance and Counseling and Implications for the Future," *Personnel and Guidance Journal* 55 (February 1977): 291.

54. W. M. Proctor, "The Use of Psychological Tests in Vocational Guidance of High School Pupils," *Journal of Educational Research* 2 (September 1920): 533–46.

55. Clark L. Hull, *Aptitude Testing* (Tarrytown-on-Hudson, N.Y.: World Book, 1928), 5.

56. Ibid., 35.

57. Clark L. Hull, "Clark L. Hull," in *A History of Psychology in Autobiography*, vol. 4, ed. Edwin G. Boring, Herbert S. Langfeld, Heinz Werner, and Robert M. Yerkes (Worcester, Mass.: Clark University Press, 1952), 151.

58. Glen L. Swigett, "Educational Preparation for Business," *School Life* 6 (15 January 1921): 6.

59. Historical accounts of the mental hygiene movement tend to date its inception from the publication of Clifford Whittingham Beers's autobiography, *A Mind That Found Itself* (Garden City, N.Y.: Doubleday, 1908).

60. Wrigley, *Class, Politics, and the Public Schools*, 173.

61. In an ethnographic case study, sociologists Aaron V. Cicourel and John Kitsuse provide a devastating critique on this tendency on the part of guidance counselors, *Educational Decision-Makers* (Indianapolis: Bobbs-Merrill, 1963). Similar themes are explored in James E. Rosenbaum's *Making Inequality: The Hidden Curriculum of High School Tracking* (New York: John Wiley & Sons, 1976).

62. This is a central theme of my book, *The Struggle for the American Curriculum, 1893–1958* (New York: Routledge, 1986, 1995).

63. John Dewey, "Why I Am for Smith," *New Republic* 56 (7 November 1928): 321.

64. John Dewey, *Individualism Old and New* (New York: Milton, Balch, 1930), 9.

65. Sinclair Lewis, *Babbitt* (San Diego: Harcourt, Brace, Jovanovich, 1922), 19.

66. Ibid., 89–90.

67. Ibid., 472.

68. Dewey, *Democracy and Education*, 372.

CHAPTER 7

1. L. H. Dennis, Editorial, *American Vocational Association Journal and News Bulletin* 10 (September 1935): 61. Hereafter cited as *American Vocational Association Bulletin*.

2. *New York Times*, 12 August 1928.

3. Kanigel, *One Best Way*, 490.

4. Conference on Unemployment, *Recent Economic Changes in the United States*, vol. 1 (New York: McGraw-Hill, 1927), ix. Quoted in Broadus Mitchell, *Depression Decade: From New Era through New Deal, 1929–1941* (New York: Rinehart, 1947), 26.

5. *New York Times*, 25 October 1929.

6. *New York Times*, 30 October 1929.

7. McElvaine, *The Great Depression*, 48.

8. Paul Webbink, "Unemployment in the United States, 1930–1940," *Papers and Proceedings of the American Economic Association* 30 (February 1941): 250.

9. Don D. Lescohier, *Working Conditions*, vol. 3 of *History of Labor in the United States, 1896–1932* (New York: Macmillan, 1935).

10. U.S. Congress, Senate, Federal Cooperation in Unemployment Relief, Hearing before a Subcommittee of the Committee of Manufacturers, 72d Congress, 1st session, on S. 4592, 9 May 1932 (Washington, D.C.: Government Printing Office, 1932): 48–51.

11. "Bad Business," *School Life* 18 (December 1932), 70.

12. David Tyack, Robert Lowe, and Elizabeth Hansot, *Public Schools in Hard Times: The Great Depression and Recent Years* (Cambridge, Mass.: Harvard University Press, 1984), 20.

13. Avis D. Carlson, "Deflating the Schools," *Harper's* 167 (November 1933): 705–13.

14. Tyack et al., *Public Schools in Hard Times*, 32.

15. Andre Roger O'Coin, "Vocational Education During the Great Depression and World War II: Challenge, Innovation and Continuity" (Ph.D. diss., University of Maryland, 1988), 44.

16. Ibid., 45–49.

17. C. M. Miller, "President's Message," *American Vocational Association Bulletin* 6 (August 1931): 1–2.

18. C. M. Miller, Letter, *School Review* 38 (April 1930), 246–47.

19. Charles H. Judd, *School Review* 38 (April 1930), 247.

20. National Advisory Committee on Education, Committee Findings and Recommendations, part 1, *Federal Relations to Education* (Washington, D.C.: National Capital Press, 1931), 33–38.

21. Ibid., 103–05.

22. Ibid., 110.

23. Ibid., 128.

24. O'Coin, "Vocational Education During the Great Depression," 52–65.

25. Ibid., 68.

26. Melvin L. Barlow, *History of Industrial Education in the United States* (Peoria, Ill.: Chas. A. Bennett, 1967), 129.

27. O'Coin,"Vocational Education During the Great Depression," 69–71.

28. Ibid., 77.

29. Fisher, *Industrial Education*, 214.

30. Larry Cuban, "Enduring Resiliency: Enacting and Implementing Federal Vocational Legislation," in Kantor and Tyack, *Work, Youth, and Schooling*, 73.

31. George Philip Rawick, "The New Deal and Youth: The Civilian Conservation Corps, the National Youth Administration, and the American Youth Congress" (Ph.D. diss., University of Wisconsin, Madison, 1957), 20–21.

32. Harry Zeitlin, "Federal Relations in American Education, 1933–1943: A Study of New Deal Efforts and Innovations" (Ph.D. diss., Teachers College, Columbia University, 1958), 68–70.

33. U.S. Congress, 73d Congress, 1st Sess., *Congressional Record*, 77: 914–15. Quoted in Rawick, "The New Deal and Youth," 54. Rawick provides an exhaustive examination of the political maneuvering involved in this legislation, as well as an extraordinarily well-documented review of its aftermath.

34. Zeitlin, "Federal Relations in American Education," 71.

35. Ibid., 72.

36. C. S. Marsh, "The Educational Program in the Civilian Conservation Corps," *Educational Record* 16 (January 1935): 3–26.

37. O'Coin, "Vocational Education During the Great Depression," 125.

38. Kenneth Holland and Frank Ernest Hill, *Youth in the* CCC (Washington, D.C.: American Council on Education, 1942), 85, 67.

39. Editorial, *American Vocational Association Bulletin* 10 (August 1935): 61.

40. Zeitlin, "Federal Relations in American Education," 96.

41. Rawick, "The New Deal and Youth," 132.

42. Paula S. Fass, *Outside In: Minorities and the Transformation of American Education* (New York: Oxford University Press, 1989), 123.

43. Edward A. Krug, *Shaping of the American High School, 1920–1941*, vol. 2 (Madison: University of Wisconsin Press, 1972), 307–36.

44. Richard A. Reiman, *The New Deal and American Youth: Ideas and Ideals in a Depression Decade* (Athens: University of Georgia Press, 1992), 52–53.

45. Tyack et al., *Public Schools in Hard Times*, 108.

46. O'Coin, "Vocational Education During the Great Depression," 134.

47. B. H. Van Oot, Editorial, *American Vocational Association Bulletin* 10 (February 1935): 11–12.

48. Charles A. Prosser, "Industrial Education and the Changing Job," *American Vocational Association Bulletin* 7 (May 1932): 9.

49. Fass, *Outside In*, 128.

50. Reiman, *New Deal and American Youth*, 39–44; Rawick, "New Deal and Youth," 173–89.

51. Zeitlin, "Federal Relations in American Education," 246–87; Paula S. Fass, *The New Deal: Anticipating a Federal Education Policy*, Institute for Research on Educational Policy and Governance (Stanford: Stanford University, 1981).

52. Reiman, *New Deal and American Youth*, 48.

53. Quoted in Reiman, *New Deal and American Youth*, 106.

54. Reiman, *New Deal and American Youth*, 114.

55. Drew Pearson and Robert A. Allen, "The Washington Merry Go-Round," *Washington Herald*, 30 September 1935. Cited in Rawick, "New Deal and Youth," 134.

56. *New York Times*, 30 June 1935. Quoted in Rawick, "New Deal and Youth," 192.

57. Willard E. Givens, "New Deal a Raw Deal for Public Schools," *National Education Association Journal* 24 (September 1935): 198.

58. O'Coin, "Vocational Education During the Great Depression," 153–54.

59. Ibid., 107.

60. Ray Fife, "President's Message," *American Vocational Association Bulletin* 9 (August 1934): 5.

61. L. H. Dennis, "Report on National Vocational Legislation," *American Vocational Association Bulletin* 10 (August 1935): 89.

62. O'Coin, "Vocational Education During the Great Depression," 201–02.

63. U.S. Congress, Senate, 5th Cong., 1st Sess, *Congressional Record*, 28 June 1937, vol. 81, pt. 6, 6403.

64. Franklin Delano Roosevelt, "Regarding Appropriation for Vocational Education: A Statement by President Franklin D. Roosevelt," *Phi Delta Kappan* 20 (October 1937): 76.

65. V. O. Key, *Southern Politics in State and Nation* (New York: Vintage, 1949), 345–82.

66. Elaine M. Smith, "Mary McLeod Bethune and the National Youth Administration" in *Clio Was a Woman: Studies in the History of American Women*, ed. Mabel E. Deutrich and Virginia C. Purdy (Washington, D.C.: Howard University Press), 153–54.

67. Ibid., 167.

68. John D. Russell and Associates, *Vocational Education*, Advisory Committee on Education (Washington, D.C.: Government Printing Office, 1938), 236.

69. Ibid., 114.

70. Ibid., 128.

71. Ibid, 129.

72. Ibid., 131.

73. Ibid., 135.

74. Ibid., 48.

75. Ibid., 49.

76. Ibid., 153.

77. O'Coin, "Vocational Education During the Great Depression," 267–68.

78. Russell, *Vocational Education*, 154.

79. McElvaine, *The Great Depression*, 307.

80. Mitchell, *Depression Decade*, 371.

81. O'Coin,"Vocational Education During the Great Depression," 346.

82. Report of Interdepartmental Committee on Mechanics Training for Aircraft Industry, 9 May 1939, OF 504, FDR Library. Cited in O'Coin, "Vocational Education During the Great Depression," 344.

83. Smith, "Mary McLeod Bethune," 168.

84. Nicholas Lemann, *The Promised Land: The Great Black Migration and How It Changed America* (New York: Alfred A. Knopf, 1991), 40.

85. Anderson, "Black Vocational Education," in Kantor and Tyack, *Work Youth, and Schooling*, 214.

86. U.S. Office of Education, Federal Security Agency, *Vocational Training for War Production Workers*, bulletin no. 10 (Washington, D.C.: Government Printing Office, 1946), 18–19.

87. Walter Dexter to John Studebaker, 16 January 1939, in Box 97, Papers of the Office of Education, Vocational Education Division, National Archives. Cited in Rawick, "New Deal and Youth," 252.

88. Aubrey Williams, "A Message from Aubrey Williams," *American Vocational Association Bulletin* 14 (February 1939), 32.

89. Aubrey Williams to FDR, 15 April 1942 and 19 December 1942, OF 444d, FDR Library. Cited in O'Coin, "Vocational Education During the Great Depression," 336.

90. O'Coin, "Vocational Education During the Great Depression," 336–37.

91. Rawick, *New Deal and Youth*, 273.

92. "Typical Wartime Activities of American Secondary Schools," *School Executive* 62 (February 1943): 15–16.

93. "U.S. High School Youth Building 500,000 Model Airplanes for the U.S. Navy," *American Vocational Association Bulletin* 17 (February 1942): 13.

94. Jeffrey Mirel, *The Rise and Fall of an Urban School System: Detroit, 1907–81* (Ann Arbor: University of Michigan Press, 1993), 156–57.

95. U.S. Office of Education. *Vitalizing Secondary Education: Education for Life Adjustment* (Washington, D.C.: Government Printing Office, 1951), 29.

96. Dorothy Elizabeth Broder, "Life Adjustment Education: An Historical Study of a Program of the United States Office of Education, 1945–1954" (Ed.D. diss., Teachers College, Columbia University, 1976), 104.

97. Charles Prosser, "Our Job Has Just Begun," *American Vocational Journal* 21 (January 1946) 21.

98. Ibid. The accuracy of these percentages has never been established. They certainly do not anticipate a trend toward post-secondary education after World War Two. In the 1940s, enrollments in post-secondary institutions rose 74 percent. By 1950, 27 percent of youth ages nineteen to twenty-one were attending such schools, a rise of 14.5 percent from 1940 levels. Robert L. Hempel, *The Last Little Citadel: American High Schools Since 1940* (Boston: Houghton Mifflin, 1986), 45.

99. FDR to Walter George, 20 May 1944; FDR to Graham Barden, 27 May 1944, PPF 109, FDR Library. Cited in O'Coin, "Vocational Education During the Great Depression," 362.

100. L. H. Dennis, "From the Desk of the Executive Secretary," *American Vocational Association Journal* 20 (January 1945): 50–51.

101. Karen Anderson, *Wartime Women: Sex Roles, Family Relations, and the Status of Women During World War II* (Westport, Conn.: Greenwood Press, 1981), 4.

CHAPTER 8

1. Dewey, *Democracy and Education*, 262–63.

2. Licht, *Getting Work*, 87–88.

3. Selden C. Menefee, *Vocational Training and Employment of Youth*, Research Monograph 25, Works Projects Administration (Washington, D.C.: Government Printing Office, 1942), 22.

4. Menefee's inclusion of clerical occupations in his study is a bit puzzling since his study was designed to compare Smith-Hughes trained workers with untrained workers, and Smith-Hughes excluded clerical training from its provisions, as did subsequent federal legislation to this point. Menefee may have been simply mistaken in assuming that clerical occupations were in fact included, or it is possible he believed that a little-known provision of Smith-Hughes authorizing the Federal Board for Vocational Education to provide states with advice and guidance in the area of clerical education made it eligible for inclusion in his study. In either case, the inclusion of data on clerical education is fortuitous, since the successes of those studies provide an interesting counterpoint to the failures in industrial education.

5. Menefee, *Vocational Training and Employment*, 29.

6. Ibid., 31.

7. Ibid., 35–36.

8. Ibid., 35–37.

9. Ibid., 46–49.

10. Ibid., 46–47.

11. Ibid., 53.

12. Ibid., 50.

13. Ibid., 87–102.

14. Ibid., 103.

15. Ibid., 105.

16. Ibid., 107.

17. Michael Polanyi, *Personal Knowledge: Towards a Post-Critical Philosophy* (Chicago: University of Chicago Press, 1958), 49.

18. Ibid.

19. Ibid., 50.

20. John Dewey, "The Schools and Social Preparedness," *New Republic* 6 (6 May 1916): 15.

21. W. Norton Grubb and Marvin Lazerson, "Education and the Labor Market: Recycling the Youth Problem," in Kantor and Tyack, *Work, Youth, and Schooling*, 129.

22. Du Bois and Dill, *Negro American Artisan*.

23. Kliebard, "Struggle for the American Curriculum," 121–24.

24. Stuart A. Rosenfeld, "Vocational Agriculture: A Model for Educational Reform," *Education Week* 4 (26 September 1984): 21.

25. Janice Weiss, "The Advent of Education for Clerical Work in the High School: A Reconsideration of the Historiography of Vocationalism," *Teachers College Record* 83 (Summer 1982): 613–14.

26. Counts, *Selective Character*, 1922.

27. Olivier Zunz, *Making America Corporate, 1870–1920* (Chicago: University of Chicago Press, 1990), 144–46.

28. Weiss, "Advent of Education for Clerical Work," 614.

29. John Dollard, *Caste and Class in a Southern Town*, 3d ed. (Garden City, N.Y.: Doubleday Anchor, 1957), 189.

30. Ibid., 191–92.

31. Regina E. Werum, "Political Process in the Pre-Desegregation South: Race and Gender Stratification in Federal Vocational Programs, 1917–1936" (Ph.D. diss., Indiana University, 1994) 182.

32. Rury, *Education and Women's Work*, 146.

33. Werum, *Political Process in the Pre-Desegregation South*, 146.

34. Ibid., 148.

35. Ambrose Caliver, *Vocational Education and Guidance of Negroes: Report of a Survey Conducted by the U.S. Office of Education* (Washington, D.C.: Government Printing Office, 1937).

36. Anderson, "Black Vocational Education," in Kantor and Tyack, *Work, Youth, and Schooling*, 211.

37. Ibid., 213.

38. Rawick, "New Deal and Youth," 236.

39. Charles H. Thompson, "The Federal Program of Vocational Education in Negro Schools of Less than College Grade," *Journal of Negro Education* 7 (July 1938): 304.

40. Fass, *Outside In*, 125.

41. Merle Curti, *The Social Ideas of American Educators*, 2d ed. (Paterson, N.J.: Littlefield, Adams, 1959), 560.

42. George B. Lockwood and Charles A. Prosser, *The New Harmony Movement* (New York: D. Appleton, 1905), 212.

43. For a revealing picture of conditions in the modern workplace, see Studs Terkel, *Working* (New York: Avon Books, 1972, 1974), *passim*.

44. Grubb and Lazerson, "Education and the Labor Market," 128–29.

45. Daniel T. Rodgers and David B. Tyack, "Work, Youth, and Schooling: Mapping Critical Research Areas," in Kantor and Tyack, *Work, Youth, and Schooling*, 293.

46. Joseph R. Gusfield, *Symbolic Crusade: Status Politics and the American Temperance Movement*, 2d ed. (Urbana: University of Illinois Press, 1986), 181–82.

47. David K. Cohen and Bella H. Rosenberg, "Functions and Fantasies: Understanding Schools in Capitalist America," *History of Education Quarterly* 17 (September 1977): 121.

48. Ibid.

49. Personal communication, Francis Keppel to Michael Fultz.

50. Gallup polls support this contention. See, for example, Elam, Rose, and Gallup, "28th Annual Phi Delta Kappa/Gallup Poll," 55–56.

51. John Dewey, *Lectures in the Philosophy of Education: 1899*, ed. Reginald D. Archambault (New York: Random House, 1966), 247.

52. See especially John Dewey, "The School and Social Progress," in *School and Society* (Chicago: University of Chicago Press, 1899), 19–44.

53. Dewey, *Lectures*, 248.

54. Ibid.

55. Ibid., 244.

56. Dewey, *Democracy and Education*, 217. So far as I know, this use of the expression "learning by doing" is the only one in Dewey's entire corpus. Examination of the context in which that phrase appears should serve to convince any serious reader that it is egregiously inadequate as a summation of Dewey's philosophy of education.

57. Dewey, *Democracy and Education*, 299, 301.

58. There are some contemporary indications that integration of the academic and the vocational is being attempted. See, for example, W. Norton Grubb, ed., *Education through Occupations in American High Schools: The Challenges of Implementing Curriculum Integration*, vols. 1 and 2 (New York: Teachers College Press, 1995).

59. Dewey, *Democracy and Education*, 63.

60. John Dewey, *Experience and Education* (New York: Macmillan, 1938), 47–51.

61. John Dewey, "Vocational Education," *New Republic* 6 (11 March 1916): 159.

62. W. Norton Grubb, "The 'New Vocationalism' in the United States: Returning to John Dewey," *Educational Philosophy and Theory* 28 (1996).

63. Dewey, *Democracy and Education*, 369.

64. Ibid., 370.

REFERENCES

Adams, David Wallace. *Education for Extinction: American Indians and the Boarding School Experience, 1875–1918.* Lawrence: University Press of Kansas, 1995.

Addams, Jane. "Address." National Society for the Promotion of Industrial Education, *Bulletin No. 1* (1907): 34–44.

Addis, Wellford. "Manual and industrial training." In *Report of the U.S. Commissioner of Education,* Vol. 1. Washington, D.C.: Government Printing Office, 1888–89.

Allison, May, and Susan Kingsbury. *A Trade School for Girls: A Preliminary Investigation in a Typical Manufacturing City, Worcester, Mass.,* U.S. Bureau of Education Bulletin no. 17. Washington, D.C.: Government Printing Office, 1913.

American Federation of Labor. *Report of the Proceedings of the Annual Meeting,* 1907, 1909, 1911, 1912, 1915.

Anderson, James D. *The Education of Blacks in the South, 1860–1935.* Chapel Hill: University of North Carolina Press, 1988.

———. "The Historical Development of Black Vocational Education." In *Work, Youth, and Schooling: Historical Perspectives on Vocationalism in American Education,* edited by Harvey Kantor and David B. Tyack. Stanford: Stanford University Press, 1982.

Anderson, Karen. *Wartime Women: Sex Roles, Family Relations, and the Status of Women During World War II.* Westport, Conn.: Greenwood Press, 1981.

Annual Reports of the Board of School Directors for the City of Milwaukee, 1883–1907.

Armstrong, Samuel Chapman. "Lessons from the Hawaiian Islands." *Journal of Christian Philosophy* 3 (1883–84): 200–229.

———. *Indian Education in the East: At Hampton, Va. and Carlisle, Penna.* Hampton, Va.: Normal School Steam Press, 1880.

———. "Address at the Anniversary Meeting of the American Missionary Society, October 24, 1877." *Southern Workman and Hampton School Record* 6 (December 1877): 94–95.

Aubrey, Roger F. "Historical Development of Guidance and Counseling and Implications for the Future." *Personnel and Guidance Journal* 55 (February 1977): 288–95.

Ayres, Leonard P. *Laggards in Our Schools.* New York: Charities Publication Committee, 1909.

"Bad Business." *School Life* 18 (December 1932): 70.

Bagley, William C. "Fundamental Distinctions between Liberal and Vocational Education." National Education Association, *Addresses and Proceedings,* 52nd Annual Meeting, 1914, pp. 161–70.

Baltimore Board of School Commissioners. *School Report.* Annapolis, Md.: Capital-Gazette Press, 1929–1930.

Barlow, Melvin L. *History of Industrial Education in the United States*. Peoria, Ill. Charles A. Bennet, 1967.

Barton, Bruce. *The Man Nobody Knows: A Discovery of the Real Jesus*. New York: Bobbs-Merrill, 1925.

Beers, Clifford Whittingham. *A Mind that Found Itself*. Garden City, N.Y.: Doubleday, 1908.

Bennett, Charles Alpheus. *History of Manual and Industrial Education, 1870–1917*. Peoria, Ill.: Charles A. Bennett, 1926.

Bloomfield, Meyer. *Youth, School, and Vocation*. Boston: Houghton Mifflin, 1915.

Board of School Directors of the City of Milwaukee. *Committee Minutes of the Statutory Committee on Trade Schools, 1907–1918*.

———. *Committee Minutes of the Committee on Textbooks, 1915*.

Bobbitt, Franklin. *How to Make a Curriculum*. New York: Houghton Mifflin, 1924.

———. *The Curriculum*. New York: Houghton Mifflin, 1918.

Bobbitt, John Franklin. *Curriculum Making in Los Angeles*. Chicago: University of Chicago Press, 1922.

———. "The Elimination of Waste in Education." *Elementary School Teacher* 12 (February 1912): 259–71.

Bonser, Frederick G. "The Industrial Arts in the Elementary School." *School Arts Magazine* 13 (November 1913): 183–86.

Brawley, Benjamin. *Early Efforts for Industrial Education*. Charlottesville, Va.: The Trustees of the John F. Slater Fund. Occasional Papers, no. 22, 1923.

Brewer, John M. *History of Vocational Guidance*. New York: Harper, 1942.

Briggs, Thomas H., Elbert K. Fretwell, and Romiett Stevens. "The Secondary Schools of Baltimore." In *Report of the Survey of the Public School System of Baltimore Maryland*, edited by George Drayton Strayer. Baltimore: Board of School Commissioners, 1921.

Briggs, Thomas M. "What Next in Secondary Education?" *School Review* 30 (September 1922): 521–32.

Broder, Dorothy Elizabeth. "Life Adjustment Education: An Historical Study of a Program of the United States Office of Education, 1945–1954." Ed.D. diss., Teachers College, Columbia University, 1976.

Bruce, William G. *I Was Born in America*. Milwaukee: Bruce Publishing, 1937.

Buenker, John D. "The Progressive Era: A Search for a Synthesis." *Mid-America* 51 (July 1969): 175–93.

California High School Teachers' Association. *Report of the Committee of Fifteen on Secondary Education in California, 1923*. San Francisco: California High School Teachers' Association, 1924.

Caliver, Ambrose. *Vocational Education and Guidance of Negroes: Report of a Survey Conducted by the U.S. Office of Education*. Washington, D.C.: Government Printing Office, 1937.

Carlson, Avis D. "Deflating the Schools." *Harpers* 167 (November 1933): 705–13.

Charters, W. W., and Douglas Waples. *The Commonwealth Teacher-Training Study*. Chicago: University of Chicago Press, 1929.

Charters, W. W., and Isadore B. Whitley. *Analysis of Secretarial Duties and Traits*. Baltimore: Williams and Wilkins, 1924.

Chiddix, John C. "School Surveys in the Smaller Communities Illustrated by a Survey of the Stanford (Ill.) Schools." *Normal School Quarterly* Series 23 (July–October): 4–20.

Cicourel, Aaron V., and John Kitsuse. *The Educational Decision-Makers*. Indianapolis: Bobbs-Merrill, 1963.

Clifford, Geraldine Joncich. "'Marry, Stitch, Die or Do Worse': Educating Women for Work." In *Work, Youth, and Schooling: Historical Perspectives on Vocationalism in American Education*, edited by Harvey Kantor and David B. Tyack. Stanford: Stanford University Press, 1982.

Clough, Robert Ripley. "The National Society for the Promotion of Industrial Education: Case Study of a Reform Organization, 1906–1917." Master's thesis, University of Wisconsin, Madison, 1957.

Cohen, David K., and Bella H. Rosenberg. "Functions and Fantasies: Understanding Schools in Capitalist America." *History of Education Quarterly* 17 (September 1977): 113–37.

Cohen, Ronald D. *Children of the Mill: Schooling and Society in Gary, 1906–1960*. Bloomington: Indiana University Press, 1990.

Commission on Industrial and Agricultural Training Report. Madison, Wis.: Democrat Printing, 1911.

Committee on Vocational Guidance. *Vocational Guidance in Secondary Education*. Bulletin No. 19. Washington, D.C. Government Printing Office, 1918.

Commons, John R. *Myself: The Autobiography of John R. Commons*. Madison: University of Wisconsin Press, 1964.

Conference on Unemployment. *Recent Economic Changes in the United States*. Vol. 1. New York: McGraw-Hill, 1929.

Cooley, Anna M. "Home Economics in the Schools of Baltimore." In *Report of the Survey of the Public School System of Baltimore, Maryland School Year 1920–1921*, edited by George Drayton Strayer. Baltimore: Board of School Commissioners, 1921.

Cooley, Robert L. "Continuation School Work in Wisconsin." National Education Association, *Addresses and Proceedings*, 53rd Annual Meeting, 1915, pp. 308–11.

———. "The Apprenticeship and Continuation Schools of Milwaukee, Wisconsin." National Education Association, *Addresses and Proceedings*, 52nd Annual Meeting, 1914, pp. 614–18.

———. "Schools and Continuation Schools." *Industrial Arts Magazine* 11 (August 1914): 49–54.

Cooley, Robert L., et al. *My Life Work*. New York: McGraw-Hill, 1930.

Coolidge, Calvin. Speech to the Society of American Newspaper Editors, January 17, 1925.

Copley, F. B. *Frederick Winslow Taylor: Father of Scientific Management*. Vol. 1. New York: Harper, 1923.

Counts, George Sylvester. *The Selective Character of American Secondary Education*. Supplementary Educational Monographs No. 19. Chicago: The University of Chicago, 1922.

Craig, Richard. "Don't Know Much about History." *New York Times*, December 8, 1997, A23.

Cuban, Larry. "Enduring Resiliency: Enacting and Implementing Federal Vocational Legislation." In *Work, Youth, and Schooling: Historical Perspectives on Vocationalism in American Education*, edited by Harvey Kantor and David B. Tyack. Stanford: Stanford University Press, 1982.

Curti, Merle. *The Social Ideas of American Educators*. 2nd ed. Paterson, N.J.: Littlefield, Adams, 1959.

Dean, Arthur D. "Vocational Education." In *Report of the Survey of the Public School System of Baltimore, Maryland, School Year 1920–1921*, edited by George Drayton Strayer. Baltimore: Board of School Commissioners, 1921.

"Declaration of Principles." National Educational Association, *Addresses and Proceedings*, 45th Annual Meeting, 1907, pp. 29–31.

Dennis, L. H. "From the Desk of the Executive Secretary." *American Vocational Journal* 20 (January 1945): 51.

———. Editorial. *American Vocational Association Journal and News Bulletin* 10 (September 1935): 60–61.

———. "Report on National Vocational Legislation." *American Vocational Association Journal and News Bulletin* 10 (September 1935): 89.

Dewey, Jane M., ed. "Biography of John Dewey." In *The Philosophy of John Dewey*, edited by Paul Schilpp. Evanston, Ill.: Northwestern University, 1939.

Dewey, John. *Lectures in the Philosophy of Education: 1899*, edited by Reginald D. Archambault. New York: Random House, 1966.

———. *Experience and Education*. New York: Macmillan, 1938.

———. *Individualism Old and New*. New York: Milton, Balch, 1930.

———. "Why I Am for Smith." *New Republic* 56 (November 7,1928): 320–21.

———. "Learning to Earn: The Place of Vocational Education in a Comprehensive Scheme of Public Education." *School and Society* 5 (March 24, 1917): 331–35.

———. *Democracy and Education: An Introduction to the Philosophy of Education*. New York: Macmillan, 1916.

———. "The Schools and Social Preparedness." *New Republic* 7 (May 6, 1916):15–16.

———. "Vocational Education." *New Republic* 6 (March 11, 1916): 159–60.

———. "Education vs. Trade Training–Dr. Dewey's Reply." *New Republic* 3 (May 15, 1915): 42–43.

———. "Splitting Up the School System." *New Republic* 2 (April 17, 1915): 283–284.

———. "A Policy of Industrial Education." *New Republic* 1 (December 19, 1914): 11–12.

———. "The School and Social Progress." In *The School and Society*. Chicago: University of Chicago Press, 1899.

Dewey, John, and Evelyn Dewey. *Schools of Tomorrow*. New York: E. P. Dutton, 1915.

Dollard, John. *Caste and Class in a Southern Town*. 3rd ed. Garden City, N.Y.: Doubleday Anchor, 1957.

Douglas, Paul H. *American Apprenticeship and Industrial Education*. New York: Columbia University, 1921.

Drost, Walter H. *David Snedden and Education for Social Efficiency*. Madison: University of Wisconsin Press, 1967.

Drucker, Peter. *Post-Capitalist Society*. New York: Harper Business, 1993.

Du Bois, W. E. B. "The Hampton Idea." In *The Education of Black People: Ten Critiques 1906–1960*, edited by Herbert Aptheker. Amherst, Mass.: University of Massachusetts Press, 1973.

———. "The Talented Tenth." In *The Negro Problem: A Series of Articles by Representative American Negroes of Today*, edited by W. E. B. Du Bois. New York: James Potts, 1903.

Du Bois, W. E. B., and Augustus Granville Dill. *The Negro American Artisan*. Atlanta University Publications No. 17. Atlanta: Atlanta University Press, 1912.

Edelman, Murray. *Political Language: Words that Succeed and Policies that Fail*. New York: Academic Press, 1977.

Editorial. *American Vocational Association Journal and News Bulletin* 10 (August 1935): 61.

Elam, Stanley E., Lowell C. Rose, and Alec M. Gallup. "The 28th Annual Phi Delta Kappa/Gallup Poll of the Public's Attitudes Toward the Public Schools." *Phi Delta Kappan* 78, (September 1996): 41–59.

Eliot, Charles W. "Industrial Education as an Essential Factor in Our National Prosperity." National Society for the Promotion of Industrial Education, *Bulletin No. 2* (1908): 9–14.

———. "The Fundamental Assumptions in the Report of the Committee of Ten." *Educational Review* 30 (November 1905): 325–43.

Fass, Paula S. *Outside In: Minorities and the Transformation of American Education*. New York: Oxford University Press, 1989.

———. *The New Deal: Anticipating a Federal Education Policy*. Institute for Research on Educational Policy and Governance. Stanford: Stanford University, 1981.

Fife, Ray. "President's Message." *American Vocational Association Journal and News Bulletin* 9 (August 1934):5.

Filene, Peter G. "An Obituary for the 'Progressive Movement'." *American Quarterly* 22 (1970): 20–34.

Fisher, Berenice M. *Industrial Education: American Ideals and Institutions*. Madison: University of Wisconsin Press, 1967.

Fitzpatrick, Edward A. *McCarthy of Wisconsin*. New York: Columbia University Press, 1944.

Fones-Wolf, Elizabeth. "The Politics of Vocationalism: Coalitions and Industrial Education in the Progressive Era." *The Historian* 46 (November 1983): 39–55.

Gilbreth, Frank B. "Bricklaying System." In *The Writings of the Gilbreths*, edited by William R. Spriegel and Clark E. Meyers. Homewood, Ill.: Richard D. Irwin, 1953. (Originally published in 1909 by the Myron C. Clark Publishing Co., New York and Chicago.).

Givens, Willard E. "New Deal a Raw Deal for Public Schools." *NEA Journal* 24 (September 1935): 198.

Goldman, Robert, and John Wilson. "The Rationalization of Leisure." *Politics and Society* 7 (1977): 157–87.

Gompers, Samuel. Editorial. *America Federationist* 20 (January 1913): 34–53.

———. "President Gompers' Report." *American Federationist* 16 (December 1909): 1060–80.

Grantham, Dewey. *Hoke Smith and the Politics of the New South*. Baton Rouge: Louisiana State University Press, 1958.

Grubb, W. Norton."The 'New Vocationalism' in the United States: Returning to John Dewey." *Educational Philosophy and Theory* 28 (1996): 1–23.

————, ed. *Education through Occupations in American High Schools: The Challenges of Implementing Curriculum Integration.* 2 vols. New York: Teachers College Press, 1995.

Grubb, W. Norton, and Marvin Lazerson. "Education and the Labor Market: Recycling the Youth Problem." In *Work, Youth, and Schooling: Historical Perspectives on Vocationalism in American Education,* edited by Harvey Kantor and David B. Tyack. Stanford: Stanford University Press, 1982.

Gusfield, Joseph R. *Symbolic Crusade: Status Politics and the American Temperance Movement.* 2nd ed. Urbana: University of Illinois Press, 1986.

Haber, Samuel. *Efficiency and Uplift: Scientific Management in the Progressive Era, 1890–1920.* Chicago: University of Chicago Press, 1964.

"Half Century Mark Reached." *Civics and Commerce* (March 1911): 7–10.

Ham, Charles H. *Manual Training: The Solution of Social and Industrial Problems.* New York: Harper, 1886.

Harris, William Torrey. "Report of the Committee on Pedagogics." National Education Association, *Addresses and Proceedings,* 28th Annual Meeting, 1889, pp. 417–23.

————. "The Intellectual Value of Tool-work." National Education Association, *Addresses and Proceedings,* 27th Annual Meeting, 1889, pp. 92–98.

Hays, Samuel P. *The Response to Industrialism: 1885–1914.* Chicago: University of Chicago Press, 1957.

Hempel, Robert I. *The Last Little Citadel: American High Schools Since 1940.* Boston: Houghton Mifflin, 1986.

Herbst, Jergen. *The Once and Future School: Three Hundred and Fifty Years of American Secondary Education.* New York: Routledge, 1996.

Hirsch, E. D., Jr. *The Students We Need and Why We Don't Have Them.* New York: Doubleday, 1996.

————. *Cultural Literacy: What Every American Needs to Know.* Boston: Houghton Mifflin, 1987.

Historical Statistics of the United States, Supplement. Washington, D.C.: Bureau of the Census, 1957.

Holland, Kenneth, and Frank Ernest Hill. *Youth in the CCC.* Washington, D.C.: American Council on Education, 1942.

Hull, Clark L. "Clark L. Hull." In *A History of Psychology in Autobiography.* Vol. 4, edited by Edwin G. Boring, Herbert S. Langfield, Heinz Werner, and Robert Yerkes. Worchester, Mass.: Clark University Press, 1952.

————. *Aptitude Testing.* Tarrytown-on-Hudson, World Book, 1928.

Johnston, Dean J. B. *Who Should Go to College?* Minneapolis: University of Minnesota Press, 1930.

Jones, Thomas Jesse. "Negro Education: A Study of the Private and Higher Schools for Colored People in the United States." U.S. Office of Education, Bulletin 36, 1916, Washington D.C.: Government Printing Office, 1917.

Judd, Charles H. Untitled. *School Review* 38 (April 1930): 247.

Kanigel, Robert. *The One Best Way: Frederick Winslow Taylor and the Enigma of Efficiency.* New York: Viking, 1997.

Kantor, Harvey A. *Learning to Earn: School, Work and Vocational Reform in California, 1880–1930*. Madison: University of Wisconsin Press, 1988.

Kantor, Harvey A., and David B. Tyack, eds. *Work, Youth, and Schooling: Historical Perspectives on Vocationalism in American Education*. Stanford: Stanford University Press, 1982.

Katznelson, Ira, and Margaret Weir. *Schooling for All: Class, Race and the Decline of the Democratic Ideal*. Berkeley: University of California Press, 1988.

Kean, Carol Judy. "The Origins of Vocational Education in the Milwaukee Public Schools. 1870–1917: A Case Study in Curricular Change." Ph.D. diss., University of Wisconsin, Madison, 1983.

Key, V. O. *Southern Politics in State and Nation*. New York: Vintage Books, 1949.

Kingsley, Clarence, D. "The Reorganization of Secondary Education." Part 6. *Journal of Education* 79 (April 23, 1914): 458–64.

———. "The High School as a Testing Time." National Educational Association, *Addresses and Proceedings*, 51st Annual Meeting, 1913, pp. 49–55.

Kliebard, Herbert M. *The Struggle for the American Curriculum, 1893–1958*. 2nd ed. New York: Routledge, 1995.

———. "Curriculum Theory: Give Me a 'For Instance.'" In *Forging the American Curriculum: Essays in Curriculum History and Theory*. New York: Routledge, 1992.

Krug, Edward A. *The Shaping of the American High School, 1920–1941*. Vol. 2. Madison: University of Wisconsin Press, 1972.

———. *The Shaping of the American High School*. Vol. 1. New York: Harper and Row, 1964.

Lagemann, Ellen Condliffe. "Contested Terrain: A History of Education Research in the United States, 1890–1990." *Educational Researcher* 26 (December 1997): 5–17.

Lamers, William M. *Our Roots Grow Deep*. 2nd ed. Milwaukee: Milwaukee Public Schools, 1974.

Lasch, Christopher. *The True and Only Heaven*. New York: W. W. Norton, 1991.

Latimer, John Francis. *What's Happened to Our High Schools?* Washington, D.C.: Public Affairs Press, 1958.

Lazerson, Marvin. "'Choosing Our Roles': American Youth Guidance in Historical Perspective." Paper Prepared for the Organization of Economic Co-operation and Development, March 1981.

———. *Origins of the Urban School: Public Education in Massachusetts, 1870–1915*. Cambridge: Harvard University Press, 1971.

Lazerson, Marvin, and W. Norton Grubb, eds. *American Education and Vocationalism: A Documentary History, 1870–1970*. New York: Teachers College Press, 1974.

Lee, Joseph. *Constructive and Preventive Philanthropy*. New York: Macmillan, 1902.

Lemann, Nicholas. *The Promised Land: The Great Black Migration and How It Changed America*. New York: Alfred A. Knopf, 1991.

Lennon, John B. "Four Alleged Crimes of Trade Unions." *American Federationist* 7 (September 1900): 273–74.

Lescohier, Don D. *Working Conditions*. Vol. 3, *History of Labor in the United States, 1856–1932*, edited by John R. Commons. New York: Macmillan, 1935.

Leuchtenburg, William E. *The Perils of Prosperity, 1914–1932.* Chicago: University of Chicago Press, 1958.

Levine, David. "Milwaukee Socialists and the Struggle for Democratic Schools, 1916–1930." Master's paper, University of Wisconsin, 1995.

Lewis, Sinclair. *Babbitt.* San Diego: Harcourt, Brace, Jovanovich, 1922.

Licht, Walter. *Getting Work: Philadelphia, 1840–1950.* Cambridge Harvard Press, 1992.

Lockwood, George B., and Charles A. Prosser. *The New Harmony Movement.* New York: D. Appleton, 1905.

Lovejoy, Owen. "Vocational Guidance and Child Labor." *Vocational Guidance, Papers Presented at the Organizational Meeting of the Vocational Guidance Association,* Bureau of Education Bulletin no. 14. Washington, D.C.: Government Printing Office, 1914.

Lynd, Robert, and Helen Lynd. *Middleton: A Study in Contemporary American Culture.* New York: Harcourt, Brace and Company, 1929.

Marsh, C. S. "The Educational Program in the Civilian Conservation Corps." *Educational Record* 16 (January 1935): 3–26.

Maxwell, William H. *A Quarter Century of Public School Development.* New York: American Book, 1912.

May, Henry F. *The End of American Innocence: The First Years of Our Own Time, 1912–1917.* New York: Oxford University Press, 1959.

McElvaine, Robert S. *The Great Depression: America, 1929–1941.* 2nd ed. New York: Times Books, 1993.

McGiveny, Joseph H. "The Politics of Vocational Education in Wisconsin, 1909–1967." Ph.D. diss., University of Wisconsin, Madison, 1967.

Menefee, Selden C. *Vocational Training and Employment of Youth.* Research Monograph XXV, Works Projects Administration. Washington, D.C.: Government Printing Office, 1942.

Merchants' and Manufacturers' Association of Milwaukee. *Bulletins.* 1906.

Miller, C. M. "Presidents Message." *American Vocational Association Journal and News Bulletin* 6 (August 1931): 1–2.

———. Letter. *School Review* 38 (April 1930): 246–47.

Milwaukee Free Press. Milwaukee, 1907.

Mirel, Jeffrey. *The Rise and Fall of an Urban School System: Detroit, 1907–81.* Ann Arbor: University of Michigan Press, 1993.

Mitchell, Broadus. *Depression Decade: From New Era through New Deal, 1929–1941.* New York: Rinehart, 1947.

Morrison, Gilbert B. "A Critical Review of the Report of the Committee on Pedagogics." In *The Educational Value of Manual Training,* Calvin M. Woodward. Boston: D. C. Heath, 1890.

Munsterberg, Hugo. *Psychology and Industrial Efficiency.* Boston: Houghton Mifflin, 1913.

Murray, Laura. "Training of Mexican Women in Household Service." *Vocational Education Magazine* 2 (December 1924): 1120–21.

National Advisory Committee on Education. *Committee Findings and Recommendations.* Part 1: *Federal Relations to Education.* Washington, D.C.: National Capital Press, 1931.

————. *Federal Relations to Education.* Part 2: *Basic Facts.* Washington, D.C.: National Capital Press, 1931.

National Association of Manufacturers. *Proceedings of the Annual Conference,* 1898, 1905, 1906, 1907, 1911, 1912.

National Education Association. *Cardinal Principles of Secondary Education: A Report of the Commission on the Reorganization of Secondary Education.* Washington, D.C.: Government Printing Office, 1918.

————. *Report of the Committee on Secondary School Studies.* Washington, D.C.: Government Printing Office, 1893.

National Society for the Promotion of Industrial Education. *Bulletins* 1, 2, 4, 5. 1907–1908.

National Vocational Education Act. U.S. Public Law 347. 64th Congress, 1917.

Nelson, Daniel. *Managers and Workers: Origins of the New Factory System in the United States, 1880–1920.* Madison: University of Wisconsin Press, 1975.

Nestor, Agnes. *Woman's Labor Leader: An Autobiography.* Rockford, Ill.: Bellevue Books, 1954.

Nichols, F. G. "Commercial Education." In *Report of the Survey of the Public School System of Baltimore, Maryland, School Year 1920–1921,* edited by George Drayton Strayer. Baltimore: Board of School Commissioners, 1921.

Noble, David F. *America by Design: Science, Technology, and the Rise of Corporate Capitalism.* New York: Oxford University Press, 1977.

O'Brien, F. P. *Survey Report of the Chanute, Kansas School System.* Lawrence: Bureau of School Service, University of Kansas, 1924.

O'Coin, Andre Roger. "Vocational Education During the Great Depression and World War II: Challenge, Innovation and Continuity." Ph.D. diss., University of Maryland, 1988.

O'Connell, Kathryn D. "Industrial Education in Boston, 1870–1890: A Case Study in Curriculur Change." Ph.D. diss., University of Wisconsin, Madison, 1975.

Ogren, Christine A. "Education for Women in the United States." Ph.D. diss., University of Wisconsin, Madison, 1996.

Pannabecker, John R. "Industrial Education and the Russian System: A Study in Economic, Social, and Technical Change." *Journal of Industrial Teacher Education* 24 (1986): 19–31.

Parsons, Frank. *Choosing a Vocation.* Boston: Houghton Mifflin, 1909.

Patton, Ruth Anne. "A Survey of Home Economics in Some Negro Schools." M.A. thesis, George Peabody College for Teachers, 1931.

Pearson, Drew, and Robert A. Allen. "The Washington Merry Go-Round." Washington *Herald* (September 30, 1935).

Perry, Charles F. "The Milwaukee School of Trades: Founded by and Conducted under the Patronage of the Merchants' and Manufacturers' Association of Milwaukee." The Merchants and Manufacturers' Association *Bulletin* (November 1906):10–15.

Peshkin, Alan. *Growing Up American: Schooling and the Survival of a Community.* Chicago: University of Chicago Press, 1978.

Peterson, Paul E. *The Politics of School Reform, 1970–1940.* Chicago: University of Chicago Press, 1985.

Picchioni, Anthony Paul. "History of Guidance in the United States." Ph.D. diss., North Texas State University, 1980.

Polanyi, Michael. *Personal Knowledge: Towards a Post-Critical Philosophy*. Chicago: University Press, 1958.

Powers, Jane Bernard. "'The Girl Question' in Education: Vocational Training for Young Women in the Progressive Era." Ph.D. diss., Stanford University, 1986.

Proceedings of the Board of School Directors of the City of Milwaukee. 1892–1913.

Proctor, W. M. "The Use of Psychological Tests in Vocational Guidance of High School Pupils." *Journal of Educational Research* 2 (September 1920): 533–46.

Proctor, William Martin, and Edward J. Brown. "College Admission Requirements in Relation to Curriculum Revision in Secondary Schools." In *The Development of the High School Curriculum*. Department of Superintendence, Sixth Yearbook. Washington, D.C.: Department of Superintendence, 1928.

"Professor Roman Attacks Vocational Training." *National Association of Corporation Schools Bulletin* 2 (October 1915): 23–26.

Prosser, Charles. "Our Job Has Just Begun." *American Vocational Journal* 21 (January 1946): 21.

Prosser, Charles A. "Industrial Education and the Changing Job." *American Vocational Association Journal and News Bulletin* 7 (May 1932): 6–9.

———. "Discussion." National Education Association, *Addresses and Proceedings*, 50th Annual Meeting, 1912, pp. 928–32.

Prosser, Charles A., and Charles R. Allen. *Vocational Education in a Democracy*. New York: Century, 1925.

Rawick, George Philip. "The New Deal and Youth: The Civilian Conservation Corps, The National Youth Administration, and the American Youth Congress." Ph.D. diss., University of Wisconsin, Madison, 1957.

Reese, William J. *Power and the Promise of School Reform: Grass-Roots Movements during the Progressive Era*. Boston: Routledge and Kegan Paul, 1986.

Reiman, Richard A. *The New Deal and American Youth: Ideas and Ideals in a Depression Decade*. Athens: University of Georgia Press, 1992.

Report of the Commissioner Appointed by the Legislature in 1899. Madison, Wis.: Democratic Printing Company, State Printer, 1901.

Report of the Commissioner of Education. Washington, D.C.: Government Printing Office, 1906.

Report of the Massachusetts Commission on Industrial and Technical Education. Boston: The Commission, 1906.

Rodgers, Daniel T. "In Search of Progressivism." *Reviews in American History* 10 (December 1982): 113–132.

———. *The Work Ethic in America, 1850–1920*. Chicago: University of Chicago Press, 1978.

Rogers, Daniel T., and David B. Tyack. "Work, Youth, and Schooling: Mapping Critical Research Areas." In *Work, Youth, and Schooling: Historical Perspectives on Vocationalism in American Education*, edited by Harvey Kantor and David B. Tyack. Stanford: Stanford University Press, 1982.

Roman, Frederick W. "Vocational Education—Its Dependence upon Elementary Cultural Training." National Education Association, *Addresses and Proceedings*, 53rd Annual Meeting, 1915, pp. 1173–77.

Roosevelt, Franklin Delano. "Regarding Appropriation for Vocational Education: A Statement by President Franklin D. Roosevelt." *Phi Delta Kappan* 20 (October 1937): 75–6.

Rosenbaum, James E. *Making Inequality: The Hidden Curriculum of High School Tracking.* New York: John Wiley, 1976.

Rosenfeld, Stuart A. "Vocational Agriculture: A Model for Educational Reform." *Education Week* 4 (September 26, 1984): 21, 24.

Runkle, John D. "The Manual Element in Education." Forty-first Annual Report to the Board of Education, State of Massachusetts, 1867–77. Reprinted in *History of Manual and Industrial Education, 1870–1917*, Charles Alpheus Bennett. Peoria, Ill.: Charles A. Bennett, 1926.

Rury, John L. *Education and Women's Work: Female Schooling and the Division of Labor in Urban America, 1870–1930.* Albany: State University of New York Press, 1991.

Russell, John D., and Associates. *Vocational Education.* Prepared for the Advisory Committee on Education. Washington, D.C.: Government Printing Office, 1938.

Smith, Elaine M. "Mary McLeod Bethune and the National Youth Administration." In *Clio Was a Woman: Studies in the History of American Women*, edited by Mabel E. Dentrich and Virginia C. Purdy. Washington, D.C.: Howard University Press, 1980.

Snedden, David. "Education for a World of Team-Players and Team Workers." *School and Society* 20 (November 7, 1924): 552–57.

———. "Cardinal Principles of Secondary Education." *School and Society* 9 (May 3, 1919): 517–27.

———. "Vocational Education." *New Republic* 3 (May 15, 1915): 40–42.

———. "Practical Arts in Liberal Education." *Educational Review* 43 (April 1912): 373–86.

———. "What of Liberal Education?" *Atlantic Monthly* 109 (January 1912): 111–117.

———. *The Problem of Vocational Education.* Boston: Houghton Mifflin, 1910.

———. "History Study as an Instrument in the Social Education of Children." *Journal of Pedagogy* 19 (June 1907): 259–68.

Snedden, David S. "Differences Among Varying Groups of Children Should be Recognized; and the Period at Which This Recognition Takes Place May Rationally Constitute the Beginnings of Secondary Education." National Education Association, *Addresses and Proceedings*, 46th Annual Meeting, 1908, pp. 752–57.

Social Democratic Herald. Milwaukee, 1904–1907.

Spinti, Robert J. "The Development of Trade and Industrial Education in Wisconsin." Ph.D. diss., University of Missouri, 1968.

Still, Bayard. *Milwaukee: The History of a City.* Madison, Wis.: The State Historical Society, 1948.

Swigett, Glen L. "Educational Preparation for Business." *School Life* 6 (January 15, 1921): 6.

Tanner, Daniel, and Laurel Tanner. *History of the School Curriculum*. New York: Macmillan, 1990.

Taylor, Frederick Winslow. *Scientific Management Comprising Shop Management, the Principles of Scientific Management, Testimony Before the Special House Committee*. New York: Harper, 1911.

———. "A Piece-rate System, Being a Step Toward Partial Solution of the Labor Problem." *Transactions of the American Society of Mechanical Engineers* 16 (1895): 856–903.

Teitelbaum, Kenneth. *Schooling for 'Good Rebels'; Socialist Education in the United States, 1900–1920*. Philadelphia: Temple University Press. 1993.

Thelen, David P. "Social Tensions and the Origins of Progressivism." *Journal of American History* 55 (September 1969): 523–41.

Thompson, Charles H. "The Federal Program of Vocational Education in Negro Schools of Less than College Grade." *Journal of Negro Education* 7 (July 1938): 303–18.

Tiefenthaler, Laura. Papers. Milwaukee County Historical Society, Milwaukee, 1900–1943.

Terkel, Studs. *Working*. New York: Avon Books, 1974.

Tyack, David B., and Elizabeth Hansot. *Managers of Virture: Public School Leadership in America, 1820–1980*. New York: Basic Books, 1982.

Tyack, David B., Robert Lowe, and Elizabeth Hansot. *Public Schools in Hard Times: The Great Depression and Recent Years*. Cambridge: Harvard University Press, 1984.

"Typical Wartime Activities of American Secondary Schools." *School Executive* 62 (January 1943): 16–17.

Ueda, Reed. *Avenues to Adulthood: The Origins of the High School and Social Mobility in an American Suburb*. Cambridge, Mass: Cambridge University Press, 1987.

Urban, Wayne. "Educational Reform in a New South City: Atlanta, 1890–1925." In *Education and the Rise of the New South*, edited by Ronald K. Goodenow and Arthur O. White. Boston: G. K. Hall, 1981.

U.S. Congress. 73rd Congress, 1st session. *Congressional Record* vol. 77: 914–15.

U.S. Congress. Senate. 77th Congress, 1st sess. *Congressional Record* vol. 81, pt. 6.

———. 62nd Congress, 2nd sess. Document no. 36, no. 40, 1911– 1912.

U.S. Department of Interior. Office of Education. *The Program of Studies Bulletin 1932*, no. 17. Washington, D.C.: Government Printing Office, 1933.

"U.S. High School Youth Building 500,000 Model Airplanes for the U.S. Navy." *American Vocational Association Journal and News Bulletin* 17 (February 1942): 13.

U.S. Office of Education. *Vitalizing Secondary Education: Education for Life Adjustment*. Washington, D.C.: Government Printing Office, 1951.

———. Federal Security Agency. *Vocational Training for War Production Workers*. Bulletin No. 10. Washington, D.C.: Government Printing Office, 1946.

Van Oot, B. H. Editorial. *American Vocational Association Journal and News Bulletin* 10 (February 1935): 11–13.

Van Rensselaer, Susan De Lancey. "Review of Normal School Class Work." *Southern Workman* 21, (June 1892): 91–100.

Viteles, Morris S. "Selecting Cashiers and Predicting Length of Service." *Journal of Personnel Research* 2 (April 1924): 467–73.

Washington, Booker T. "Industrial Education for the Negro." In *The Negro Problem*, edited by Booker T. Washington et al. 1903. Reprint ed. New York: Arno Press, 1963.

———. *The Story of My Life and Work*. Atlanta: J. L. Nichols, 1901.

———. *The Future of the American Negro*. 1899. Reprint ed. New York: Haskell House, 1968.

Webbink, Paul. "Unemployment in the United States, 1930–1940." *Papers and Proceeding of the American Economic Association* 30 (February 1941): 248–300.

Weiss, Janice. "The Advent of Education for Clerical Work in the High School: A Reconsideration of the Historiography of Vocationalism." *Teachers College Record* 83 (summer 1982): 613–38.

———. "Educating for Clerical Work: A History of Commercial Education in the United States Since 1850." Ed.D. diss., Harvard Graduate School of Education, 1978.

Werum, Regina. "Political Process in the Pre-Desegregation South: Race and Gender Stratification in Federal Vocational Programs, 1917–1936." Ph.D. diss., Indiana University, 1994.

Wilentz, Sean. "Speedy Fred's Revolution." Review of *The One Best Way: Frederick Winslow Taylor and the Enigma of Efficiency*, by Robert Kanigel. *New York Review of Books* 44, (October 20, 1997): 32–37.

Williams, Aubrey. "A Message from Aubrey Williams." *American Vocational Association Journal and News Bulletin* 14 (February 1939): 32.

Wirth, Arthur G. *Education in the Technological Society: The Vocational-Liberal Studies Controversy in the Early Twentieth Century*. Scranton: Intext, 1972.

Wisconsin Journal of Education. 1884–1897.

Wisconsin Laws. 1907. Chapter 122.

Wisconsin Senate. *Joint Resolution No. 53*, 1909.

Wisconsin State Board of Vocational Education. "Coordination in Part-Time Education." *Administrative Series Circular* 8 (1924).

Woerdehoff, Frank J. "Dr. Charles McCarthy: Planner of the Wisconsin System of Vocational and Adult Education." *Wisconsin Magazine of History* 41 (Summer 1958): 270–74.

———. "Dr. Charles McCarthy's Role in Revitalizing the University Extension Division." *Wisconsin Magazine of History* 40 (Autumn 1956): 13–18.

Women's Educational and Industrial Union, Department of Research. *The Public Schools and Women in Office Service*. Boston: WEIU, 1914.

Woodward, Calvin M. "The Rise and Progress of Manual Training." In *Report of the U.S. Commissioner of Education, Part 1*. Washington, D.C.: Government Printing Office, 1893–94.

———. "The Results of the St. Louis Manual Training School." National Education Association, *Addresses and Proceedings*, 28th Annual Meeting, 1889, pp. 73–91.

———. *The Manual Training School*. Boston: D. C. Heath & Co., 1887.

———. "Manual Training in General Education." *Education* 5 (July 1885): 614–26.

———. "Manual Training." National Education Association, *Addresses and Proceedings*, 22nd Annual Meeting, 1883, pp. 84–99.

———. *Manual Education*. St. Louis: G. I. Jones, 1878.

Wraga, William G. *Democracy's High School: The Comprehensive High School and Educational Reform in the United States.* Lanham, Md.: University Press of America, 1994.

Wrigley, Julia. *Class Politics and Public Schools: Chicago, 1900–1950.* New Brunswick: Rutgers University Press, 1982.

Yerkes, Robert M. *Psychological Examining in the United States Army.* Vol. 15 of *Memoirs of the National Academy of Sciences.* Washington, D.C.: Government Printing Office, 1921.

Yoakum, C. S., and Robert M. Yerkes. *Army Mental Testing.* New York: Holt, 1920.

Young, Ella Flagg. "Industrial Training." National Education Association, *Addresses and Proceedings,* 53rd Annual Meeting, 1915, pp. 125–27.

Zeitlin, Harry. "Federal Relations in American Education. 1933–1943: A Study of New Deal Efforts and Innovations." Ph.D. diss., Teachers College, Columbia University, 1958.

Zunz, Olivier. *Making America Corporate, 1870–1920.* Chicago: University of Chicago Press, 1990.

⬥⬥⬥ INDEX ⬥⬥⬥

ABOUT THE AUTHOR

Herbert M. Kliebard is currently an emeritus professor at the University of Wisconsin, Madison. Upon completion of his baccalaureate degree at the City College of New York in 1952, he began his teaching career at the Bronx Vocational High School. After serving in the United States Army Medical Corps between 1953 and 1955, he returned to teach at the Bronx Vocational High School for another year. Between 1956 and 1962, he taught at Nyack Junior–Senior High School in Nyack, New York. After one year as a research associate at Teachers College, Columbia University, he was granted a doctorate by that institution in 1963 and in that same year accepted a faculty position at the University of Wisconsin, Madison. Professor Kliebard has been affiliated with the Departments of Curriculum and Instruction and Educational Policy Studies ever since. At the University of Wisconsin, Madison, his teaching and research have centered around curriculum theory, secondary education, and, particularly, history of curriculum. His awards include a distinguished faculty award from the University of Wisconsin, a distinguished alumni award from Teachers College, and a lifetime achievement award from the Curriculum Studies division of the American Educational Research Association. His most recently published books are *The Struggle for the American Curriculum, 1893–1958* (1986, 1995) and *Forging the American Curriculum* (1993).